The Catskill Mountain House

THE CATSKILL
MOUNTAIN HOUSE

ROLAND VAN ZANDT

BLACK · DOME

BLACK DOME PRESS CORP.
RR 1, Box 422
Hensonville, NY 12439
Tel: (518) 734-6357
Fax: (518) 734-5802

SECOND EDITION PAPERBACK 1997

Black Dome Press Corp.
RR 1, Box 422
Hensonville, NY 12439
Tel: (518) 734-6357
Fax: (518) 734-5802

Library of Congress Catalogue Card Number: 66-18877

ISBN 0-9628523-6-8

Cover design by Artemisia, Inc., Windham, NY

Printed in the USA

*The author acknowledges with gratitude permission to quote from
"East Coker" in* Four Quartets, *copyright ©1943 by T.S. Eliot.
Reprinted by permission of Harcourt, Brace & World, Inc.*

To
MULFORD Q. SIBLEY

Preface to the 25th Anniversary Edition

It was one of those chance encounters that can change a person's life. I was not expecting anything unusual that lovely summer's day in 1958 while exploring some old trails 50 miles or so from my summer home in the Catskill mountains. Nor when I first saw that scene did I suspect that my inner excitement forbode some new intellectual commitment that would occupy the next seven years of my life.

The scene was disturbingly, hauntingly American, full of pathos and loneliness. When enterprise dies in this country and is no longer profitable, it is simply abandoned, left to rot in the wind and rain without consecration or memory. Our land is strewn with uncommemorated ruins, and here was another in the most unexpected of places: a huge wooden structure, still buttressed by thirteen splendid Corinthian columns, built like the wish of a child on the very edge of an overhanging ledge of the mountains, commanding a view that (I later learned) was once the most famous in all America.

The ravished lineaments of former elegance and luxury placed in "splendid isolation" in the midst of a far-flung wilderness was another profoundly American note that could not be missed. The United States, it has often been said, is "the land of contrasts." It has always been torn by the conflicting attractions of city and country, civilization and the virgin wilderness. Such are the polarities of American history, and here they were encapsulated, made graphic, in the dramatic scene of these great ruins. I had come upon something indigenous to not only the Catskills, but to our national culture.

Thirty years ago the Catskills, so to speak, had no history. They weren't supposed to: true to American presuppositions, the Catskills were what

Washington Irving called "a dismembered branch of the great Appalachian family," and belonged to *natural* rather than *human* history. The revelation that I might therefore have found something of historic value came as a considerable surprise. The stirring events of American history avoided the mountains in favor of the Hudson and Mohawk valleys, the obvious paths of empire. To this day population is very thin in the Catskills; small hamlets and villages are confined to narrow cloves and valleys; occupations are restricted to forest products, the tourist trade, recreation (hunting, fishing, skiing, camping, etc.). Unfit for industry or cities, the mountains have always provided a refuge from the vicissitudes of urban life. People sought the mountains to escape mainstream America—in other words, to escape history.

In any event, the Catskills had so little to say to history that Washington Irving expressly wrote a legend (*Rip Van Winkle*) to endow the region with some human interest. Historians found little to attract them to the subject, or so I assumed until I saw those bewitching ruins. They were a manifestation of considerable power and ambition, and must have been the excrescence of some formidable movement in the larger national background. Such turned out to be the case.

Revelation followed revelation in the next few years as I spent the summers exploring the mountains and interviewing people, and winters researching the seemingly limitless stores of information locked up in the archives of museums, libraries and historical societies. The Mountain House, as I soon realized, was much more than a hotel: it was the focus and emblem of a complete culture, a national treasure.

Even though the great building has disappeared along with the 19th-century American culture that gave it life and meaning, and of which it became a transcendent symbol, the story remains a demonstration of the magical harmony that can exist between a specific region and its larger national setting. It is this harmony that explains the preeminent role of the Mountain House in the romantic era of American culture from 1825 to at least the turn of the century. It is this harmony, in other words, that is the key to the single most important period in the history of the Catskill Mountains.

ROLAND VAN ZANDT

Shandaken, NY
January, 1991

Foreword

For 140 years the Catskill Mountain House stood on a rock shelf in Pine Orchard above the Hudson Valley and facing the Hudson River. Everything about this illustrious hotel is fascinating—how it came to be built on such a lofty, remote perch in 1823, who built it, how people got there over the years, what they ate and drank when they got there, what they thought and wrote, how it all fell apart and had to be burned—most reluctantly, by the New York State Department of Conservation at 6 a.m. on January 25, 1963.

Being emotionally attached to this beautiful building and institution, Mr. Van Zandt has tracked down thousands of homely details throughout the 140 years, and charged them with personal feeling. No one can reconstruct the Catskill Mountain House but Mr. Van Zandt has recreated it. Although the Catskills have become a second-rate resort area, "The Catskill Mountain House" is a first-rate book, first-rate history, first-rate biography, first-rate folklore.

It takes this rank because Mr. Van Zandt is not content with recording facts but has put the Mountain House in perspective as history of American manners and thought. The second section of the book is entitled "The Romantic Quest," which defines the attitudes that cultivated people had towards nature in the early part of the nineteenth century. The prevailing attitude was a European formulation. Cultivated people went to the Mountain House in search of the "sublime" and the "picturesque."

What was nature? The discussion of this question is the most original part of the book. Europeans regarded nature as monotonous unless some human touch—a ruin, perhaps—intruded on nature and provided contrast. William Gilpin argued that a natural scene could not be intrinsically beautiful unless it was endowed with some "recollection of man, of human feelings." The enjoyment of American nature needed indoctrination. Thomas Cole, who painted the Catskills ardently, felt the necessity of defending the Catskill landscape against people who thought that "American scenery possesses little that is interesting or truly beautiful; and it is rude without picturesqueness, and monotonous without sublimity; that being destitute of the vestiges of antiquity, which so strongly affect the mind, it may not be compared with European scenery." His superb paintings supplied his answer and, in fact, changed the public attitude. Mr. Van Zandt has given this discussion a solid grounding by going to primary intellectual sources.

To a modern reader, however, the attitudes of the defenders of the American landscape seem obsolete now. Thomas Cole, William Cullen Bryant, Washington Irving, James Fenimore Cooper and other liberated Americans could not quite inhabit nature. They looked at nature as something outside themselves. Mr. Van Zandt's book is richly illustrated with reproductions, several of them in color, of paintings by Cole, Asher B. Durand, W.H. Bartlett, B.B.G. Stone, Harry Fenn, Fritz Meyer, E. Heinemann and others. In most of their paintings nature is a little forbidding; the wildness just a bit hostile.

In Durand's memorial painting of two "Kindred Spirits" Thomas Cole and William Cullen Bryant seem to be standing on nature, subtly isolated from their environment. Their clothes are civil; their posture is cultivated. In those days ladies and gentlemen went on idyllic rambles through the woods, carrying walking sticks or Alpine staffs, which were a means of patronizing nature as something too crude for cultivated people. They had not yet found a way of living with nature in terms of equality. To be in the wilderness was to be in a romantic frame of mind, which involved improvising educated comparisons. Most of the men who wrote about nature used baroque imagery and made references to works of art or figures in history or the Bible. Nature was something that lay outside their egos.

This discussion applies to only one section of a singularly comprehensive book. The rest is on a more elementary plane. But some parts of the story provoke unanswerable speculations. For instance, where did Charles L. Beach, proprietor of a livery stable, get the perfect taste he applied to the building? After he took control in 1838 he removed the original gables, balustrades and catwalks and gave the building the classical lines of a Greek design; he also installed the thirteen glorious Corinthian columns that made the old Mountain House one of the supreme architectural treasures of America.

The decline of the Mountain House suggests an American paradox. It was most heavily patronized when the journey from New York was most formidable. Before the day of the railroads, the journey consisted of an overnight voyage on a Hudson River steamboat and then four hours by stage from Catskill. Ultimately, the railroads reduced the journey to about four hours from New York, climaxed by that mechanical haul up the face of North Mountain by the Otis Elevated Railroad. The Mountain House was most prized when it was most inaccessible. When the automobile solved the problem of transportation perfectly, people began to lose interest in the Mountain House. Lovers of the sublime and the picturesque deteriorated into transients.

Mr. Van Zandt's book proves that something of great value was discarded. The Catskills lost a fine institution and a standard of excellence that has never been retrieved.

BROOKS ATKINSON

Acknowledgments

The author cannot hope to acknowledge adequately the innumerable obligations he has happily incurred during four years of research. They extend from the villages of upstate New York to the libraries and historical associations of New York City, and to the staffs of art galleries and museums throughout the country.

The early stages of research were confined almost exclusively to the New York Public Library, the richest of repositories for students of New York State history. The Genealogy Room with its extensive collection on the Catskills, the Art Department, Periodical, and Map Rooms were especially helpful. Other New York City sources that proved fruitful were the New-York Historical Society and the Frick Art Reference Library. The author wishes to express his gratitude for the many courtesies and attentions bestowed upon him by the staffs of these distinguished institutions.

In upstate New York the most important sources were the public libraries of Catskill, Kingston, Phoenicia, and Haines Falls; the Greene County Historical Society (which very recently acquired some of the scattered registers of the Mountain House); the Albany Institute of History and Art; the New York State Library; and a host of generous individuals. The latter included Mrs. Era Zistel Posselt of Haines Falls; Mr. Virgil B. Van Wagonen of Bearsville, great-grandson of Charles L. Beach; Mr. Charles G. Coffin, a Catskill lawyer with many memories of the

Mountain House; Mr. Norman S. Rice of the Albany Institute of History and Art; Mrs. Ruth Fairbanks, the former librarian of the Catskill Public Library, and Mr. Walter D. Franklin, the present librarian; Mrs. Charles A. W. Beach of Catskill, who hospitably supplied the author with refreshments as well as a wealth of historical material during a hot summer's day; Mrs. Richard Albright of Athens, who opened her rich collection of material on the steamboat history of the Hudson to the author's perusal; Mr. Alf Evers, town historian of Woodstock; Mr. Bert Beardsley of Kingston, a hearty octogenarian who parted with old memories of childhood days at the Mountain House as well as a prime collection of original source material that had been jealously guarded for over sixty years; the late Mr. Felix Hughes of Allaben, whose concise memories of the Stony Clove Railroad went back to the 1890s; Mrs. Elsie S. Feistmann of Queens and Haines Falls, to whom the author is indebted for extensive information on the last owner of the Mountain House; Mr. C. E. Dornbusch, librarian of the Vedder Memorial Library in the Bronck House, Coxsackie, New York, who offered his own hearth and home as a refuge for study during a mid-winter blizzard; and Mr. Edward G. West of Shandaken, Superintendent of Land Acquisition in the State of New York Conservation Department, who supplied much useful information on the last period of the Mountain House and permitted the author to complete his pictorial record by contributing a photograph of the final holocaust of January 25, 1963. A special debt of gratitude is gladly tendered Mrs. Mabel Parker Smith, historian of Greene County, whose pioneer researches first illuminated the historical depth and richness of the Catskill Mountain House and who gave unstintingly of her time and energy during a crucial stage of writing.

For the timely advice and encouragement that are indispensable to any protracted work of scholarship, the author is deeply indebted to Mr. Clemens Heller of the University of Paris, Professors Mary C. Turpie and Bernard Bowron of the University of Minnesota, and the extraordinary man and teacher to whom this volume is respectfully dedicated.

The author's wife has shared the pleasures as well as asperities of this work at every stage of its preparation; in matters both practical and spiritual her assistance has exceeded the bounds of possible acknowledgment.

R.V.Z.

Shandaken, New York
April, 1966

List of Illustrations

COLOR PLATES

Frontispiece: *Beach Mountain House, the Artist Sketching,* Sarah Cole, 1848; Albany Institute of History and Art.

Plate 1: *A View of the Two Lakes and Mountain House, Catskill Mountains, Morning 1844,* Thomas Cole, 1844; The Brooklyn Museum.   162A

Plate 2: *Catskill Mountain House,* unknown artist, Hudson River School, undated; collection of Gary & Barbara Slutzky.   162C

Plate 3: *Catskill Mountain House (from North Mountain),* Jaspar F. Cropsey, 1855; Minneapolis Institute of Arts.   162E

FIGURES

1. *Village of Catskill,* W.H. Bartlett, 1836; engraving by J.C. Bentley.   4

2. *View of the Catksill Mountain House, New York,* Thomas Cole, c. 1828; engraving by Fenner Sears & Co.   14

3. *The Mountain House,* Harry Fenn, 1870.   35

4. *Catksill Mountains,* William J. Bennett, c. 1828.   38

5. *View from the Mountain House, Catskill,* W. H. Bartlett, 1836; engraving by R. Brandard.   39

6. The Catskill Mountain House, 1892; photograph by J. Loeffler.   40

7. *Catskill Mountain-House,* C. Parsons, c. 1844.   56

FIGURES

8. *Catskill Mountain House*, De Witt Clinton Boutelle, 1845; Vose Gallery, Boston.   57
9. Mountain House pamphlet (1845–50), title page.   58
10. Two Staffordshire China plates depicting the Mountain House.   59
11. *Catskill Mountain House*, George Harvey, c. 1845; engraving by J. Smillie.   60
12. The Hudson Valley from a third-floor bedroom window of the Mountain House, 1961.   64
13. An early spring fog shrouds the ruins of the Mountain House, 1961.   66
14. The Mountain House from the bend in the road, c. 1905.   74
15. The Mountain House from the bend in the road, 1961.   75
16. The beginning of the toll road up the mountain, 1961.   78
17. Rip Van Winkle House, Sleepy Hollow, 1884.   94
18. Rip Van Winkle House, Sleepy Hollow, 1906.   98
19. *Catskill Mountain House*, Thomas Cole, probably 1843; collection of Mrs. Calvin Stillman, New York City.   111
20. *Catskill Mountains*, Sanford R. Gifford, 1868; collection of Mrs. E. W. Isom, New York City.   111
21. *The Two Lakes and the Mountain House on the Catskills*, W. H. Bartlett, 1836; engraving by J. C. Bentley.   113
22. *Scenery of the Catskills*, unsigned, undated print by Currier & Ives.   113
23. The Mountain House from North Mountain; photo by Herman Bickelman, c. 1910.   116
24. North Lake and the Catskill Mountain House from the ledges of North Mountain, 1960.   116
25. Newman's Ledge on the trail to North Mountain, 1960.   118
26. *Catskill Lake*, Thomas Cole, probably 1825; Allen Art Museum, Oberlin College.   120
27. *Kaaterskill Clove*, Asher B. Durand, 1866; The Century Association, New York City.   121
28. *Under the Falls, Catskill Mountains*, Winslow Homer, 1872.   133
29. *The Falls of Catskill, New York*, Thomas Cole, probably 1825; engraving by Fenner Sears & Co.   133
30. *Kaaterskill Falls*, Thomas Cole, 1827; collection of Lee B. Anderson, New York City.   134

FIGURES

31. *From the Top of Kaaterskill Falls*, Thomas Cole, 1828; Detroit Institute of Arts. 135
32. *The Catterskill Falls*, W. H. Bartlett, 1836; engraving by J. T. Willmore. 135
33. *Catskill Falls*, Harry Fenn, 1870. 137
34. *Catterskill Falls*, unsigned, undated print by Currier & Ives. 138
35. "Kaaterskill Fall," scene from a composite print, *The Catskill Mountains*, by Fritz Meyer, 1869. 140
36. *View from Prospect Rock—Kaaterskill Falls*, E. Heinemann, 1884. 141
37. The Laurel House as it appeared after the Victorian addition, c. 1882. 143
38. Haines Falls, showing ice column; February, 1961. 149
39. *The Catskill Mountains*, Thomas Cole, 1833; Cleveland Museum of Art. 165
40. *Kindred Spirits: Thomas Cole and William Cullen Bryant*, Asher B. Durand, 1849; New York Public Library. 167
41. *Catskill Mountains*, Asher B. Durand, c. 1828. 174
42. *River in the Mountains*, Thomas Cole, c. 1843; Museum of Fine Arts, Boston. 175
43. *Catskill Mountain House*, B. B. G. Stone, 1860. 181
44. *The Catskill Mountains*, composite print by Fritz Meyer, 1869. 187
45. The Mountain House in the early 1880s. 218
46. Hotel Kaaterskill (1881–1924). 231
47. The transportation system during the heyday of the Catskills. 232
48. The Laurel House Station of the Kaaterskill Railroad, 1961. 237
49. The Otis Elevating Railway (1892–1918). 238
50. The Mountain House about the time of the Civil War; photograph by J. Loeffler. 243
51. A Mountain House souvenir spoon of the 1890s. 251
52. *On the Road from Kaaterskill Hotel*, E. Heinemann, 1884. 259
53. Colonnade of the Mountain House, c. 1922. 259
54. The piazza of the Mountain House, c. 1922. 260

Figures

55. *Rear View of the Mountain House*, Walter Launt Palmer, 1883; collection of Norman S. Rice, Albany, N.Y.   272
56. Rear view of the Mountain House, c. 1910.   273
57. West view from the Mountain House, c. 1922.   277
58. West view from the Mountain House, c. 1910.   277
59. The board walk to South Lake, c. 1922.   279
60. General William T. Sherman at the Mountain House, c. 1890.   282
61. *Sketches Among the Catskill Mountains*, composite print by Thomas Nast, 1866.   286
62. "The Piazza," Mountain House; Thomas Nast, 1866 (detail of Figure 61).   287
63. "Arriving," Mountain House; Thomas Nast, 1866 (detail of Figure 61).   287
64. "Departing," Mountain House; Thomas Nast, 1866 (detail of Figure 61).   287
65. Full-page advertisement, 1905.   290
66. The Mountain House in ruins, 1961.   292
67. An Andron advertisement of the late 1930s.   307
68. The piazza, Mountain House, 1961.   311
69. Catskill Mountain House, 1922.   318
70. The beginning of the end: the Mountain House after a hurricane in November, 1950.   319
71. Where the North Wing joined the central part of the Mountain House, 1961.   324
72. Sixteen hundred feet below the Mountain House, 1961. 325
73. Looking west over the remains of the North Wing, 1962.   327
74. The corner of the South Wing facing the Hudson Valley, 1962.   330
75. The rear of the Mountain House, 1961.   331
76. The ledges in front of the Mountain House, 1961.   332
77. The gutted remains of the South Wing, 1961.   333
78. The piazza, 1961.   334
79. The Mountain House ballroom, sometime between 1902 and 1913.   336
80. The Mountain House ballroom, 1961.   336
81. The Mountain House after removal of the columns and the piazza, 1962.   337

FIGURES

82. The main entrance of the Mountain House, 1961.   338
83. Looking west from a window over the ballroom, 1961.   338
84. The burning of the Mountain House by the New York State Conservation Department, Friday, January 25, 1963, 6:00 A.M.   341
85. Four days after the New York State Conservation Department burned down the remnants of the Mountain House, January 29, 1963.   341

MAPS

1. Northeast United States within a 200-mile radius of Pine Orchard.   6
2. Detail from 1826 map showing the road from Catskill to Pine Orchard.   17
3. Detail from 1802 map of the Pine Orchard area.   18
4. Automobile route map of 1909, Pine Orchard area.   72
5. The Pine Orchard-Kaaterskill Clove area at the height of its history.   102
6. Detail from 1879 map of the Pine Orchard-Kaaterskill Clove area.   104
7. Detail from 1892 U.S. Geological Survey Map, Kaaterskill Quadrangle.   107
8. Modern trail map of the Pine Orchard-Kaaterskill Clove area.   108
9. Map of the Catskill resorts in 1894.   227

PLANS

A. Sketch Plan of the Growth of the Mountain House.   262
B. Sketch Plan, Ground Floor of the Mountain House.   264
C. Sketch Plan, Second Floor of the Mountain House.   266
D. Sketch Plan, Third Floor of the Mountain House.   268
E. Sketch Plan, Fourth Floor of the Mountain House.   270

Contents

Preface vii

Foreword by BROOKS ATKINSON ix

Acknowledgments xii

List of Illustrations xv

PART I—THE ANTEBELLUM PERIOD

1. The Setting. 3
   The Catskills and the Nation in the Early Nineteenth
   Century—The "Pine Orchard" Area of the Catskill
   Mountains

2. The First Two Decades 28

3. The Early Years under Charles L. Beach 45
   The Early Career of Charles L. Beach—The Mountain
   House under the Proprietorship of Beach—Years of
   Fulfillment

4. The Old Mountain Road 71

5. The Scenic Domain of the Mountain House 101
   The Trails—The Lakes—Kaaterskill Clove—
   Kaaterskill Falls

PART II—THE ROMANTIC QUEST

Introduction 151

6. The Discovery of the Romantic Motif 156

7. The Hudson River School of Painting 170

8. The Romantic Debate 189

   The Doctrine of Association—The Picturesque versus
   the Sublime—Summary

9. The Romantic Apotheosis 210

Part III—The Gilded Age

Introduction 217

10. The Coming of the Railroads 225

    The Ulster and Delaware Railroad Opens the Interior
    of Ulster County—Charles L. Beach and the Catskill
    Mountain Railroad—The Kaaterskill and Otis Elevated Railroads

11. The Flush Years of the Catskills 242

12. "One of the Greatest Hotels of the Country" . . 258

    "A Massive and Elegant Structure of Wood"—"All
    the Comforts and Luxuries"—"Its Own Park of 3,000
    Acres of Magnificent Forests"—"The Favorite Summer Resort on the River"—"This Shrine of Summer
    Pilgrimage"

Part IV—The Twentieth Century

Introduction 291

13. Years of Decline, 1918–1942 298

    Early Signs: 1894–1918—1918 to 1930—1930 to 1940—
    1941 to 1942

14. Years of Embattled Ruin, 1942–1962 310

    Decade of Undecided Fate (1942–1952)—Decade of
    Wreckage and Ruin (1952–1962)

Postscript—Friday, January 25, 1963 337

Appendix: Rate Policy of the Mountain House . . . 343

Notes 347

Bibliography 381

Index 399

Part I

The Antebellum Period

Chapter 1

The Setting

The final scene was played to its end during the early hours of the morning. The exact time was 6:00 A.M., January 25, 1963. The scene was a dark, massive ruin silhouetted against the dawn on a high windswept ridge of the Catskill Mountains. The temperature stood close to zero, the snow was deep, the valley far below lay dark and quiet. At that time, and in that lonely setting, one of the monuments of nineteenth century American culture was being put to the torch. History was coming full cycle for what had once been known as "the noblest wonder of the Hudson Valley," the world-famous Catskill Mountain House.

Only necessity could justify such destructiveness, and the necessity seemed to lie close at hand. After two decades of neglect and decay the venerable edifice commanding the eastern escarpment of the Catskill Mountains had become a hulking ruin, a threat to the lives and limbs of every curious visitor or trespasser. And its appeal was magnetic: no hiker or camper, no tourist or sightseer, no student of architecture or history, could resist the temptation of its labyrinthine corridors. Signs against trespassing had proved unavailing; a huge fence around the ruins only offered further challenge. Finally, bowing to necessity, officials of the New York State Conservation Department ordered the great structure burned to the ground.

Figure 1. *Village of Catskill*, W. H. Bartlett, 1836. From the engraving by J. C. Bentley in N. P. Willis, *American Scenery* (London, 1838–40). The Mountain House is barely visible as a white speck on the brow of the mountain at center.

The New York Times noticed the event; every newspaper of the Hudson Valley carried articles and editorial comments, and the Conservation Department received a smattering of irate letters. Among the older residents who had been raised within sight of this "fairy palace" clinging to the edge of the mountain, and among those farther away who had once visited it or known its ancient history, the sense of sudden loss was acutely personal and deeply, disturbingly, national. A few years previous when a midwestern scholar and artist first saw the abandoned ruins, he had lamented an American indifference to cultural heritage and said, "it would be criminal not to maintain this landmark, which has not lost one iota of its inspirational value." A sense of guilt pervaded the high villages of the Catskills. The great white mansion, a delight to successive thousands of Americans as they traveled up the Hudson through 140 years of unbroken history, had disappeared from the earth. "What is that white speck?" a famous English traveler had asked a century and a quarter earlier as her delighted eye first glimpsed its presence on the distant mountaintop, more than twenty miles away. "What is this place?" strangers still ask as they stumble upon the remnants of the gigantic foundations along the mountain's edge.

The keys to history are as diverse as the affairs of men, but in the early stages of history before civilization has conquered the land, none is likely to be more important than geography, one of the oldest of human sciences. Such was the case in America during the first quarter of the nineteenth century when the Mountain House first appeared on a high rim of the Catskill Mountains and the Hudson Valley provided a natural highway from the developing cities of the Atlantic seaboard to the nation's first mountain resort. The rise of the Mountain House to the stature of an American classic within that setting presupposes a deep commitment to time and place, and in early nineteenth century America that meant a nation still dominated by the geographical necessities of the East. Many factors contributed to the rise of the Mountain House, cultural and social as well as economic; but all were dependent upon the *sine qua non* of this basic geographical harmony.

In the decade of 1820–1830 during which the Mountain House was established, the Hudson Valley was the focal population center of the nation. In the early nineteenth century, America was a regional rather than continental power, and within that narrow region the Hudson Valley was the main artery of trade and traffic, the fastest-growing commercial and social center of the whole nation.

In 1830 the population of the United States was overwhelmingly confined to the area between the Mississippi and the Atlantic, and at least 65 per cent of the population was still concentrated on the Atlantic slope between the Alleghenies and the sea. The only sizable area with ninety or more inhabitants per square mile was the region extending from New York City across New Jersey to Philadelphia.[1]

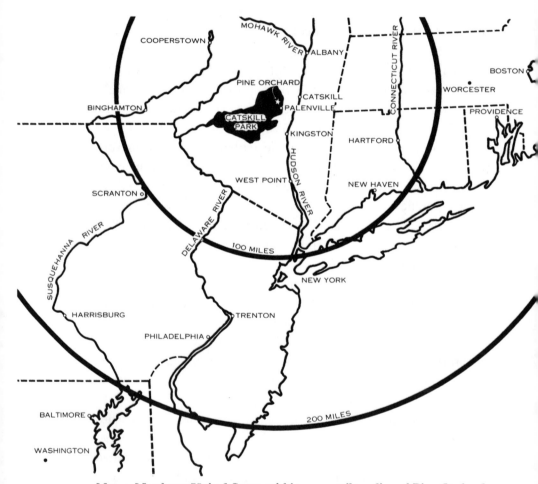

Map 1. Northeast United States within a 200-mile radius of Pine Orchard.

In 1820, the three leading cities of the Northeast, Boston, New York, and Philadelphia, had more than twice the population of the four leading Southern cities, Baltimore, Charleston, Mobile, and New Orleans. By 1830 the margin was even greater.[2] In the Northeast there was a further regional differentiation of special significance to this story. In the decade 1810–1820 New York State took the lead in population over its nearest competitor, Virginia, and retained that lead throughout the 140-year history of the Mountain House.[3] Finally, by 1830 the City of New York had become the largest and wealthiest city in all America. In short, the distribution of population gave the Catskills a geographical importance that could not be duplicated in any other mountains of the Atlantic seaboard.

They were preëminently accessible to the thriving centers of American population, and in the early nineteenth century this advantage had a special significance for the rise of such a social phenomenon as the Catskill Mountain House. Visitors to the hotel were attracted from the start not only by the dramatic location, but by the surprising elegance and luxury of its facilities, for the great hotel stood in the midst of hundreds of square miles of raw wilderness, and it could be reached only after a four-hour stage ride up a precipitous mountain. This ideal combination of wilderness and luxury—so beguiling to the romantic imagination of the early nineteenth century—was a key to the immediate success of the Mountain House, but it was possible only in the Hudson Valley, less than a day's journey from the markets and resources of the greatest city in the nation.

Luxury and the amenities of life receded in 1830 as one traveled away from the centers of population. Travel was slow and uncomfortable relative to today; it required a week to reach Cincinnati from New York City and two weeks to reach the Mississippi frontier; and the farther a man traveled, the more completely he found himself in a world of stark necessities. The frontier was not—as used to be assumed—a boundary between civilization and savagery, but between an inferior state of civilization and its total absence. In 1830, therefore, such amenities as fine hotels and resorts were virtually unknown west of the Alleghanies.

And they were also virtually unknown, though for different reasons, south of the Mason-Dixon Line. Resorts and large hotels and the tourists and vacationers who patronize them have only arisen in modern history as an urban-industrial civilization has come into being. Throughout the antebellum period the rise of such a civilization was retarded, if not frustrated altogether, by the agrarian economy of the southern plantation. The North therefore received a disproportionate share of the rising benefits of a highly complex civilization: just as southern trade and capital flowed north, so the southerner often sent his sons to northern colleges and his family to northern spas and hostelries. The dearth of inns and hotels in the South was notorious throughout the antebellum period. Such social amenities kept pace in the North with the rising wealth and complexity of its population.

This was particularly noticeable in the developing "Commercial Emporium" of New York City. Here geography again played a crucial role, seen especially in the decisive influence of the Hudson River.

The strategic importance of the "lordly Hudson" was already apparent at the time of the American Revolution, when it became the pivot of military operations. In conjunction with the Mohawk, it was the only river to penetrate the Appalachian barrier and provide easy access to the great American interior. This economic advantage became especially impressive after the completion of the Erie Canal in 1825. Another advantage was the southern terminus of the Hudson: close by the sea yet sufficiently inland to escape its destructive storms, the Hudson River forms one of the finest deep-water harbors on the face of the globe. Manhattan Island became a natural center for both transatlantic and continental trade and commerce, and the rise of New York City as America's greatest metropolis was inevitable.

The Hudson Valley as a region of trade and wealth kept pace with the rise of New York City. This progress was facilitated by the constant development of new and more effective means of transportation. The ample depth and width of the Hudson, and the fact that it rises only five feet between New York and Albany and is navigable to the latter point, led the early Dutch to develop a sailing vessel that could utilize these advantages. The famous Hudson River sloop, seventy to a hundred feet in length with a carrying capacity of four to five hundred barrels of flour, dominated the river, and hence the trade and traffic of the whole of New York State, for the first two centuries of the river's history. Every town and village from New York to Albany possessed its own fleet of freight, market and packet sloops, and two or three hundred sails might be seen on the river on a single day.

The famous sloop held sway over freight and passenger service on the Hudson until 1807 when Robert Fulton's first voyage with the *Clermont* introduced the steamboat to Hudson River travel. By 1840 there were about a hundred steamboats, considerably larger and more practical than Fulton's *Clermont*, plying the river between New York and Albany.[4] Much cheaper and swifter, the steamboats soon stole the passenger service of the cumbersome sloops. When the railroads later joined the steamboats as a chief means of transportation, the long history of the sloop ended. In 1830, however, the prodigious river traffic was still a colorful mixture of sail and steam, a sight unequaled on any other American river.

The convenient location and exceptional beauty of the Hudson soon encouraged wealthy New Yorkers to build summer homes along its commanding heights, and the lower valley became the scene of America's first vacationland. Even in the early years of the nineteenth century the area south of the Highlands acquired a suburban aspect unknown to the rest of America until long after the advent of the railroad age.[5] While making a trip up the Hudson to visit the Mountain House in 1860, Bayard Taylor discovered that "the elegant summer residences of New Yorkers . . . now extend more than half-way to Albany."[6] Yet as early as 1838 while viewing the Hudson from the steps of the Mountain House, Nathaniel P. Willis found that "there is a suburban look and character about all the villages on the Hudson," and that the steamboat had "destroyed the distance between them and the city" and converted the Catskills themselves into a "resort." [7]

The scenic beauty of the Hudson Valley was a prime factor in the development of America's first vacationland. Even in the post-Civil War period, after people had become aware of the wonders of the West, the Hudson River remained a "must" of American travel. Before the war, when travel was largely confined to the Atlantic seaboard and most American scenery was considered far inferior to Europe's, the Hudson Valley gained special praise. "However widely European travellers have differed about other things in America," Harriet Martineau observed in 1838 while visiting the Mountain House, "all seem to agree in their love of the Hudson. The pens of tourists dwell on its scenery, and their affections linger about it like the magic lights which seem to have this river in their peculiar charge." [8] A famous example of such praise appeared in Mrs. Trollope's *Domestic Manners of the Americans* (1832):

I had heard so much of the surpassing beauty of the North river [as the Hudson was also called], that I expected to be disappointed, and to find reality flat after description. But it is not in the power of man to paint with a strength exceeding that of nature, in such scenes as the Hudson presents. Every mile shows some new and startling effect of the combination of rocks, trees, and water; there is no interval of flat or insipid scenery, from the moment you enter upon the river at New-York, to that of quitting it at Albany, a distance of 180 miles. . . . I felt no lack of that moral interest so entirely wanting in the new states, and without which no journey can, I think, continue long without wearying the spirits. . . . The Hudson river can be surpassed in beauty by none on the outside of Paradise. [9]

Occupying about three thousand square miles of the west bank of the river, the Catskills, as William Cullen Bryant once said, "are among the most remarkable objects seen in the voyage up the Hudson . . ." [10] Travel literature of the nineteenth century abounds in descriptions of these mountains as they are first seen from the river, for other than the narrow passage through the

Highlands the Catskills provide some of the most beautiful scenery of the whole voyage upriver. To many travelers such as the youthful Thomas Cole in 1825, they were the climax of that voyage. Of all accounts that convey the impact of these mountains upon the romantic sensibility of the early nineteenth century, none has surpassed the description by Washington Irving:

To me they have ever been the fairy region of the Hudson. I speak, however, from early impressions, made in the happy days of childhood, when all the world had a tinge of fairyland. I shall never forget my first view of these mountains. It was in the course of a voyage up the Hudson, in the good old times, before steamboats and railroads had driven all poetry and romance out of travel. A voyage up the Hudson in those days was equal to a voyage to Europe at present, and cost almost as much time; but we enjoyed the river then; we relished it as we did our wine, sip by sip; not as at present, gulping it down at a draught, without tasting it. My whole voyage up the Hudson was full of wonder and romance. I was a lively boy, somewhat imaginative, of easy faith, and prone to relish everything that partook of the marvellous. Among the passengers on board the sloop was a veteran Indian trader, on his way to the Lakes, to traffic with the natives. He had discovered my propensity, and amused himself throughout the voyage by telling me Indian legends and grotesque stories about every noted place on the river, such as Spuyten Devil Creek, the Tappan Zee, the Devil's Dans Kammer, and other hobgoblin places. The Catskill Mountains, especially, called forth a host of fanciful traditions. We were all day slowly tiding along in sight of them, so that he had full time to weave his whimsical narratives . . . All these were doled out to me as I lay on deck, throughout a long summer's day, gazing upon these mountains, the everchanging shapes and hues of which appeared to realize the magical influences in question. Sometimes they seemed to approach, at others to recede; during the heat of the day they almost melted into a sultry haze; as the day declined they deepened in tone; their summits were brightened by the last rays of the sun, and later in the evening their whole outline was printed in deep purple against an amber sky. As I beheld them, thus shifting continually before my eye, and listened to the marvellous legends of the trader, a host of fanciful notions concerning them was conjured into my brain, which have haunted it ever since.[11]

The particular favor with which Americans of the early nineteenth century looked upon the Catskills may be seen in an 1830
statement of William Cullen Bryant that the Catskills are "the
highest in the state of New-York." [12] Bryant did not know, and
Americans as a whole did not know until after the Civil War, that
the highest mountains in New York are the Adirondacks, another
hundred miles north. As late as 1850 when hundreds of visitors
were frequenting the area of the Mountain House during the summer months, the Adirondacks were known only to a few lumbermen, hunters or trappers.[13] The Green Mountains of Vermont and
the White Mountains of New Hampshire—not to mention the
Smokies or mountains west of the Mississippi—were also generally
unknown when the Catskills had already become a popular American resort.

The various handbooks of travel and picture books of American scenes that began to appear in the pre-Civil War period attest
the singular popularity of the Hudson Valley and the Catskills.
Appleton's Illustrated Hand-Book of American Travel asserted
in 1857 that "We can commend to the traveller no pleasanter or
more profitable summer excursion for a day, or a month, or even
a season, than a visit to the Catskills—one of the grandest and
most picturesque of the mountain ranges of the United States." [14]
Such a statement can be understood only in terms of the restricted
boundaries of the American nation in the 1850s, the relative obscurity of the upper and lower reaches of the Appalachians, the
unknown domains of the Rockies and High Sierras. Even as late
as 1872–1874 Bryant's *Picturesque America* could still substantiate the singular importance of the Catskills by declaring "there
are few places in the whole range of American scenery so attractive
and refreshing as the Catskill Mountains." [15]

The heart, though not the full extent, of the Catskills today is
bounded by the Catskill State Park and embraces about 900 square
miles of Greene, Ulster, Delaware, and Sullivan counties. Meas-
ured by the foothills and the outer perimeter of today's resort
area, the Catskills include almost thrice that amount of land and ex-

tend from the eastern escarpment along the Hudson west to the upper reaches of the Susquehanna, and as far south as the vicinity of Liberty and Monticello. The remarkable fact about this geographical extent of the Catskills is that until the coming of the railroads in the 1880s only one very small part of it formed the famous resort area. This was a sixteen- to twenty-square-mile area of the eastern escarpment just opposite the city of Catskill and close by the precipitous cliffs of Kaaterskill Clove. The geographical center of this small area was called "Pine Orchard," a high plateau-like area between two peaks that included two lakes and large rock "platforms" that protruded beyond the edge of the mountain and provided the foundations of the Catskill Mountain House.

Paralleling the Hudson for over twenty miles between the present-day cities of Catskill and Kingston, the mountains rise like a wall almost from sea level to elevations of three to four thousand feet. Geologically this "Wall of Manitou," as it was called by the Indians, is the abrupt eastern terminus of a slightly inclined surface that slants downward into western New York and eastern Pennsylvania. At the latter place the incline goes so deep in the ground that it forms the base-strata of the Pennsylvania coal fields. From the compact wall of the eastern escarpment the Catskills spread westward in a maze of declining ridges and spurs that seem to be going in all directions at once. These ridges and spurs deflected the northward flow of population to the west of the mountains up the difficult headwaters of the Delaware and Susquehanna rivers or else around the "Wall of Manitou" up the natural highway of the Hudson Valley. Because of the far more navigable approach up the Hudson where such "seaports" as Esopus (Kingston) and Catskill had already been established in the late seventeenth century, all the earliest penetration of the Catskill Mountains came from the east rather than the west. The proximity of the Hudson Valley to the base of the mountains, and the presence of "cloves" or passes that breached their eastern wall, facilitated penetration from that direction. The village of Catskill became the main gateway to the mountains; Kingston, its nearest rival, did not seriously compete until after the Civil War

Figure 2. *View of the Catskill Mountain House, New York*, Thomas Cole, c. 1828 (oil on canvas, 23″ x 14½″). From the engraving by Fenner Sears & Co., published in *History and Topography of the United States*, J. H. Hinton, ed. (London, 1830), no. 59. The Mountain House Staffordshire plates (Figure 10) were copied from this engraving.

when it became the eastern terminus of the Ulster and Delaware Railroad.

The location of the village of Catskill near the northern reaches of the mountains favored the development of trade around the northern flank of the mountains to the rich and relatively populous farmlands of the Mohawk Valley. One of the earliest roads in the area was established along this natural overland route between the Mohawk and the Hudson, and on it sprang up two of the oldest communities of "upper" Greene County—Greenville, founded in 1786, and Durham in 1788. Then the eastern end of this avenue of trade, Catskill was probably the fastest growing community in the Hudson Valley during the first quarter of the nineteenth century. In 1787 it had only five houses, one store, and two sloops; in another fifteen years it had 180 houses, 12 warehouses, 31 stores, 2,000 people and 15 vessels employed in transporting agricultural products to New York, Boston and the Southern States.[16] At the falls of Catskill Creek, three miles west of the village, could be found the most extensive flour mills in the state.[17]

But of equal importance to the early ascendancy of Catskill was its location vis-à-vis the mountains themselves and especially Kaaterskill Clove and what is still known as "the top of the mountain"—a high plateau and river valley that runs from the head of the clove westward to the convergence of Delaware, Schoharie and Greene counties, and the headwaters of the Susquehanna and Delaware rivers. This area also saw some of the earliest settlements, the villages of Hunter and Jewett between 1783 and 1787, and Lexington in 1788.[18] Most of these primitive communities were pioneered by Massachusetts victims of Shays' Rebellion of 1786. They sought refuge in the mountains and until 1817 had a very tenuous existence; the real development of this "back side" of the mountains came later with the rise of the tanning industry. It was this economic development that first linked the "top of the mountain" with the village of Catskill and contributed once again to the latter's importance.

Until the advent of the tanning industry, these mountains

were a solid mass of hemlock forests. The first enterprise using hemlock bark for curing hides was founded in Athens, New York, in 1750. State historians, however, usually date the effective rise of the industry as 1817 when the first tanneries appeared on the top of the mountain back of Kaaterskill Clove. In subsequent years the tanneries spread throughout the Catskills and accounted for the first penetration, if not settlement, of that region. As the tanneries moved westward they left little permanent settlement behind them, for once the surrounding supply of hemlock had been exhausted, there was nothing to keep people in the area. While the hemlock forests lasted, industry grew, forming one of the two or three most important economic phases of the mountains. Hides were imported from as far away as South America, cured in the mountains, and retransported by wagon to Catskill and from there down the river to New York City. Millions upon millions of cubic feet of giant hemlock were laid to the ax, pealed, and in most instances left to rot. By 1890 this unbridled exploitation had destroyed the virgin forests, the tanning industry collapsed, and the mountains grew up again to the hardwoods of today.[19] The more benign farmer, sportsman and vacationer secured the permanent settlement of the mountains.

This was especially true of the area that most concerns us, the "top of the mountain" back of Kaaterskill Clove. From roughly 1817 to 1835 the tanning operations that first opened up the Catskills were restricted to Palenville, Tannersville, and Prattsville. According to H. A. Haring, a reliable authority on their history, the tanneries were very slow to extend beyond this area, and it was not until 1835 that they suddenly began to spread out over every other part of the mountains.[20] That this section became more significant than any other was due, at the start at least, to the presence of the tanning industry.

Other factors, too, account for the continued ascendancy of the top of the mountain once the tanneries had departed. It happened that the eastern terminus of this region (roughly equivalent to the present township of Hunter) contained "without question," as one commentator has said, "the wildest and most pic-

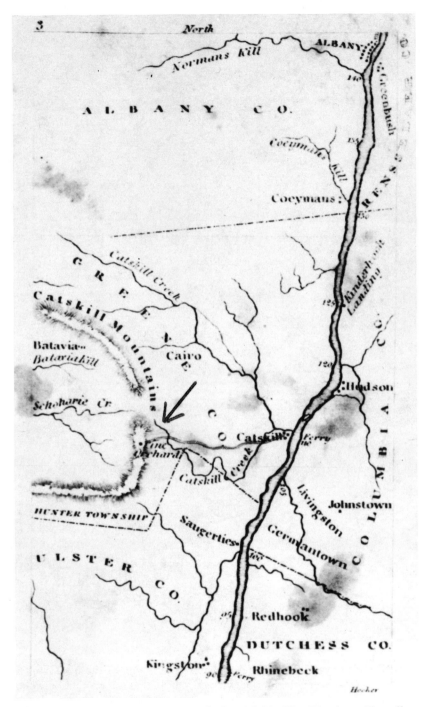

Map 2. Detail from a map in A. T. Goodrich's *The Northern Traveller* (New York, 1826), showing the road from Catskill to Pine Orchard.

Map 3. Detail from a map of 1802, now in the map collection of the New York Public Library. The twin lakes are already known, and a primitive wagon trail or wood road goes up Sleepy Hollow rather than Kaaterskill Clove. The road going south to Little Shandaken (now Lake Hill) is the Mink Hollow route used by the early tanners before improvement of the Mountain House road to Catskill via Sleepy Hollow.

turesque beauty of the whole Catskill region." [21] It followed
that the first area of the Catskills to be opened by the tanneries
was also the first to attract sightseers and to be developed as a
vacationland; and it is this second development that explains the
continued importance throughout the antebellum period of the
one region of the Catskills that had been originally penetrated by
the tanning industry.

The story of this convergence of industry with the resort
business is a fascinating study in the local problems of transportation. The first road to the newly opened tanneries took a circuitous route from the village of Catskill, north around the hook
of the mountains to South Durham, then up the slope to East
Windham, and finally to Prattsville and Grand Gorge. Keeping
to the outskirts of the mountains, the road was nearly seven
years in the making (1815–1822) and fell far short of satisfying the needs of the tanneries for a more direct and economical
route from the Hudson to the "back of the mountains." Another
road was attempted from the present area of Elka Park at the
head of Plattekill Clove, a precipitous vent in the wall of the
mountains just south of the larger Kaaterskill Clove. Avoiding the
impossible engineering problems of the route down the mountain
through Plattekill Clove (a road could not be built there until
1880 and even today it is closed to winter traffic), the new road
went south through Mink Hollow (today only a foot trail),
eight miles to Bearsville, west of Woodstock; then to Woodstock
itself around the southern hook of the mountains to Saugerties
on the Hudson. This route involved something like thirty miles
of detour and a loss of four days' traveling time. As Colonel
William Edwards, the founder of Hunter and the biggest tanner
in the state said, "A turnpike down the mountain is necessary to
keep the tanneries running." [22]

At this point the Catskill Mountain Association comes into the
picture. This association was formed by a group of Catskill
businessmen with the aim of buying the land of Pine Orchard
and building thereon "a large and commodious hotel." The association was incorporated by New York State on March 24, 1823,

and one of the provisions of its charter required the building of a road from the valley below to the site of the new hotel. The new road could take only one possible direction. As a New York State map of 1802 clearly shows, some kind of road to Pine Orchard already existed from the earliest years of the nineteenth century. The same road is also clearly shown on a map of 1819, five years before the formation of the Catskill Mountain Association. This road was probably built by the earliest settlers of Hunter shortly after the Revolution.[23] Although the road fell into disuse when the tanners built presumably better roads around the northern and southern flanks of the mountains, it still continued to be used by "numerous parties in summer" who climbed on foot or horseback to enjoy the "inexpressibly grand" view from the heights of Pine Orchard.[24] In 1823 when the Catskill Mountain Association decided to take advantage of the popularity of that view and build a "house of entertainment" on the site, the old abandoned road of the original settlers of Hunter became once again the main artery into the mountains.[25] The finely graded road not only provided the easiest and most direct route to the new hotel, but answered all the prayers of the tanners for an economical route down the eastern escarpment.[26]

The tanning industry no doubt helped to establish the importance of the Sleepy Hollow route once it was inaugurated, but of far greater significance was the access it afforded to Pine Orchard and the most scenic and dramatic region in all the Catskills. Until well after the Civil War this relatively small region of the Catskills—3,500 acres of which were eventually owned by the Mountain House—composed the very heart and circumference of the famous resort area. For years following the opening of the Mountain House in 1824 all the various guidebooks and pamphlets featuring "The Catskill Mountains" were restricted to this single part of them. An article called "The Catskills" that appeared in an 1854 issue of *Harper's*, for instance, declared that "geologically speaking, the Catskills occupy the counties of Sullivan, Ulster, Greene, Schoharie, and Albany; but pictorially considered, they are in the county of Greene alone, within whose limits are found all the loftiest peaks and all the chief resorts of the tourist and artist"; and the article thereupon restricted itself to a detailed description of the area immediately surrounding Pine Orchard.[27]

Perhaps the most accurate account of the outer perimeter of the resort area of the Catskills prior to the era of the railroads in the 1880s may be found in the Rev. Charles Rockwell's *The Catskill Mountains and the Region Around*, published in 1867:

In May and early in June the large hotels and numerous boarding and farm-houses in and about Catskill, and on and near the eastern slope of the mountains, and among and beyond the upper heights, are opened for the season of four or five months. The region thus occupied extends from Durham, on the north, to Woodstock, on the south, and from Catskill, on the east, to Hunter and Windham, on the west, and many thousand persons, from all parts of the world, visit this region each summer, many of them remaining here for weeks and months. The region thus described is from twenty to thirty miles or more in length and breadth. The main points of interest and attraction, however, are the upper heights, in the region of the Mountain House, from the Cauterskill [Kaaterskill] Clove, on the south, and from those heights eastward, down the slope and along the base of the mountains, for several miles on either side of . . . the valley of Kiskatom.[28]

"The region of the Mountain House" is still the center of attraction; and what is conspicuous is the absence of any mention of the vast mountainous area northwest from Hunter to Grand Gorge and southwest to Phoenicia, Margaretville and beyond. General ignorance regarding this area is shown by a statement of *The American Cyclopaedia* (1879) that "the highest summits [in the Catskills] are Round Top, High Peak, and Overlook . . ."—or, in other words, the peaks in the immediate vicinity of the Mountain House.[29] It wasn't until the late 1870s and early 1880s that local people began to realize that Slide Mountain, in the southwestern Catskills, was the highest in the mountains and that there were at least fifteen peaks higher than those around the Mountain House.[30] Stony Clove, one of the few natural routes

from the area of the Mountain House to the mountains around
Phoenicia, is rarely mentioned in guidebooks until the late 1850s.

As a contemporary historian, Alf Evers, has well said:

These peaks [the Shandaken Mountains] were not thought of, in
those days, as parts of the Catskills. They were described in school
geographies as the end of a chain of the "Blue Hills" which moved
from Pennsylvania through Sullivan County to the Esopus Valley.
They were usually thought of as quite distinct from the Romantic
Catskills which Washington Irving, Cole and Bryant had endowed
with glamor.

It was not until the coming of the railroads in the post-Civil
War period that they were thought of as "the Southern Catskills." [31] The name thus kept pace with the spreading circumference of the resort area, beginning in an eastern corner of Greene
County and terminating, late in the century, in the headwaters
of the Delaware River.

Until the post-Civil War period, then, the developed resort
area of the Catskills was restricted to the "top of the mountain"
in the vicinity of Pine Orchard and, as Rockwell noted, to the
lovely farm area of the Kiskatom Valley on the classic route between the village of Catskill and the Mountain House. Throughout that period Pine Orchard remained the center of the whole
region, the goal of thousands of tourists and sightseers even when
they chose to stay at cheaper boardinghouses in the valley below.
Until the opening of the Mountain House there was not a single
hotel in the area. The erection of the Mountain House, one of the
first "mountain hotels" in America, signalized the advent of the
resort history of the Catskills, and led to the development of the
whole historic region.

From the very start, the geographical location and scenic beauty
of Pine Orchard contained the key to all subsequent history. The
combination of topographical features found within a four-mile
radius—of precipitous cloves, high mountain peaks, lakes and
waterfalls, secluded dales and panoramic views—are characteristic of the Catskills as a whole; but nowhere else can they be

found in such concentrated grandeur and so conveniently located to the town of Catskill.

Descriptions of the area abound in nineteenth century American letters. One of the earliest was also one of the most famous— a three-page encomium in James Fenimore Cooper's *The Pioneers*, the first of the Leather-Stocking novels. Written in 1823 coincident with the construction of the Mountain House, Cooper's description was the progenitor of literally hundreds of such descriptions; and as one of the few passages in the Leather-Stocking tales that localized the topographical setting of the stories, it is a revelation of the scenery of Pine Orchard under the telling guise of nineteenth century romanticism. The speaker is Leather-Stocking himself:

"I have travelled the woods for fifty-three years, and have made them my home for more than forty; and I can say that I have met but one place that was more to my liking; and that was only to eye-sight, and not for hunting or fishing."

"And where was that?" asked Edwards.

"Where! why up on the Cattskills. I used often to go up into the mountains after wolves' skins and bears; once they paid me to get them a stuffed panther, and so I often went. There's a place in them hills that I used to climb to when I wanted to see the carryings on of the world, that would well pay any man for a barked shin or a torn moccasin. You know the Cattskills, lad; for you must have seen them on your left, as you followed the river up from York, looking as blue as a piece of clear sky, and holding the clouds on their tops, as the smoke curls over the head of an Indian chief at the council fire. Well, there's the High-peak, and the Round-top which lay back like a father and mother among their children, seeing they are far above all the other hills. But the place I mean is next to the river, where one of the ridges juts out a little from the rest, and where the rocks fall, for the best part of a thousand feet, so much up and down, that a man standing on their edges is fool enough to think he can jump from top to bottom."

"What see you when you get there?" asked Edwards.

"Creation," said Natty, dropping the end of his rod into the water, and sweeping one hand around him in a circle: "all creation, lad. I was on that hill when Vaughan burned 'Sopus [Kingston] in the last war; and I saw the vessels come out of the Highlands as plain as I can see that line-scow rowing into the Susquehanna, though one was twenty times farther from me than the other. The river is in sight for seventy miles, looking like a curled shaving under my feet, though it was eight long miles to its banks. I saw the hills in the Hampshire grants, the Highlands of the river, and all that God had done, or man could do, far as eye could reach—you know that the Indians named me for my sight, lad; and from the flat on the top of that mountain, I have often found the place where Albany stands. And as for 'Sopus' the day the royal troops burnt the town, the smoke seemed so nigh, that I thought I could hear the screeches of the women."

"It must have been worth the toil to meet with such a glorious view."

"If being the best part of a mile in the air, and having men's farms and houses at your feet, with rivers looking like ribbons, and mountains bigger than the 'Vision,' seeming to be haystacks of green grass under you, gives any satisfaction to a man, I can recommend the spot. When I first came into the woods to live, I used to have weak spells when I felt lonesome; and then I would go into the Cattskills, and spend a few days on that hill to look at the ways of man; but it's now many a year since I felt any such longings, and I am getting too old for rugged rocks. But there's a place, a short two miles back of that very hill, that in late times I relished better than the mountain; for it was more covered with the trees, and natural."

"And where was that?" inquired Edwards, whose curiosity was strongly excited by the simple description of the hunter.

"Why, there's a fall in the hills where the water of two little ponds, that lie near each other, breaks out of their bounds and runs over the rocks into the valley. The stream is, maybe, such a one as would turn a mill, if so useless a thing was wanted in the wilderness. But the hand that made that 'Leap' never made a mill. There the water comes crooking and winding among the rocks; first so slow that a trout could swim in it, and then starting and running like a creatur' that wanted to make a far spring, till it gets to where the mountain divides, like the cleft hoof of a deer, leaving a deep hollow for the brook to tumble into. The first pitch is nigh two hundred feet, and the water looks like flakes of driven snow afore it touches the bottom; and there the stream gathers itself together again for a new start, and maybe flutters over fifty feet of flat rock before it falls another hundred, when it jumps about from shelf to shelf, first turning thisaway and then turning thataway, striving to get out of the hollow, till it finally comes to the plain."

"I have never heard of this spot before; it is not mentioned in the books."

"I never read a book in my life," said Leather-Stocking; "and how should a man who has lived in towns and schools know anything about the wonders of the woods? No, no, lad; there has that little stream of water been playing among the hills since He made the world, and not a dozen white men have ever laid eyes on it. The rock sweeps like mason-work, in a half-round, on both sides of the fall, and shelves over the bottom for fifty feet; so that when I've been sitting at the foot of the first pitch, and my hounds have run into the caverns behind the sheet of water, they've looked no bigger than so many rabbits. To my judgment, lad, its the best piece of work that I've met with in the woods; and none know how often the hand of God is seen in the wilderness, but them that rove it for a man's life."

"What becomes of the water? In which direction does it run? Is it a tributary of the Delaware?"

"Anan!" said Natty.

"Does the water run into the Delaware?"

"No, no; it's a drop for the old Hudson, and a merry time it has till it gets down off the mountain. I've sat on the shelving rock many a long hour, boy, and watched the bubbles as they shot by me, and thought how long it would be before that very water, which seemed made for the wilderness, would be under the bottom of a vessel, and tossing in the salt sea. It is a spot to make a man solemnize. You can see right down into the valley that lies to the east of the High Peak, where, in the fall of the year, thousands of acres of woods are before your eyes, in the deep hollow, and along the side of the mountain, painted like ten thousand rainbows, by no hand of man, though without the ordering of God's providence."

"You are eloquent, Leather-Stocking," exclaimed the youth.[32]

Evidently many others besides Edwards thought Leather-Stocking's description of the mountains was eloquent, for it became a common quotation of the nineteenth century literature of the Catskills. Even in the second half of the twentieth century Leather-Stocking's description of "all creation" is still quoted by those who attempt to describe the view from the crest of the mountains. In some cases Cooper's description is ascribed to the region of the Overlook House considerably south of Pine Orchard in the vicinity of Woodstock.[33] There is, indeed, no part of the Catskills which would not like to claim the famous description as its own. A careful reading of the full passage, however, makes it unmistakable that Cooper was referring to Pine Orchard and the view from the Catskill Mountain House. Indeed, so accurate and graphic is Cooper's description of this particular region that it seems obvious he drew it from first-hand acquaintance. It is quite possible that Cooper visited the area some time before the erection of the hotel. Many people did, as several dates that are engraved in the protruding "platform" attest. Since Cooper lived just to the west of the mountains at the foot of Otsego Lake and traveled to and from that place by way of the Hudson and Mohawk rivers, we may safely conclude that on one or more of those trips he made a slight detour to visit the dramatic heights of Pine Orchard.

It was this dramatic region that became the setting of the Catskill Mountain House and a glowing page in the history of American Romanticism. Though, as Leather-Stocking suggested, it extended from High Peak and Round Top on the south, to Kaaterskill Falls on the west, and from there north to the two lakes and North Mountain, it was the eastern boundary of the region along the high escarpment of the mountains that became the focal center of the whole select region. Here midway between Sleepy Hollow and Kaaterskill Clove at the head of an old abandoned road, "a large and singular plain" called Pine Orchard terminated in a remarkable "rock platform." [34] The subject of some of the oldest Indian legends of the Hudson Valley,[35] commemorated in the lore of the American Revolution,[36] known and sought out by early travelers of the nineteenth century as one of the most beautiful sights of the Atlantic seaboard,[37] the high stone "platform" of Pine Orchard became in 1823 the foundation of the Catskill Mountain House and the geographical center of the first great resort area in American history. As this development spread throughout the Catskills, bringing artists and writers, people of wealth and fashion, new towns and villages, extravagant hotels and art colonies, the Mountain House maintained its command of the eastern approaches to the mountains and became the hub and center of the whole movement, the acknowledged monarch of the mountains, one of the great hotels in American history.

The setting, the geography of mountain and seacoast, wilderness and city, was everything. The Mountain House and its growing domain occupied an ideal location on a high but accessible ledge of the American wilderness, just off the center of American population, one hundred and ten miles north of the fastest-growing city in the western hemisphere. This "juxtaposition of civilized and savage life," as one famous commentator called this abiding pattern of American life, was repeated in the nineteenth century history of the Catskills at a time when the Romantic Movement was making it a universal principle of art and culture. It became almost a metaphysical experience to realize, as William Cullen Bryant expressed it,

that on that little point, scarce visible on the breast of the mountain, the beautiful and the gay are met, and the sounds of mirth and music arise, while for leagues around the mountain torrents are dashing, and the eagle is uttering his shriek, unheard by human ear.[38]

The Catskills were all the American past, the deep primitivism of the American environment; the Mountain House was a symbol of a young nation's wealth, leisure and cultural attainments. The triumph of one would eventually destroy the other, but in the second quarter of the nineteenth century both were still equal manifestations of the American environment, and under the aegis of Romanticism Americans believed for one glowing moment in their history that they could have both. At this moment when the ancient dichotomies of nature and art, wilderness and luxury, primitivism and civilization, became harmonized in the fervor of man's belief, "straightway there rose up, like an exhalation, a splendid hotel, on the very brink of the precipice, some five-and-twenty hundred feet above the river." [39]

Chapter 2

The First Two Decades

Traveling through the wilds of the Catskills collecting material for his *Gazetteer of the State of New York* (1824) about the time Cooper's *The Pioneers* appeared on the bookstands of New York, H. G. Spafford noted that he was hearing

much of the *Pine Orchard* in this town [Hunter], near the [Kaaterskill] Falls, but I have not yet been able to view it, and no one has given me any information about it, calculated for my purpose, though I have applied to several. . . . Report says that a house of entertainment is about to be erected at the Pine Orchard, for the accommodation of visitants, and if so I may by-and-by see, and describe it, for my readers.[1]

Just before the *Gazetteer* was released from the printer, however, Spafford received his information; and he had the following footnote inserted:

After the copy of this Work was prepared for the press, a labor of 2 years, a gentleman favored me with the loan of his Journal, and remarks, having just returned from the above places, well pleased with a jaunt of some 3 or 4 days. . . . It will do well to follow [him] in this sketch, designed for the information of Tourists.—"From the Village of Catskill, traversing the Kaatskill [Creek], and the Kaaterskill, keeping along the right of the valley of the latter stream, to Lawrence's, at the foot of the mountains, the distance is 7 miles, thence to what is called the foot of the mountains, 2 miles, and thence to *Pine Orchard*, 3 more, making 12 miles. . . . *Pine Orchard*, is a sort of platform, too small to be called a table-land, of about 7 acres, situated on the Kaatsbergs, or Catskill Mountains, elevated about 3,000 feet above the tides of the Hudson, at the distance of 9 or 10 miles, supported on the E. by an awful precipice of graywacke . . . from which the view is as awe-inspiring as it is extensive. *Mr. Van Bergen* has a house of entertainment here, and by the season of company in 1824, will have a superb Hotel, of 60 by 24 feet, 3 stories, elegantly furnished and attended, erected by the '*Catskill Mountains Association*,' an incorporated Company, with a capital of $10,000." [2]

The passage marks the first mention in print of the Catskill Mountain House and so the very beginning of a long illustrious history. Local legend provides a foreground that is more romantic than these bare facts, and relating it may serve to introduce the prolific Beach family which from 1839 to 1929 held complete sway over the destiny of the great hotel.

During Lafayette's celebrated visit to the United States in 1824 he toured the Hudson Valley in the steamship *James Kent* and stopped briefly at the village of Catskill to receive the acclaim of its citizens, many of whom held that they had served under the great Marquis during the Revolution. Approaching from the south this is what he saw, in the words of his secretary:

Scarcely had we left Clermont, when we came in sight of the beautiful Catskill mountain, which arising at some miles from the river, finally terminates the horizon by its beautiful brown mass which is amphitheatrically developed, in the center of which shows forth the white house of the pine garden situated 2500 feet above the level of the Hudson. This house is an object of curiosity to the traveller, and a place of promenade for the neighboring inhabitants. [3]

Arriving at the long pier that extends from the village to the channel of the Hudson, Lafayette had time only to be paraded from there to the head of Main Street and back. The coach in which he rode was owned and operated by one Erastus Beach, the proprietor of the first livery service in Catskill. The second coach containing the welcoming committee was driven by Charles L. Beach, the sixteen-year-old son of Erastus. [4] This young man was to become one of the leading entrepreneurs in the history of transportation in the Hudson Valley, and from 1839 to 1902 the single most important force in the history of the Catskill Mountain House. At the time of Lafayette's visit, however, all this was still in the future; the Mountain House had been open only a few weeks, and it was the father, Erastus, who was associated—albeit apocryphally—with the story of its founding.

Erastus Beach, who had originally come from Goshen, Connecticut, about 1800, left Mt. Morris, New York, for Catskill in 1817. He established a livery service in that village in 1819, employing eight horses. In the summer of 1822 he purchased a coach and took it and four of his horses to find business at Saratoga where people of fashion had already begun to assemble during the summer months, drawn by the growing fame of the mineral waters in the area. He left his Catskill livery service in the hands of his son Charles, then fourteen years old. What happened after that may best be told by the author of the 1884 *History of Greene County* who probably received it from Charles L. Beach himself:

There his [Erastus's] services were engaged by a party of four ladies and four gentlemen, who retained him thirty days. At the end of that time they had seen all the points of interest and driven over all the attractive roads of that vicinity, and longed for some new field of pleasure. Mr. Beach, remembering the beautiful view he had obtained from the flat rock on South Mountain, to which he had once in his ramblings climbed, ventured to describe it to his party. They were interested and engaged him at once to take them thither. Approach to the mountain was not then the easy thing it is now. Going as far as the open road would allow, with the carriage, they placed the ladies on the horses and continued the ascent of the mountain. It was a laborious undertaking, but before nightfall they found themselves with wearied limbs and ruffled and tattered garments upon the commanding rock from which so many thousands have since looked off upon the glorious landscape of "Creation." Gathering boughs and hedging themselves in from the cool night wind, they made their beds upon the rock, and spent the night under the stars amid the grandeur of that virgin scene of solitude. That was probably the first night ever passed by a pleasure party of ladies and gentlemen from abroad upon the mountains. It is claimed that the idea of establishing a house for the accommodation of visitors to the mountain originated with this episode, but for that we cannot vouch, though it does not seem improbable.[5]

Though the writer is deservedly cautious about linking this episode with the actual founding of the Mountain House, many commentators have assumed it as a fact and held that the 1822 visit led Erastus Beach to help organize the Catskill Mountain Association and hence the first construction of the hotel. One such commentator is apparently Erastus's own son, Charles. The evidence for this is in the form of a typewritten manuscript that recently came to light in the home of a contemporary member of the Beach family.[6] Seemingly written or dictated by Charles L. Beach, this document follows the above account of the 1822 visit in all but one or two particulars. The first deviation declares that an "abandoned road" already existed up the face of the mountain to Pine Orchard, the second asserts that the party slept the first night "under a projecting ledge of rocks located about one hundred feet south of the summit"—later famous as Moses Rock.[7] Then occurs the following unequivocal statement:

Soon after this Erastus Beach was instrumental in organizing a stock company called the Catskill Mountain Association. This company was organized in 1823 and that year erected a Shanty with bunks and straw for bedding, for the accommodation of visitors, and also began building the original Catskill Mountain House which was opened in 1824. The hotel was kept the first year by Wilhelmus Van Bergen, father of J. C. Van Bergen, who had also kept the shanty of 1823 when the place was visited by Aaron Burr.[8]

While Erastus Beach may have been in some way "instrumental" in organizing the stock company, we know for a certainty that he was not part of its formal organization. Our proof is the original act of incorporation:

Be it enacted by the People of the State of New York, represented in Senate and Assembly, that James Powers, Caleb Benton, John Adams, Edwin Croswell, James Pierce, Apollas Cook, John A. Thomson, Jacob Haight, Henry McKinstry, and their associates and all such other persons as shall hereafter become stockholders in the Company hereby incorporated, be, and they are hereby ordained and declared a body corporate and politic, by the name of the president, directors, and company of the Catskill Mountain Association.[9]

Not only is the original charter silent about Erastus Beach, but "in none of the early organization and re-organization records of the Catskill Mountain Association," according to Mabel P. Smith, a local authority, "does a Beach name appear."[10] The fact is striking because local legend ascribes, even to this day,[11] the founding and subsequent history of the Mountain House to the Beach family alone. Mrs. Smith's conclusion is undoubtedly correct that the effective participation of the Beach family in the hotel's history does not begin until Charles L. Beach's leasing of it in 1839.[12]

As an adjunct of the livery service that Erastus opened in Catskill in 1819, he established the first stage service from Catskill to the Mountain House in 1823, an operation that remained in the exclusive hands of the Beach family until 1882 when it was supplanted by the Catskill Mountain Railroad. Erastus no doubt encouraged the formation of the original association that built the Mountain House, for it gave him a monopoly of the transportation facilities into the mountains. But it was the son, Charles L., who united the two enterprises and brought both the hotel and the transportation business to their highest pitch of development.

The first few years of the history of the Mountain House therefore belong exclusively to the Catskill Mountain Association. When the association was chartered by the state in 1823, it was authorized to buy land at Pine Orchard, to erect "a large and commodious hotel" as well as other buildings, and to build a road from the base of the mountains to the heights of Pine Orchard. The capital stock of the company was $6,000 in shares of $25.00 each, with a power to increase the amount to $10,000 at the discretion of the five directors. Within three years the legislature of New York increased the capital stock to $15,000 and granted other privileges, all of which attests the early success of the "commodious" edifice on the edge of the mountain. Land was acquired piecemeal, most of it coming from a large tract that had been originally granted to one Elisha Williams in 1813. The initial purchase was a 300-acre tract, more or less, of Pine Orchard.[13] It was sold to the association by James Powers and his wife on July 29, 1823.[14] Within a year more land was purchased from Hiram Comfort and Silas Scribner, the latter owning a large tract in the vicinity of South Lake. The association thus embarked the Mountain House upon a policy of continuous expansion until, under the leadership of Charles L. Beach, the hotel owned some 3,500 acres of the eastern escarpment of the mountains. It is a remarkable feature in the history of the Mountain House, and it did not come to an end until the third decade of the twentieth century when the descendants of Charles L. Beach were forced to face the harsh realities of the great depression.

There can be no doubt that the association opened the first Mountain House proper in the early summer of 1824, but there is considerable confusion regarding the first building of 1823. We know from an early account book of the treasurer of the Catskill Mountain Association that "old buildings" existed at Pine Orchard prior to the erection of the hotel of 1824 and that they passed into the ownership of the association sometime in 1823. According to the Rev. Charles Rockwell these buildings had been erected "for the accommodation of summer parties and excursions [sic], but not for lodgers." [15] The author of the 1884 *History of Greene County*, on the other hand, declares that they had merely afforded "a temporary protection from the weather," [16] and J. Van Vetchen Vedder declares they had been built "for the accommodation of travellers." [17] Charles L. Beach, the later owner of the Mountain House, confuses the issue still further by asserting that in 1823 the association itself "erected a Shanty with bunks and straw for bedding, for the accommodation of vistors, and also began building the original Catskill Mountain House which was opened in 1824." [18] Beach, however, was writing many years after the event, and it seems more likely that the association refurbished the old buildings as the first "Shanty" of 1823 rather than erected new temporary buildings.

The temporary house of 1823 was leased by Wilhelmus Van

Bergen, who also leased and managed the first permanent building of 1824. It was built of hemlock boards whose length determined the height of the building, and the interior was divided into two dormitories, a kitchen, ballroom and parlor. The dormitories were outfitted with bunks and divided into separate quarters for men and women. In stark contrast to the luxury for which the first Mountain House proper became famous, the bedding in the Shanty of 1823 was simply loose straw "for the gentlemen" and coarse ticks filled with straw for "the ladies." [19] Notables such as Aaron Burr and De Witt Clinton were known to have visited this temporary hotel, and Charles L. Beach declared he made his first visit to Pine Orchard when as a lad of fifteen he drove one of his father's coaches to the grand opening on July 4, 1823.[20]

While there may be confusion regarding the history of this temporary building, there can be no doubt about the first Mountain House proper. The house that Lafayette saw from the Hudson River in the summer of 1824—already the gleaming white structure that it was to remain throughout its history—was the first permanent Mountain House, erected during the fall and winter of 1823 and finished in time for the initial season of 1824. All the timber for this building was hewed on the spot, from the forests of South Mountain. There is a legend that many of the white pines that were used for the sills and upper floor beams of the hotel were marked with the ancient imprint of the arrow of the British crown and had been originally consigned to the royal navy for use as ship masts.[21] Construction of the hotel was in charge of Wells Finch, a local carpenter, and Samuel Chichester, a young man of Welsh background who had just completed his apprenticeship under Finch in the nearby town of Cairo and who eventually became, in the 1850s and 1860s, one of the leading furniture manufacturers in the state.[22] When the building was completed in the spring of 1824 it contained a minimum of ten rooms, was three stories high, sixty feet long facing the Hudson, twenty-four feet wide,[23] and had a large columned piazza

Figure 3. *The Mountain House*, Harry Fenn, 1870. From the engraving in *Picturesque America*, William Cullen Bryant, ed. (New York, 1874), Vol. II, p. 116.

that was to remain a characteristic feature of the Mountain House throughout all its later additions and expansions.

The elite of American society began to patronize the Mountain House with its very first season, drawn in part by William L. Stone, friend of James Fenimore Cooper and editor of the New York *Commercial Advertiser,* who used the pages of his popular newspaper to publicize the beauties of the new resort in the Catskills. In an article of 1824, Stone was one of the first to note that "the rock on which the Mountain House stands projects out like a circular platform beyond the regular line of the ridge." [24] A dramatic, if exaggerated, depiction of this well-known feature in the setting of the Mountain House may be found as late as 1874 in an engraving done by Harry Fenn for William Cullen Bryant's *Picturesque America.* This famous feature of the hotel has subsequently all but disappeared, for it has fallen piecemeal through the years from its own unsupported weight, leaving today a cleaner, if less dramatic, line along the the ridge of the mountains.

The striking success of the Mountain House during its first season was impressively demonstrated in the purchase of more land in August of 1824, in the petition of the association for extra privileges and increased capital stock, and the immediate initiation of plans to more than triple the size of the original building. In 1825 fifty rooms were added, at a cost of about $22,000,[25] and the Mountain House assumed at this time the shape and size it was to maintain with only minor changes until 1839 when Charles L. Beach took it over.

Local information regarding the construction history of the Mountain House is virtually nonexistent,[26] but several prints and engravings that depict the house during the period 1825–1839 show what it looked like before Beach bought it. One of the earliest paintings of the house done by Thomas Cole about 1828 (later engraved and printed in J. H. Hinton's *History and Topography of the United States* in 1830); an engraving done by W. Bennett for the *New Mirror* before 1835; another by W. H. Bartlett, c.1836–38, all show substantially the same house.

It was divided into two sections with a combined frontal length of one hundred and forty feet; the first and main section had four floors, the top floor being servant quarters under the gabled roofs. The roof of this part of the house was characterized by pitched balustrades and a square level area much like a widow's walk, which permitted patrons to ascend to the roof for the best view of the Hudson Valley. In subsequent years under Beach, these walks and gables were eliminated and the house acquired the clean lines that made it one of the best examples of American Neo-Classic. As originally built, however, it was distinctly Federal. There was also a flagpole (later transferred to the rock ledges in front of the house) which arose from the roof of the oldest and most central section.

The second section was an attached three-story wing, slightly to the rear of the main section. In subsequent years this wing underwent a remarkable evolution and housed (near the rear or service entrance) a prodigious kitchen and servants' quarters. Later still a large wing was added to the south side of the house. In this final form the Mountain House contained more than three hundred rooms and accommodated at least five hundred people. Before 1839, it was a far more modest structure of fifty or sixty rooms and gave little hint of its ultimate grandeur. Classical influence was already present before 1839 in a columned façade: eight columns rose before three of the four floors of the first section, and seven or eight more columns extended the full three floors of the second section. Bartlett's picture of 1836–38 clearly displays these as fluted Doric columns, but this design is difficult to confirm in earlier illustrations of the Mountain House. A piazza extended across the front of both sections, but was raised above the ground so that the floor of the piazza was midway between the first and second floors of the hotel—a rather Italianate feature that gave promenaders a better view of the Hudson Valley. Access to the piazza was provided by two staircases that were placed at right angles to the oldest section of the building. When the hotel later achieved its pure classical form, thirteen Corinthian columns rose from the floor of the piazza rather than the ground and thereby extended over the second and third floors only. The two staircases were also eliminated in favor of a single broad staircase that was placed in the middle of the piazza. The columns were always a noteworthy feature of the Mountain House; they added an extra attraction to the front bedrooms of the hotel: descriptions abound of how beautiful the sunrise appeared when one reclined in bed and watched the dawn's early light filter through the great Corinthian columns.[27]

Unfortunately, we possess very little information on the interior aspect of the Mountain House, probably because most commentators were much more concerned to exercise their literary talents on the "indescribable sublimities" of the great out-of-doors. We may be certain, however, about the luxury and

Figure 4. *Catskill Mountains*, William J. Bennett, c. 1828. Drawn and engraved for the *New Mirror*. The Mountain House from the bend in the road.

Figure 5. *View from the Mountain House, Catskill,* W. H. Bartlett, 1836. From the engraving by R. Brandard in N. P. Willis, *American Scenery* (London, 1838–40).

elegance of the hotel's general appointment and facilities. One early comment asserts that "the apartments are appropriately and richly furnished, and splendid mirrors sparkle in the drawing rooms, and rich carpets spread the floors, while couches of ease and elegance afford a grateful rest to the weary traveler."[28] One of the most sophisticated dandies of nineteenth century *belles lettres,* Nathaniel P. Willis, discovered what he thought was almost too much luxury. You may find at the Mountain House, he wrote in 1843, a choice of " 'white' or 'red' Burgundias, Madeiras, French dishes, and French dances, as if you had descended upon Capua." Such luxury was almost unnatural:

How the proprietor can have dragged up, and keeps dragging up, so many superfluities from the river level to the eagle's nest, excites your wonder. It is the more strange, because in climbing a mountain the feeling is natural that you leave such enervating indulgences below.[29]

All of this meant that the prices were high at the Mountain House [Appendix]. Many people complained about this; but many more,

Figure 6. The Catskill Mountain House, 1892. Photograph by J. Loeffler, Tompkinsville, Staten Island, New York.

like the class-conscious Harriet Martineau, found that the high prices were the justifiable cost of the hotel's most welcome comforts. "When we were departing," the Englishwoman asserted during a visit of 1834 or 1835,

a foreign tourist was heard to complain of the high charges! High charges! As if we were to be supplied for nothing on a perch where the wonder is if any but the ravens get fed! When I considered what a drawback it is in visiting mountain-tops that one is driven down again almost immediately by one's bodily wants, I was ready to thank the people devoutly for harboring us on any terms, so that we might think out our thoughts, and compose our emotions, and take our fill of that portion of our universal and eternal inheritance.[30]

Correct about the high prices at the Mountain House (they were high throughout its nineteenth century history), Harriet Martineau was less than accurate about another aspect of its fame. Noting that most travelers and tourists of the time were well acquainted with the Hudson Valley, she yet ventured the opinion that "very few travellers have seen its noblest wonder," the Catskill Mountain House. "What is this Mountain House? this Pine Orchard House? many will ask; for its name is not to be found in most books of American travels." [31]

Such was hardly the case. Not only in travel books, but in the media of art, literature, and journalism the fame of the Mountain House was fully established by the time Mrs. Martineau published that statement in 1838. The evidence is eloquent and extensive. As early as 1828 one visitor noted that

The Pine Orchard is the resort of so much company during the pleasant seasons of the year, that the attractions of its scenery are redoubled by the presence of agreeable and refined society. Individuals of taste and leisure, and still more, parties of travellers, will thus often enjoy a gratification which is rarely to be found in a place naturally so wild and difficult of access.[32]

Ten years later, or the very year that Mrs. Martineau published her presumed discovery of the unknown wonder of the Hudson Valley, one of the most popular novelists of the day, James Fenimore Cooper, informed the readers of his latest novel that the three most important sights of the Atlantic seaboard were Lake George, Niagara Falls and, quite simply, "the Mountain House." [33] As for references to the Mountain House in books of travel, Harriet Martineau's own compatriot, Captain Basil Hall, provided a description of the hotel in his popular *Travels in North America*, published in London as early as 1829. An account also appeared in *Impressions of America*, 1833–35, by the famous Irish actor, Tyrone Power. The following year William Henry Bartlett, a young but already famous English artist and author, visited the Mountain House with N. P. Willis (who also had an international reputation), to make drawings of the hotel for *American Scenes*, a picture book on the scenery of America.[34] But as early as 1830 William Cullen Bryant avowed in his *American Landscape* (text by Bryant, drawings by Asher B. Durand), that the view from Pine Orchard had already "become familiar" to a large number of people, because "a house of entertainment has been erected . . . which within a few years has become a place of fashionable resort during the summer heats." [35] Indeed, if one of the first guidebooks to be published in America may be trusted, the fame and popularity of the Mountain House was a spontaneous development of the hotel's actual founding. *The Northern Traveller* declared in 1826 that "an excursion to the summit of the mountains is performed by great numbers of travellers; and indeed has become so favourite an enterprise, that it may very properly be ranged among the principal objects in the great tour which we are just commencing." [36] Within two years of its opening, the Mountain House had already become a central object of American travel.

Extensive publicity certainly favored that development. An early example, already alluded to, was William L. Stone's article in the *Commercial Advertiser* (1824). Other examples abound in the first two decades of the hotel's history. So extensive had the literature on the Mountain House become by 1845, and so well represented by the famous writers of the time, that beginning that year a series of booklets with a selection of the more important writers (e.g. James Fenimore Cooper, Washington Irving, Willis Gaylord Clark, Tyrone Power, N. P. Willis, Park Benjamin, Harriet Martineau, William Cullen Bryant, Elizabeth F. L. Ellet, Thomas Cole and many others) were published at periodic intervals by the Mountain House itself, probably under the instigation of its new proprietor, Charles L. Beach.[37]

The literature of the decade 1835–1845 especially reflects the growing stature of the Mountain House. It is readily apparent from references to Pine Orchard, the village of Catskill, and the Mountain House in guidebooks, gazetteers and other sources during this period that although this whole area had become a well-established resort at this time, it was the Mountain House alone that made it so. In another ten years more and more hotels and boardinghouses appeared in the village of Catskill and the Kiskatom Valley. In another thirty years extraordinarily large hotels—in one or two instances even larger than the Mountain House—were built in the many valleys and cloves of the central

Catskills. But from 1835 to 1845 all evidence indicates that when people spoke of "the Catskills" they meant the Catskill Mountain House and its immediate domain.

When the *Hudson River Guide* referred to the village of Cats-kill in 1835, for instance, it merely asserted that "the village is in the immediate neighborhood of the Catskill Mountains, and has become the resort of people of fashion and pleasure, who design a tour of *Pine Orchard*, 12 miles distant . . ." [38]

Perhaps the most informative as well as amusing account of the status of Pine Orchard and the Mountain House during this period was written by N. P. Willis. In a long description which appeared in *American Scenery* (1840), Willis evoked the mid-nineteenth century life of the whole Hudson Valley and thus the fullest regional significance of the unique role and location of the Mountain House. Observing the view from the heights of Pine Orchard during a hot summer's day, he declared:

At this elevation, you may wear woollen and sleep under blankets in mid-summer; and that is a pleasant temperature where much hard work is to be done in the way of pleasure-hunting. No place so agreeable as Catskill, after one has been parboiled in the city. New York is at the other end of that long thread of a river, running away south from the base of the mountain; and you may change your climate in so brief a transit, that the most enslaved broker in Wall Street may have half his home on Catskill. The cool winds, the small silver lakes, the falls, the mountain-tops, are all delicious haunts for the idler-away of the hot months; and, to the credit of our taste, it may be said they are fully improved—Catskill is a 'resort.'

From the Mountain-House, the busy and all glorious Hudson is seen wending half its silver length—towns, villages, and white spires, sparkling on the shores, and snowy sails and gaily-painted steamers, specking its bosom. It is a constant diorama of the most lively beauty; and the traveller, as he looks down upon it, sighs to make it a home. Yet a small and less-frequented stream would best fulfil desires born of a sigh. There is either no seclusion on the Hudson, or there is so much that the conveniences of life are difficult to obtain. Where the steamers come to shore, (twenty a day, with each from one to seven hundred passengers,) it is certainly far from secluded enough; yet, away from the landing-places, servants find your house too lonely, and your table, without unreasonable expense and trouble, is precarious and poor. . . . No place can be rural, in all the *virtues* of the phrase, where a steamer will take the villager to the city between noon and night, and bring him back between midnight and morning. There is a suburban look and character about all the villages on the Hudson which seems out of place among such scenery. They are suburbs; in fact, steam has destroyed the distance between them and the city.[39]

Such was the particularly American aspect and development of the Hudson Valley by 1838 when the Mountain House had already become an indigenous part of its culture.

Thus contrary to the opinion of Harriet Martineau, that development had already fulfilled itself by the mid-1830s when the *Retrospect of Western Travel* was first published. As N. P. Willis said elsewhere in *American Scenery*,

Catskill is more known as the landing-place for travellers bound to the mountains above, than for any remarkable events in its own history, or any singular beauties in itself. It is a thrifty little village, in which the most prosperous vocations are those of innkeeper and stage-proprietor, and, during the summer months, these two crafts of Catskill entertain and transport to the hotel on the mountain half the population of the United States—more or less. The crowded steamers stop at the landing on their way up and down [the river between Albany and New York]; and a busier scene than is presented on the wharf twice in the day, for a minute and a half, could not easily be found.[40]

Erastus Beach's stages met those boats twice a day and took their passengers for $1.00 to the Mountain House, but we may note from Willis's remarks that that was the end of the line: the destination of all these tourists and sightseers of the 1830s was still Pine Orchard and its immediate area.

Then in 1845, just five years after he had leased the hotel from the Catskill Mountain Association, Charles L. Beach acquired complete ownership of the famous edifice and inaugurated the greatest period of its history.

Frontispiece: BEACH MOUNTAIN HOUSE, THE ARTIST SKETCHING, *Sarah Cole, 1848 (oil on canvas, 15" x 23¼"); inscribed on the back, "A view of the Catskill Mountain House copied from a picture by T. Cole by S. Cole, 1848." Courtesy of the Albany Institute of History and Art. A copy by Thomas Cole's sister of his original, which is in a private collection.*

Plate 1: A VIEW OF THE TWO LAKES AND MOUNTAIN HOUSE, CATSKILL MOUNTAINS, MORNING 1844, *Thomas Cole, 1844 (oil on canvas, 36¼″ x 54″). Courtesy of the Brooklyn Museum.*

Plate 2: CATSKILL MOUNTAIN HOUSE, *unknown artist, Hudson River School, undated (oil on canvas, 16¼" x 22¼"). Collection of Gary & Barbara Slutzky.* (Figure 21).

Plate 3: CATSKILL MOUNTAIN HOUSE (FROM NORTH MOUNTAIN), Jaspar F. Cropsey, 1855 (oil on canvas, 29" x 44"). Courtesy of the Minneapolis Institute of Arts, William Hood Dunwoody Fund.

Chapter 3

The Early Years under
Charles L. Beach

The pattern of a successful life often returns, for its earliest manifestation, to the humblest acts of youth. So there was importance in the appearance of Charles L. Beach on the ledges of Pine Orchard during the opening ceremonies of the Catskill Mountain House on July 4, 1823. Charles Beach was sixteen, an employee in his father's stagecoach business; he had come merely to transport guests and patrons from the village of Catskill. Yet the event was pregnant with a future alliance that would bring one of the most singular figures in the history of New York State, and one of the greatest hotels in American history, to their highest fulfillment.

Faithful to the pattern of his youth, Beach devoted his major energies to the transportation business throughout a long and extraordinary life, and it was the early success of this endeavor that permitted him to become in 1845 full owner of the Mountain House. But even after the hotel business and, later on, banking and milling, had been added to his wide range of interests, transportation still remained the economic center of his life, the mainstay of all other activities. The Mountain House was a resplendent symbol of wealth, leisure and culture, and brought him fame and a secure niche in the cultural history of the Hudson Valley; but the transportation business brought him financial security and the power to invade the impractical realms of poetry. In a pattern characteristic of the age-old schism between art and business in American life, Beach's transportation enterprise became the unsung catalyst of the world-renowned "palace built for angels."

Like most young men first setting out in life, Charles L. Beach did not immediately find his life's vocation. Passing quickly from one job to another, he soon displayed an uncommon ability for converting each position into a handsome source of profit. After several such coups he had the capital to enter the transportation business, and was on his way. Fearless and highly competitive, Beach soon surpassed his father at his own vocation and finally established a local economic empire that would employ his descendants to the third or fourth generations.

Charles L. Beach was nine years old when his father gave up his pioneer store in Mt. Morris, New York, to become a constable in Catskill; and he was eleven when the country-wide traveling entailed by this position encouraged his father to establish the first livery service in Catskill. The son's life was to span the history of transportation from the saddle horse to the steam engine, but it began in the livery service of his father where he spent his apprenticeship tending horses and driving stagecoaches in the village of Catskill. Though the father's business had grown in five or six years from four or five horses to eight horses and two or three stagecoaches, the son repeated an earlier pattern of his father's and in the fall of 1824 at the age of sixteen went out on his own to work in a general store in the nearby whaling village of Hudson. The experience ended in the economic exploitation that many beginners encounter in life, for after a year and a half of service the only compensation young Beach had received was his board and a gift of $5.00.

During this period while the future entrepreneur learned the facts of life, momentous developments were occurring in New York State: in 1825 the Erie Canal was opened; about the same time New York City supplanted Philadelphia and Boston as the nation's foremost center of literature, art, and population; and Catskill rapidly acquired the status of a major resort center, attracting artists and writers as well as tourists and sightseers from all over the East. Charles Beach decided he had better seek his fortune in his own home town.

Leaving the employ of John Powers in Hudson, he started work in a dry-goods store in Catskill in the spring of 1826 at the age of eighteen. The store was owned by Sam Smith, a Quaker, who paid him $50.00 a year plus board. Then occurred the first of those exploits which were to become an abiding feature of Beach's business talents: in five years' time he passed from employee to employer, purchased the business outright with one George Marvin, and three months later ended the whole affair with a profit of $1,000 by selling his interest to Marvin. It was the first coup of his career, and in three months' time in 1831 he was able to make forty times the amount that he had earned in the previous five years.

Or almost so. Part of young Beach's wealth at this time came from The United States Insurance Company, for which he had become an agent some time between 1826 and 1831. With the compensation he received from this agency plus the $1,000 he had received from Marvin, Beach found himself with enough capital to enter the transportation business; and he did it forthwith, liquidating all interests in both the insurance and the dry goods business.

Beach had now embarked upon his life's work, but it is noteworthy that from the start he did so without becoming in any way subservient to his father. At this time the elder Beach and a Mr. Rowe ran a stage line from Catskill to Stamford in the northwestern foothills of the Catskills. Charles Beach decided to make his debut into the transportation business by opening his own line from Stamford to Ithaca, forming one unbroken stage line from the Hudson to the central part of the state. It was a bold and even ruthless act that displayed another abiding characteristic of young Beach's business dealings, for it was a deliberate threat to another company that already ran a line from Ithaca to Newburgh on the lower Hudson. The stratagem was brilliantly successful: after eighteen months of strenuous competition, during which young Beach used Ithaca as his base of operations, the older stage line sued for peace. In the spring of 1833 at the age of twenty-five Charles Beach sold his company to his competitor and returned to Catskill with $3,000 in cash. It was the second great coup of his career.

This left the elder Beach and his partner with their original stage line from Catskill to Stamford. Ordinarily this line could be expected to continue operating just as it had before Charles Beach extended it by way of his line to Ithaca. But this was not to be. By a strange coincidence (which gains no clarification in the son's autobiography), the father's line lost its mail contracts "about this time" to a powerful opposition line by the name of Tompkins and Morgan which ran from Catskill to Delhi, twenty miles to the west of Stamford.[1] The loss of this important source of revenue was as catastrophic to the old stage line as it would be to a modern airline, and it caused the failure of the firm of Rowe and Beach and left the two partners with a debt of $4,500 that had been contracted with Francis Sayre, a former partner.

The son's reaction was remarkable. Activated by guilt or simply a desire to avenge the ruin of his father, Charles Beach used the whole of the $3,000 he had acquired from the sale of his own line to pay off the debt to Francis Sayre (leaving $1,500 in notes), acquired complete control of the defunct line, and began running it between Catskill and Delhi in open defiance of the line of Tompkins and Morgan. This plan was only partially successful: "after a very lively opposition of about six months," according to the discreet wording of Beach's autobiography, Tompkins and Morgan "purchased C. L. Beach's stage property at a price that enabled him to retire from the business without loss."[2] In point of fact, Beach was forced out of business without losing or gaining a cent, for he came out with "$3,000 in cash," or the same amount with which he originally went in. The remarkable thing is that he hadn't lost everything he had: Tompkins and Morgan was the most powerful stage line in that part of New York State, and the fact that the young Beach could fight it to a standstill gives proof of his superior drive and ability. The moral victory belonged to him.

Still, both he and his father had been driven from the field and they now faced the necessity of changing their scene of operations. Encouraged by his successful bout with the powerful Tompkins and Morgan, full of self-confidence and the impetuosity of youth, Charles Beach decided to challenge big business itself and invade the "commercial emporium" of New York City. Taking the $3,000 he had won from Tompkins and Morgan, he set up his father in the livery business in the most competitive city in America, but before the winter of 1833–34 was over both father and son had been reduced to bankruptcy.

This was Charles L. Beach's time of trial. In spite of the auspicious triumphs of his early youth, the unmistakable signs of mastery and high achievement, he arrived on the threshold of manhood without any means of livelihood, bereft of career and fortune. Turning his back upon a field of endeavor that had brought ruin both to himself and his family, he pitched about for a new means of livelihood and in the spring of 1834 somehow managed to lease a hotel that stood on the later site of the Irving House in his native town of Catskill.

Then fortune smiled upon Charles L. Beach precisely when he was in greatest need. With many successful lives, this seems to be the design of providence: one miraculous stroke of good luck wrests victory from defeat and establishes the pattern of a lifetime. It happened to Beach in the spring of 1835 when he was twenty-seven years old.

In April of that year Major Augustus Morgan, one of the principal partners in the firm of Tompkins and Morgan, received a letter from the other principal partner directing him (Morgan) to offer Tompkins' interest in the firm to the man they had driven out of business two years before, "on such terms as might be convenient and satisfactory to Mr. Beach." The event throws considerable light on the harsh events of Beach's frantic competition with Tompkins and Morgan in 1833, for Tompkins' generous offer was prompted by a deathbed twinge of conscience over the ruthless tactics that had been employed to drive the Beaches out of business. The offer was accepted with alacrity and Beach acquired a one-third interest in one of the most powerful transportation companies in the upper Hudson Valley. From this moment, failure for Charles L. Beach became a thing of the past.

True to his youthful patterns, Beach promptly exploited his opportunity with all his characteristic force and ingenuity. He soon purchased the one-third interest in the firm held by Sidney Robinson. After continuing in partnership with Major Morgan for two years, Beach purchased his one-third interest in 1837 for $6,000, giving notes for that amount, and became sole owner of the firm at the age of twenty-nine. In seven eventful years (1835–1842) this is what he accomplished: he became complete owner of the firm; he enlarged the stage company until he controlled all lines up both sides of the Hudson from New York to Albany and acquired all mail contracts for the same; he married, started a family and built a large home in Catskill; he became master of the Catskill Mountain House; and he accumulated a fortune of $35,000.

Two events stemming from this period of Beach's life dramatize not only the conditions of American travel in the first half of the nineteenth century, but the young entrepreneur's force and ingenuity. The first occurred during the exceptionally severe winter of 1836–37 when stagecoaches were converted into sleighs and people traveled the frozen Hudson between Poughkeepsie and Albany for almost four months of the year. At the height of the winter the Canadian border dispute (known to history as "The Caroline Affair") threatened to become a full-fledged war between the United States and Canada. Alarmed by the extent of the emergency, President Van Buren ordered General Winfield Scott, an experienced trouble-shooter and pacifier of the Indian frontiers, to hasten to Canada to avert hostilities. Arriving in New York, Scott soon learned that Charles L. Beach was the only man who could supply transportation up the Hudson Valley during the winter months and asked him to make all arrangements by eight o'clock that evening. Beach eagerly accepted the challenge, dispatched couriers up the hundred-and-fifty-mile course of the valley and alerted the relay stations that were placed about every fifteen miles on the frozen river. The general's sleigh converted into a huge bed complete with mattress, blankets and pillows, left New York City promptly at eight, drawn by four of the fleetest horses. Scott himself later informed the public that he was asleep before he had even left the Bowery and that he did not awaken until eight o'clock the next morning when the sleigh was drawn up at a hotel in Albany and he was greeted with the words, "General Scott, your breakfast is served." [3]

Although the second episode which illustrates Beach's ingenuity in improvising more rapid means of transit belongs to local rather than national history, it still reveals the rugged individualism that typified successful businessmen of early nineteenth century America. The authoritative account comes from the pen of Mabel Parker Smith:

Newspaper rivalry reached a high pitch in the 1840's and the Governor's annual message convening the Legislature was a high prize in New York City. The advance release to newspapers had not yet been thought up so the race began when the Governor finished speaking. The contest reached its climax on January 3 and 4, 1843, when Mr. Beach contracted with the New York Sun to outdistance every other newspaper's combined horse, rail and boat delivery. Dimock, a famous driver, was assigned. The undertaking was to put the message in New York within 11 hours of its proclamation in Albany. Dimock received the document shortly after 2 p.m. The weather was fine as he shot down the West side route, meeting relays of horses every six or eight miles. The course bore inland to Goshen 107 miles away where he drew to a halt in little more than six hours. There Mr. Beach was waiting with an Erie Railroad engine fired and champing at its steel bit; he seized the paper, mounted the engine, and away they went snorting steam down to Piermont on the Hudson where a steamboat was all fired up at the dock with the most incredible cargo and passenger list: 12 printers with complete fonts of Sun type. The message was set up in type as the vessel plied the river and on the morning of January 4 the Sun burst on the city with headlines screeching: "By the Sun's Exclusive Express, from Albany through the Horse and Sleigh in 10 hours and one-half."

It was disclosed later that the rival dailies had attempted the dash by the Housatonic Railroad with two locomotives which were found next day stalled in snowdrifts at State Line.[4]

Such were the qualities that enabled Beach during the decade of 1835–1845 to acquire a small fortune and lease and then purchase the Catskill Mountain House. He did it mostly by revolutionizing the mail and passenger service of the whole Hudson Valley during the long winter season when the steamboats were not running. Perhaps Beach acquired the Mountain House to help fortify his reduced business activities during the slack summer months; in any event, it was his striking success with the transportation business that made the purchase possible. When Beach first became a partner in the firm of Tompkins and Morgan the company had mail contracts for only the limited run between Catskill and Ithaca—the far more lucrative runs down both sides of the Hudson were controlled by other companies. Under Beach's proprietorship the company absorbed both competing lines, amalgamated them into one efficient system, and acquired the mail contracts for the whole valley. The older and more developed eastern shore of the Hudson required one mail and two passenger lines daily, in each direction; the western shore also required two lines daily in each direction. Both lines together were equivalent to one continuous system of fifteen hundred miles. In addition to this, Beach continued to run the old line between Catskill and the Finger Lakes, a daily line in each direction equivalent to more than three hundred miles. All lines together came to a grand total of more than eighteen hundred miles of daily service.

The mail service between New York and Albany was scheduled at eight miles per hour, restricted for the most part to night travel and the harsh winter months. Coach service was greatly improved: the old platform wagons were replaced by the safer and more comfortable Concord coaches, and each coach was drawn by four horses in relays of about every fifteen miles. Taverns along the route were also improved, and a dependable schedule of twenty-four to twenty-eight hours was strictly maintained. The stages departed from a home base that was located at the old Western Hotel on Cortlandt Street, and they broke into open country around the present site of 14th Street. Much like present-day buses, the stages added additional coaches when the traffic demanded it, and five or six coaches could often be seen leaving together from the Western Hotel during a busy weekend. An armed government guard usually sat on the high front seat of the first or mail coach; his duty was to guard the mails and see that the schedule was rigorously maintained.

Winter travel was especially picturesque, however uncomfortable. When the ice was especially thick on the upper river, it often formed a far safer roadway than the hilly route along each bank. At such times the wheels of the coaches were replaced by sled runners and swift time was made up the very course of the river. Temporary "tavern shanties" or relay stations were set up at periodic intervals along the icy highway. One winter the snow was so deep around the old post office, located at that time in a converted church, that the mail had to be delivered through the second floor windows. The mails generally weighed a ton and a half per trip, and so successful was the operation that Beach was never fined by the government for failures—a common practice in those days. In later years when the Hudson River Railroad was completed as far as Poughkeepsie and the mails had to go by stage from that point to Albany, Beach was rewarded for his extraordinary record by securing the mail contracts for two years "at his own price without competition of other bidders and also without any security being required." [5]

The railroads, however, spelled the ruin of the stagecoach business. The first steam railroad to reach the Hudson River was that of the 16-mile Mohawk and Hudson Railroad which started service between Schenectady and Albany in 1831. The Erie Railroad reached the western shore of the Hudson at Piermont in 1841. As the Hudson River Railroad penetrated each new area of the valley it absorbed the passenger and mail service of the stage line; by 1851 when the railroad reached all the way to Albany the era of the stagecoach in the Hudson Valley had come to an end. Always sensitive to the trend of the times, Charles Beach liquidated his interests in the stage and mail business as early as 1842. He transferred the business to his younger brothers, A. F. and G. L. Beach, whom he assisted and advised until they too yielded to the railroad in 1849. This did not by any means bring an end to Charles Beach's general involvement in transportation (in the 1850s and 1860s he acquired a monoply of the steamship and freighting service between Catskill and New York); but 1842 saw the termination of the first phase of his interest in the field of transportation, and through it he acquired the financial means of entering the hotel business and becoming owner of the Catskill Mountain House.

One of the earliest notices of the new ownership appeared on the inside cover of a booklet called *The Scenery of the Catskill Mountains*, published in New York City:[6]

For the information of strangers, the proprietor begs leave to say, that within the last two years he has torn down the old house referred to by the tourists, and erected a far better, longer and more convenient building for the entertainment of his guests. No exertion or expense has been spared to render the Mountain House an agreeable retreat to those who seek health, pleasure, or retirement from business.

It is a building one hundred and fifty feet front, with a wing of one hundred and thirty feet, and both three stories high. A splendid colonnade extends along the whole front of the main building. It is hoped and believed that its accommodations will be found at least equal to those of any other fashionable establishment in the country.

The statement appears to derive from first-hand information, yet it bristles with inaccuracies. There is, for instance, no evidence whatsoever that Beach tore down the old house. His own autobiography merely asserts that "in 1845 C. L. Beach rebuilt a portion of the original hotel which is still standing, and in subsequent years enlarged it at various times as business increased."

An engraving of the Mountain House done most probably in 1844 when William Scobie managed the hotel for Beach, shows a large wing, easily a hundred and thirty feet long, already attached to the northern side of the building. This wing does not appear in Bartlett's print of 1836 and it was probably constructed some time between 1839, when Beach first leased the hotel, and 1845 when he added the "splendid colonnade" noted in the above booklet.

It is instructive to compare the Scobie print of 1844 with a picture of the hotel that appeared on the cover of *The Scenery of the Catskill Mountains*, published by the Mountain House itself in 1847 or 1848. The two houses are identical except for the following features: the flagpole and federalist appurtenances on the roof of the older house (gables, balustrades, catwalks) have been eliminated; thirteen Corinthian columns have replaced twenty pillars along the piazza of the first house; and a single staircase has replaced the former two staircases that used to approach the piazza from the north and south sides. The dimension of the piazza (on either house) was one hundred and forty feet, not one hundred and fifty. This is exactly the dimension of the *whole front* of the house after its 1825 enlargement when that front was broken into two sections. By 1844 the second section had been moved forward to be flush with the first, forming the famous one-hundred-and-forty-foot piazza that remained unaltered (except for the addition of the Corinthian columns) throughout all the subsequent years of the Mountain House. The new north wing (i.e. of 1844) has added another fifty or sixty feet to the one-hundred-and-forty-foot building of 1825, thus making a total frontage of one hundred and ninety to two hundred feet. Aside from the statement that Beach has "torn down" the original 1825 hotel, which is simply apocryphal, the publisher of the first booklet entitled *The Scenery of the Catskill Mountains* has probably condensed several years of construction history into one dramatic but fictitious incident.

We have no record of the architect or artisan who helped to give the house its classical shape and form, but the builders were

Figure 7. *Catskill Mountain-House*, C. Parsons, c. 1844 (drawn on stone). From a lithograph by Endicott. A view of the Mountain House the year it was run by William Scobie just prior to Charles L. Beach's acquisition. Courtesy of the Old Print Shop, Harry Shaw Newman.

undoubtedly local craftsmen, and it is not improbable that the classical architecture of the hotel was the happy result of its thirteen Corinthian columns. The manufacture of such columns was apparently native to the area, for the village of Cauterskill (near Catskill) once possessed woodworking mills that supplied columns for the Southern market of the antebellum years. The columns that still may be seen on the façade of the Christ Presbyterian Church in Catskill, of which Beach was a member, came from the same lot of columns that were added to the Mountain House, and we may assume that Beach gave one set of columns to the church at about the time he placed the remaining thirteen on the famous façade of the Mountain House. It is the opinion of a contemporary Kingstonian who can still remember Charles Beach and his son, that the hand-carved columns were made in Cauterskill by a Dutchman named Oberbaugh.[7] In any event, the thirteen columns of the Mountain House which local legend says commemorated the thirteen original Colonies, formed the most striking feature of the structural transformations of 1844–1845 and probably determined the new architecture of the Mountain House in all important details.

Artists soon became enamored of the white Grecian edifice with its strangely congruous background of wild American scenery. One of the first was Thomas Cole whose "Beach Mountain House, the Artist Sketching" has been attributed by E. P. Richardson to a period "after 1840" [8] [Frontispiece]. Since Cole died in 1848 and the Corinthian columns were not added until 1845, the painting belongs to the period 1845–1848. Another early artist was the English water-colorist, George Harvey, whose "Catskill Mountain House" of 1845 was also clearly inspired by what visitors to the hotel soon began calling "the noble Corin-

Figure 8. *Catskill Mountain House*, De Witt Clinton Boutelle, 1845 (oil on canvas, 36½" x 47½"). The Mountain House immediately before the renovations of Charles L. Beach. Courtesy of the Vose Gallery, Boston.

THE

SCENERY

OF

THE CATSKILL MOUNTAINS.

NOTE BY THE COMPILER.

The matter in the following pages has been collected and published in this form for the information and amusement of the lovers of natural scenery. It is hoped that the collection will be acceptable to all such. If it should aid in directing public attention to one of the most beautiful spots upon the continent, and thus induce a love for American scenery, instead of the rage for trans-Atlantic, now so prevalent, the object of the publication will have been attained.

Figure 9. Title page of a pamphlet published by the Mountain House between 1845 and 1850, showing the hotel soon after it was renovated by Charles L. Beach (original page 9″ x 6″).

Figure 10. Two Staffordshire China plates, labeled "Pine Orchard House, Catskill Mountains" (top, blue; bottom, rose; diameter 10″), by Enoch Wood, potter, who copied the design from the engraving (Figure 1) in *History and Topography of the United States*, which itself had been copied from Thomas Cole's original painting, *View of the Catskill Mountain House, New York*, c. 1828. The plates are described in E. B. Larsen, *American Historical Views on Staffordshire China* (New York, 1939), no. 34, p. 20.

thian pillars." [9] Both Cole and Harvey concealed the bulky mass of the north wing and chose a perspective that emphasized the classical purity of the façade.

The classical motif of the new hotel was repeated on the western side or rear of the building where four more Corinthian columns supported a portico above the main entrance of the hotel. In spite of this improvement, however, the rear of the Mountain House never achieved the architectural unity or beauty of the front of the house, and artists rarely chose to show it. An exception is Walter Launt Palmer's watercolor of the rear of the Mountain House, painted in 1883 [Figure 55]. As wings kept being added to the house they were placed at right angles to the beau-

Figure 11. *Catskill Mountain House*, George Harvey, c. 1845. From an engraving by J. Smillie.

tiful eastern façade and achieved, from this angle at least, a triumphant harmony of design. Viewed from the rear where the north wing terminated in a veritable conclave of shedlike attachments, utility houses and annexes, the Mountain House suffered from its piecemeal expansion and lost all pretensions to style.

To avoid this defect one viewed the hotel either from the eastern escarpment or the high ledges of North Mountain. The latter location was a favorite with the artists of the Hudson River School, for it was the only place from which they could see the full dimensions of the Mountain House or its complete romantic setting. The eastern escarpment afforded the best view of the house itself. Facing the great edifice from the southeastern corner of the lawn (close by the huge boulder that is seen in so many pictures), or from the famous bend in the road as it winds up the escarpment, one saw the house that most impressed the thousands of visitors of the nineteenth century—the triumph of classical design that had been achieved by Charles L. Beach during the drastic renovations of 1844–1845.

The comfort and luxury of the first Mountain House, noted, as we have seen, by such fastidious visitors as Harriet Martineau and N. P. Willis, continued to be a feature of Beach's regime. The post-1845 period gives ample evidence that, as one writer for *Harper's* put it, the hotel "affords all the conveniences and elegances of our most recherché metropolitan hotels." [10] An article in *Appleton's Illustrated Hand-Book of American Travel* for the year 1857 became even more specific: the Mountain House, it asserted, has "capacious and well-furnished parlors, halls, attentive hosts and waiters—and bathing, billiard and bowling appointments." [11] One of the most graphic pictures of the luxurious interior of the Mountain House during this period came from the pen of Mrs. Elizabeth F. Lummis Ellet, the well-known critic, historian and poetess of the nineteenth century. Visiting the hotel in 1849 or 1850 shortly after a prolonged residence in the "barren wastes of southern pine-lands," she was enthralled by the unexpected splendor of the Mountain House:

It is spacious enough to accommodate a very large number of guests, having double and triple rows of goodly dormitories, all of a better size, and more comfortably furnished, than the sleeping-rooms usually appropriated to travelers at the fashionable watering-places. The drawing-rooms are spacious; the principal one consisting of three large saloons opening into each other, or rather forming one. The dining-hall is large enough for a feudal banqueting hall, its effect being increased by a range of pillars for the whole length down the centre; and these pillars are wreathed with evergreens, while between the numerous windows stand hemlock or cedar trees during the season, quite baronial in taste. As far as I know, this style of embellishment is unique; it is certainly very picturesque.

She also had warm praise for the cuisine, noting that an "excellent supper" had been provided by "Mr. Beach, the enterprising landlord. Here is an almost wasteful profusion of strawberries, and other fruits of the season, freshly picked by the mountaineers, with cream and butter that does ample justice to the rich pasturage of this region." [12] The Mountain House, as these words suggest, had practically become a self-sufficient community: large gardens supplied fresh vegetables for the daily table; herds of cattle provided fresh dairy products; bakeries supplied pastry and bread. An exception was the daily supply of fresh meat: lacking modern means of refrigeration, the Mountain House had to import its meat from the distant village of Catskill. The meat was brought up early each morning while the guests of the hotel were still asleep. The wagons, horses, and even some of the roads were directly owned or controlled by the Mountain House itself.

Under Beach's regime the Mountain House became an early prototype of the modern resort-hotel, combining the amenities of the city with the pleasures of the country, and offering services and facilities for every conceivable taste. Outdoor activities featured bathing, boating and fishing, tennis, horseback riding, sightseeing by carriage to more distant sights and landmarks, or hiking and picnicking along the many miles of beautiful mountain trails. Indoor activities ranged from bowling and billiards, impromptu skits and organized shows, to song fests, tea dances and, in the evening, formal balls. Music was supplied by the hotel's own hired bands and orchestras, retained for the season in residence. Night after night the windows of the palatial hotel were ablaze with light and festivity, the sounds of revelry penetrating the accustomed quiet of the Catskills' deep repose.

The day's activities could begin early at the Mountain House, for they started with a ritual that few guests ignored. "In the dark of the morning," as one ministerial visitor described the ritual in 1849,

I heard gentle feet going through the long passage, and, afraid of being late, I hastened to the east side of the house, where the greater part of the guests were before me; and after looking at the sky, and then at the spectators, I thought of the Psalmist's words, "I wait for thee, as they that wait for the *eyelids* of the morning." [13]

It was the rite of the morning sunrise, a "must" of any visit to the Catskill Mountain House. For hundreds of guests who visited the hotel during the romantic years of the nineteenth century nothing was more inspiring than the famous sight of "all creation" under the first break of day. Any clear morning saw a score or more of enthusiasts gathered on the cold windy ledges of the hotel waiting for the first sign of light over the dark unseen depths of the Hudson Valley. Many more, however, immersed themselves in the scene simply by looking out of the front windows of their bedrooms. At least thirty bedrooms on the second and third floors of the Mountain House faced directly east and provided, as Bayard Taylor noted during a visit of 1860, a series of unusual advantages:

We have front rooms at the Mountain House; have you ever had one? Through the white, Corinthian pillars of the portico—pillars, which, I must say, are very well proportioned—you get much the same effects as through those of the Propylaea of the Athenian Acropolis. You can open your window, breathing the delicious mountain air in sleep (under a blanket), and, without lifting your head from the pillow, see the sun come up a hundred miles away.[14]

So the present author also discovered when, more than a century later, he spent a night in the ruins of the hotel in order to enjoy the same experience.

Figure 12. The Hudson Valley from a third-floor bedroom window of the Mountain House. Early spring, 1961. Author's photo.

Moods varied at the Mountain House, depending upon the day, the time of season, the people. At times it could be frantic with souvenir hunters, especially when a crowded weekend coincided with the visit of some idol of the people and the hotel was all astir with elaborate preparations. Special days, such as the Fourth of July, had their own round of ritual beginning with the explosive antics of the children in the early morning and ending in the evening with a brilliant display of fireworks that could be seen for countless miles up and down the Hudson Valley. If the season was still early, as noted by Taylor on his brief visit in 1860, the mood of people could be strikingly serene:

Several entire families were quartered there for the season, but it was perhaps too early for the evening hops and sunrise flirtations which I noticed ten years ago. Parties formed and strolled off quietly into the woods; elderly gentlemen sank into armchairs on the rocks, and watched the steamers on the Hudson; nurses pulled venturous children away from the precipice, and young gentlemen from afar sat on the verandah and wrote in their note-books. You would not have guessed the number of guests if you had not seen them at table. I found this quiet, this nonchalance, this "take care of yourself and let other people alone" characteristic very agreeable. . . .[15]

For peace and quiet to the point of somberness, one had only to visit the hotel after the official season had come to an end and no one remained but a solitary group of people who were friends of the proprietor. Such was a dark, gloomy day in September, a century and a quarter ago:

The wave-like sound of the gong floated upward from hall to hall through the Mountain House, and our party of three were all that answered it (the season had closed) in doing honor to the creature comforts that paid tribute to the keen mountain air that had assailed our appetites.

When the last egg had disappeared I found the leisure to take a peep at the appointments of the place.

A solitary lamp glimmered on the table, and its feeble rays made the gloom which hovered around the columns that supported the immense apartment but more shadowy. The couple opposite me were one in every sense, save corporeally; therefore the darkness

Figure 13. An early spring fog shrouds the ruins of the Mountain House. 1961. Author's photo.

of Tartarus would have been sunshine to them. For myself, the leaden gloom was oppressive. The ebon statue at the head of the table [a waiter] stood so motionless that I shuddered. A sense of loneliness—a desolate retreat of the heart—the eye moistens if you think of your hearthstone—an indescribable something we have all felt some time or other, crept over me. I courted the friendly companionship of a fire that was blazing in the drawing-room, but the wind moaned piteously around the peaks of the pine orchard in their attempts to keep off the *dyer* [sic] from its coronal; but a return spark of the sensation was fanned by the sighing breeze, and the solitude of the immense apartment gave it a shrine to burn upon. Who has not felt this at midnight, when the only tenant of such a place as the Mountain House, a solitary communicant with its unbroken stillness!

After such exquisite melancholia the following conclusion comes as something of a surprise:

Contemplative reader! Go to the Catskills in September, when the mountain air will give you an appetite for the creature comforts of the Mountain House; when you will not be jostled by the unthinking crowd, who go there because it is fashionable; when the deep verdure of its woods is relieved by a rainbow here and there; and when, if you will not complain of the company, I will greet you a welcome at the table-rock.[16]

But one did not have to wait for a dark gloomy day in September to visit the Mountain House in its more somber moods: any Sunday could be equally satisfactory. A century ago the Sabbath was still the Lord's Day, bound from sunrise to sunset in sacred ritual. The Sabbath at the Mountain House was no exception to this hardy rule, even though for six days of the week at least, the hotel functioned superbly as a "house of entertainment." This is what a Sunday was like in the middle of the nineteenth century:

Yesterday was a golden Sabbath. . . . By five o'clock we were out upon the ledge in front of the hotel, for you must remember that the Mountain House is hung, like an eagle's nest, right on the verge of the precipice. . . . A half-dozen of our fellow-lodgers, who, like ourselves, wished to begin the day's worship early, were standing beside us on the rocks, wrapped in cloaks and shawls. . . .

After breakfast, the large company gathered in groups upon the ledge until the hour of service, or, with book in hand, strolled up into the thickets toward South Mountain. A few drove off to the Kauterskill Falls about three miles distant; but the Sabbath arrangements of our Sabbath-observing host were cordially responded to by nine-tenths of all his guests. This house is a "sweet home" all the week, and a sanctuary on the Lord's day.

At eleven o'clock a gong sounded through the halls, and the parlors were soon filled by a quiet, reverential audience. A pulpit was extemporized in one corner of the drawing-room. . . . We had delightful music, for the leader of the "First Dutch Church" of Brooklyn, with his accomplished *soprano*, was present. Their rich voices led ours, as we joined in good old "Coronation;" and with swelling chorus shouted out, "Rise, my soul, and stretch thy wings," in a style that would have gladdened Father Hastings' soul. A stout substantial Scotch divine gave us a discourse quite Chalmerian in character, on the "wondrous works of God" in creation,

providence, and redemption. . . . In the afternoon our hotel congre-
gation gathered again to hear a discourse from your Brooklyn friend
on "Love for Christ as the inspiration and joy of the Christian's
life." Even a third service in the evening was crowded to the
door! Again our good dominie from the "land o'brown heath"
addressed us, his subject being the "Sepulchre in the Garden;"—
again our eyes were lifted toward the everlasting hills whence cometh
our help—again our voices rang out upon the still mountain air as
we joined in singing "Comfort ye, comfort ye, my people." When
the company separated, unwearied, to their rooms, the general
utterance was: "What a blessed Sabbath we have had! A more delightful we never passed than this Sabbath on the Catskills!" [17]

The rest of the week was another story; and by a law of
physics that says "to every action there is an equal and opposite
reaction," the enforced sobriety of the Sabbath often led to week-
day reactions that, to the management at least, bordered on madness. The offenders were the youthful patrons of the hotel who
yesterday as today loved nothing better than a good cathartic
party. This required at the Mountain House the privacy of some
bon vivant's bedroom and, before the era of electricity, a plenti-
ful supply of tallow candles. It was the candles, and not the customary noise of a party, that caused such anxiety to the proprietors. Always fearful of fire, the proprietors restricted the use of
candles to one per room per night. These were placed in iron
candlesticks that were stacked in the main hall so that members of
the staff as well as guests could pick them up on the way to bed
and so light their rooms upon retiring. They were returned to
their places in the morning, and many still contained the remnants
of last night's candles. What's a party without blazing lights! The
remnants became fair game for whatever *bon vivant* was planning
a midnight revel and they disappeared en masse until the culprit
believed he had enough to schedule his festivities. The candles
were then placed in rows on the bureaus, window sills and foot-
boards of the old-fashioned bedsteads, and the party was on.

The wonder is that this and similar practices never started a
fire in the Mountain House. The threat of fire was a constant
nightmare to the owner, supported by a thousand tragic episodes

in the history of the mountains. Even today there is hardly a community in the Catskills that does not suffer its annual loss of some old landmark or summer home. One of the most famous fires in the Catskills occurred within a mile of the Mountain House when during the early fall of 1924 the huge Hotel Kaaterskill (built, as local legend says, to ruin the Mountain House) burned to the ground in a three-hour holocaust that could be seen all the way into Massachusetts.

During the nineteenth century, there were even closer calls. The excessively dry summer of 1864, for instance, gave rise to what was called "a fearfully sublime example" of a forest fire that raged within a few feet of the Mountain House; only when a special fire engine was hastily drawn from the village of Catskill, twelve miles away, was the hotel saved from total destruction.[18] Nor was Charles L. Beach always as lucky as this: on April 14, 1851, a fire swept through the southern part of the village of Catskill and destroyed his complete livery service—including all the horses and carriages that provided transportation to and from the Mountain House.[19] Through it all, however, as if protected by a special act of providence, the Mountain House itself escaped all holocausts. It lived on for another century of charmed existence and seemed to become as permanent as the mountains themselves.

The years of 1845–1865 were ones of fulfillment for the proprietor of the Catskill Mountain House. Charles L. Beach would continue to be a major figure in the history of the Catskills for many more years to come; but from the time he first acquired ownership of the Mountain House until the Civil War inaugurated a new period of history, he virtually controlled the destiny of all the Catskills. The large house that he built on a high hill in the village of Catskill became the symbol of his success: from its upper chambers he could keep an eye on the great "white palace" that dominated the resorts of the mountains, and he could also survey and direct the many business enterprises that assured his control of the surrounding valley and plain.

Transportation remained the key to his success. In 1846 he became a partner in the steamboat freighting firm of J. M. Donnelly and Company. In 1853 he joined his brothers, A. F. and G. L. Beach, in getting control of the ferry service that linked the Hudson River Railroad (at Oak Hill, on the east bank of the Hudson) with his own stage line going from Catskill into the mountains. The following year he joined another man in getting complete control of J. M. Donnelly and Company, changing its name to "C. L. Beach and Company." Within the next twelve years (1854–1866) he absorbed all competing lines in the steamship freighting service between Catskill and New York and formed his own monopoly under the name of "The Catskill Steam Transportation Company." [20]

The jewel and capstone of it all, was the three thousand acre principality of the Catskill Mountain House. Here on the heights of Pine Orchard the economic passions of the valley yielded to aspirations of a higher order, bringing fame and a measure of immortality to the "pioneer landlord of the mountains." Throughout the antebellum period the Mountain House remained the center of the expanding resorts of the Catskills, proudly pre-empting the region's scenic heartland, the mecca of the artists and writers of the American romantic movement. By the time of the Civil War the roads, valleys, peaks, falls and cloves of its lordly dominion had become one of the most celebrated landscapes in the East, familiar to thousands of summer visitors over every mile of its enchanting diversity, known to the populace at large through art and literature. It is this aspect of the history of the great hotel that now demands our attention.

Chapter 4

The Old Mountain Road

When Charles L. Beach made his first visit to the heights of Pine Orchard to attend the opening ceremonies of July 4, 1823, he used a road that was to become the classic approach to the great scenic domain of the Catskill Mountain House for almost all the remaining years of the nineteenth century. Known variously as "the toll road," "the old stage road," or more commonly as "the old mountain road," it became during the romantic years of the antebellum period one of the most famous in America. Today when the modern motorist travels westward from the town of Catskill over route 23A or "The Rip Van Winkle Trail," he passes unaware over the first half of that famous road, traversing in fifteen minutes' time a six-mile stretch of beautiful farmland that had once taken two hours of cumbersome stagecoach travel. Veering southwest to ascend the mountains by way of Kaaterskill Clove, the motorist leaves the old mountain road behind and arrives at the top of the mountain in the present resort town of Haines Falls, missing thereby the most dramatic part of the old road. The latter had followed a more westerly course toward a rural community known as "Pelham's Four Corners" and ascended the mountain by way of the scenic splendors of "Sleepy Hollow." This part of the road—still visible today as an enchanting foot trail—belonged outright to the Catskill Mountain House and was guarded at the bottom by Charles L.

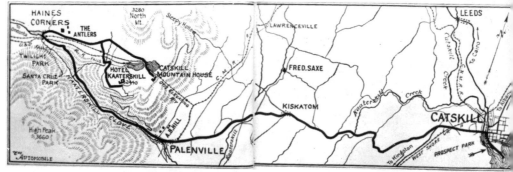

Map 4. "Automobile Route from Catskill to Hotel Kaaterskill and Catskill Mountain House," from *Van Loan's Catskill Mountain Guide* (New York, 1909) between pp. 37 & 38.

Beach's own tollgates. The total distance from the town of Catskill to the Mountain House was twelve miles and ordinarily required a minimum of fours hours' stage time.

The history of the road belongs exclusively to the era of the stagecoach, for its effective use was brought to a close by the coming of the railroads in the 1880s, and though the early automobiles occasionally used it until the severe winter of 1922, the main automobile approach to the mountain had already been established by that time over the present route of the Rip Van Winkle Trail. Throughout its history, all stage travel was controlled by the Beach family, until 1882 when Charles A. Beach, the nephew of Charles L. Beach, gave up the stagecoach business. It is this man, Charles L. Beach, who is most responsible for the history of stagecoaching over the road, and it was his own building of the Catskill Mountain Railroad and the later Otis Elevating Railroad that brought that history to an end.

Descriptions of the scenery along the old mountain road abound in the literature of the Catskills, for nineteenth century visitors to the mountains, fresh from the turmoil of the city and the frantic trip up the Hudson on the crowded steamers or congested railroads, felt they had at last reached their destination when they stepped ashore at the village of Catskill, and hastened to record their impressions as soon as the stages got underway. For such enthusiasts the four- to six-hour stage ride from the village to the Mountain House was but an extension of their ultimate goal on the crest of the mountains, confirmed throughout the journey by the visible presence of the distant hotel.

The following description was written about 1872 when the use of the old mountain road was at its height a few years before it was made all but obsolete by Beach's Catskill Mountain Railroad. Penned by Henry A. Brown, it appeared in William Cullen Bryant's *Picturesque America* accompanied by illustrations by Harry Fenn. Brown and Fenn had arrived by train from New York City, and the description therefore begins with their first sight of the Catskills from the eastern bank of the Hudson. At this time, passengers still had to detrain at Oak Hill and take one of Beach's ferries across the river to Catskill Landing. The view that Brown describes in the first paragraph was familiar to thousands of visitors who habitually arrived by steamboat.

Now and then, as we strain our eyes forward [as the train approaches Oak Hill], we can catch for a moment a faint outline, toward the north, of high mountains, dark blue in the lessening distance. Suddenly we rush through a dark cleft in the rock, and then out again on the other side. On the western bank of the river you can see a series of ridges covered with trees, rolling away, one after another, eight or ten miles; and beyond these, lifting their wooded sides up into the clouds that have begun to settle on their peaks, are the famous mountains. Yonder round one to the right is Black Head; then, in succession, North Mountain, South Mountain, and Round Top, with High Peak towering over all. Between this last and the South Mountain you see a sharp notch, or depression, terminating in a deep shadow. There lies the clove, through which the Kaaterskill comes tumbling to the plain. High on the face of the South Mountain, or rather between it and its northern neighbor, your eye detects a small speck, hanging like a swallow's nest upon a wall, white and glistening in the sun. It is the Mountain House, from the broad piazza of which three or four hundred human beings are perhaps, at this moment, looking out over the landscape which lies beneath them like a map, and noting the faint line of white smoke that marks the passage of the train.

Figure 14. The Mountain House from the bend in the road, after the Otis Elevated Railroad had forced the abandonment of the old stage route up the mountain. From the Ulster & Delaware Railroad's *The Catskill Mountains* (Roundout, N.Y., 1905), p. 102.

Figure 15. The Mountain House from the bend in the road. Spring, 1961. Author's photo.

[They then detrain at Oak Hill and take a ferry to Catskill Landing.]

Old-fashioned stage-coaches stand by the landing, awaiting our arrival. In a little while our trunks are strapped on behind; and, seated each in his place, we swing about, and are jolted up and down, as the huge vehicles roll through the little village of Catskill. We have presently crossed the bridge which spans the mouth of the Kaaterskill, and have fairly begun our ride toward the mountains. The day is intensely hot. The road stretches before us white and dusty in the sunshine. On either side the trees stand drooping, unstirred by a breath of air; and, often as our horses slowly pull their heavy burden up a rise in the road, and stop a moment to rest, a locust, perched on a tree by the road-side, begins his grating cry. In the meadows the cows stand under the trees, switching away the buzzing flies; and recently-cut grass breathes out its life in the soft perfume of new-mown hay. In the distance, the clouds have begun to gather on the tops of the mountains, and, now and then, a long rumble of thunder reverberates through them, and comes rolling down into the valley. Here Mr. Fenn pauses to make his first sketch. Beside us, the little Kauterskill, wearied with its rough journey down from the heights yonder, winds among the trees that line its banks, placidly smiling in the sun. Half a dozen cows are standing in the stream to cool themselves. In front the valley rolls gradually (about a thousand feet in seven or eight miles) up to the base of the mountains, which rise in the distance like a wall. Round Top and High Peak are buried in a dark cloud, but the scarred head of the North Mountain is in full view, and the Mountain House is clearly defined against a background of pines.

A ride of several hours across the fertile valley, climbing the ridges that lead like steps from the level of the river to the foot of the mountains, brings us at length to a tollgate, from which we see the road straight before us, ascending steadily. We have now begun to climb in earnest. This excellent road takes advantage of a deep glen, or ravine, through which in the winter the melting snow finds its way into the valley. By clinging closely to the mountain—now creeping around a projecting rock; now crossing the beds of little streams, which, in the midsummer heat, trickle down the mossy rocks beneath the overshadowing trees—it brings us, at last, nearly to the highest point of the ravine. On every side huge trees overhang the road. On the right, the mountain towers straight up above our heads; on the left, the precipice plunges headlong down among the scattered rocks. As you climb up this steep road, and see, here and there, great boulders lying on the slope of the mountain, covered with moss and fern, and in the perpetual shade of the forest, trees that interlace their leafy arms above you— catching a glimpse, every now and then, through some opening in the treetops, of the valley, a thousand feet below, and the river glistening in the distance—you can hardly blame him who, seeking a scene for Irving's immortal story, wandered into the romantic beauties of this wild ravine, and called it "Rip Van Winkle's Glen." . . . Here by the side of a little stream, which trickles down the broad, flat surface of a large rock, is the shanty called "Rip Van Winkle's House," which is represented in Mr. Fenn's sketch. . . . On the right, one may notice the corner of a house, built for a tavern some time ago, which serves for a resting-place and half-way house between the foot of the mountain and the hotel on the summit. From this point the glen grows narrower and steeper, until it is finally lost among the crevices on the cliffs of the mountain.

The road now winds around the side of the North Mountain, creeping at times on the edge of the precipice, and steadily ascending. . . . At a certain place it turns abruptly, and commences to climb in zigzags, at the first turn you suddenly see the Mountain House directly before you, apparently at a distance of half a mile. Perched upon a piece of rock which juts out far over the side of the mountain, in the bright sunshine glistening and white against the pine-clad shoulders of the South Mountain, the pile of buildings forms a singular feature of the view . . .[1]

From this point, according to Brown, the Mountain House is another "steady climb of three miles"; in point of fact, however, it was something less than a mile. The error was common among the visitors to the Mountain House. Arriving at the bend in the road after a long fatiguing journey and suddenly coming upon the Mountain House but an apparent few yards away, most visitors were unprepared for the devious three quarters of a mile that still remained before the road twisted up the final summit to the rear of the hotel, so its distance was greatly exaggerated. The deception was also encouraged by the common practice of dismounting from the coaches during the last and most precipitous part of the journey

Figure 16. The beginning of the toll road up the mountain, by the former Saxe Farm at the base of Sleepy Hollow. The toll gate was located just beyond the end of the stone wall at right center. Early spring, 1961. Author's photo.

and ascending the rest of the mountain on foot. This relieved the burden on the straining horses, but it made the last mile seem like half the journey.

As recently as 1962 the approach to the tollgate at the base of the mountains by way of Pelham's Four Corners appeared the same as it had more than a century ago. Since the area had escaped the transformations of history and lay in a kind of *cul-de-sac* between the mountains and the modern population centers of the Kiskatom Valley, it was possible to explore it with the aid of maps dating back to the time of the Civil War. The open stretch of flat farmland lying between Pelham's Four Corners and the base of the mountains was still remarkably the same; on a hot summer's day clouds of dust churned up about the wheels of an automobile just as they had about the large clanking wheels of the old stagecoaches. Arriving at the base of the mountains, one found the house and barns of "Saxe's Farm" exactly as they were a century ago. The old Beach tollgate had long since disappeared, but it was easy to point out its exact location.

It was also easy to imagine the joy of the traveler as he left the heat of the open plain at Saxe's Farm and started the cool ascent of Sleepy Hollow.[2] As anyone may discover who visits the "wild ravine" today, the innumerable pools, glens and falls that border the first mile of the steep ascent are as refreshing and beautiful as they were during the hottest summers of the nineteenth century. Halfway up the ravine the modern hiker comes upon a small tributary bridged precariously by a few old rotting logs, and immediately recognizes the remains of what the nineteenth century called Black Snake Bridge. Going on for another half mile, he discovers the famous horseshoe turn where the road leaves the head of Sleepy Hollow and starts ascending the shoulder of North Mountain. At this place one may still find the old stone foundations of "The Rip Van Winkle House." As one goes on, the ascent is gradual for a quarter of a mile and then becomes more precipitous as it enters upon a stretch called Dead Ox Hill on the oldest maps of the area. The name presumably derives from the fact that some poor belabored ox had died at this place, having been forced to haul too heavy a load up the long, difficult road.[3] A little further on one encounters Little Pine Orchard, a rich stand of pine trees to the left of the road. Just beyond this point Dead Ox Hill terminates in another horseshoe bend called Cape Horn and then starts a gradual ascent that is called Short Level. After one more horseshoe bend the road crosses the eighteen-hundred-foot level of North Mountain and ascends another two hundred feet along an area called Feather Bed Hill. The next mile of the road is relatively straight and much less precipitous, giving rise to its name, Long Level. This good section of the road terminates in the famous ninety-degree turn that gave the weary travelers of the past their first deceptive sight of the Mountain House. (It also, as we noted in the previous chapter, became a favorite place for painting the Mountain House.) Beyond this point the road ascends another two hundred feet through a series of curves and steep climbs, then skirts the edge of North Lake, and finally reaches (in a little less than a mile) the high promontory of the Catskill Mountain House. Since leaving the village of Catskill, practically at sea level, the traveler has climbed some 2,250 feet above the level of the Hudson—700 feet during the eight-mile trip between the river and the base of the mountains; 1,550 feet during the four-mile climb from the base to the summit.

From at least 1826 until 1835 the coach fare from Catskill Landing to the Mountain House was one dollar. Throughout that period coaches usually ran twice a day;[4] by 1857 there were several stages a day;[5] and by 1880 when the history of stagecoaching was almost at an end, stages met every steamboat arriving from Albany and New York and the fare was $2.50 (excluding trunks, which were charged extra).[6] The stages at that time varied from two to four horses and carried from eight to fourteen passengers. All baggage had to be consigned to a special baggage wagon for the safety of the passengers and to lessen the load in the passenger coaches. Once underway, drivers were not permitted to leave their seats, for the safety of the passengers depended upon a firm control of the reins throughout the journey.

Until the late 1870s when stagecoach travel was almost at an end, the coaches were large and cumbersome in the traditional manner of all American vehicular construction. Basil Hall was especially struck by this fact when he rode in such a coach during his 1827 trip to the Mountain House:

An American stage is more like a French diligence than any thing else. Like that vehicle it carries no outside passengers, except one or two on the box. It has three seats inside, two of which are similar to the front and back seats of an English coach, while the third is placed across the middle from window to window, or I might say, from door to door, only these stages very seldom have more than one door. Instead of panels, there hang from the roof leather curtains, which, when buttoned down, render it a closed carriage; or when rolled up and fastened by straps and buttons to the roof, leave it open all round. This for summer travelling is agreeable enough; but how the passengers manage in the severe winters of the north, I do not know; for certainly we found it on many occasions, even in the south, uncomfortably cold. The middle seat is movable on a sort of hinge, that it may be turned horizontally, out of the way when the door is opened. The three passengers who sit upon it, rest their backs against a stuffed leathern strap, permanently buckled to one side of the carriage, and attached to the other side by means of a stout iron hook. These ponderous stages are supported on strong hide straps, in place of steel springs, and all parts are made of great strength, which is absolutely necessary to enable them to bear the dreadful joltings on the miserable roads they have but too frequently the fate to travel over.[7]

In the late 1870s just before the railroads put an end to the great era of stagecoach travel, these "ponderous" stages were replaced by "Light Platform Wagons," reducing the time of travel from Catskill Landing to the Mountain House to approximately three and a half hours or "one hour less than in former years." [8]

The traditional coaches were not only heavy and cumbersome, but notoriously noisy. A contemporary Catskillian who received her information from one of the last of the Mountain House's stage drivers, says that

everything about the coaches rattled and clanged and clattered. To the ears of the driver it was one long wearisome din, but the sounds, hedged in by woods and ravines, made music as they rose straight up in welcome greeting to the ears of the eager company on the Mountain House verandas—for the stage also carried the mail.[9]

The descent was especially noisy, for in addition to the usual clangor of the iron-rimmed wheels and axles, there was the scraping of iron slippers or "shoes" which had been placed on a rear wheel for braking. The brake became more efficient as the load got heavier, but it also became noisier. The whole apparatus made the descent of the mountain a rather unforgettable experience, as attested by Willis Gaylord Clark who made the adventurous journey in 1837:

It looks to be a perilous enterprise to descend the Kaatskills. The wheels of the coach are shod with the preparation of iron slippers, which are essential to a hold up; and as you bowl and grate along, with wilderness-chasms and a brawling stream mayhap on one hand, and horrid masses of stone seemingly ready to tumble upon you on the other; the far plain stretching like the sea beneath you, in the mists of the morning; your emotions are *fidgetty*. You are not afraid—not you, indeed! Catch you at such folly! No; but you wish most devoutly that you were some nine miles down, not-withstanding, and are looking eagerly for that consummation.[10]

To some people the trip was rather frightening no matter which way you traveled over the mountain. Upon arriving at the tollgate where the real ascent of the mountain began, many people chose to get out of the coaches and walk the remaining distance. "Rolling on with the merciless velocity of stage-coaches," Elizabeth Ellet noted during a trip of the antebellum period,

we came to the spot where the steep ascent commences; and here I was fain, with many others, to alight and walk, dreading that in the climbing process No. 1 might chance to fall back on No. 2, No. 2 on No. 3, and so on. However, none but an habitual coward like myself need fear such a catastrophe, as the vehicles are strongly built, and provided each with a pointed bar of iron that would effectually prevent any retrograde motion.[11]

Storms thundering over the mountain could turn a journey into an awesome experience. "We had scarcely commenced the ascent," James S. Buckingham noted in 1838,

before the clouds began to lower overhead, and there was every indication of an approaching thunder-storm. In less than half an hour it burst upon us with all its fury. The lightning was most vivid, the rattling of the thunder deafening and its prolonged reverberation in the hollows of the surrounding mountains, grand in the extreme. The rain, too, fell in torrents, the drops being so heavy as to make an impression as large as a dollar on the rocky masses which formed part of our road; and these were succeeded by a rattling hail-shower, which completely chilled the air. During the first burst of the storm, the horses stopped; but there being a guard against the descent of the coach behind . . . we were at ease respecting our safety.[12]

The case could be somewhat different when a sudden blanket of fog descended upon the old mountain road. The danger was so real during these sinister occurrences that even the most experienced of drivers took fright. The fog might only last for "ten minutes," as one old driver recalled,

but it was bad while it lasted . . . A good driver could keep close watch and if the coach began to sag the least bit he'd know he was getting off the road and he'd pull to the other side. There's some pretty steep drops and narrow passes, you can see. Yes, it was bad in those fogs, but we took the coaches through . . . all except the fellow who quit and tied up for the night on one trip and we never got done roasting him for it.[13]

Knowing that the hazards of stage travel could discourage many prospective patrons, especially in the light of the extraordinary location of the Mountain House, the managers of the hotel always made a policy of drawing attention to the fact that the Sleepy Hollow route was "acknowledged to be the best mountain road in the country." [14] Such claims certainly helped to allay many fears of the public, but since they were based upon comparisons with the usual quality of mountain roads in nineteenth century America (which were probably atrocious), it is difficult to know how to judge them. One observer asserted rather late in the century that the Sleepy Hollow route was "a most enjoyable one, for the road is firm and the ascent so gradual that a good team can trot almost the entire distance." [15] Yet that could hardly be true. Even when passengers disembarked from the coaches to lighten the load and the horses were simply walked up the mountain, they still arrived at the summit with steaming flanks and hard, convulsive breathing. Horses had to be treated with great care both before and after each journey; watering of the horses was strictly forbidden either ascending or descending. The road was hard on horses and people alike. Dust, noise, strain, and discomfort were intrinsic to this mode of travel.

It is difficult to know how to characterize the relative comforts and discomforts of the old Mountain House road. Reactions were as diverse as human beings themselves. To Willis Gaylord Clark, for instance, "the road was smooth and good" and he took great delight in observing the rich foliage and wild, dramatic scenery; [16] Tyrone Power, on the other hand, dismissed the whole subject with a phrase—a "winding rocky road." [17] To yet another commentator the road was neither good nor bad, but simply something one had to put up with: "the journey up the mountain is safe," he said, "yet rather tedious and difficult. For a greater part of the way the road is uneven, and the last portion of it a very steep ascent in a zig-zag direction." [18] To another the road was frightening: "A good though circuitous road of three miles, but which, after running upon the brink of a deep ravine, or beneath frowning precipices, excites an unwelcome degree of terror" [19] To one Englishman the road was a living torture. "We had been told, on inquiry," James S. Buckingham complained in 1838,

that the road to the foot of the mountain, which is about nine miles, was level and excellent, and that it was only the ascent of the mountain itself, about three miles more, that was at all rough or disagreeable. The standard of excellence differs, however, in different countries and in different minds. In any part of Europe the road would have been thought bad, but in England it would have been called execrable. There was no remedy, however, but patience; though it required a large exercise of this to sustain the jolts and shocks which were almost enough to dislocate a weak frame and shake it to pieces. The road was not only full of deep ruts and large masses of rock, by which elevation and depression sometimes succeeded each other so rapidly that the transition was fearful; but there was a perpetual succession of steep ascents and descents, instead of a level road, nearly all the way to the foot of the mountains. [20]

Compared to Buckingham's reaction, Bayard Taylor's opinion of 1860 could not be more blandly American:

There are few summits so easy of access—certainly no other mountain resort in our country where the facilities of getting up and down are so complete and satisfactory. The journey would be tame, however, were it not for the superb view of the mountains, rising higher, and putting on a deeper blue, with every mile of approach.[21]

To Bayard Taylor the old mountain road was exactly what the managers of the Mountain House always said it was: "the best mountain road in the country."

Yet how good, we still may ask, was that? In another twenty years (1880s) the railroads had come to the Catskills, and they lost no time in drawing attention to the fact that no other mode of transportation could possibly equal the speed and comfort of iron rails. Relative to a more advanced stage of technology, in other words, all stagecoach travel—even the best—was a cruel test of human endurance. It was left to the new railroads of the Catskills to draw the most negative picture of the older means of transportation:

A hot and dusty day's ride in a lumbering stage-coach, over a horrid, stony, rutty road, and up a steep mountain side was the inevitable method. The trip was uncertain and not wholly un-attended with danger. A passing shower or storm might at any time wash out the narrow road or hurl the rude brush bridges down into the ravine. It was not enough to be an enthusiastic lover of mountain grandeur, but it took a man of health and vigor, with a goodly share of courage and endurance, to stand the journey. Invalids, who would be most benefited by the air and scenery, rarely attempted the trip. This, however, was about the situation of traffic to the Catskill Mountains from 1823, when the first cabin hotel was built, until 1870, when the iron rails began to reach out among the hills. Of course the stage ride was somewhat shortened and improved by better roads and appliances during the latter portion of that period, but the steep and stony miles were all there, the jaded horses and the rocking stage. The discomfort and fatigue of the journey were only lessened in degree. Visitors were still expected to relieve the poor horses by walking up the steepest hills. Nobody was really requested to do this, of course, in view of the ample price paid for riding. But the drivers were experienced and loquacious old mountain whips, and they had a way of getting their passengers out on their feet for an occasional heavy mile or so, "just to rest their legs."[22]

Perhaps; but there is as much propaganda as truth in this derisive picture of early stagecoach travel over the old mountain road. The Ulster and Delaware Railroad—which was responsible for that picture—penetrated the Catskills from the western side of Greene County, and terminated at South Lake. It therefore placed itself in competition with the classic route from the village of Catskill and tried to supplant it as the major artery into the mountains. The proprietor of the Mountain House soon met this threat by building his own railroad from Catskill to the base of the mountain (and later clear to the summit); and in doing so he acknowledged the superiority of this new mode of travel.

Travel over the old mountain road was certainly much better than pictured by the Ulster and Delaware Railroad. Charles L. Beach was one of the most efficient and progressive stagecoach operators in the Hudson Valley. The road up to the Mountain House was so well built and maintained that even today after half a century of disuse there are still parts of the road that can admit the passage of a modern automobile. While the road was never paved, it was always firm and smooth, securely anchored in rock and gravel, and finished off with a top-dressing of native red shale (still favored in the Catskills for its soft granular texture). As for the "danger," someone observed about 1845 that since the Mountain House was first visited, "thousands have gone and returned" in Charles L. Beach's stagecoaches, yet "not a single accident has ever occurred." [23] Nor is there any evidence that there was ever any serious accident in all the subsequent years of stagecoach travel. This is hardly a statement that can be applied to the history of the railroads. Furthermore, the bridges of the old mountain road were not built of "brush," but of strong stout logs placed on firm stone abutments. Nor is it true that only "a man of health and vigor" could stand the journey: women traveled to the Mountain House in even greater numbers than men (and this is saying something in the light of the pampered femininity of the Victorian period). It is true that "the steep and stony miles" were there, if by the latter we mean the many picturesque ledges that lined the walls of Sleepy Hollow; but this was part of the adventure that city people deliberately sought in going to the Catskills. It is true that the "jaded horses and the rocking stage," the "fatigue and discomfort of the journey," were also there; but this again was the willing cost of an adventurous flight from the banal comforts of city life. The railroads were wrong: to an early generation of American romanticists, it *was* enough "to be an enthusiastic lover of mountain grandeur."

The railroad appeal to the mundane advantages of speed and comfort could prove to be a boomerang. To an American writer like Lucy C. Lillie, concerned above all with the "Catskill of Indian romance and one's imagination," the old stagecoaches provided "ample opportunity" for filling "her eyes and heart—indeed, perhaps, to touch some glimmerings of her soul—with the majesty, the gigantic wonders, of the scene before her." The railroad, on the other hand, was a harsh intruder upon the face of the land, violating its ancient tone and character. "I think it is disappointing to most people," she said, "to be met with so much bustle and crudity when their destination is such an old and grand region." [24] Many more people believed the same. The railroads brought a new tone, a new culture, to the Catskills, destroying the higher aspirations of a more romantic generation. To Henry James traveling down the Hudson by railroad at the end of the century, the Catskills—compounded of memories of "the delightful old pillared and porticoed house that crowned the cliff and commanded the stream," the "wonder of Rip Van Winkle" and "the Hudson River School of landscape art"—were now "a felicity forever gone," destroyed by the harsh realities of the new age of the railroads. [25]

All elements of this previous "felicity" converge upon the history of the old mountain road from Catskill to Pine Orchard. Terminating in the classical splendor of the Mountain House and its commanding view of the Hudson River, the mountain road belongs exclusively to the era of the stagecoach and the romantic associations of Washington Irving and the first school of American landscape painting. As long as the road was in existence, Irving's legend had a local name and habitation halfway up the wild ascent of North Mountain. By the time the road was abandoned to nature, and the railroads formed a network of transportation throughout the Catskills, technology and tourism had destroyed the romance of the wilderness and Irving's legend never regained the conviction of a specific location. The passing of the old mountain road and the primitive conditions that went with it also heralded the end of the Catskillian center of the Hudson River School. When the solitude of the mountains disappeared, so did the artist's belief in the possible union of God and man through nature and the whole metaphysical animus of the first school of American landscape painting.

In describing the spot on the old mountain road, about halfway between the base and the summit of the mountain, where local legend ascribed the scene of Rip Van Winkle's encounter with the bizarre crew of the *Half-Moon*, Henry A. Brown, one of the writers of Bryant's *Picturesque America*, declared that "you can hardly blame him who, seeking a scene for Irving's immortal story, wandered into the romantic beauties of this wild ravine, and called it 'Rip Van Winkle's Glen.' " [26] It would be pleasant to think that this historic spot had such a poetical beginning, but there can be little doubt that far more mundane considerations governed its first selection.

Looking at the story itself we can find very little reason for selecting Sleepy Hollow as its scene of action. In Irving's story "the Kaatskill mountains" are so generally rather than specifically described that one could choose any number of possible locations for its geographical setting. Palenville at the base of Kaaterskill Clove is still taken as the "little village of great antiquity" where Rip began his adventures, but any one of several old Dutch villages "at the foot of these fairy mountains" could serve with equal validity. Nor do things get any better when we take a close look at the "deep mountain glen" of Irving's story. We may note, first of all, that Irving does not say that his hero used such a glen to ascend the mountains; on the contrary, Rip only saw such a glen after having "scrambled to one of the highest parts of the Kaatskill mountains" and peered down "the other side." And what about that "highest" part? The actual spot in Sleepy Hollow that is supposed to correspond to this place is 1,300 feet above sea level—less than half the height of the highest peaks around the village of Palenville. While it is true that Rip could have looked from that point through "an opening between the trees" and perhaps seen the "lordly Hudson, far, far below him," the actual spot still does not correspond to a "green knoll, covered with mountain herbage, that crowned the brow of a precipice." The actual spot is the head of a ravine that is still, as noted above, considerably below the top of the surrounding mountains. Rip could have looked down the ravine, perhaps, to see the "lordly Hudson"; but it would have been impossible for him to have looked down "on the other side" to see a "deep mountain glen." The only other view was straight up to the towering cliffs that still hung above the actual site in Sleepy Hollow. A more plausible site for Rip's high adventure would have been those same heights, a good 2,000 feet above the one that had actually been chosen.

But this was not to be; and there can be little doubt by now that the only reason why the horseshoe bend, halfway up Sleepy Hollow, was chosen for the celebrated site was that it was an important staging area in the laborious climb to the heights of Pine Orchard. All stages commonly stopped at this point to give both horses and riders a well-earned rest; and later on when a tavern and inn were built at this strategic location many people chose to spend the night in the picturesque place and resume their journey the following morning. In the end it was probably this establishment that "did more than anything else," as one historian has suggested, "to fasten Rip's adventure on this particular ravine." [27]

Once commercial expediency established the exact location of Rip's famous sleep, people accepted or rejected it according to their individual preferences for realism or romance. People of easy faith—the simplest of romantics—accepted it without question. Other more complex souls rejected it, and then argued, with

even more ingenuous romanticism, for alternative locations in
the heart of the Catskills. Many natives of the area advanced from
the gullibility of childhood to the skepticism of maturity. One
old-timer whom Lucy C. Lillie encountered in the 1880s confessed that he had once taken the whole story as gospel truth,
but now found himself assailed with doubts. Replying to a direct
question about the current status of his convictions, he could only
confess that "there's some as does now, some as believes it all,
and I don't know myself just what to think—just what to think;
I railly don't." [28] Controversy regarding the truth or falsehood
of the legend raged throughout the century. A publication of the
West Shore and Buffalo Railroad of 1883 asserted—no doubt with
tongue in cheek—that "the question thus opened still remains unresolved, and to determine the exact location of Rip Van Winkle's surprising adventure may furnish occupation for investigat-
ing minds among this summer's visitors to the Catskills." [29] Not,
however, for the more realistic souls of the nineteenth century.
To many of these, such as the authoritative Ernest Ingersoll,
the whole controversy was a gratuitous piece of nonsense. "No
intelligent person," he declared year after year in the pages of
the *Rand, McNally Guide*, "believes that such a character ever
existed or had any such experience . . ." Irving, he concluded,
had written nothing but an "imaginary" story, and had, "perhaps
purposely, left indefinite the precise spot, if any, he had in view
as the locality . . ." [30]

Such, alas, was the truth of the matter, as anyone could have
discovered if he had taken the trouble to read Pierre M. Irving's
Life and Letters of Washington Irving that appeared as early as
1863. In a letter written by Washington Irving to his brother
Peter on July 9, 1832, we find the following statement:

I have been for a few days up the Hudson. I set off in company
with James Paulding, Mr. Latrobe, and the Count de Pourtales,
whom I have found most agreeable travelling companions. We
left New York about seven o'clock, in one of those great steamboats
that are like floating hotels, and we arrived at West Point in about
four hours. Gouverneur Kemble's barge, with an awning, was waiting

for us, and conveyed us across the river into a deep cove to his cottage, which is buried among beautiful forest trees. Here we passed three or four hot days most luxuriously, lolling on the grass under the trees, and occasionally bathing in the river. . . . From thence we took steamboat, and in a few hours landed at Catskill, where a stage coach was in waiting, and whirled us twelve miles up among the mountains to a fine hotel built on the very brow of a precipice, and commanding one of the finest prospects in the world. We remained here until the next day, visiting the waterfall, glen, etc., that are pointed out as the veritable haunts of Rip Van Winkle.[31]

As the editor, Pierre M. Irving, points out, "this was the author's first visit to the scene of his renowned story, published twelve years before." [32] Consistent with the custom of the period, Washington Irving was showing distinguished foreign visitors the beauties of the American landscape by making a grand tour of the Hudson. This required among other things a visit to the historic Highlands and West Point, an occasional stopover at some renowned manor house or estate on the eastern bank of the river, and an all but mandatory side trip to the Catskills and the Catskill Mountain House—now made even more mandatory by the international fame of his own legend of Rip Van Winkle. This visit, however, occurred twelve years after the publication of the legend and seven years after the erection of the Mountain House; and it was the latter event and the building of the stage road, rather than Irving's own descriptions of the mountains, that determined the exact location of Rip's exploits. As a result of this trip of 1832, Irving discovered that "the wild scenery of these mountains outdoes all my conception of it." [33] For until he made this trip his knowledge of the Catskills was limited to what he had seen from the Hudson Valley.

Nor, given Irving's whimsical and imaginative genius, would he have cared to pin-point the setting of his story even if he had been able to. Literalness was never a quest of this most romantic of American writers. The legend of Rip Van Winkle gripped the imagination of the nineteenth century precisely because of its enveloping air of mystery and romance. That Irving himself was

well aware of this is attested by his final say regarding the celebrated issue of its exact setting. One year before he died he received a letter from a boy living in Catskill asking him to settle
a dispute the boy was having with a "very old gentleman" about
Rip's place of origin. The boy contended it was his own home
town of Catskill; the old man, that it was Kingston. In showing the
letter to his nephew Irving remarked, "He little dreamt when I
wrote the story, I had never been on the Catskills." [34] The following, however, is the reply Irving actually sent: [35]

Sunnyside, Feb. 5, 1858

Dear Sir:—
I can give you no other information concerning the localities of
the story of Rip Van Winkle, than is to be gathered from the
manuscript of Mr. Knickerbocker, published in the Sketch Book.
Perhaps he left them purposefully in doubt. I would advise you
to defer to the opinion of the "very old gentleman" with whom
you say you had an argument on the subject. I think it probable
he is as accurately informed as anyone on the matter.

Respectfully, your obedient
servant,
Washington Irving

The reply, of course, satisfied no one; and the controversy pursued its merry course throughout the remaining years of the
century.

When Irving's brother Peter received the news of the 1832
trip to the Catskills and learned how the legendary Rip was being
given a specific geographical home within the vicinity of the
Mountain House, he was as delighted as Irving himself and said
he had "little doubt that some curious travellers will yet find
some of the bones of his dog, if they can but hit upon the veritable
spot of his long sleep." [36] Hit upon it they did, and this within
five or six years of this prognostication. The actual site of Rip's
long sleep was found to exist on a huge boulder within sight of
the famous horseshoe bend on the old mountain road. [37] There
is no evidence that the bones of Rip's dog were ever found in the
vicinity, but a little later when the Rip Van Winkle House was
built in the same place one could at least go inside and there be-

hold—for a small fee—the very chair used by Dame Van Winkle and the very flagon from which Rip drank the most potent of somniferous brews. Irving never saw these mementoes of his literary precocity, but we may safely assume he never would have questioned their authenticity.

The actual date of the first founding of the Rip Van Winkle House is an enigma of local history. H. A. Haring believes that some kind of a structure, however crude, existed at the horseshoe bend from the time the first wood road was built up the mountain, or, in other words, even before the founding of the Mountain House. Apparently used as a "resting place," this original structure was most probably a shedlike building made of logs and was "barely more than a shelter against weather." Then "in due time," according to Haring's vague phase, "a single-room house was built; barns for the stagecoach horses next appeared; then a barroom was set up; later, about the year 1845, a boarding house." [38] This last-named was the Rip Van Winkle Boarding House.

It is highly doubtful, however, whether the boardinghouse was built as early as 1845, in spite of Haring's assurance. The one statement that can be clearly documented is the reference to the "single-room house." There can be little doubt that this structure, commonly called Rip Van Winkle's shanty, existed throughout the antebellum period, and probably from the time the Mountain House was built. The following is a description of 1828:

The traveller sprung from his seat into the door way of Rip Van Winkle's shanty, which occupied a nook in that part of the mountain to which the stage had arrived. A species of wild cherry hung its ripe red fruit over a mass of rock, variegated with lichens and moss, through which the water of a clear spring trickled, and was collected in a long strip of bark; by this rustic expedient it was conveyed to Rip's dwelling, and afforded an unfailing fountain. The present Rip was not even a descendant of the mountain sleeper, but could show the spot from which the old man of the glen repeated "Rip Van Winkle," and the very hollow where Rip saw the "company of odd-looking personages playing at nine-pins." [39]

Figure 17. Rip Van Winkle House, Sleepy Hollow. From a picture folder published by Wittemann Bros., New York, 1884.

The main points of this description—the shanty, the proprietor with the same name as the legendary hero, the faithful spring— are repeated again and again in the early accounts of travel over the old road.

The spring was a famous feature of the place. When the present author visited the area in early April of 1961 he could find no trace of this "unfailing fountain"; nor could it be found thirty years earlier when one of the Mountain House's last stagecoach drivers made a commemorative visit to the famous area.[40] Yet from the second to the eighth decades of the nineteenth century it was an unfailing source of refreshment to the hot and thirsty travelers up the mountain. In describing Rip's Cabin in an 1873 edition of his *The Catskill Mountains*, Charles Rockwell still found it appropriate to point out that "From a rude spout by the cabin there pour cooling draughts from a mountain spring, more delicious than ever came from the juice of the grape." [41]

The most charming and graphic account of this famous spring comes from the pen of Thomas Cole. During early July, 1835, he and a friend decided one late afternoon to visit the Mountain House. Since there were no stages at that time of day, they determined to walk the full twelve-mile distance from river to mountaintop! The account begins from the time the two companions arrived at the base of the mountains.

Being thirsty, and finding no spring at Lawrence's, where they were soundly asleep, we walked three miles further, to Rip Van Winkle's Hollow. The long mile from the tollgate to Rip's is very steep. Thirst, however, gave wings to our feet, and we reached there with parched mouths and wet skins. It was midnight when we sat down by the stream which comes leaping from the grand amphitheatre of wooded mountains. There was a tin cup glittering by the rill, placed there for the use of travelers, by some generous soul, and we drank from it again and again, of the pure, cold water, and the draughts were even more delicious than those of Rip from the famous keg. It was a solemn scene. Dark forests, rugged rocks, towering mountains were around us, and the breeze brought to our ears the sound of waving trees, falling waters, and the clear chant of the whip-poor-will. We did not, like old Rip, sleep twenty years after our drinking, but reached the Mountain House at one o'clock.[42]

As we noted previously, transportation was indeed no problem to this early generation of American romantics; it was enough "to be an enthusiastic lover of mountain grandeur."

Returning to the issue of the building of the first boardinghouse at the famous site, we may note from Cole's description that it contains no hint of any building at all. Yet the statement "to Rip's" means something, and it undoubtedly meant the old shanty that we know existed from the second decade of the century. Cole simply did not bother mentioning it. This rude building was called Rip Van Winkle's shanty from at least 1828. We encounter it again a year or two after Cole's death (1848) when Elizabeth Ellet descended the old mountain road. In a "dreamy nook," two-thirds of the way down the ravine, she noted the presence of "a rude-looking house of refreshment" from which was hung a sign depicting "old Rip at his waking." [43] (The sign, incidentally, was still there when Lucy C. Lillie made her visit of 1882.) [44] In 1867 and again 1873 Charles Rockwell described Rip's cabin as "a small, white building, with two rooms, where travellers formerly obtained refreshments." [45] The last phrase is significant. In 1866 when B. J. Lossing described Rip's cabin as "a decent frame-house, as the Americans call dwellings made of wood, with two rooms, standing by the side of the road," he went on to say

The Rip Van Winkle of our day, who lived in the cottage by the mountain roadside as long as a guest lingered at the great mansion above him, was no kin to old Rip, and we strongly suspect that his name was borrowed; but he kept refreshments that strengthened many a weary toiler up the mountain. . . .[46]

The true-life Rip, who was keeping the shanty as early as 1828, apparently died sometime between that date and the Civil War, and so terminated the refreshment business of Rip's cabin.

Perhaps it was the death of this solitary proprietor of Sleepy Hollow that led to the founding of the first boardinghouse at the famous site. In the 1870 issue of *Appleton's Hand-Book of American Travel* we encounter the following statement:

Two miles from the summit the coach stops at *Sleepy Hollow*, a spot usually conceded to be the site of Rip Van Winkle's famous nap. Here a house of refreshment has recently been built; it is known as the "Rip Van Winkle House." [47]

The last sentence is arresting; the "house of refreshment" cannot possibly refer to the shanty which was built long before, and which was almost never referred to as a house. The one exception was Elizabeth Ellet's statement of c. 1849 that the shanty was "a rude-looking house of refreshment." The new boardinghouse, however, was most certainly not rude-looking, and there can be no doubt that Mrs. Ellet was referring to the original shanty. The full name, the Rip Van Winkle House, was always applied throughout the post-Civil War period to the large three-storied structure that was featured in all illustrations of Sleepy Hollow from 1870 until the end of the century, but never before that time. We therefore conclude that, contrary to Haring's belief, the first Rip Van Winkle House was built, not in 1845, but sometime between 1865 and 1870.

Little is known about the Rip Van Winkle House because it was built too late in the history of stagecoaching to acquire much historical significance. Traffic was still heavy—and perhaps even heavier—over the old mountain road during the decade 1870–1880, but the following decade saw the beginning of a long decline that was not to terminate until the road had been abandoned to nature and the Rip Van Winkle House had disappeared from the face of the earth.

The cause of the decline was readily apparent in the summer of 1882 when Charles L. Beach built a railroad from the town of Catskill to the base of Sleepy Hollow. This eliminated the usefulness of two-thirds of the old stage route and was accompanied by the termination of the stagecoach business that had been run by various members of the Beach family since 1823. Passengers still had to detrain at the Mountain House station and complete their journey up the mountain by means of the familiar carriages and coaches, but the following year even this part of the journey became obsolete. In 1883 the Ulster and Delaware and Stony Clove railroads completed a line of tracks all the way from Kingston to the borders of South Lake, within a mile of the Mountain House. This created an alternative route to Pine Orchard that eliminated all necessity of stagecoach travel, and it materially reduced the amount of traffic over both the Catskill Mountain Railroad and the old stage route up Sleepy Hollow. To recapture this lost trade, Beach built an "inclined railway" up the face of South Mountain in 1892 and thus provided an all-rail route from the steamboat landing in Catskill to the very doors of the Mountain House. The stratagem restored Beach's control of traffic to the heights of Pine Orchard, but it also sealed the fate of Sleepy Hollow.

From the 1880s onward, therefore, the history of the old mountain road was one of accelerating decay and ruin. By 1884 it was

Figure 18. Rip Van Winkle House, Sleepy Hollow. From a postcard (A. C. Bosselman & Co., New York, 1906). "Rip's Rock" was up the ravine to the left of the house.

already apparent that the railroads had "cut down the stage travel to a comparatively small traffic . . ."[48] Revenues from tolls dropped from a high of $1,169.51 in 1881 to less than $700 in 1885 and the road soon became a financial liability. In 1885 the Beaches turned the road over to the county, renouncing all rights of ownership. The road department of Greene County kept the road under repair until 1918 when all maintenance was finally abandoned.[49] In 1900 when the road was still kept in good repair many bicyclists used it as a speedy way of descending the mountain.[50] In 1908 or 1909 when the author of *The Picturesque Hudson* sought to visit the abandoned Rip Van Winkle House he was advised to leave his horse at the base of the mountain and make his journey on foot.[51] Reports of the bad condition of the road, however, seem to have been exaggerated, for the

road was still passable a number of years after 1919, and some
early automobiles were known to have traveled over it until
1922 when an unusually severe spring thaw washed out a
great deal of its surface.[52] By that time, also, the Rip Van
Winkle House and cabin had totally disappeared. In 1901 they
were still in a fairly good state of repair; by 1908, they were
noticeably derelict ("much marked and scribbled with names
of idling sightseers"[53]); and the Rip Van Winkle House had
lost its whole façade of pillar and porch. In another seven years
both buildings were little more than crumbling ruins;[54] and
finally about 1916 or 1917 a fire destroyed the remains of
the buildings, leaving nought but crude stone foundations to
mark the site of the famous "resting place" of Sleepy Hollow.[55]

The road fared otherwise. By 1927, according to one report,
it was fast becoming a foot trail, and the whole of Sleepy
Hollow was reverting to primitive nature.[56] In 1931 the road
was officially closed to all traffic, and left to the sporadic care
and attention of lumbermen.[57] Still it did not die. In 1951 or
1952, when it was considered "dangerous to any one but an
extremely skillful and daring driver in a very high-wheeled
car," an army jeep descended the whole three-mile course
without a single mishap.[58]

In 1961 the author left his automobile at "Saxe's Farm,"
close by the site of the old tollgate, and ascended the road
on foot; he found it in remarkably good condition. The first
sharp curve with its protruding ledge of rock would have
discouraged a modern automobile; the fallen timbers of "Black
Snake Bridge" would have been impassable; but the road was
cleared of brambles and undergrowth throughout its course; the
surface was generally smooth and firm; and the whole road
was obviously in far better condition than it had been reported
as being thirty years before.[59] A little care and attention—it
seemed to this nostalgic writer—could restore this "best mountain road in the country" to its prime historic condition.

Time and history, however, had passed it by. The famous

hotel that sired the most romantic of all mountain roads now stood in ruins on the mountain's brow, an object of idle curiosity to the occasional hiker and camper from the neighboring peaks and cloves. The old unseen road that wound down the mountain's cliff and brought half a nation to the first of America's mountain resorts now lay concealed in the overhanging canopy of returning forest and woodland, as meaningless to the occasional hiker of 1961 as the mossy remains of Rip's crude cabin or the whole storied past of Sleepy Hollow.

Chapter 5

The Scenic Domain of the Mountain House

Trails, Lakes, Cloves, and Falls

Our object—in this part of the Guide—is . . . to assist the visitor (who has made the ascent of the best mountain road in this country) *in finding* the principal points within four miles' radius of the Catskill Mountain House. We take this central point, as the space covered includes that portion which for fifty years has been visited by thousands in search of the sublime and the picturesque.

—WALTON VAN LOAN (1876)

Arriving at the heights of Pine Orchard by means of the old mountain road, nineteenth century visitors found themselves at the exact geographic center of the famous scenic domain of the Catskill Mountain House. If we consult the very accurate and popular maps published by Walton Van Loan during the second half of the century, we may note that the relatively small area of this crescent-shaped domain (most points are within three miles of the Mountain House) contains a remarkable diversity of scenic features. During its heyday when the hotel itself owned more than three thousand acres of this land—or three lineal miles of the eastern escarpment of the mountains—it could offer its appreciative patrons everything from wild mountain retreats, secluded glens and dales, gentle forest streams and moonlit lakes, to high mountain promontories, precipitous ravines, and one of the most famous vistas of the whole Atlantic seaboard. Beyond its own boundaries, yet tied to the Mountain

Map 5. The Pine Orchard–Kaaterskill Clove area at the height of its history. Detail of map from *Van Loam's Catskill Mountain Guide* (New York, 1897), p. 45.

House by miles of well-kept trails and carriage roads, were the peripheral attractions of Kaaterskill Clove and several waterfalls higher than Niagara. To Americans still unacquainted with the wonders of the Rockies and High Sierras, it was a region of almost inexhaustible beauty. Many would agree with a well-known writer of the antebellum period and say, "To those who have leisure. . . for exploring the wild and numerous beauties of this region, I would recommend a residence of weeks at Pine Orchard." [1] It was this larger setting of the Mountain House, its surrounding landscape of beautiful trails, lakes, cloves and falls, that provides one of the most important keys to its long distinguished history.

To satisfy the demand of its nature-loving clientele for easy access to every scenic corner of its great property, the Mountain House established from the earliest years a network of trails that for sheer beauty and popularity could not be duplicated in any other region of the Atlantic seaboard. The trails were set out in two groups, consistent with the natural topographical division of the area. Consulting Van Loan's maps once again, we can see that the Catskills form a crescent at this point, the bulge with the Mountain House in the center facing the Hudson, the points of the crescent sweeping westward to the rear of the hotel. One point is formed by the 3,450-foot bulk of North Mountain, the other by the 2,460-foot mass of South Mountain. South Mountain also forms the north wall of Kaaterskill Clove. The Mountain House and its two lakes occupy a depression or small plateau between these land masses and therefore a strategic position midway between the two groups of trails that connect the hotel with North and South mountains. While the second group—and especially the trail that went a half mile to the summit of South Mountain—was apparently more popular in the nineteenth century,[2] the first group is the favorite of today's hikers and campers. This may be due, in part, to the fact that New York State now maintains a public camp site on the shores of North Lake. During the nineteenth century, however, most points

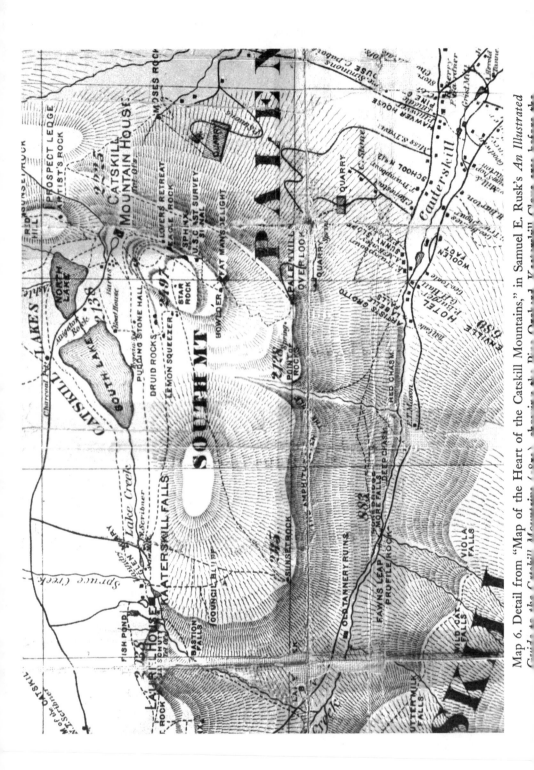

Map 6. Detail from "Map of the Heart of the Catskill Mountains," in Samuel E. Rusk's *An Illustrated Guide to the Catskill Mountains* (1885), showing the Pine Orchard, Kaaterskill Clove area before the

of interest were located along the southern group of trails. The Kaaterskill Falls (now all but unknown and no longer accessible by trails and stairs) was a favorite attraction of the southern group; and late in the century the Hotel Kaaterskill attracted hundreds of sightseers to the top of South Mountain. Today all trails are owned and operated by the Conservation Department of New York State. There are very few hikers and campers who are aware that these were once the most popular trails in all North America.

The guidebooks and resort literature of the period commonly featured exact and detailed descriptions of every foot of these famous trails.[3] Distance was always computed from the Mountain House. The distance from the hotel to the Kaaterskill Falls, for instance, was stated as being one and a half miles by way of the path that went to the south of South Lake or one and three-quarters miles by way of the one along the north shore of that lake. The shorter route required two hours of walking. The distance to Sunset Rock, a 2,123-foot elevation on the rim of Kaaterskill Clove whence one could look to the westward peaks of the Catskills or down the clove to the Hudson Valley, was two miles by way of the path over South Mountain and required three hours' hiking. People were advised year after year that

no visitor to the mountains should miss going to Sunset Rock, as the view of the Clove is magnificent, and the grandeur of High Peak, seen from its base in the Kaaterskill, two-thousand feet below you, to its summit, four-thousand feet, is wonderful in its mass of unbroken foliage.

The view west takes in Haines' Falls, the Hunter Valley and distant mountains.

A remarkable echo is produced here by the firing of a gun.[4]

Other points along the rim of the clove were Inspiration Point, Point of Rocks or Indian Head, and High Rock or the famous Palenville Overlook. The latter was a favorite destination more than two thousand feet above the village of Palenville at the entrance of Kaaterskill Clove. Going by way of certain rock formations known as Pudding Stone Hall and Fat Man's Delight, the distance was a mile and a half. (Hikers going over these trails today will find a useful guide in Eric Posselt's *The Rip Van Winkle Trail.*)

Every unusual formation along the miles of trails very early acquired names and designations that remained unchanged for generations. One of the first landmarks you encountered on the trail from the Mountain House to the summit of South Mountain was Druid Rocks, a formation of several detached rocks of conglomerate one of which was said to resemble "a gigantic toad or rabbit, according to the position from which you observe it." [5] Next appeared two landmarks known as the Lemon Squeezer and Fairy Spring, the first being a very narrow fissure that was also known as Elfin Pass, and the second forming a natural spring that fell over a ledge into a moss-lined basin. The Sphinx, Eagle Rock, and Lovers' Retreat were also well-known features of the trail from the Mountain House to the Palenville Overlook. Lovers' Retreat was a fifteen-minute walk south of the hotel on the same ledge that faces the Hudson Valley. It consisted simply of two large fir trees that had been joined together at the base by an interlocking system of exposed roots, creating two comfortable seats for the susceptible lovers of Pine Orchard.

The various trails from the Mountain House to the Kaaterskill Falls and the scenic points of South Mountain were supplemented toward the end of the century by miles of finely graded carriage roads. When the Hotel Kaaterskill acquired all that part of South Mountain not preëmpted by the Mountain House, it first built its own carriage road from Palenville to the top of the mountain and then extended that road to connect the new hotel with all the other major points of the area. The whole area from the Mountain House to South Lake, the Kaaterskill Falls, and the new Hotel Kaaterskill became a maze of interlocking carriage roads permitting day-long tours to every point of the compass.

This was never the case with that great scenic area that

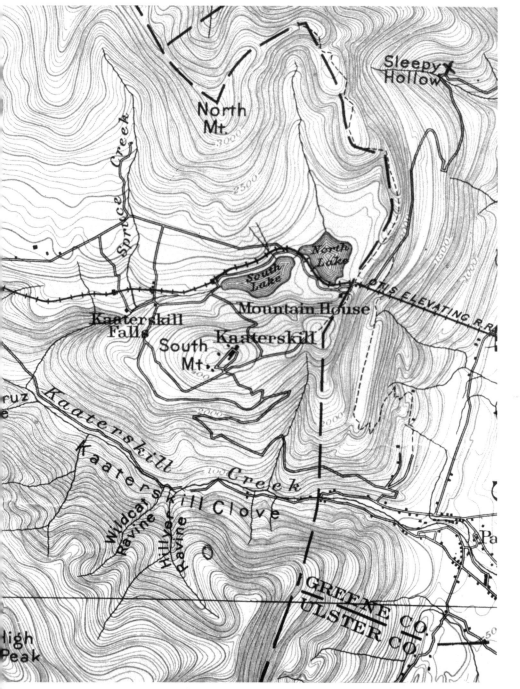

Map 7. Detail from U.S. Geological Survey Map, Kaaterskill Quadrangle, 1892; contour interval is 20 feet.

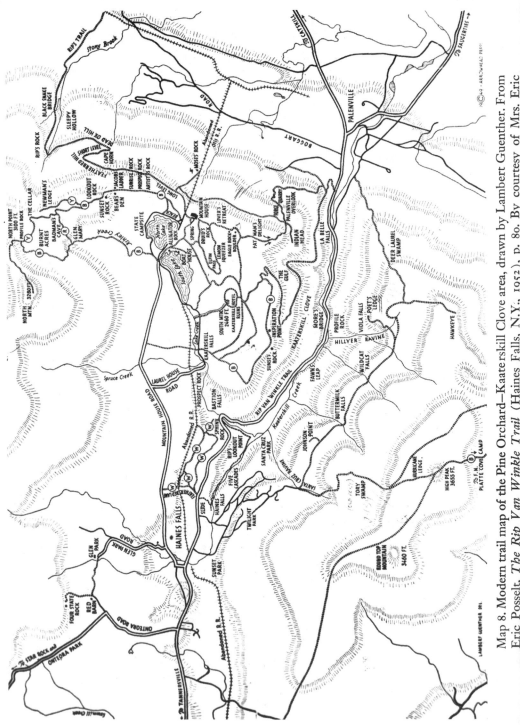

Map 8. Modern trail map of the Pine Orchard–Kaaterskill Clove area, drawn by Lambert Guenther. From Eric Posselt, *The Rip Van Winkle Trail* (Haines Falls, N.Y., 1952), p. 80. By courtesy of Mrs. Eric

lay to the north of the Mountain House. Because of the sharp, spiny contours of North Mountain, roads were not feasible, and the area always remained the exclusive preserve of the hiker and camper. The trails in this vicinity are still, in the author's opinion, some of the most beautiful of the Atlantic seaboard. The main trail from North Lake to North Point and back again is only about five miles; yet in that distance one may enjoy more panoramic views than are usually encountered in whole days of hiking in the umbrageous mountains of the East. Much of the trail (clearly marked by the blue disks of the State of New York) follows the smooth, flat ledges of the eastern escarpment, and there is only a thousand-foot climb between the shores of the lake and the summit of the mountain (North Lake is 2,100 feet above sea level; North Point is 3,100 feet). The whole trail may be encompassed in a comfortable five-and-a-half hours.[6]

In the nineteenth century, hikers usually left the rear entrance of the Mountain House, walked down the circular drive to the main barns of the hotel; then they followed the old stage road to the top of the second hill where it began its descent of the mountain, close by the shores of North Lake. In the latter part of the century the powerhouse of the Otis Elevating Railroad stood near this point; in more recent years it was part of the property of Rip's Retreat, a commercial concession and bathing beach on the eastern side of North Lake. One can park one's car at this point today and walk in fifteen minutes to Artist's Rock, the first promontory of the trail. In the nineteenth century it took about an hour to walk from the Mountain House to this outlook. The name was well-chosen, for the place affords a dramatic view of the protruding ledges of the Mountain House and was a favorite of nineteenth century artists. A few hundred feet beyond Artist's Rock one comes out upon a second promontory called Prospect Rock. This ledge is hallowed by the memory of Thomas Cole, for the artist was known to come here with friends and point out the exact location of his home in Catskill, twelve miles away.

Beyond this point the trail ascends a sharp elevation called Red Hill and after a short distance passes to the left of an eminence called Sunset Rock (not to be confused with the Sunset Rock of South Mountain). By making a slight detour one can ascend to the top of it and facing directly west obtain, at the end of the day, a magnificent view of the setting sun. Since a shoulder of the mountain arises just beyond a chasm at one's feet, the place is also known to produce remarkable echoes. Beyond Sunset Rock the trail turns sharply away from the eastern escarpment and runs straight for a solid wall of rock that seems to bar all further progress. Until only a few years ago all hikers were forced to scale this obstacle by means of a large wooden ladder that was kept against the face of the cliff. Under the recent jurisdiction of New York State, however, "Jacob's Ladder," considered too hazardous, was removed and the trail reconstituted to provide easy stages to the top of the ledge.

At the top, one still encounters the same remarkable terrain that delighted the hikers of the past. The area abounds in deep crevasses and caves that are easily explored by youthful climbers, especially the largest of them all, the Bear's Den, which is a famous landmark on the trail. In spite of these subterranean chambers, the surface of the area is notably flat and treeless, affording easy walking to the noble prospects of the region. Visiting the site in the middle of the twentieth century, one can see why it was once thought to contain "the grandest combination of mountain scenery to be met with here or elsewhere." [7] The vista from the top of Bear's Den embraces both North and South Lakes, the site of the Mountain House, all of South Mountain, the distant ridges of High Peak and Round Top (on the other side of Kaaterskill Clove), and the full basin of the Hudson Valley together with the outlying promontories of the western tier of mountains in the states of Connecticut and Massachusetts. No vista is more

Figure 19. *Catskill Mountain House*, Thomas Cole, probably 1843 (oil on canvas, 29″ x 36″). The hotel seen from the slopes of North Mountain. Courtesy of Mrs. Calvin Stillman, New York City. Preparatory sketches for this painting are now in the Princeton University Art Museum.

Figure 20. *Catskill Mountains*, Sanford R. Gifford, 1868 (oil on canvas, 9½″ x 18½″). Courtesy of Mrs. E. W. Isom, New York City.

flattering to the high romantic setting of the Catskill Mountain House, and it became from the earliest years of the century a favorite motif of the Hudson River School of painting. Thomas Cole painted it several times in typically divergent styles; W. C. Bartlett made it the subject of one of the illustrations of *American Scenery;*[8] Jaspar F. Cropsey commemorated it in one of his finest paintings; S. R. Gifford infused it with the mellow warmth of his Turneresque palette; and the firm of Currier and Ives finally made it a commonplace of every middle-class American parlor.

Beyond this famous promontory, the trail veers eastward through an area of rich glacial deposits and finally returns to the high eastern escarpment of North Mountain where Lookout Rock presents another fine view of the great Hudson Valley. Looking north along the high rim of the mountain, one may see a large outcropping that promises even more spectacular views of the valley. To reach this point (Newman's Ledge) one continues along the trail until it ascends a rather steep part of the mountain and joins a second trail with yellow markers. Turning right on the yellow trail, one arrives in twenty minutes at the sensational ledge that was named after an English divine called the Rev. Newman Hall. From the top of this ledge there is an immediate perpendicular drop of one hundred feet, followed by a two-thousand-foot slant to the floor of the Hudson Valley. Looking down to the thick covering of forest a couple of hundred feet below, one may detect a long opening (or "cut") that runs along a lower ridge or bulge of the mountain. It is the remains of Long Level, the last good stretch of the old mountain road. Slightly to the left, there is a long dark ravine sloping down the mountainside to the floor of the valley. This is the famous Sleepy Hollow of the nineteenth century. At its exact base where the forest first encounters the open fields of the distant valley, one may easily espy the house and barns of "Saxe's Farm" and the precise location of the former tollgates of the old mountain road.

Figure 21. *The Two Lakes and the Mountain House on the Catskills*, W. H. Bartlett, 1836. From the engraving by J. C. Bentley in N. P. Willis, *American Scenery* (London, 1838–1840).

Figure 22. *Scenery of the Catskills*, unsigned, undated print by Currier & Ives (8½" x 12½") in the author's collection. Listed in Frederick A. Conningham, *Currier and Ives Prints, An Illustrated Check List* (New York, Crown, 1949), no. 5419.

Retracing the yellow trail to the point where the main or "blue" trail had been left, one now continues on the final leg to the summit of North Mountain. After ascending another steep incline, the trail comes out into a large open area of sparse timber, and the hiker must be careful to follow the cairns and blue disks that have been set out for his guidance. Negotiating that area, the hiker ascends another steep climb, comes out into a second open area, and finally arrives at Badman Cave. At this point another trail (marked with red disks) offers a shortcut to Glen Mary, a small, picturesque dale located on a stream that parallels the return route to the Mountain House. Ignoring this shortcut and continuing on up the blue trail, the hiker arrives in ten minutes' time at a third open level where on clear days he can see the State Office Building in Albany. The trail then proceeds through an area of scrub spruce, skirts a small swamp rich in wild blue iris, and emerges (three miles from its point of departure on North Lake) at a junction with another yellow trail. The hardy climber may turn right on this trail and in a quarter of a mile of stiff climbing arrive at the 3,000-foot summit of North Point. And "splendid is the reward!" as one intrepid climber exclaimed more than a century ago:

So vast is the height on which you stand, that the "Mountain House," with its lakes, itself appears upon a plain. In clear weather the view is almost boundless, including Albany on one hand, the Highlands on the other. . . .[9]

In spite of its noble prospect, the summit of North Mountain does not have the rich historical associations of the lower promontories. Requiring twice the amount of time to get to as, for example, Jacob's Ladder and Bear's Den, it proved impractical to the heavily laden artists of the nineteenth century; and its precipitous last quarter of a mile discouraged all but the most confirmed climbers.

Many hikers choose to bypass the last detour to the summit and continue on the blue trail for the return journey to the Mountain House. Since the trail no longer follows the eastern escarpment of the mountain, it lacks the spectacular rewards of the upper trail. Quickly descending the mountain, it soon arrives at the headwaters of Ashley's Creek, the principal source of North and South Lakes. Following this mountain stream for about half a mile, the trail then intersects the red trail that provides a shortcut to the eastern escarpment (not known in the nineteenth century), and soon reaches the head of Ashley's Falls, the main feature of the idyllic Glen Mary. The falls are not large, but they are proportionate to the intimate seclusion of the surrounding dale and afford a delightful contrast to the more spectacular scenes of the upper trail. A subsidiary yellow trail (much used in the nineteenth century) provides a detour to the top and bottom of the falls, then back to the main trail. During the last century this trail was a popular walk for those who did not wish to encounter the rigors of the eastern escarpment and was "a favorite walk with the ladies." [10] The distance from Glen Mary to the present site of the caretaker's cabin on North Lake (maintained by the Conservation Department) is a half mile of easy walking. Today as in the nineteenth century the blue trail terminates at the old mountain road close by the present site of the caretaker's cabin. (It is another three quarters of a mile to the Mountain House.)

"The two lakes, which we have just overlooked from the North Mountain," *Appleton's Illustrated Hand-Book of American Travel* declared in 1857,

make one of the leading items in the Catskill programme. They lie side by side, in gentle beauty, in the heart of the lofty plateau, upon the eastern brink of which the Mountain House is perched. They may be reached in a pleasant little walk back of the hotel. Onwards, and on the way to the Great Falls of the Kauterskill, a few minutes' stroll, indeed, is sufficient to bring us to the nearest of these twin waters, the Upper or Sylvan [or North] Lake. This is a spot for repeated and habitual visits, with its pleasures by the forest shore; in skiff, upon the quiet and lonely flood; or, with angle in hand and trout in prospect. [11]

Figure 23. The Mountain House from North Mountain. Photo by Herman Bickelman, c. 1910. Courtesy of C. E. Dornbusch. The Otis Summit Station is visible just below the Mountain House, and the Kaaterskill Hotel dominates the ridge at right center.

Figure 24. North Lake and the Catskill Mountain House from the ledges of North Mountain. Summer, 1960. Author's photo.

The lakes are indeed two of the greatest topographical assets of the whole area. Today North Lake, the smaller lake (twenty-six acres), is the more active, as it is the site of the state-owned public campsite and, until recently, a public beach run by Rip's Retreat. Throughout the nineteenth century, the lower lake (thirty-five acres) was the more important—regardless of *Appleton's* intimations to the contrary. South Lake was always the site of the main boathouses and pavilions of the Mountain House until as late as 1931. Furthermore, all the various roads and trails that went from the Mountain House to the Laurel House and Kaaterskill Falls ran close to the shores of the larger lake, making it a greater source of interest. At the end of the century the Kaaterskill Railroad Station was located on its southwestern tip; and the lake was connected to the Mountain House by means of an extraordinary covered walk that was at least 1,700 feet long! Still, both lakes received equal attention in the annual advertisements of the Mountain House—the hotel simply stating that both lakes were "plentifully stocked with various kinds of Fish, and well supplied with Boats, canoes, etc." [12] Since the lakes were used for boating, fishing, and swimming, they were never trusted as sources of drinking water. The water for the Mountain House was always piped from the headwaters of Spruce Creek on the lower slopes of North Mountain, one-and-a-half miles from the hotel.[13] All the springs and brooks that fed the two lakes also originated in that area. After passing from the two lakes to Lake Creek, this water tumbled over the crest of Kaaterskill Falls, then descended the wild cascades of Kaaterskill Clove, emptied into the Hudson at the village of Catskill, and finally reached the sea.

The impression that most nineteenth century visitors had of South Lake—"a perfect gem of a lake"—[14] can only be retained today by viewing it from the distant heights of North Mountain. Close by, it has suffered from years of neglect since the demise of both the Hotel Kaaterskill and the Mountain House, and has become the prey of the ubiquitous picnicker and soda-pop vendor. To get a close view of its former beauty one must consult W. H. Bartlett's charming picture, "Winter Scene on the Catterskills,"

Figure 25. Newman's Ledge on the trail to North Mountain, about 2,700 feet above the Hudson River (background). Summer, 1960. Author's photo.

or read the following description by Thomas Cole, the first of its devotees. During one of his many visits to the Mountain House more than a century and a quarter ago, Cole paid a special visit to the lake in the company of a friend who had never seen it before. While the event was still fresh in his mind, he penned this delightful vignette:

I pointed out a view which I once painted, which was, I think, the first picture ever painted of the lake, which will hereafter be the subject of a thousand pencils. Several years since I explored its shores for some distance, but thick woods and swampy grounds impeded me. I enriched my sketchbook with studies of fine dead trees, which stand like spectres on the shores. As we made our way to an opening through the woods, which disclosed the lake in a charming manner, we perceived a rude boat among the bushes, which was exactly what we wanted. We pushed off and leaped into it, as if the genius of the deep had placed it there for our special use. Before us spread the virgin waters which the prow of the sketcher had never yet curled, enfolded by the green woods, whose venerable masses had never yet figured in annuals, and overlooked by the stern mountain peaks never beheld by Claude or Salvator, nor subjected to the canvas by the innumerable dabblers in paint of all past time. . . .

A little promontory, forming a fine foreground to a charming view down the lake, invited us. We had some fine perspective lines of forest on our right, with many dead trees standing near the shore, as if stripped for the elements. These dead trees are a striking feature in the scenery of this lake, and exceedingly picturesque. Their pale forms rise from the margin of the lake, stretching out their contorted branches, and looking like so many genii set to protect their sacred waters. On the left was another reach of forest of various hues, and in the center of the picture rose the distant Round Top, blue and well defined, and cast its reflection on the lake, out to the point where our boat swung like a thing in air. The headland was picturesque in the extreme. Apart from the dense wood, a few birches and pines were grouped together in a rich mass, and one giant pine rose far above the rest. On the extreme cape a few bushes of light green grew directly from the water. In the midst of their sparkling foliage stood two of the bare spectral trees, with limbs decorated with moss of silvery hue, and waving like gray locks in the wind. We remained here long enough to finish a sketch, and returned to our harbor to refit.

After dinner we again launched our vessel for a longer voyage of discovery. We now crossed the lake, paddling, after the manner of the Indians. Our boat glided beautifully over the tranquil waters, and swept aside the yellow water-lilies. In a strait between the mainland and a low islet, where the water was very still, the woods were reflected beautifully. I never saw such depth and brilliancy in the reflections. The dead trees on the margin added by their silvery tints to the harmony of color, and their images in the water, which had a gentle undulation, appeared like immense glittering serpents playing in the deep. At every stroke of the oar some fresh object of beauty would break upon us. We made several sketches, and about sunset turned our prow. As we returned we struck up the 'Canadian Boat Song,' and though our music was rude, the woods answered in melodious echoes. What a place for music by moonlight! It would be romance itself! This may be, and I may enjoy it.[15]

Such was the beauty of South Lake when it was first discovered by the founder of the Hudson River School of painting.

The historic painting to which Cole referred was done in the fall of 1825 during his first memorable trip to the Catskills. It was the "Lake with Dead Trees," one of three original paintings that led to Cole's discovery by Colonel Trumbull and the start of his career as the first of America's landscape painters.[16]

The dead trees along the shore of the lake which Cole found so "exceedingly picturesque," also forms a prominent feature of Bartlett's "Winter Scene on the Catterskills" and "The Two Lakes and the Mountain House on the Catskills." These trees have long since vanished; but if the lake is viewed at dusk when no one else is there, it still suggests the haunting primitivism of the early nineteenth century. For those who wish to view it to best advantage, the finest prospect is the classic one from the ledges of North Mountain. Distance obscures human neglect, the mountains rise round about in their unalterable grandeur, and one may

Figure 26. *Catskill Lake,* Thomas Cole, probably 1825 (oil on canvas, 27″ x 34½″). Courtesy of the Allen Art Museum, Oberlin College, gift of Charles F. Olney. This is undoubtedly the historic painting, *Lake with Dead Trees,* in the early catalogues of Cole's work.

Figure 27. *Kaaterskill Clove*, Asher B. Durand, 1866 (oil on canvas, 3'3" x 5'). Reproduced courtesy of The Century Association, New York City. Frick Art Reference Library photo. Painted from the present site of Twilight Park, looking down the Clove toward the Hudson Valley. The high point behind the fir tree at left is Palenville Overlook, the southern boundary of the Catskill Mountain House property.

see as in ages past the two small lakes lying "side by side, in gentle beauty. . . ."

Forming the southern boundary of the scenic heights of Pine Orchard, and easily accessible to the Mountain House by means of horse and carriage, Kaaterskill Clove became, by the end of the nineteenth century, one of the most famous mountain passes in the East. Cumberland Gap in the southern Appalachians was undoubtedly more historical; Delaware Water Gap and some of the passes of the Green and White Mountains became almost as fashionable (e.g., Crawford Notch in New Hampshire and Smugglers Notch in Vermont); but none equaled the wildest clove of the Catskills in sheer popularity, or accumulated such a rich store of artistic associations.

Nineteenth century travel literature abounds in eulogies to the superior beauty of Kaaterskill Clove. To someone like

Elizabeth Ellet, the diverse beauty of Kaaterskill Clove was almost inexpressible:

Surprise and delight at the wondrous scene accompany you on every step onward. The mountains rise abruptly on either side almost to the clouds; the primeval forest is around you; and the depth of the gorge, which is sometimes narrow and cavernous, is filled by a brawling mountain stream, the same Cauterskill that takes the leap down the falls above. For two or three miles this scene of beauty and grandeur, varying at every moment, meets your eye; now the stream runs over its bed of rocks, now dashes wildly in rapids, now runs smoothly for a space; while the road winds on its verge, sometimes far above it, sometimes descending nearly to its level.[17]

Finding that many visitors to the Mountain House (i.e., during the antebellum period) neglected Kaaterskill Clove in order to see the more accessible sights on the top of the mountain, she urged sightseers to take more time and make the fourteen-mile drive down the old mountain road to the base of the mountains, then up Kaaterskill Clove and back to the hotel by way of Haines Falls and the two lakes. This became a favorite tour during the 1880s and 1890s when improved carriage roads and the Otis Elevating Railroad permitted sight-seers to make the complete circuit in something less than five hours.[18]

The route from Pelham's Four Corners (where the nineteenth century sightseer turned right after descending the mountain) to Palenville is much the same today as it was at the height of its popularity. Directly below the ledges of Pine Orchard one may still see the buildings of the Otis Elevating Railroad (now privately owned) and the long open slash that marks the previous route of the railroad straight up the precipitous incline to the Mountain House. A little farther on one may see the roof (on the right, through the trees) of Bogart's Farm, a Dutch dwelling of the late seventeenth century. All during the nineteenth century it was possible to take a path from this place to a famous lookout called Moses Rock just a hundred feet below the Mountain House;

and then another path to the Long Level of the old mountain road and thence back to the crest of the mountains. Passing beyond this point the modern motorist continues on Bogart Road to an intersection with route 23A and finds himself in the middle of Palenville, the legendary home of Rip Van Winkle.

As he turns right on 23A, the motorist immediately confronts the huge chasm of Kaaterskill Clove. Up ahead the lofty crags of the Catskills loom over the village of Palenville "like towers and battlements of cyclopean structure." [19] The motorist passes up the main street of the village, makes a sudden turn to the left, crosses a bridge, and begins the actual ascent of the steep cloven mountain. At this point in the 1880s and 1890s stagecoaches commonly stopped briefly to water the horses and allow travelers to refresh themselves at Burger's Hotel. Beyond, the road rises gently through a series of curves and climbs twenty or thirty feet above the level of the Kaaterskill Creek. To the right one can see a gigantic bowl still known as the amphitheatre against the north wall of the clove. Above, and still to the right of this, high against the sky, one can discern two promontories known respectively as Point of Rocks (or Indian Head) and High Rock (or the Palenville Overlook). This overlook always marked the southeasternmost point of the 3,000-acre domain of the Catskill Mountain House.

A short distance beyond the bridge one comes to the site of the former tollgate of Kaaterskill Clove. During the nineteenth century a little path led from this point to two sights which Thomas Cole and many others found "truly picturesque," the still lovely Artist's Grotto and La Bella Falls.[20] Today access to both places involves crossing private property, and visitors are advised to get permission before trespassing.

Several landslides are encountered in this area along the walls of the clove, and a small stream tumbles down a ravine called the Gulf and empties into the Kaaterskill Creek. During the late nineteenth century the Hotel Kaaterskill built a road from Palenville to the head of the Gulf and thus to the top of South Mountain. As the contemporary motorist continues to ascend the clove, he passes on the right a sign reading "Entering Catskill Park" and a little later a second sign:

1885–1935

State Land   A part of 2,370,000 Acres
Entering Forest Preserve   of wild forest maintained
Acquired 1931   for free public use

Still following the original toll road up the clove, the modern concrete highway makes a sharp turn to the right and recrosses the Kaaterskill Creek over More's Bridge, a favorite subject of nineteenth century artists. On the other side of the bridge the motorist may find a space just large enough to park his car and thus take time to study the many interesting features of the area. Directly below the bridge the Kaaterskill Creek tumbles down a series of ledges and forms the picturesque cascades known as More's Falls. To the left up the south wall of the clove is the lofty outcropping of Church's Ledge, and close by is an unusual formation of rock that nineteenth century visitors called Profile Rock, probably because it resembled a man's head (complete with a mossy cap). Next on the left come two of the many ravines that form such dramatic features of the south wall of the clove—Hillyer's Ravine and Wildcat Ravine. Both contain turbulent streams that hurtle down the steep slopes of High Peak to the Katterskill Creek.

In between the two points where these streams join the creek one may find some of the most beautiful falls, pools, and grottoes of the whole Kaaterskill Clove. Part of them form a miniature canyon known as Fawn's Leap. It is located a couple of hundred feet above More's Bridge and may best be seen by scrambling down the steep banks from the road and viewing it from the bottom of the ravine. Legend explains the name by asserting that a young fawn fell to its death between the canyon walls while attempting to follow its mother by leaping across the chasm. Whatever the value of the legend, the old guidebooks are right when they say "it will repay the time taken to leave your conveyance and examine the beauty of the fall and its surroundings." [21]

Resuming the motor tour, one now finds that the surface of the road has been deliberately serrated or corrugated to permit greater traction during the long winter months, and that the ascent has become exceptionally arduous and steep. On the left one soon passes Buttermilk Ravine, and high on the southern rim of the clove one can see the cascading foam of Buttermilk Falls, at least a thousand feet above the surface of the road. Straight below this, along the base of Kaaterskill Clove, one can see a small level area to the left of the road. This was once the location of the first boardinghouse in the clove (Brockett's) and also a large tannery and its adjacent settlements. Today little remains of this active community, but as late as the 1880s the ruins of the huge tannery were an impressive sight. [22]

The tanneries of Katterskill Clove were among the oldest in the Catskills. The founders of Palenville, a family by the name of Palens, built a large tannery at the lower end of the clove even before 1817. [23] In subsequent years, according to *Appleton's*, "this clove was a den of tanneries," and as late as 1857 "a few establishments" were still operating. [24] By 1866, however, all tanneries had ceased operations, leaving what B. J. Lossing called "the ruins of a leather manufacturing village" where the Buttermilk joins the Kaaterskill Creek. [25] This was confirmed the following year by Charles Rockwell who found "the decayed and decaying ruins of what was once a busy and thrifty village of tanners" in the "wild ravine of the Cauterskill Clove." [26] Visiting the site today we may still observe some of the old stone foundations of this once thriving enterprise.

Higher up the clove from the site of the tannery ruins, we pass beneath the towering heights of Sunset Rock and Inspiration Point on the high picturesque trails of South Mountain. In the same area the motorist passes the entrance of an abandoned road and may notice an iron plaque containing the ambiguous statement, "Indian Trail to Fort on Round Top, now Kaaterskill Clove." The sign is misleading, for old guidebooks assure us that the "Indian Trail" is actually the original road of Kaaterskill Clove before it was replaced by the modern concrete highway. From this point onward the new road turns away from the original toll road and crosses Lake Creek at Bastion Falls, three quarters of a mile to the north of the old road. The new road makes a dramatic horseshoe bend across the top of the falls (one of the most photographed sights of present-day Kaaterskill Clove), loops around the end of Prospect Mountain and re-encounters the original road near the head of the clove at a place called Dripping Rock.

By taking advantage of Lake Creek Ravine to ascend the north wall of Kaaterskill Clove, the new road solved many of the engineering problems that harassed the builders of the first road, and it also provided some of the most interesting prospects of the whole ascent from Palenville. As the motorist approaches the hairpin turn at Bastion Falls, he gets a spectacular view of the head of the clove and the cliff-hanging dwellings of Santa Cruz and Twilight parks. The falls themselves are a most impressive sight and confirm the appropriateness of their name by tumbling down great battlements of high rocky ledges and then plunging, directly under the highway, into a deep chasm. The site also affords the modern hiker the most convenient way of reaching the base of the superlative Kaaterskill Falls. All during the nineteenth century, the customary approach was by way of the elaborate system of steps and staircases directly in front of the Laurel House. With the abandonment of those facilities, the 250-foot walls of the surrounding ravine became an almost insurmountable barrier to the foot of the falls until the new highway was built to the head of Bastion Falls, three-quarters of a mile below Katterskill Falls. The rudimentary path that leads from Bastion Bridge to the base of these falls is now the favorite means of approach for those few romantic souls who still know about the unpublicized wonders of the highest falls in the Catskills.

From Bastion Falls the modern highway ascends another

mile to the head of the clove at the village of Haines Falls. Just before reaching the top of the mountain, close by a sign saying "Welcome to Haines Falls," the motorist may notice the entrance of another small road going off to the right. It is an old carriage road called Featherbed Lane, and it leads around the edge of Prospect Mountain to join the main road from Haines Falls to the Catskill Mountain House. Halfway up this small lane one of the favorite trails of the nineteenth century goes off to the right across the top of Prospect Mountain. From Sphinx Point along this trail one can look down the whole length of the Kaaterskill Clove to the distant reaches of the Hudson Valley; and from Prospect Rock, opposite the Laurel House, there is an unrestricted view of the full length of the Kaaterskill Falls. It was a favorite subject of the Hudson River School of painting.

Some of the most spectacular scenery of the Kaaterskill Clove is all but unknown today. It is at the bottom of the chasm between the base of the falls at Haines Falls and the junction of the Kaaterskill and Lake creeks. To get there one must walk down route 23A (say, from the Post Office in Haines Falls) toward the entrance of Twilight Park (sign and stone gates on your right); then on to the upper junction of the old toll road and the modern highway (i.e. near Dripping Rock); down the old road to its junction with Lake Creek; down this creek to its junction with Kaaterskill Creek; and finally back up this stream in the very bottom of the gorge toward the base of the falls at Haines Falls.

The way is still anything but easy. Once you start back up the gorge (to quote a local authority)—

it becomes increasingly rough until washed out overhanging sides force the visitor to jump from rock to huge rock way in the middle of the creek, and an occasional gap must be crossed on a fallen, age-old tree.

High overhead on the left hang the eyrie-like houses of Santa Cruz and Twilight Park perilously perched, or so it seems, directly above the void. *Dripping Rock*, constantly oozing water through its many crevices, towers high up on the right. At the foot of the old landslide, *Triton Cave, Shelving Rock* and finally *Naiad's Bath* become visible in their eery beauty while the *Five Cascades* turn the scene into a fairyland with their constant rush of water in its ever changing sparkling beauty.

But this is as far as the average visitor can go, since the old path on the left bank is completely washed away, and further penetration would require the use of ropes and possibly ladders, and the going further up to the bottom of Haines Falls might become really dangerous, particularly in spring and fall when the water is deep and treacherous.

Thus it is necessary to retrace one's step to the starting point, unless the adventurous want to climb up the face of the landslide, a feat not too difficult, though strenuous. Total walking time about two hours.

The ascent of the old landslide is one of two alternatives, both disagreeable. The other is "a rather precarious path from the near side of the falls leading to the bottom." It is so precipitous that "only people completely free of vertigo and skilled in rock climbing should attempt it." [27] It is little wonder that so few people know the beauties of this climactic part of Kaaterskill Clove.

Yet it has not always been so. Eighty years ago during the flush years of the Catskills people could descend to the bottom of Haines Falls almost as easily as they could at the Kaaterskill Falls. This is the way it was done in 1881:

A path to the left of the bridge [where the old toll road crossed Lake Creek] leads down to the [Kaaterskill] creek, and follows the same to Haines' Falls, passing on the way the foot of the great land slide, "Triton Cave," "Shelving Rock," and "The Five Cascades." . . .

Parties who wish a hard climb occasionally scramble down the Landslide and up Haines' Ravine. From Shelving Rock and past the Cascades, the ascent is one long to be remembered. The hand of man is not visible here except in the rustic stairs winding up through the immense precipices.

Some of the steps are really part of the mountain, being cut in the rocks by the strong arm of the mountaineer; but it will be found far easier to descend the stairs at Haines' Falls, and, continuing down the Cascades, return the same way.[28]

Thus there were "rustic stairs" going up the side of the ravine near the great landslide, and more stairs at the site of Haines Falls itself. Both disappeared many years ago, as they did at the more famous Kaaterskill Falls. One may still get to the bottom of Haines Falls by making the strenuous climb up and down the landslide, but otherwise must approach the falls from the Lake Creek bridge or descend a dangerous old trail on the "near side" of the falls—a feat which requires the skill of an experienced alpinist. It is as difficult today to get to the bottom of the falls and to the region of the Five Cascades as it was during the 1840s and '50s when such artists as Kensett, Gifford, McEntee, Whittredge, Cassilear, and Thomas Cole were known to have used ropes and ladders to descend.[29]

But times have changed; we live in the middle of a new century; and the worthy artists who once endured such hardships for the fulfillment of their faith in the "sublimities" of nature, have no successors. Nor do we any longer hear, as "thousands" did in the flush years of the 1880s, that "the paths are now good, and none should fail to visit this favorite resort of the artists." [30] The easy paths, the hewn steps and stairs have vanished with the passing years, and few who still come to this part of the Catskills remember "the favorite resort of the artists." At the head of the falls, close by the present-day gates of Twilight Park, there are still the twisted remains of old guardrails standing along the upper edge of the falls. One can park one's car close by and with great caution explore the edge of the ravine and enjoy the dramatic vista down the clove. But to the few who still do, the beauty of the scene is narrowly topographical rather than historical; and the long rich foreground of all past associations makes no echo in the remembered vistas of the most beautiful clove in all the Catskills.

A few minutes' drive from the center of Haines Falls takes the modern motorist along the upper end of the old mountain road to the still existing Laurel House and the imperishable beauty of Kaaterskill Falls. As unknown today to the casual visitor as the history of Sleepy Hollow, Kaaterskill Falls was at one time far more popular than its picturesque rival at the head of Kaaterskill Clove and, indeed, one of the most famous sights of the East. Higher than Niagara Falls (though lacking the breadth), it attracted hundreds of sightseers during any given summer of the last century and became a well-featured subject of American journalism and a favorite motif of American landscape painting. It was the jewel of the upper Catskills, an indestructible symbol of the prodigious scenic assets in the outer domain of the Catskill Mountain House.

Long before the founding of the Mountain House, the falls had already acquired a modest fame in the local lore and legend of early New York history. The early Dutch settlers of the Hudson Valley learned about them through the legends of the Mahican Indians,[31] and during the eighteenth century they became a famous landmark to the hunters and trappers who first invaded the mountains. By 1800, when James Fenimore Cooper and Washington Irving were young men, there can be no doubt that the beauty of the falls had become common knowledge among the more cultured classes of the Hudson Valley. In another decade sightseers began to chisel their names in the rocky ledges at the head of the falls, leaving indelible evidence of the growing popularity of the spectacular phenomenon.[32] By 1820 the falls had become familiar enough to give rise to some extraordinary antics on the part of the young people of the neighboring villages of the Hudson Valley. One story still goes the rounds of the Catskills. From time immemorial until July 4, 1820, a great boulder weighing some fifty tons and estimated to be about 175 feet in circumference rested precariously on the very lip of the Kaaterskill Falls. Deciding it was fair game for a novel way of celebrating the national holiday, a group of gay young blades from Catskill and Cairo spent the night of July 3 in the vicinity of the falls, and early the next morning gathered together at the head of the falls and proceeded to execute an extraordinary bit of mischief. With much heaving and pushing, huffing and puffing, they managed to topple the boulder into the mighty abyss.

The effect [according to a contemporary account] was awful and sublime, the crash tremendous, exceeding the loudest thunder—the tremulous motion of the earth and the long murmuring echo rolling from point to point through the ravine gave the scene an indescribable degree of grandeur. The rock was shattered in a thousand pieces. Toasts were then drunk and volleys of musketry fired.[33]

In 1820 the wild, unpreëmpted state of Kaaterskill Falls encouraged such youthful capers: no hotel stood at the head of the falls; no road connected it with the primitive communities of Hunter or Tannersville or made it accessible to the old wood road going down the mountain from the ledges of Pine Orchard. Nor would it have made much difference if such roads had existed: in 1820 the falls were still a local rather than national phenomenon, and the Catskills as a whole an undeveloped wilderness suitable only to hunting, trapping, and lumbering.

The Kaaterskill Falls are especially enchanting because of their location within the hidden recesses and folds of the mountains. Completely invisible until one has reached the crest of their 260-foot drop, they confirm a childlike phantasy of a high mountainous landscape full of unexpected wonders. Descending the steep walls of the ravine on either side of the falls, one encounters the great cavern first described by James Fenimore Cooper. It is a feature that cannot be duplicated in any other falls of the Catskills and helps to make it one of the most picturesque formations in the East. The impression this cavern made upon the early visitors from the Mountain House is the subject of the following description written for *The Atheneum Magazine* during the summer of 1825:

The most curious part [of the falls] is a vast dome, or more properly semi-dome, formed in the rock, directly behind, and under the cascade. It is like a huge roof, perfectly semi-circular, under the eaves of which, *inside*, you walk along a narrow stony ledge or shelf for about 300 feet, as if on the seat or bench of an amphitheatre, while the enormous and lofty ceiling projects like a canopy 75 feet, sloping upwards, and forming in front a vast arch nearly a hundred feet high, and directly behind the falling water. In order to enter this ponderous dome, you descend from the top of the rock, where the stream commences its career, along the steep side of the ravine 170 feet to the first basin, and arrive at one side or wing of the front arch. The first impression is overwhelming— you hesitate for a moment, and are awe-struck: such a wide and towering vault of solid rock, as if built by art!—what supports it? may it not possibly fall, and crush and bury you forever under its massy ceiling, nearly one hundred feet thick? But your feelings become too sublime to be restrained by your timidity, and you rush forward with a dauntless and ambitious step, as if bent on an achievement that is to immortalize your name, especially if you should have the good luck to be crushed, and buried like king Cheops, under a pyramid of rocks.[34]

The description was written in an era not noted for its literary restraint, but the present writer can vouch for its lack of exaggeration. When he visited the scene in 1961 by scrambling up the base of the deep ravine to the foot of the falls, his first sudden vision of the gigantic amphitheatre (it was invisible until one edged around a protruding ledge of rock and encountered it full-face) was indeed "overwhelming," and everyone in his party *did* "hesitate for a moment" before deciding to go on to the rear of the falls. Until this moment the author had assumed that Winslow Homer's illustration of the cavern was a typical exaggeration of the period, but he now knew it was, if anything, an understatement. The scene seemed strangely out of place in the context of the Catskills or the usual Eastern landscape, and "such a wide and towering vault of solid rock" could only remind him of the great rock walls of the ancient cliff dwellers in the famous Mesa Verde region of Colorado.

Winslow Homer was not the first American artist to be attracted by this unique feature of the Kaaterskill Falls; the honor, once again, belongs to Thomas Cole. We have previously noted that Cole's "Lake with Dead Trees" was one of three historic paintings that he made on his first memorable trip to the Catskills in 1825. Another was "The Falls of Cattskill, New York," now hanging in the Wadsworth Atheneum in Hartford, Connecticut. Though painted from approximately the same angle as Winslow

Figure 28. *Under the Falls, Catskill Mountains*, Winslow Homer, 1872 (engraving, 9⅛″ x 13⅞″). Author's collection. Published in *Harper's Weekly*, September 14, 1872.

Figure 29. *The Falls of Catskill, New York*, Thomas Cole, probably 1825. From the engraving by Fenner Sears & Co., published by I. T. Hinton and Simpkin & Marshall (London, 1831). The original painting, now in the Wadsworth Atheneum, Hartford, Conn., is entitled *Cascade in Catskill Mountains*.

Figure 30. *Kaaterskill Falls*, Thomas Cole, 1827 (oil on canvas, 43″ x 36″). The painting, now in the collection of Lee B. Anderson, New York City, was originally owned by William Cullen Bryant.

Figure 31. *From the Top of Kaaterskill Falls*, Thomas Cole, 1826 (oil on canvas, 31″ x 41″). Courtesy of the Detroit Institute of Arts.

Figure 32. *The Catterskill Falls*, W. H. Bartlett, 1836. From the engraving by J. T. Willmore in N. P. Willis, *American Scenery* (London 1838–40).

Homer's painting (from the back of what Cole called "the vast arched cave that extends beneath and behind the cataract"[35]), the two paintings could hardly be more dissimilar. Homer's painting leads the eye of the observer from the large static figures on the left to the dynamic falls, and then back along the catwalk to the static figures. Cole's, on the other hand, leads the eye from the vertical mass of the falls on the left to the small figure at the head of the second invisible falls, then down the dark ravine to the dramatic peaks and clouds of the distant horizon. Cole's painting is quintessentially "romantic," a moody evocation of the wild and dynamic aspects of nature; the falls are subservient to this end, and have little topical interest; the whole is a "landscape" in the fullest sense of the word. In Homer's painting, however, we are invited with the well-groomed figures on the left to observe an interesting freak of nature; the intent of the painter has been journalistic or topical; he has given us what the modern cinema calls a "documentary" rather than a landscape. The two paintings are so different that they almost register a great social change in the history of the Catskills: the romantic adulation of the poet and artist has yielded in fifty years' time to the popular idolization of the tourist and vacationer.

Cole's original painting of 1825 marked the advent of the Kaaterskill Falls as one of the most popular subjects of nineteenth century American painting. In another year or so W. G. Wall, an Irish émigré with considerable contemporary renown as a painter of topographical views in and around New York City, adopted Cole's original perspective in his "Landscape View, Cauterskill Falls from under the Cavern" and in 1827 exhibited the painting in the National Academy of Design.[36] Cole himself returned to the subject during this period of initial excitement about the phenomenon, and gave us several examples of his earliest and perhaps finest style of painting. "Wolf in the Glen," now hanging in the Wadsworth Atheneum, Hartford, Connecticut, is undoubtedly an early picture of the falls. The "Kaaterskill Falls" of 1827 and the unusual "From the Top of Katterskill Falls" of 1826 both show what the falls must have looked like to James Feni-

Figure 33. *Catskill Falls*, Harry Fenn, 1870. From the engraving in *Picturesque America*, William Cullen Bryant, ed. (New York, 1874), Vol. II, p. 121.

more Cooper or any other early visitor long before the various stairs and pavilions along the sides and upper rim of the falls were erected. By 1836 when Henry Bartlett arrived to make a painting for the English publication, *American Scenery* (London, 1840), these appurtenances had become an established feature of the famous scene. Bartlett's wash drawing managed to combine a vista of the ravine together with a front view of the falls, a most unusual but completely successful composition. The more common composition had been established by Cole's second painting of the falls: a full vertical view of both the upper and lower falls painted from the bottom of the ravine. Notable examples of this standard but highly flexible composition occur in Harry Fenn's "Catskill Falls" of 1870 and the "Catterskill Falls" by Currier and Ives. Though the first of these is much more

Figure 34. *Catterskill Falls*, unsigned, undated print by Currier & Ives (7¹⁵⁄₁₆″ x 12½″), in the author's collection. Listed in Frederick A. Conningham, *Currier and Ives Prints, An Illustrated Check List* (New York, Crown, 1949), no. 858.

dramatic and gives the impression of exaggeration, it is actually the more "realistic" of the two pictures—indeed, the only picture the author knows that captures the actual violence of the scene. The predominant planes of the deep chasm are vertical, not horizontal, and it is therefore the Currier and Ives print that bears least resemblance to the actual scene. Verticality is again a prime aspect of the two illustrations by Fritz Meyer and E. Heinmann. Both pictures were drawn from the high vantage point of Prospect Rock and include the Laurel House in their wider field of vision. By the time Heinmann painted his charming picture of the Kaaterskill Falls (1884) almost sixty years had elapsed since Thomas Cole first discovered "the most famous beauty" of the Catskills,[37] in the interval it had come to attract what appeared to be all the major artists of the century, including (other than those named above) Frederick E. Church,[38] Jaspar F. Cropsey,[39] Jervis McEntee,[40] and S. R. Gifford (who alone painted or drew at least five pictures of the falls within one ten-year period).[41]

As the Kaaterskill Falls became more and more famous as a mecca of American artists, it inevitably attracted the attention of the general public and a growing number of visitors to the great scenic surroundings of the Catskill Mountain House. In the earliest years the Mountain House itself supplied the majority of visitors to the falls, for there were no other accommodations in all the mountains and few people could endure the hardships of the early artists and spend a sleepless night on the exposed heights of Pine Orchard. As the region steadily grew in popularity, and more and more boardinghouses appeared in the valley below, the demand arose for more convenient—and less expensive—accommodations close by the falls themselves. The result was the building of the Laurel House, the second oldest resort hotel in all the Catskills.

Its beginnings were humble enough, if we can trust the words of Walton Van Loan, author of *The Catskill Mountain Guide* of 1892. Desirous of clearing up the problem of the origin of the Laurel House, Van Loan went directly to his friend, "the vener-

Figure 35. "Kaaterskill Fall," scene from a composite print, *The Catskill Mountains*, by Fritz Meyer, 1869, in the author's collection. The complete print is shown in Figure 44; this scene also appears as Plate 1 in Meyer's *Catskill Mountain Album* (New York, 1869).

Figure 36. *View from Prospect Rock–Kaaterskill Falls*, E. Heinemann, 1884. From the engraving in A. E. P. Searing, *The Land of Rip Van Winkle* (New York, 1884), p. 17.

able proprietor of the Catskill Mountain House." These were the picturesque circumstances related by Charles L. Beach:

In 1846 two maiden ladies from Philadelphia that were at his Mountain House, asked him if he did not think they could get board at some farm house on the mountain not far away from his place. He told them of a Mr. Theodore Overbaugh, who had a house at that time at the turn of the road from the main one to the Laurel House [or rather, to the falls; for the Laurel House was not yet in existence], and said they might probably get board there for $5 per week. The ladies said that would be too much, but they started out, and before long returned saying they had made a bargain with Mr. Overbaugh for $2 per week each. They took up quarters there, and in a day or two Peter Schutt, the father of the present proprietor of the Laurel House, came to Mr. Beach and said, "Charley, Theo. Overbaugh has got city boarders. Why can't I build at the falls and take city boarders?" Mr. Beach said, "Uncle Peter, put up a house to hold fifty and I will guarantee you can fill it at five dollars a week." The next season, sure enough, the first house for boarders at the well-known Kaaterskill Falls was erected.[42]

The resulting Laurel House is the humble structure we may see in Fritz Meyer's stone engraving of 1869. The new hotel satisfied growing demands for accommodations close to the falls, and in subsequent years underwent considerable enlargement. It always remained, however, a modest second-class boardinghouse compared to its monolithic neighbor; it drew its patronage from the less affluent levels of American middle-class society, and so offered no competition to the Catskill Mountain House. In 1857, for instance, charges at the fashionable Mountain House were $2.50 per day, but visitors could go to the Laurel House for half that amount.[43] Charles Rockwell noted in the early 1860s that the Laurel House was "a retired, pleasant summer home" where "from fifty to one hundred boarders" commonly remained "much longer than do the guests at the Mountain House, where the expenses are much greater." (The Mountain House accommodated at this time four or five hundred guests "with all the best comforts and luxuries of the best hotels in our large cities.") [44]

The original Laurel House underwent little structural change until after the Civil War when the Catskills as a whole enjoyed their greatest period of development. About the middle of the seventh decade a wing of 50 x 50 feet was added to the rear of the original structure, conforming to its rather undistinguished architecture.[45] Then sometime between 1881 and 1884 the hotel received its final shape and form in the addition of a huge wing that more than doubled the original size of the building and that converted the Laurel House into a beautiful example of ornate Victorian architecture. The new addition was placed at right angles to the much smaller addition of the mid-1870s (marked by a chimney in the 1884 illustration) and formed a long front with the original hotel of the late 1840s, directly facing the Kaaterskill Falls. A comparison of the 1869 and 1884 illustrations reveals this dramatic change. The Laurel House miraculously survived

Figure 37. The Laurel House as it appeared after the Victorian addition, c. 1882; the original building is the wing at left. From a picture folder published by Wittemann Bros., New York, 1884.

the great social and economic upheavals of the twentieth century and looked as late as 1963 exactly as it had in the 1880s.

The Laurel House could hardly avoid such a long prosperous history in view of its superlative location overlooking one of the main tourist attractions of the Catskill Mountains. During the summer of 1882, for instance, the average number of visitors to the falls was 75 to 100 per day, a remarkable number in terms of the very few people who visit the falls today during the course of a whole summer.[46] Many of these visitors, of course, were the paying guests of the Laurel House; many more were guests of the Mountain House or sightseers from other parts of the expanding Catskill resort area. They became the source of a lucrative income for the enterprising landlord of the Laurel House, for whether or not they were his own guests at the Laurel House, they could hardly resist his ingenious facilities for making their visit to the falls more comfortable and—for a slightly additional charge—more edifying.

A refreshment stand existed at the falls from the time the Mountain House first began to attract a considerable number of visitors to the area. After Peter Schutt built his own hotel at the head of the falls, these primitive facilities underwent a remarkable development. The following is a first-hand account of what it was like to visit the falls by the summer of 1854:

Approaching from the Mountain House, you of course see them first from above. Before you commence the descent of the long flights of wooden steps which lead to the base of the cataracts, you enter a very pleasant sort of café where you may strengthen your physical man with any species of refreshment, from brandy-punch (in the quality of which you may place the extremest confidence of true love) to a cooling ice-cream or a draught of sparkling lemonade. At the same time you may relieve yourself still further by lightening your purse to the extent of a quarter, which the placards posted around will instruct you it is expected that gentlemen will pay to keep the stairs, the Falls, and the guides, in order. This assessment also rewards the Neptune of the spot— our venerated friend Peter Schutt, whom you must cultivate—for "letting off the water!" For, be it known unto you, that a dam is built above these Falls; by which ingenious means the stream, restrained from wasting its sweetness on the desert air, is peddled out, wholesale and retail, at the tale of two and a half dimes a splash! . . . When you reach the base of the first Fall, your guide will perhaps conduct you over a narrow ledge behind the falling torrent, as at "Termination Rock" at Niagara. Then reaching the green sward on the opposite side of the stream, you may make a signal to Peter Schutt, who will be looking over the piazza of his café above, and if you have duly settled between you the telegraphic alphabet, in such case made and provided, he will attach a basket to the projecting pole, and incontinently there will descend sundry bottles of the very coolest Champagne of which the vineyards of France ever dreamed. You may then repose yourself half an hour or more upon the mossy couch aforesaid, imbibe Neptune's nectar, and when your quarter's worth of cascade is spent, you may remount the steps to the summit of the Falls, or may accompany us and the stream down the ravine to the great clove below.[47]

Not every visitor to the falls accepted Peter Schutt's innovations with equal grace and humor; some of the more romantic souls regretted the intrusion of such a vulgarism as an artificial dam into a scene of wild grandeur. But this device and all the other facilities of the enterprising steward of the Kaaterskill Falls were there to stay: they became throughout the rest of the century as generic to the scene as the mighty cataract itself.

The days when one could view the falls in their pristine state of nature had long since passed, but one season of the year at least afforded an impressive surrogate. During the winter when all activity had come to an end in the high resorts of the Catskills and all the peaks and cloves lay deep in silent folds of snow and ice, the Kaaterskill Falls returned to nature's own undisturbed dominion and were transformed into a new vision of splendor. The spectacle was little noted or recorded during the nineteenth century, for only the most confirmed romantics could tolerate the acute discomforts and hazards of a winter journey to the mountains. We know, however, that William Cullen Bryant was one such enthusiast, for his well-known poem on the Kaaterskill Falls is a long encomium to the remarkable beauty of their wintry aspect. The phenomenon that he notes in the second stanza of the poem—"A palace of ice . . . / With turret, and arch, and fretwork fair / and pillars blue as the summer air"—could only be the result of direct observation.[48] We also know that Bryant's friend, Thomas Cole, was another and even more devoted enthusiast, for this artist was in the habit of keeping a diary about his experiences in the mountains, and he has left us a notable account of a midwinter visit to the falls. Written a hundred and twenty years ago, it may be quoted in its entirety as a fitting conclusion to this brief history of the nineteenth century fame of the Kaaterskill Falls.

We have often heard that the Falls of Cauterskill present an interesting spectacle in winter; and, February 27, a party of ladies invited Mrs. C—— and myself to join in this tour, in search of the wintry picturesque. Cloaks, moccasins, and mittens were in great demand, and we were soon glancing over the creaking snow, the sleigh-bells ringing in harmony with our spirits, which were light and gay.

A snow-storm near the mountains, which proved transitory, added to our enjoyment; for, by partially veiling the heights above us, it gave them a vast, visionary, and spectral appearance. The sun broke forth in mild splendor just as we came in view of the Mountain House, on the bleak crags, a few hundred feet above us. Leaving the house to the left, we crossed the lesser of the two lakes. From its level breast, now covered with snow, the mountains rose in desolate grandeur, their steep sides bristling with bare trees, or clad in sturdy evergreens. Here and there are to be seen a silvery birch, so pale and wan that one might readily imagine that it drew its aliment from the snow around its roots. The Clove Valley, the lofty range of the High Peak and Round Top, which rise beyond, as seen from the road between the [Mountain] house and the falls, are, in summer, grand objects; but winter had given them a sterner character. The mountains seemed more precipitous, and the forms that enclosed their sides more clearly defined. The projecting mounds, the rocky terraces, the shaggy clefts, down which the courses of the torrents could be traced by the gleaming ice, were exposed in the leafless forests and clear air of winter, while along the grizzly peaks the snow was driving rapidly. There is beauty, there is sublimity in the wintry aspect of the mountains, but their beauty is touched with melancholy, and their sublimity has a dreary tone. . . .

To visit the scene [of the falls] in winter, is a privilege permitted to but few; and to visit it this winter, when the spectacle is more than usually magnificent, and, as the hunters say, "more complete than has been known for thirty years," is, indeed, worthy of a long pilgrimage. What a contrast to its appearance in summer! No leafy woods, no blossoms glittering in the sun, rejoice upon the steeps around.

> "Hoary Winter
> O'er forests wide has laid his hand,
> And they are bare—
> They move and moan, a spectral band
> Struck by despair."

There are overhanging rocks and the dark-browed cavern, but where the spangled cataract fell stands a gigantic tower of ice, reaching from the basin of the waterfall to the very summit of the crags. From the jutting rocks that form the canopy of which I have spoken, hang festoons of glittering icicles. Not a drop of water, not a gush of spray is to be seen. No sound of many waters strikes the ear, not even as a gurgling rivulet or trickling rill. All is silent and motionless as death; and did not the curious eye perceive, through two window-like spaces of clear ice, the falling water, one might believe that all was bound in icy fetters. But there falls the cataract, not bound but shielded, as a thing too delicate for the frosts of winter to blow upon.

It falls, too, as in summer, broken into myriads of diamonds, which group themselves, as they descend, into wedge-like forms, like wild-fowls when traversing the blue air. This tower, or perforated column of ice, one hundred and eighty feet high, rests on a field of snow-covered ice, spread over the basin and rocky platform, that in some places is broken into miniature glaciers. Near the foot it is more than thirty feet in diameter, but is somewhat narrower above. It is in general of milk-white color, and curiously embossed with rich and fantastic ornaments. About its dome are numerous dome-like forms, supported by groups of icicles. In other parts may be seen falling strands of flowers, each flower ruffled by the breeze. These are of the most transparent ice. This curious frostwork reminded me of the tracery and icicle-like ornament frequent in Saracenic architecture, and I have no doubt that nature suggested such ornament to the architect as the most fitting for halls wherever flowing fountains cooled the sultry air. Here and there, suspended from the projecting rocks that form the eaves of the great gallery, are groups and ranks of icicles of every variety of size and number. Some of them are twenty or thirty feet in length. Sparkling in the sunlight, they form a magnificent fringe. . . .

Beyond the icicles and the column is seen a cluster of lesser columns and icicles, and columns of pure cerulean color, and then come the broken rocks and woods. The icy spears, the majestic tower, the impending rocks above, the wild valley below, with its contorted trees, the lofty mountains towering in the distance, compose a wild and wondrous scene, where the Ice King

> "Builds in the starlight clear and cold,
> A palace of ice where the torrent falls;
> With turret, and arch, and fretwork fair,
> And pillars blue as the summer air."

We left the place with lingering steps and real regret, for in all probability we were never to see these wintry glories again. The Royal Architect builds but unstable structures, which, like worldly virtues, quickly vanish in the full light and fiery trial.[49]

The gigantic column or cylinder of ice, as Cole goes on to explain, is formed from the base up, in reverse order of the actual fall of water. As the first or upper falls strikes the huge platform of rock 160 to 180 feet below the crest, an ice pack is formed that gradually ascends with the developing winter. The height and thickness of the resulting column, which tapers as it rises toward the summit, varies with the intensity of the cold. During the winter of 1960–61, which was apparently almost as severe as the extraordinary winter of 1843, the author visited both the Kaaterskill Falls and the nearby Haines Falls and was struck by the accuracy of Cole's description. Haines Falls (which, unfortunately, was the only one the author was able to photograph) was not so beautiful as the much higher falls in front of the Laurel House, but it still provided its own notable example of the famous tower of ice. If it is true that these scenes were "worthy of a long pilgrimage" in the first half of the nineteenth century when one had to drive all the way from Catskill in an open sleigh, it is doubly true today when one can drive in much less time in well-

Figure 38. Haines Falls in February, 1961, showing the type of ice column (over 100 feet high) described by Thomas Cole at Kaaterskill Falls in 1843. Author's photo.

heated automobiles to within walking distance of the magnificent spectacles.

But rare today is the visitor who disturbs the frozen peace of the great falls of the Catskills during the long quiescent months of the winter, and rare is he who even among the occasional summer visitors knows the almost forgotten history of their grandeur. The Laurel House stands,* a tottering but still beautiful Victorian memorial to the departed glory of the Catskills, its few stray summer patrons oblivious of the ancient trails and wagon roads, the gay pavilion at the head of the falls, the steep winding staircases to the bottom of the ravine, the hundreds of tourists, personages, foreign visitors, writers, artists, statesmen and people of fashion who any given summer a century or more ago made the scene around them one of the most colorful in the history of the Catskills.

* The Laurel House was purchased by the New York State Conservation Department as this book was going to press in the winter of 1965–66. It was burned to the ground in late February, 1967.

Part II

The Romantic Quest

Introduction

It has been acutely observed that "the atmosphere in which American romanticism developed [was] the scenic mountains of New York." [1] The truism carries a wealth of connotation for the great scenic domain that we have just described within a four-mile radius of the Catskill Mountain House.

Several mountainous areas of New York may justifiably contend for places of honor under the purview of that statement. The Adirondacks, for instance, are New York's largest and most impressive range of mountains, but they were not settled until after the Civil War and were too remote from the centers of population to play anything but a minor role in the rise of American romanticism. More important were the Highlands, a small but picturesque spur of the Appalachians that sit astride the Hudson River just thirty miles north of New York City. The fiordlike beauty of the Hudson as it cuts through these mountains was a favorite subject of the "topographical" painters of the early romantic movement. If it is possible to choose one specific group of mountains as providing "the atmosphere in which American romanticism developed," the honor must fall upon the subject of this history. In 1847, close to the height of the romantic movement, the authoritative voice of Henry T. Tuckerman asserted that "few native localities are more endeared to the lovers of scenery where beauty and grandeur are happily combined, than the Catskill Mountains." [2] And within that region it was "the lofty plain called Pine Orchard" that remained the chief source of inspiration. From 1830 onward, as noted by Walton Van Loan, "thousands" visited this single area "in search of the sublime and picturesque." [3]

The words "sublime" and "picturesque" in the context of Van Loan's statement have a formal meaning that is far removed from the popular usage of today. In the nineteenth century the words were governed by the academic doctrines of an established school of philosophy (the so-called "Scotch school of psychological aesthetics"), and were two of the most important concepts in the universal philosophy of romanticism. The "search of the sublime and picturesque" in the domain of the Catskill Mountain House was therefore a remarkable phenomenon, for it carried the full aesthetic and philosophical force of nineteenth century romanticism and produced, among other things, the first literary and artistic glorification of the native American landscape. It is this achievement that raises the history of the Catskill Mountain House above the ordinary annals of American resorts and makes it and the region around an eloquent chapter in the history of American culture.

The key to this, as to so many chapters in the history of American culture, lies in the ancient reality of the American wilderness. For the first two hundred years of American history (roughly from 1600 to 1800) the vast unbroken wilderness that spread from the Atlantic Ocean to the Mississippi River had been the dominant aesthetic as well as economic factor of American life. By the end of the first quarter of the nineteenth century, however, the frontier had reached the Mississippi and the American population was about to invade the treeless prairies and plains of the great American West. It was the ending of one great movement in American history and the beginning of another, for the event coincided with the successful repulsion of the last European invasion of the North American continent and the advent in America of an unprecedented period of national growth and prosperity.

In 1826 the nation celebrated its fiftieth anniversary with the joyous knowledge that it had overcome all adversaries and that a new civilization had finally been carved out of the great receding forests of the Atlantic seaboard.

At this moment when the nation was most predisposed to celebrate the native grandeurs of its own historic setting, it fell under the irresistible influence of the romantic movement and found therein a glowing confirmation of its unique landscape. "Perhaps of all species of landscape," W. Gilpin, a popular authority on romantic aesthetic theory, declared, "there is none which so universally captivates mankind as forest scenery." [4] This central theme of European romanticism, elaborated into a complex cult of the wilderness, reached America just as it faced the loss of its ancient wilderness and was embarking upon its first great period of national glorification. The Catskills, a by-passed bastion of wild beauty close by the most civilized centers of the Eastern coast, became a symbol of the whole and a leading motif of the American romantic movement.

The discovery of this romantic motif by the early writers of America, and the rise in the Catskills of the first school of American landscape painting are only a part of the story. The romantic discovery of the American landscape was an intellectual as well as literary or artistic movement, and it was accompanied by one of the longest controversies in the history of American ideas. The American landscape, so to speak, was an *argumentum* as well as an object of praise or beauty; it had to be *argued* into a state of aesthetic respectability. The reasons for this were the formal philosophical aspects of European romanticism and the inevitable clash with the unique characteristics of the American landscape. The key word in this controversy is once again the word *wilderness*, for it was the unique quality of the American wilderness that became a major obstacle in the intellectual assimilation of European canons of aesthetic judgment. The European doctrine of "Association," for instance, was intrinsically inimical to the American environment, for it defined an ideal landscape in terms of its rich association with the ruins and relics, myths and legends, of all past human history—a condition that could hardly be found in the raw American wilderness. The concomitant doctrine of "the picturesque" was also, in some of its aspects, a major stumbling block: wherever it stressed the importance of human art and artifice in landscape, it encountered a severe American opposition.

The debate concludes in what we may call "the romantic apotheosis" of the American landscape. The key word is still *wilderness*. If many aspects of European romanticism were intrinsically hostile to the characteristic primitivism of the American landscape, one of the most important of all was the source of unqualified approval. Dear to the heart of every true romantic was the overriding belief in the transcendental world of nature—the belief that the visible landscape of the earth was an emanation of God, complete unto itself, without the need of human intervention for its own self-contained glory. It was a belief that Americans could accept with unmitigated pride. Where but in America was the world of nature more free of human association, more true to God's first intentions? What could be more "sublime," in the crucial word of the romantic era, than the deep virginal forests of this vast primeval landscape? Here in the highest category of nineteenth century romantic philosophy the American landscape achieved an unequivocal apotheosis.

The discussion that follows will at times take leave of the central theme of this study, the specific history of the Catskill Mountain House. There can be, however, no accounting for the rise of that venerable subject without the due consideration of the larger cultural context from which it drew its chief sustenance and finally sprang to eminence as one of the most famous hotels in American history. Neither the Mountain House itself nor its great scenic domain had any intrinsic power for attracting the legendary thousands to the heights of Pine Orchard. Great hotels are easily built; the scenery of the Catskills had existed from time immemorial. The impetus came from a revolutionary change in man's attitude toward nature and the timely romantic discovery of—or belief in—the aesthetic values and transcendental attributes of the American landscape. When we revert to the main theme of this study and chart the history of the Mountain House during the post-Civil War period, we shall find it the resplendent center of the first populous "playground" in American history. However, that whole climactic development was an outgrowth of the era of discovery when the high romantic quest of "the sublime and picturesque" first drew the attention of the American populace to "the lofty plain called Pine Orchard." It is this important quest that now demands our close attention.

Chapter 6

The Discovery of the
Romantic Motif

It was the spectacular wildness of the Catskill Mountains that first commended them to the romantic spirit. One of the most common observations of the nineteenth century was that the Catskills contained "some of the most picturesque bits of mountain scenery in the world." [1] Picturesqueness in this context meant, as Edward Everett Hale, Jr., observed, "something wild, rugged, rough, something that stirred the imagination and took it away from the ordinary commonplaces of everyday life." [2] It was the landscape that avid readers of Sir Walter Scott sought in the popular Waverley novels, or that the enthusiastic followers of Lord Byron feasted upon in the extravagant verses of *Childe Harold's Pilgrimage*. The same landscape was the source of the phenomenal popularity of Salvator Rosa's canvases among the romantic artists and poets of the nineteenth century—a landscape of fierce wildness expressed through such melodramatic devices as high beetling cliffs, deep impenetrable chasms, torrential mountain streams, and all the agonized shapes and forms of nature in her most violent aspects. It was a landscape that even gained formal expression in the academic treatises of the popular English and Scotch aestheticians of the period. Culling the works of such authorities as Lord Kames, Sir Archibald Alison, Edmund Burke, and William Gilpin we find repeated references to: "amplitude or greatness of extent," "vast

and boundless prospects," "great power and force exerted"; the
thundering cataract or violent storm; a great profusion of natural
objects thrown together in wild confusion; obscurity, vagueness,
indistinctness, darkness; mystery, suggestion of terror; evidences
of cataclysmic force or superhuman power.[3] Such were the well-
recognized features of a wild romantic landscape when American
writers and artists first began to ascend the Hudson River and
discover the native splendors of their own Catskill Mountains.

One of the earliest visitors was Washington Irving, the first
of America's great men of letters. Irving made his initial trip
up the Hudson as early as 1800, a good nineteen years before
Bryant wrote *Thanatopsis*, and twenty-three to twenty-five
years before Emerson wrote *Nature* or Thomas Cole painted
his first pictures of the "undiscovered" Catskills. It was on this
trip that Irving discovered that the Catskill Mountains had "the
most witching effect" on his boyish imagination, occasioned
in part by his spending a full day gliding by their atmospheric
heights and hearing countless tales of their past from an old
Indian trader.[4] Some of the literary fruits of this first impres-
sionable encounter with the legendary Catskills appeared in
the famous story of *Rip Van Winkle*. This typically Irvingesque
treatment of some of the more profound aspects of American
experience (the flight from civilization; the ritual of self-identi-
fication; the phantasy of the libertarian wilderness) enjoyed
an immediate and overwhelming success when it appeared in
The Sketch Book (1819–1820). Irving was not a romantic in the
New England or Concordian sense of the word, for he had
little sympathy for the high moral predilections or philosophical
prejudices of his northern compatriots; his genius was a finely
wrought product of the more worldly and sophisticated culture
of New York City. On an aesthetic rather than philosophical
level, however, and especially in respect to his feeling for the
wilder aspects of nature, he could not have been a truer romantic. *Rip Van Winkle*, for instance, is full of such observations
as the following: "He looked down into a deep romantic glen,
wild, lonely, and shaded, the bottom filled with fragments from

the impending cliffs, and scarcely lighted by the reflected rays of the setting sun." [5] It is the eye of Salvator Rosa transferred to the American wilderness.

Irving was not aware of this cultural conditioning; or if he was, he implicitly assumed that the Catskills were in fact what his romantic eye told him they were in fancy. Speaking matter-of-factly about his first trip to the Mountain House in 1832 he said, "the wild scenery of these mountains outdoes all my conception of it." [6] And a little later:

The interior of these mountains is in the highest degree wild and romantic; here are rocky precipices mantled with primeval forests; deep gorges walled in by beetling cliffs, with torrents tumbling as it were from the sky; and savage glens rarely trodden by the hunter. [7]

The passage could not be more typical of natural description of the early nineteenth century. For Irving there was no discrepancy between the reality of the American wilderness and the extravagant imagery of romanticism. Speaking at another time of how the Catskills share the same characteristics as all the Appalachians, he said:

In many of these vast ranges or sierras, nature still reigns in indomitable wildness: their rocky ridges, their rugged clefts and defiles, teem with magnificent vegetation. Here are locked up mighty forests that have never been invaded by the axe; deep umbrageous valleys where the virgin soil has never been outraged by the plough; bright streams flowing in untasked idleness, unburthened by commerce, un-checked by the mill-dam. This mountain zone is in fact the great poetical region of our country; resisting, like the tribes which once inhabited it, the taming hand of cultivation; and maintaining a hallowed ground for fancy and the muses. [8]

Irving's influence in associating the Catskills with the emerging cult of the wilderness was enormous: even as late as 1905 Henry James still found himself surprisingly responsive to that protracted influence. [9] Writer after writer naturally fell into Irving's mode of romantic description as they traveled to and from the Mountain House during the antebellum years. Such, for example, was Willis Gaylord Clark's description of Sleepy Hollow, written in the 1830s:

Huge rocks, that might have been sent from warring Titans, decked with moss, overhung with rugged shrubbery, and cooling the springs that trickle from beneath them, gloom beside the way; vast chasms, which your coach shall sometimes seem to overhang, yawn on the left; the pine and cedar-scented air comes freely and sweetly from the brown bosom of the woods; until, one high ascent attained, a level for a while succeeds, and your smoking horses rest, while, with expanding nostril, you drink in the rarer and yet rarer air a stillness like the peace of Eden. . . .[10]

We may easily see from this, however, why Irving, rather than his friend, Clark, became one of the most famous stylists in the history of American writing.

After Irving, the next major writer to associate the Catskills with the cult of the wilderness was James Fenimore Cooper. We have already referred at length to *The Pioneers* and its elaborate description of the region around Pine Orchard. Appearing two years after *The Sketch Book* (and one year before the opening of the Mountain House), *The Pioneers* was the first of a succession of novels that "introduced to human recognition," as Barrett Wendell noted, "certain aspects of Nature unknown to literature before his time"—the forests of North America.[11] The judgment is probably just, in spite of the earlier appearance of *The Sketch Book*; for Cooper was the first to devote himself exclusively to the great romance of the American wilderness, and he extended its literary scope far beyond the narrow intentions of Washington Irving. "The strongest impression made upon Cooper was the vastness of the virgin forest," Edward Everett Hale, Jr., noted some years ago,

something that in spite of the American love of largeness, was hardly appreciated in his day. . . . In the characteristic American novels of Cooper, the action generally goes on with a forest background. The forest is always there, a bleak wilderness, vast and interminable, stretching its gloomy extent over uncounted leagues of mountain and valley. . . . Cooper was haunted by the solitude, the stillness, the repose of the forest depths, the deep and breathing silence. It was the solitary grandeur, the solemn obscurity, the sublime mystery (to use phrases or thoughts that recurred often to his mind) of the virgin wilderness that made the chief impression which the forest left upon his mind.[12]

To use the nineteenth century's own distinction, it was the "sublime" rather than "picturesque" aspects of the American forest that attracted his attention. All the qualities and attributes mentioned by Hale—vastness, gloom, solitude, grandeur, obscurity, mystery—were automatic aspects of this highest category of the romantic cult of the wilderness.

In extending the cult of the wilderness to embrace the "sublime" aspects of the American forest, Cooper operated under the principle that "he who succeeds in giving an accurate idea of any portion of this wild region must necessarily convey a tolerably correct notion of the whole," [13] and relied almost exclusively on his childhood memories of the Catskill Mountains. Many American writers have been as deeply rooted in their native states and regions as James Fenimore Cooper, but few have been so successful in extending that influence into an image of the national domain. One admirer of Cooper has said that "he used the Catskills as an emblem of that dark and unknown virgin forest which once covered all of New York State." [14] But the achievement was even greater than that, for the same "dark and unknown virgin forest" once covered all the Atlantic seaboard; and it was this larger American setting that became the recognized world of the Leather-Stocking tales. Cooper used the Catskills (as Irving, Bryant, Cole, and many others did to a lesser extent) as the prototype of the whole American wilderness.

The conclusion is borne out by the facts of his life. By the time Cooper first started writing the Leather-Stocking stories, the great forests of America had shrunk, as Irving noted, to the narrow dimensions of the "mountain zone" of the Eastern seaboard. Cooper himself, however, had very little knowledge of this zone with the exception of his boyhood haunts in New York State. When he was one year old his father took him up the Hudson to the pioneer community of Cooperstown close by the western foothills of the Catskills, and there he remained until he went to Yale (where he was dismissed after his third year) and spent a brief tour of duty with the United States Navy. Cooper subsequently spent many years in Europe; but other than a trip he made in 1847 to Detroit, his travels in his own country were limited to the Hudson valley and frequent journeyings between New York City and his ancestral home on Lake Otsego. Becoming more and more enamored of the American forest while still living in Europe, he wrote from Paris in 1831 that

Now my longing is for a wilderness—Cooperstown is far too populous and artificial for me, and it is my intention to plunge into the forest, for six months in the year, at my return. I will not quit my native state, but shall seek some unsettled part of it.[15]

But except in the Catskills (and the Adirondacks, which Cooper did not know), the forests had disappeared in New York State, and Cooper decided in 1834 to take up permanent residence in Cooperstown. Even when he was a child and all the land round and about Lake Otsego was being laid to the ax, the nearby Catskills stood inviolate as an unpreëmpted realm of wild beauty. They now became the inspiration of Cooper's fanciful stories of the ancient American wilderness. Perhaps because those stories *were* so fanciful—Cooper was, after all, reconstructing an American past that existed only in his imagination—his references to the Catskills remain vague, and he never localized the settings of his novels in any particular region of the mountains. However, the significance of the Catskills as a source of inspiration gains eloquent tribute in Natty Bumppo's choice of Pine Orchard as the greatest wonder of the American landscape. It was Cooper's own settled opinion.

A historical incident occurred two years after the publication of *The Pioneers* and was to have a profound influence upon the association of the Catskills with the rising cult of the wilderness—the simultaneous appearance in New York City of William Cullen Bryant and Thomas Cole. It was perhaps inevitable that two native citizens of the Empire State, Irving and Cooper, should have pioneered the romantic discovery of the Catskills; but the honor of making good that discovery in the full popularization of the Catskills as a central theme of romantic poetry and painting belongs to two out-of-staters who came to New York by choice. Bryant was a New Englander, and Cole was an

English emigré who spent his earliest years in America in the prairie states. Both arrived in New York City in 1825, "a year," as W. Born has suggested, "that seems to have been a turning point in American taste." [16]

Since Bryant met Cole as a result of the latter's triumph with his first paintings of the Catskills and since Cole was therefore the prime mover in the discovery of the mountains, our emphasis will fall upon the artist. The two men became lifelong friends, and it is difficult to think of one without the other in connection with the mountains. But it was Cole who finally settled permanently in the Catskills and made the major contribution to our subject, for as L. Goodrich has noted, he was the first "to embody in pictorial form the cult of the wilderness." [17] A legion of artists would follow Cole to the Catskills, but to Cole belongs the honor of being the first and foremost of them all. The time was ripe, and by temperament and taste Cole could not have been more suited to the opportunity. The incipient romantic sensibility of the nineteenth century found in this imaginative young man a most susceptible subject. Even as a boy in England Cole had been deeply moved by early romantic accounts of the American wilderness; and by 1825 when he came to the city to establish himself as an artist, his earlier wanderings in the empty wastelands of the prairie states and subsequent failures as a portrait painter prepared a fertile ground for the sudden revelations of the romantic Catskills.

"Cole started one October day," Mrs. L. C. Lillie recounted after interviewing the artist's friends about his first trip up the Hudson.

The Indian summer had begun, and maple and sumac lent their glow to the still deep-greens of the country that borders that enchanted river. The breaks in the land's fertility were few. It was not then as now [1890], a country of summer villas and hotels, but a place of never-ending delight, of natural forms untouched, and for miles together almost unbroken in simple growths of nature. There seems to have been no definite idea in Cole's mind as to a resting-place, but on nearing Catskill his choice was made. He landed at the little village, and started at once upon a tour of investigation, making footprints for many others to follow.

It was a journey of strange and unexpected delight to the young artist. Brought face to face with this most lovely, untried country, Cole's heart awoke to new inspirations, his mind to wider visions and loftier dreams. He roamed about the valleys and mountain paths, feeling, as he often said in later years, that he was taking them to himself, to be his for all time, and it has been remarked that in all his work some touch or hint of the country of the Catskill lingers.

Cole went at once into the heart of the mountain country, and painted some sketches in the neighborhood of the Clove [specifically, the lakes and falls back of the Mountain House], which certainly contained as good work as anything he did later. The difficulty of an over-stimulated imagination was not in his way during his first greeting of a country which, as an artist, he felt he had discovered. The infection of the place took hold of him; he came back to the village filled with a desire to make some permanent place of work for himself in this lovely untried region. . . .[18]

There can be no doubt that the Catskills liberated Cole's romantic sensibility, gave him a theme and message, and permitted him to satisfy some deep desire for glorifying the American landscape. While it is true, as more recent critics than Mrs. Lillie have noted, that Cole's highly wrought imagination eventually led him to foresake the simpler and more satisfying landscapes of his earlier period for the larger allegorical subjects of his later and (to us today) more questionable period, still, it was this same excess of sensibility that took him to the Catskills in the first place; and it was this prodigality of talent that permitted him to launch the first school of American landscape painting. Other artists such as Durand and Doughty had already acquired some reputation as landscape painters, but it was Cole with his greater range and intensity of romantic interests who first deflected American painting away from the niggardly topographical tradition of the day and made landscape painting as economically rewarding as portrait or historical painting. And it was the same romantic susceptibility that led him to respond to the dramatic scenery of the Catskill Mountains. Showing a characterstic nineteenth century talent for literary as well as artistic expression, Cole has left us this revealing description of his first encounter with the beauty of North and South Lakes:

Shut in by stupendous mountains which rest on crags which tower more than a thousand feet above the water, whose rugged brows and shadowy peaks are clotted by dark and tangled wood, they have an august aspect of deep seclusion, of utter and unbroken solitude, that when standing on their brink a lonely traveler, I was overwhelmed with an emotion of the sublime, such as I have rarely felt. It was not that the jagged precipices were lofty, that the encircling woods were of the deepest shade, or that the waters were profoundly deep; but that over all rocks, wood, and water, "brooded the spirit of repose, and the silent energy of nature stirred the soul to its utmost depths." [19]

It is no wonder that the already famous John Trumbull, William Dunlap, and Asher B. Durand were excited by the first canvases of this unknown artist fresh from the Catskills: here was an astonishing neophyte who had utterly dispensed with the prevailing taste for portraiture and topographical painting and plunged directly for some new romantic ideal of pure landscape. And it had the added shock of presenting to the public, as Mrs. Lillie noted, a "hitherto unthought of region," [20] a brand-new aspect of the national landscape, that more and more people came to consider uniquely American. "I well remember," William Cullen Bryant said at the time of Cole's death,

what an enthusiasm was awakened by these early works of his, inferior as I must deem them to his maturer productions—the delight which was expressed at the opportunity of contemplating pictures which carried the eye over scenes of wild grandeur peculiar to our country, over our aerial mountain-tops, with their mighty growth of forest never touched by the axe, along the banks of streams never deformed by culture, and into the depths of skies bright with the hues of our own culture; skies such as few but Cole could ever paint, and through the transparent abysses of which it seemed that you might send an arrow out of sight. [21]

Cole's success was immediate. "Pictures were sold as fast as they could be painted," George Washington Greene testified, orders came in from all sides. Every lover of American scenery seemed to take pride in showing that he knew how to appreciate these faithful transcripts of its loveliness. They became the chief attraction of the public exhibitions, and you could always tell, by the throng around them, in what part of the room they hung. "I could tell one of these pieces," said [James Fenimore] Cooper, "as far as sight enabled me to see it." [22]

Cooper's quick recognition of Cole's genius was based upon the meeting to two kindred souls, for as E. E. Hale, Jr. has pointed out, "just as Cooper expressed the romance of American scenery in his novels, so had Cole shown it in his pictures." [23] No other artist of the day, not even Durand or Doughty, had such affinity with Cooper in his celebration of the American wilderness, though all at one time or another had tried their hands at

Figure 39. *The Catskill Mountains,* Thomas Cole, 1833 (oil on canvas, 39⅜" x 63"). Romanticized landscape of the Catskills near the Mountain House; South Lake is in the left foreground. Courtesy of the Cleveland Museum of Art, Hinman B. Hurlbut Collection.

illustrating Cooper's novels. In such a painting as "The Catskill Mountains" (1833), for instance, Cole's affinity is unmistakable. The picture displays the dramatic scenery of Pine Orchard from the exact location where Cole later painted the very romantic "Catskill Mountain House" [Figure 19]. In the earlier picture, however, the artist has excluded the Mountain House altogether and allowed the landscape itself to be the center of interest. The wild grandeur and loneliness of this rendition is strongly reminiscent of Cooper's abiding sense of the wilderness; and when one's eye catches sight of the scarlet plumes of several Indians lurking in the tangled underbrush of the foreground, one is immediately transported into the specific world of *The Last of the Mohicans*.

Another writer who echoed Cole's romantic response to the scenery of the Catskills was William Cullen Bryant. Born in 1794, Bryant had a slight edge on Cole in the discovery of his life work: *Thanatopsis* appeared in 1819; *A Forest Hymn* in 1824. In the latter year Bryant also visited New York for the first time; and in 1825—the very year Cole discovered his life work in the Catskills—Bryant decided to take up permanent residence in the metropolis and devote himself entirely to a career of writing.[24] Within a few years he had achieved something of a national reputation and in 1832 a volume of his verse was published in Europe under the glowing auspices of Washington Irving. The older writer with an international reputation knew a fellow romantic when he saw one, and he also knew that Bryant would be of particular interest to a European audience. Bryant's poems, Irving pointed out in a warm introduction,

transport us into the depths of the solemn primeval forest, to the shore of the lovely lake, the banks of the wild nameless stream, or the brow of the rocky upland, rising like a promontory from amidst a wide ocean of foliage, while they shed around us the glories of a climate fierce in its extremes and splendid in all its vicissitudes.[25]

It sounds like a description of the early paintings of Thomas Cole, and it well might have been, for it was through Cole that Bryant first discovered the unique qualities of the American wilderness. Bryant had known "the leafy retreats in the neighborhood of

Figure 40. *Kindred Spirits: Thomas Cole and William Cullen Bryant*, Asher B. Durand, 1849 (oil on canvas, 46″ x 36″). Probably Kaaterskill Clove. The painting was commissioned by Jonathan Sturges and presented to Bryant; in 1940 it was bequeathed to the New York Public Library by Julia Bryant, the poet's daughter. Reproduced courtesy of the New York Public Library.

New York"[26] from the time he first arrived in that city, but it was his new-found friend, Thomas Cole, who introduced him to what he called "the sublime mountain tops and the broad forests and the rushing waterfalls" of the Catskill Mountains.[27] Accompanied by Cole, Bryant soon became acquainted with "every cleft and crevice" of the mountains.[28] If it is true, as Emerson said, that Bryant was the first poet to make known to mankind the beauty of "our northern nature,"[29] it was due predominantly to this discovery of what Bryant called "a region singular for its romantic beauty," the primeval Catskills.[30]

The friendship of Cole and Bryant in this idyllic setting became a symbol of the unity of arts and letters in the American romantic movement. The two men "took great pleasure," as Bryant's biographer said,

in sauntering together among the mountains, scaling their heights, or threading their thickets, from dawn to dark. To some of the less frequented cloves—deep chasms between perpendicular precipices, shaggy with rocks and trees, and echoing with the roar of hidden cascades—they ventured to give appropriate names, which, it is understood, they still retain. Cole derived from these wanderings some of the most impressive effects of his pictures, and they enabled Mr. Bryant to commend the attractive region to public admiration in the columns of his journal.[31]

Nothing is more evocative of the friendship of these two leaders of the romantic movement and of the common love of nature that brought them together in the Catskills than Asher B. Durand's famous painting, "Kindred Spirits." One of the finest works of art to come out of the romantic movement, it was commissioned in 1849 by Jon Sturges, a famous patron of the period, as a gift for Bryant "as a token of gratitude for the labor of love" that the poet had performed in delivering Cole's funeral oration the previous year. Sturges told Bryant that his instructions to Durand had been specific: "to paint a picture in which he should associate our departed friend and yourself as kindred spirits."[32] Durand, a friend of both Cole and Bryant who had often joined their excursions into the scenic heights of Pine Orchard,[33] brilliantly fulfilled his instructions by choosing "one of the wildest and most romantic rambles in the world" as his setting [34]—Kaaterskill Clove. The two men are shown standing upon a picturesque promontory on the south side; Cole—recognizable by the portfolio that he carries under his arm—is pointing his cane toward the distant cascades and falls and is obviously engaged in an ardent discussion with Bryant about the finer aesthetic points of the famous scene around them. The picture is a superb example of the meticulous craftsmanship and subtle lyricism of the first school of American landscape painting and may well stand as a fitting tribute not only to a famous friendship, but to the larger taste and unity of the whole American romantic movement.[35]

By the time Cole had passed from the scene and Durand had commemorated the event with "Kindred Spirits," the Catskills had become—as the picture itself eloquently testifies—a common haunt of many of the leading writers and artists of America. A romantic discovery that had begun with the fanciful and generalized impressions of Irving and Cooper soon developed into a passion for first-hand observation as more and more artists followed Cole's example and spent days and even weeks and months at a time in the heart of the mountains. The Catskill Mountains had become the center of America's first school of landscape painting, the Hudson River School.

Chapter 7

The Hudson River School
of Painting

Even if the artists painted far afield, the title "Hudson River School" fitted, for the cradle of the style was the Catskill Mountains.

—JAMES THOMAS FLEXNER

Originally coined as a term of derision by a vituperative critic of the *New York Tribune*,[1] the "Hudson River School" is now generally accepted as a convenient title for the large and relatively cohesive group of painters who first devoted themselves to the subject of the American landscape during the second and third quarters of the nineteenth century. Henry T. Tuckerman (1813–1871) apparently never used the term, though he once went so far as to say "up to 1828 we had no landscape school in America while by 1836—mainly due to Luman Reed—it made surprising progress."[2] Luman Reed was a wealthy merchant and famous art patron who lived in New York City, as Tuckerman himself did; and there can be no doubt that the latter was referring to the innumerable artists who lived and worked during this period on the banks of the Hudson. General usage of the explicit term itself, however, dates from the time Samuel Isham employed it in his *History of American Painting* (1905). Since all such terms are necessarily arbitrary, they never gain universal acceptance. Edgar P. Richardson, for instance, believes it is "a misleading local name for our first really national school

170

of painting," and ought to be abandoned.[3] Richardson's objection stems from the fact that the term casts a rather wide net and snares many artists who habitually resorted to far more distant waters than those of New York State.[4] Statistically, the overwhelming number of artists was concentrated in the general area of the Hudson Valley during the long rule of America's first school of landscape painting, and New York City remained throughout the nineteenth century the art capital of the nation. Most art historians therefore have little difficulty in bestowing upon a national movement the name of the region that not only originated it, but remained its chief source of inspiration as well as profit, and provided the necessary resources and facilities of a large metropolitan culture. The term merely recognizes, in fine, that without the Hudson Valley of the nineteenth century this country would have had no school of landscape painting, regional *or* national.

It is, however, the Catskill Mountain phase of the Hudson River School that is our main interest in the present chapter. We have seen how the cult of the wilderness found a willing subject in Thomas Cole and led him to launch the whole movement. As Frederick A. Sweet has noted, "landscapes dating from the first quarter of the nineteenth century are the occasional work of men who were primarily portrait or historical painters."[5] Cole was the first to seek out an unpreëmpted domain of pure landscape where there was no incentive or market for portrait or historical painting, and his success established not only the first school of American landscape painting but the outstanding role of the Catskill Mountains within that movement.[6] Even as late as 1882 when the Hudson River School had reached some kind of final apotheosis in the far-western panoramas of Church and Moran, and American artists as a whole faced the collapse of their traditional markets and patronage, the opinion still could be ventured that "nowhere in the world can be found so many subjects for the artist's brush so exquisitely beautiful and extremely grand as here among the historical Catskills."[7] As extravagant as that statement sounds to us today, it was supported in the nineteenth century by a veritable legion of artists, all of whom were indebted to the original commitment of Thomas Cole to the unpreëmpted Catskills.

I

Although that commitment was first made when Cole visited Pine Orchard in the fall of 1825, he did not take up permanent residence in the village of Catskill until 1836. In that year he married Maria Bartow of Catskill, a young woman he had met on his first visit, and moved into the mansion on the banks of the Hudson that is still owned by his descendants. Between the spring of 1825 when he arrived in New York City and the year of his marriage, he made repeated excursions into the Catskills with the exception of a four-year period (June 1829–November 1832) when he made the traditional tour of European art centers. From 1836 until his death in 1848, Catskill remained his year-round residence with the exception again of another brief sojourn in Europe (midsummer 1841–early summer 1842). Cole's name became as firmly attached to the Catskills as did Cézanne's to Aix-en-Provence, and he became almost immediately the center of a movement. "With each returning summer," Mrs. L. C. Lillie noted,

expeditions on foot, in buck-boards, or other mountain conveyances, were made by the band of artists, all men representative of their period, who gathered in the Catskills in answer to Cole's summons thither, so that scarcely a nook or gorge or valley was unvisited, and many canvases went forth to bring the beauties of that region before the eyes of the world.[8]

One of the most important of these artists was also one of the few pupils Cole ever had, Frederick Edwin Church. Born in Hartford, Connecticut, the year after Cole first discovered the Catskills (1826), and dying the last year of the century, Church came to mark "the culmination of romantic landscape in America," as Frederick A. Sweet has said, "and the final expanse of the Hudson River School."[9] As a very young man, he sought out the leading landscape painter of the period and was accepted into Cole's household in 1844, where he remained until Cole died in 1848. The lengthy apprenticeship made Church a true exemplar of the Hudson River School, and it also made him, as Mrs. Lillie observed, "an enthusiastic lover of that region of the country, with which his name is permanently associated." [10] Church subsequently wandered throughout the world painting huge panoramas of the most melodramatic scenes of nature and commanding some of the highest prices ever paid an American artist; but in the antebellum period he returned to New York State and built, directly across the river from the Cole mansion, a huge semi-Moorish castle that remained his home for as long as he lived. This archaic monument to Church's success still stands, commanding the eastern approach of the present-day Rip Van Winkle Bridge and facing the full range of those mountains which inspired the first, and in some critics' opinion, the finest paintings he ever made. [11]

Of the other artists Cole drew to the Catskills, probably the most important was Asher B. Durand. Often linked with Cole, Thomas Doughty, and John Frederick Kensett as one of the four leading exponents of the Hudson River School, [12] Durand first met Cole—and the Catskills—in the famous encounter of 1825 when Colonel Trumbull introduced the unknown Cole and his first canvases to Dunlap and Durand. Five years older than Cole, Durand was already an established engraver and portrait painter at the time of this meeting; and his passionate interest in landscape painting, restricted in his earlier years to the conventional subjects along the lower reaches of the Hudson, always had to remain subordinate to the prime economic mainstay of portrait painting. One reason why Cole is considered the founder of the Hudson River School is that he was the first to make a living from landscape alone. Durand, on the other hand, was more representative of an older generation that could never make the transition from portraiture to landscape. In spite of Cole's earnest efforts to get Durand to forsake New York City for the mountains [13]—a move that actually appealed to Durand's deepest nature—the older painter was not able to free himself from his economic bondage to the portrait market of the metropolis.[14]

But this did not prevent Durand from pursuing his fervent interest in landscape painting during the innumerable summers and falls of a long productive life. The first—and one of the few of all our nineteenth century artists—to paint directly from nature,[15] Durand eventually visited, often with considerable physical hardship, the major landscape motifs of the North Atlantic seaboard, from the cliffs of Hoboken to the Adirondacks and the Green and White Mountains.[16] From the time he first met Cole, however, until the 1850s and beyond, he got to know "every

Figure 41. *Catskill Mountains,* painted and engraved by Asher B. Durand, c. 1828. From the engraving originally published in Durand's ill-fated *The American Scenery* of 1830. It shows the Catskill Creek from Jefferson Heights and was painted from the same location as Thomas Cole's *River in the Mountains,* c. 1843 (Figure 42); the Mountain House appears as a white speck on the mountain at right.

Figure 42. *River in the Mountains,* Thomas Cole, c. 1843 (oil on canvas, 28¼″ x 41¼″). The old Catskill-Canajoharie narrow-gauge railroad and the Catskill Creek are shown from the same location as Durand's *Catskill Mountains* (Figure 41). Courtesy of the Museum of Fine Arts, Boston, Mass., M. & M. Karolik Collection.

nook, corner, and 'clove' " of the Catskill Mountains, beginning with Cole's own territory around the Catskill Mountain House.[17]

That Durand had been in the Catskills as early as 1830 is attested by an engraving he did from his own painting of the subject called "Catskill Mountains" which appeared in the ill-starred *American Landscape* of that year.[18] The painting was done at the exact place (on the present-day Mohican Trail close by the Catskill Creek) where Cole painted both his "River in the Catskills" and "River in the Mountains," and shows the Mountain House as a white dot on the distant rim of the mountains. From about 1836 onward, when Durand began to spend more time on landscape painting, he appeared in the Catskills with increasing frequency. By the late 1840s, even while Cole was still alive, Durand became the center of America's first art colony in the village of Palenville at the southern end of Kaaterskill Clove. After Cole's death and into the 1850s, Durand pioneered a movement into the hinterland of the catskills by way of the Esopus Valley and painted the area around Shandaken long before the arrival of tourists and vacationers and long before the surrounding mountains were considered an organic part of the Catskills.[19] It is the Palenville period, however, that now concerns us.

II

When Samuel E. Rusk said in his 1879 *Illustrated Guide to the Catskill Mountains* that "the first summer boarders" in Palenville "were artists, who found this an admirable region in which to obtain choice studies," he probably had in mind the early visits of Durand and his companions.[20] By the late 1840s, according to a contemporary historian of the Catskills, Durand had made Palenville "what amounted to the Catskills' first year round art colony."[21] Whether the colony was year round or not, by the fall of 1848 Durand had certainly made it a flourishing colony during the summer and fall months. Durand's son lists the artists at Palenville during that season as David Johnson, John Frederick Kensett (still highly respected by American critics and collectors), Christopher Pearse Cranch (the writer turned artist who was a friend of Emerson's), Thomas Addison Richards (writer, painter, and illustrator who did several articles on the Catskills for *Harper's* during the 1850s), Richard William Hubbard (businessman turned artist), and Alfred Jones (a painter, and also one of the finest engravers in America).[22] Other artists as well as writers who were known to have been "frequent visitors" were Durand's pupil, the young John W. Casilear; the Dutch painter Vilmerung; George William Curtis, "fresh from two years at New England's transcendental utopia at Brook Farm"; and of course the master of them all, Thomas Cole.[23] Curtis is an example of the many writers who joined the group and became enthusiastic converts to the beauties of the Catskills, endlessly discussing the aesthetic properties of the scenes around them, searching out all the comely motifs in the area and finally "driving over gorges and bridges to the Mountain House."[24]

It is difficult to imagine just how primitive life was in this early American art colony. A submarginal standard of living and a certain bohemian attitude toward the amenities of life have always been associated with the normal life of the artist. But Palenville during the middle of the last century defied even this romantic picture. Unable to afford the luxury of the Mountain House, Durand and his group settled in Palenville while it was still something of a frontier community. Tourists and vacationers, modern hotels, paved roads, electricity, telephones, were things of the future. The eagle still soared over Kaaterskill Clove when the artists first arrived; the surrounding mountainsides still echoed with the cries of catamounts, bears, and even an occasional mountain lion. Palenville itself was a shambling village of woodsmen, millers and farmers, many of whom spoke the archaic Dutch language.[25] One of the more frequent visitors to the primitive art colony, T. Addison Richards, noted as late as 1854 that

very few of the thousands who annually visit the Mountain House ever explore this, the most charming part of the Catskills. The village of Palenville, apart from its location, is a hamlet of the most shabby sort. It barely supports one ill-furnished store, two primitive way-side taverns, a Methodist chapel, a school, a post-office, and a small woolen factory. With the exception of such gentry as the blacksmith, the wagon-maker, the cobbler, and the tailor, the inhabitants employ themselves in the factory, in neighboring sawmills, tanneries, and in the transportation of lumber and leather to the river landings. In the vicinity are a few of the better class of homesteads and small farms.[26]

What it meant to live as an artist in the Palenville area is evoked by an occasional detail from Durand's letters and journals:

The Clove [October, 1848] is rich in beautiful wildness beyond all we have met before. . . . With the exception of two days, the weather has been so cold that we have worked in overcoats and over-shoes, and, in addition, have been obliged to have a constant fire alongside for an occasional warming, all of which I have endured pretty well, with no worse effect than a slight cold.

I caught a trout which I ate for breakfast—the only decent one I have had since I came here: sour bread, salt pork, and ham being the staple commodities.[27]

Even after Cole died and Durand changed his field of operations to the yet more primitive area around Shokan and Shandaken, Palenville remained physically crude and uncomfortable to the artists who used it as their summer headquarters. *Appleton's Illustrated Hand-Book of American Travel* noted in 1857 that artists still flocked to the inns of Palenville even though the accommodations were unfit for "the ease and comfort-loving tourist." [28]

Yet in spite of all the crudities, Palenville remained a popular art colony throughout the remaining years of the century. In 1897, it was spoken of as "a famous gathering place for landscape artists, as the wildness of the many ravines, and the massive projecting rocks that can be seen above you on the South Mountain side of the Clove, afford an endless variety of subjects for their pencils." [29] One of the last artists to settle in Palenville was George H. Hall (1825–1913) who first discovered the Catskills in the company of Gifford, McEntee, and others. Hall was another New Englander who moved to New York City in the early 1850s and spent the summers and falls in the Catskills. "Realizing," as Mrs. Ellet said, "that few comforts could be had within the native woodsman's hut . . ." Hall built his own home close by the bridge that marks the entrance of Kaaterskill Clove. A mecca for the artists who visited the clove in the 1890s, the house stands today as a picturesque landmark of the declining years of the Palenville art colony.[30]

III

While Palenville remained throughout the nineteenth century a favorite headquarters for those who sought the mountains only during the summer months, the village of Catskill on the Hudson River became the home of the occasional artist who, like

Thomas Cole, chose to take up a permanent residence in the vicinity of the mountains.

Albertis De Orient Browere (1814–1887) followed Cole's example and left New York City for Catskill in 1841. Unlike Cole, who interrupted his stay in Catskill by making the traditional tour of the art centers of Europe, Browere was representative of a later generation of artists and felt the lure of the newly discovered wonders of the great American West. Fired by the discovery of gold in California, he spent four years (1852–1856) in that territory prospecting for gold, but also managed to take time for some landscape painting. Returning to the Catskills, he spent two years painting in the mountains and then went West again for another brief sojourn (c. 1858–1861). The last twenty years of his life were spent in Catskill, "painting the native scene with gusto, and ignoring the academic rules and standards," according to Wolfgang Born, and therefore attracting "more and more admiration as his scattered and forgotten paintings come to light." [31]

Sanford Robinson Gifford's life (1823–1880) practically coincides with that of Browere. Although Gifford spent two periods in Europe (1855–1857 and 1868–1870) and like Browere felt the attraction of the American West (in Colorado, Wyoming, and the region of Lake Superior in the early 1870s), his main association was with the Catskill Mountains where, as Mrs. Lillie noted, "he lived and worked, and, we may safely say, had his being, since from inclination he identified himself entirely with it." [32] Gifford was born just north of Albany in the town of Saratoga, but grew up in the village of Hudson across the river from Catskill. Gifford was two years old when Cole made his first trip to the mountains; he was thirteen when Cole took up permanent residence in Catskill; and he was twenty-one when he decided to become a landscape painter four years before Cole's death. It is not surprising that, as Frederick A. Sweet has said, he "derived his greatest inspiration from Thomas Cole." [33] How important the Catskills were to Gifford may be seen by the Metropolitan Museum of Art's "Memorial Catalogue" of his work which was printed the year after his death.[34] More than a hundred of the paintings and sketches listed in that catalogue were done in the Catskills, and the majority were painted within a four-mile radius of the Catskill Mountain House. There are at least twenty-five explicit references to the Katterskill Clove, five to the Katterskill Falls, four to the lakes, several to North and South Mountains. No. 278 of the catalogue refers to the Mountain House itself, and there are at least half a dozen references to the paths, views, and so forth, that are on the immediate approaches to the Mountain House. The dates of these paintings go from 1845, the year Gifford left college and took up landscape painting, to the last year of his life (1880).

In a pattern similar to that of F. E. Church, who went from New England to New York City and finally to Catskill, B. B. G. Stone (1829–1906) was born in Belmont, Massachusetts, went to New York to pursue an art career, and finally moved to the village of Catskill. A painting of 1854 called "Souvenir of the Catskills" shows that Stone had already visited the mountains by that time, even though we know he was then living at 359 Broadway. By 1858 he had taken up permanent residence in Cole's and Browere's adopted town, and except for the period of the Civil War during which he served as an officer, he remained in Catskill devoting himself to journalism and politics as well as landscape painting, and achieving a local as well as national fame.[35] While he was still alive Mrs. Ellet said of him:

For over forty years he has devoted his life and energy, through pen and brush, in making known the open beauties and most hidden charms of these "mountains of the sky." He has tramped the valleys, climbed its peaks, until the very trees and rocks are known and loved by him, and his gathered treasuries fill to overflowing his cosy little studio.[36]

Stone, who was a student of Jaspar F. Cropsey when the latter painted the Mountain House (1855), was himself a frequent visitor to the hotel, never doubting that "his presence conferred honor on the house," [37] and leaving many illustrations of its post-Civil War appearance.[38]

A final example of the many artists who at one time or another in their lives took up residence in the village of Catskill is Charles Herbert Moore (1840–1930). As a teacher at Harvard and the first director of the Fogg Museum, Moore is better known today as an educator and scholar than as a landscape painter. However, his early career gives him a small but secure niche in the Hudson River School. Born in New York City eight years before the death of Cole, Moore succumbed to the prevailing influence of the Hudson River School and decided, while still a young man, to move to Catskill and make a career of landscape painting. During the 1860s "he painted several delightful land-

Figure 43. *Catskill Mountain House*, B. B. G. Stone, 1860 (hand-colored lithograph, 13½" x 19"), in the author's collection. Originally published by J. H. Bufford's Lithographers, Boston.

scapes, usually small, simple scenes of the local countryside." [39]
Moore's departure in 1871 for a teaching position at Harvard and
his subsequent residence in Europe coincided with the loss of
native patronage of the Hudson River School and symbolizes
the end of an era, even though many artists still continued to
paint within its broad tradition.

IV

The crucial role of the Catskills in the development of America's first school of landscape painting cannot be fully conveyed
by the number of artists who took up permanent residence in
the area or by those who supported the long history of the Palenville art colony. Of equal importance are the legion of artists whom
we might term the "occasional" visitors to the mountains, those
who went individually at one time or another and represented
the rank and file of the Hudson River School.

The first of these, Thomas Doughty (1793–1856), occupies an
anomalous position in the history of American art. One of the
first to take up landscape painting (he was listed in a Philadelphia
directory as early as 1820 as a landscape painter), he is often
considered a pioneer, if not the founder, of the Hudson River
movement.[40] The oldest of all the members and an established
landscape painter even before Cole stole the limelight in 1825,
Doughty's career never achieved a clear focus in the history of the
movement. Starting his career in Philadelphia at the time when
the city was the cultural center of America,[41] Doughty perversely
chose to settle in Boston rather than New York just as the latter
city supplanted Philadelphia as the art capital of the nation. When
he did finally move to New York in 1837 he dissociated himself
from the main artistic life of the city and never became a member
of the National Academy—a routine matter for almost every
other member of the Hudson River School.

The ambiguity in Doughty's career extends to his relationship
with the Catskill Mountains. Frederick A. Sweet (who got his
information from Doughty's great-grandnephew) declared that

the artist never frequented "the Hudson River until the latter part of his life" [42]—an odd admission when we learn from Wolfgang Born and others that "his name is firmly linked with the origin and development of the Hudson River School." [43] Sweet's opinion also seems to be contradicted by the fact that Doughty did at least one painting in the Catskills as early as 1836.[44] It is difficult, however, to determine the significance of this isolated example. Doughty roamed all over the Eastern seaboard from Maine to Pennsylvania seeking landscape subjects, and there is no immediate evidence confirming a statement made by W. B. M'Cormick in 1915 that "the Catskills were the scene of most of his life work, and in the list of pictures that remain, the name of that region appears more frequently than that of any other section of the East." [45] True or not, it was Thomas Cole who first opened that region to the artist's brush and thereby founded the first school of American landscape painting. Until further research throws more light on the subject, Doughty's role must remain ambiguous. All we can safely say is that he is an example of an early American landscape painter for whom the Catskills had at least an occasional interest.

Occupying a somewhat less ambiguous position is John Frederick Kensett (1819–1872). Born in Connecticut, Kensett learned to paint while he was in his twenties, touring Europe with such artists as Durand, Casilear, and Rossiter. Upon his return to America in 1847 Kensett followed the example of most artists of the day and settled in New York. Within two years he was elected to the National Academy and was fast establishing himself as one of the two or three most popular artists of the nineteenth century.[46]

Although Kensett, like most of his contemporaries, covered the major landscape motifs of the day from the White Mountains to Lake George and the Adirondacks, the Catskills always remained a paramount source of interest. We have already seen how he frequented the Palenville art colony when he first returned from his long stay in Europe. Among the works found in his studio upon his death (not to mention those hanging in galleries or private homes), there were at least a dozen sketches and paintings that had been done in the Catskills (plus one painting, "Catskill Mountains, N.Y.," that had been given to him by his friend Gifford).[47] His deep interest in the Catskills is also seen in what Sears calls "an exceedingly interesting work, though unpublished," that he wrote on the legends of the mountains.[48]

An artist who had something more than a sporadic interest in the Catskills was Jervis McEntee (1828–1891). A pupil of Frederick E. Church in New York City (1850–1851), McEntee opened his own studio in the city in 1858, made the usual trip to Europe (in this case in the company of Sanford R. Gifford) and became a member of the National Academy. Born in Rondout (now part of Kingston), the Ulster County entrance to the southern Catskills, McEntee spent many summers and autumns in that area, becoming especially attached to Lanesville in the southern end of Stony Clove. McEntee is an example of a later generation of artists who extended the Catskill motif into the interior of the mountains to the southwest of the Mountain House property. A catalogue of the paintings that were found in his possession upon his death gives an accurate picture of his geographical interests. One title specifies "The Brook in Mink Hollow," along the old tanners' wagon road from Woodstock to the head of Plattekill Clove. Two others are respectively called "The Catskills from Kingston" and "Ulster County Scenery." That McEntee had at least an occasional interest in the Pine Orchard region is shown by two titles which refer to "The Kaaterskill Falls" and "Kaaterskill Clove."[49]

Alexander H. Wyant (1836–1892) is another example of this later generation of artists who extended the Catskill motif to the west of Pine Orchard. Less interested in the Catskills than McEntee, Wyant made the usual pilgrimage to Europe, joined the National Academy, and painted in the Far West (1873) and the Adirondacks (he owned a house in Keene Valley in the early 1880s), as well as in the Catskills. Though he painted in the Catskills as early as the 1860s,[50] his main interest in the region dates from 1889 when he established his summer headquarters in a studio in Arkville along the route of the Delaware and Ulster Railroad at a time when the resort area of the mountains was no longer confined to the cloves and peaks of Greene County. Apart from occasional drives he seldom ventured far from his favorite haunts along the border of Ulster and Delaware counties.[51]

Jaspar F. Cropsey (1823–1900), who was born in Rossville, New York, was a more important member of the later generation of the Hudson River School. In between trips to Europe, in the early 1850s, he spent some time in the Catskills, painted the Kaaterskill Falls and the brilliantly conceived "Catskill Mountain House" of 1855 [Plate 3]. We have previously mentioned this painting in our discussion of the favorite haunts of the artists along the trails of North Mountain. It would almost seem as if Cropsey had painted this picture to challenge Bryant's dictum that only Thomas Cole could paint "the transparent abysses" of our American skies. The painting succeeds in this respect as well as anything Cole attempted, and it admirably confirms Born's opinion that Cropsey certainly knew how "to capture the translucent air of a clear September day in the mountains." [52]

Winslow Homer (1836–1910), our final example of the artists who had an occasional interest in the Catskills, followed the usual nineteenth century pattern and sought his fortunes as an artist by moving to New York (from Cambridge, Massachusetts) in 1859. Although he is usually considered in a class by himself and is chiefly remembered for his sportsman's scenes of the Adirondacks and the famous seascapes of his Maine period, he began his apprenticeship under the aegis of the Hudson River School while working as an illustrator for *Harper's* at the end of the Civil War. From 1858 to 1875 he was a frequent visitor to the Catskills, favoring the village of Hurley, four miles west of Kingston.[53] Even here Winslow Homer was in a class by himself, for the works of this period carry forth his earlier interest in genre painting rather than pure landscape, and he has left us a notable example of his topical art in the "Kaaterskill Falls" of 1872. This painting becomes something of an historical document when contrasted with Cole's original painting of the same subject ("The

Falls of Cattskill"). Cole's painting depicts the famous scene at the dawn of the historic development of the Catskills when the mountains were still a virgin wilderness. Winslow Homer's painting registers fifty years of subsequent social development and marks the advent of the Catskills as a fashionable playground of the post-Civil War era.

V

Though not strictly a part of the Hudson River School, no art history of the Catskills can be complete without some reference to the legion of commercial artists who worked tangentially to the formal landscape painters of the period and popularized the beauties of the Catskills through the ubiquitous picture books, newspapers, and magazines of the nineteenth century. Examples of such artists range from the English illustrators, Bartlett and Bennett in the 1830s, to Fritz Meyer and Harry Fenn in the post-Civil War period. Reference has already been made to William Henry Bartlett (1809–1854). One of the "leading topographical artists of his time," [54] Bartlett made four trips to America between 1836 and 1854 and during the first trip visited the Pine Orchard area to record several scenes for Virtue's *American Scenery*, published in London in 1840. The wide circulation attained by that publication, and the common nineteenth century practice of plagiarizing Bartlett's aquatints,[55] made the scenery of the Catskills familiar to a wide audience on both sides of the Atlantic. The same popularization was promoted by William J. Bennett whose water colors of American scenes became very well known during the 1830s.[56] Bennett's "Catskill Mountains," a charming view of the early Mountain House that appeared in the *New Mirror*, has been discussed. After the Civil War Fritz Meyer was one of those who reached a mass audience with his *Catskill Mountain Album* of 1869. The pictures in this album, "drawn from nature and on stone," were also reprinted as a single composite, suitable for framing. The overwhelming success achieved by such picture books during the affluent years

Figure 44. *The Catskill Mountains*, Fritz Meyer, 1869 (composite print, 19½" x 25"), in the author's collection. The individual scenes appeared as separate plates in Meyer's *Catskill Mountain Album* (New York, 1869). Print originally published by Herman Bencke.

of the Gilded Age reached something of a climax in William Cullen Bryant's huge, ostentatious two-volume edition of *Picturesque America.* Printed by D. Appleton and Company in 1872–74 with a sumptuousness that modern publishers can hardly afford to emulate, the same work was printed in four volumes in England between 1894 and 1897. Twenty-eight pages of Volume II were devoted to the Catskills, with a text by Henry A. Brown and illustrations by Harry Fenn. A far cry from Bryant's slim *American Scenery* of 1830 which failed after the first experimental issue, *Picturesque America* marked the heyday of the picture-book craze. In subsequent years as the summer vacation became an established habit of more and more segments of the American population, an increasing number of people began to enjoy their scenery at first-hand, and the invention of the camera drove the commercial engraver and watercolorist out of existence. But by that time the Hudson River School had long since disappeared, and the once vibrant Catskills had ceased to exert their charm as one of the main scenic attractions of the nation.

Chapter 8

The Romantic Debate

The artists of the Hudson River School had achieved their purpose by the second half of the nineteenth century; the American landscape had become a source of national pride and veneration. But the victory had been won in the face of difficulties that make it seem no less than miraculous. Born into a hard-working, utilitarian society still dominated by the harsh necessities of a pioneer life, our early artists encountered very little understanding of their vocation. When Thomas Cole once sought shelter for the night in a settler's cabin deep in the wilds of the Catskills, he was accepted only when the contents of his portfolio were judged to be the work of a surveyor and mapmaker. Many artists themselves never saw a painting until they went to Philadelphia or New York, and they rarely saw whole collections of paintings until they visited the galleries of Europe. The lowly craft of sign painting was often the first proving ground of a later career in landscape painting. Lacking the guidance of well-established traditions or the resources and facilities of schools and museums, most artists received a bare minimum of formal instruction and were very fortunate if they could spend a year or two under the apprenticeship of some portrait or topographical painter. Few, however, ever believed they had completed their apprenticeship until they had been able to tour the art centers of Europe.

There was one handicap that unquestionably exceeded all others, for it struck at the very roots of the precarious profession of the landscape painter. Cole put his finger on it when he paused in the village of Catskill to give a lecture on American scenery just before making his final trip to Europe in the spring of 1841. "There are those who, through ignorance or prejudice," he told his audience with unusual ardor,

strive to maintain that American scenery possesses little that is interesting or truly beautiful; that it is rude without picturesqueness, and monotonous without sublimity; that being destitute of the vestiges of antiquity, which so strongly affect the mind, it may not be compared with European scenery.[1]

Cole dismissed the opinion with the statement that it came from people who preferred to get their knowledge of scenery by reading books about the glories of Europe rather than looking at their own landscape. That he felt impelled to raise the subject many years after he himself had become a famous landscape painter attests its unrelenting influence. Denigration of the American landscape had practically become a tradition among the educated classes of Europe, and it also found support among some of the most sophisticated classes of the American population. European denigration was in part an inevitable by-product of the more general political opposition of the Old World to the "great experiment" of the new American society, but it was also a genuine expression of the prevailing European commitment to formal doctrines of aesthetic appreciation that left little room for an unqualified approval of the American landscape. The resulting dissension put the Americans on the defensive throughout the nineteenth century and led to an intellectual debate that became as important to the romantic discovery of the American landscape as the literary cult of the wilderness or the flowering of the Hudson River School of painting. It was, indeed, inseparable from those two movements and affords one final key to the preëminent role of the Catskills in the unfolding context of nineteenth century American culture.

I
The Doctrine of Association

Throughout the nineteenth century the most serious charge that could be brought to bear against American scenery was that it was generally devoid of "romantic association." [2] This is the charge that Cole alluded to when he said that a common complaint against American scenery was that it is "so destitute of the vestiges of antiquity, which so strongly affect the mind, [that] it may not be compared with European scenery." There were many other charges that could be brought against American scenery, but none was quite so unanswerable as this single charge of a general historical deficiency. To such a crusty realist as Cooper, the absence of "romantic association" in the American landscape was of little consequence. "We concede to Europe much the noblest scenery," he freely admitted, "in all those effects which depend on time and association, in its monuments, and in this impress of the past which may be said to be reflected in its countenance"; and he sought the virtues of American scenery in other quarters.[3] But to most Americans the want of romantic association in their native landscape was too serious a charge to be so lightly dismissed; somehow or other the charge had to be encountered in its own terms and disqualified.

As disseminated from Europe, the doctrine of romantic association could not be more hostile to the American environment. W. Gilpin, a noted authority of the day, explained the doctrine by saying that "there is no such thing as absolute or intrinsic beauty. . . . It depends altogether on those associations with which it is thus found to come and disappear." [4] When we look at a natural scene, he went on to explain, it is "the recollection of man, of human feelings," that endows the scene with beauty.

It is sympathy with the present or past, or the imaginary inhabitants of such a region, that alone gives it either interest or beauty, and the delight of those who behold it, will always be found to be in exact proportion to the force of their imaginations, and the warmth of their social affections.[5]

A scene can only be beautiful, in other words, when it is associated with human life—past, present, historical, or imaginary. European scenery, it goes without saying, is inordinately beautiful: where else in the world can we find such a high concentration of historical associations? But what about America? Devoid of history and tradition, lore and legend, ruins and artifacts, the American landscape has little power to challenge the imagination or "social affections" in terms of such romantic associations. How, then, are we to commend the American landscape in the light of such a demanding doctrine?

Defenders of American scenery were hard beset to answer this question, but the attempt was nonetheless made, and it was the scenery of the Hudson Valley that supplied the main body of evidence. Answering the charge that American scenery has a "grand defect" in the "want of associations such as arise amid the scenes of the old world," Thomas Cole had the Hudson Valley in mind when he said:

> American scenes are not destitute of historical and legendary associations; the great struggle for freedom has sanctified many a spot, and many a mountain stream and rock has its legend, worthy of a poet's pen or painter's pencil.[6]

Bayard Taylor made a similar point when he took some friends up the Hudson to make his fourth visit to the Mountain House in the summer of 1860. Passing through the Highlands he noted that they impressed his critical European friends "as much as I could have wished"; and then he made the following observation:

> It is customary among our tourists to deplore the absence of ruins on those heights—a very unnecessary regret, in my opinion. To show that we have associations fully as inspiring as those connected with feudal warfare, I related the story of Stony Point, and André's capture; and pointed out, successively, Kosciusko's Monument, old Fort Putnam, and Washington's Headquarters. Sunnyside was also a classic spot to my friends, nor was Idlewild forgotten.[7]

Bryant also liked to refer to the "numerous remains of old fortifications, which, in the revolutionary war, crowned nearly all the prominent points" along the Highlands and enhanced the beauty of that part of the Hudson.[8]

But as Bayard Taylor suggests in his reference to Sunnyside— the home of Washington Irving—the associations of the Hudson were not restricted to the military events of the Revolution. When Irving first traveled up the Hudson, "prone to relish every thing which partook of the marvelous," he was enthralled not by historical or military events, but by the stories and legends that were told him by an old Indian trader. Irving made the most of these tales, as well as the many Dutch legends that pertained to the seventeenth century life along the river; and he was delighted to find that "the Catskill Mountains especially called forth a host of fanciful traditions."[9] Consciously aware that the American scene ordinarily lacked such legendary resources, he deliberately set out to revive and preserve them through his own literary genius, so enhancing the romantic value of his native landscape. How successful he was may be seen in the extraordinary influence of such a story as *Rip Van Winkle*. T. Morris Longstreth noted in 1918 that "every summer half a million people" visited the Catskills "partly on account of that story," thus giving the mountains "a distinction" possessed by hardly any others in America.[10]

Perhaps the most eloquent testimony we have of Irving's success—as well as that of his whole generation—in endowing the Hudson Valley with rich romantic associations is contained in a tribute written by Henry James. Upon returning to America in 1905 after nearly a quarter of a century of self-imposed exile, James was surprised to find that the Hudson Valley looked to him like "a great romantic stream." Pondering the cause of this, he linked it first of all with the "romantic effect" of the luminous atmospheric haze that lay along the river bottom, and then added, in his own quite irreducible prose:

Such accordingly is the strong silver light, all simplifying and ennobling, in which I see the place—see it as a cluster of high promontories, of the last classic elegance, over-hanging vast receding reaches of the river, mountain-guarded and dim, which took their place in the geography of the ideal, in the long perspective of the poetry of association, rather than in those of the State of New York. . . . It was type and tone of the very finest and rarest; type and tone good enough for Claude or Turner. . . . What it came back to was that the accents, in the delightful and pillared and porticoed house that crowned the cliff and commanded the stream were as right as they were numerous. . . . For the iridescence consists, in this connection, of a shimmer of association that still more refuses to be reduced to terms; some sense of legend, of aboriginal mystery, with a still earlier past for its dim background and the insistent idea of the River as above all romantic for its warrant. Helplessly analyzed, perhaps, this amounts to no more than the very childish experience of a galleried house or two round about which the views and the trees and the peaches and the pony seemed prodigious, and to the remembrance of which the wonder of Rip Van Winkle and that of the "Hudson River School" of landscape art were, a little later on, to contribute their glamour.[11]

There can be no doubt that the Hudson Valley had accumulated some such store of romantic association by the end of the nineteenth century, but as James also knew there was something deeply deceptive about that nebulous accomplishment. It was no less than absurd, as he said, to encounter the Hudson Valley as if you were "meeting again a ripe old civilization." Compared to Europe, America had no such antiquity; and James drew his favorite conclusion that "values of a certain order are, in such conditions, all relative."[12] This relative poverty of the American landscape in "romantic association" could not be ignored even by those who like Irving, Cole, and Bayard Taylor, were most wont to assert otherwise. America was all too obviously a manifestation of natural rather than human history, and as Cole himself was forced to admit, echoing many others, "American associations are not so much of the past as of the present and future," a qualification that only confirmed the original charge of historical and legendary impoverishment.[13]

The defense of the American landscape had to be sought in other quarters; it had to be sought where the landscape was least, not most, civilized—in the vast forests and mountains that first fired its romantic adulation and that still suggested the original condition of the unique American environment. Yet even here the defense had to run a thorny path of critical self-analysis before it achieved a clear basis of unqualified approval. Even when the concepts of European romanticism proved most amenable to the American environment they still revealed enough inconsistencies to arouse dissension and debate and hence prolong the arduous romantic quest of the American landscape.

II
The Picturesque versus the Sublime

Excluding the Doctrine of Association, most of the intellectual debate regarding the nature of the American landscape that occurred in the nineteenth century revolved around the twin concepts of the "picturesque" and the "sublime." Some of the difficulty that the Americans encountered was intrinsic to the concepts themselves, for their precise definition eluded the grasp of even the experts of the period.[14] The concept of the "sublime" was least ambiguous, but the concept of the "picturesque" was often absorbed into a third category, the "beautiful," where it could simply denote a smaller and more intimate aspect of a larger beautiful scene.[15] Usage in this book has followed the apparent preference of the Americans for the term "picturesque." The main battle of the nineteenth century was fought not between the "beautiful" and the "picturesque," but between the scenic qualities that make up the "beautiful" and/or the "picturesque" and those that form the "sublime." This becomes fully apparent in the following comments penned by that shrewd American observer, Henry T. Tuckerman.

"The peculiar beauty of American mountains is rather incidental than intrinsic," Tuckerman avowed in 1852 during the height of the romantic debate:

We seldom gaze upon one with the delight awakened by an undivided charm, but usually on account of its grand effect as part of a vast landscape. Our scenery is on so large a scale as to yield sublime rather than distinct impressions; the artist feels that it is requisite to select and combine the materials afforded by nature, in order to produce an effective picture; and although our country is unsurpassed in bold and lovely scenes, no ordinary patience and skill are needed to choose adequate subjects for the pencil. The outline of the mountains is almost invariably rounded; the peaks of the Alpine summits and the peaceful linear curves of the Apennines render them far more picturesque. As we stand on the top of Mount Washington, or the Catskills, the very immensity of the prospect renders it too vague for the limner; it inspires the imagination more frequently than it satisfies the eye. Indeed, general effect is the characteristic of American scenery; the levels are diffused into apparently boundless prairies, and the elevations spread in grand but monotonous undulations; only here and there a nook or a ridge, a spur, a defile or a cliff, forms the nucleus for an impressive sketch, or presents a cluster of attractive features limited enough in extent to be aptly transferred to canvas.[16]

Behind those comments stands the ancient reality of the vast American wilderness, a predominant feature of the American landscape until well into the middle decades of the nineteenth century. One thinks of Cooper's pervading sense of the "monotonous undulations" of the American forest, stretching from the Atlantic to the Mississippi. Tuckerman's comments sum up the major aesthetic attitudes of the day regarding this ancient reality, and central to them all is a major distinction between the "picturesque" and the "sublime."

We may note, for instance, that Tuckerman's comments revolve around a series of dichotomies: the incidental versus the intrinsic, general effect versus specific impact, open lineal planes versus contained verticals, massiveness versus minutiae, imagination (mind) versus the eye (sense), America versus Europe, or—containing all—the sublime versus the picturesque. All these terms have logical connection with each other. The beauty of the American landscape is "incidental" rather than "intrinsic" because the vast lineal planes of that landscape are deficient in those qualities that present readily composed pictures; the attention of the artist, captured by immensity, vagueness, silence, and intimations of infinity, abandons the self-contained aesthetic delight of the senses for the imaginative realm of philosophical and religious reflection—the realm of the sublime as against the picturesque, of America rather than Europe.

Such became the logical frame of the great nineteenth century debate regarding the nature of the American landscape. Only one major point has been excluded from Tuckerman's exposition, the absence in America of the influence of man (in work and art) in redeeming the deficiencies of nature. Otherwise Tuckerman strikes all the major notes of the great romantic debate. Variations and sharp disagreements occur, intrinsic to the American as well as the European points of view; but they occur within Tuckerman's general frame of reference and obey his general distinction between the strategic concepts of the "picturesque" and the "sublime."

One can begin almost anywhere in the relevant literature of the nineteenth century to illustrate the general pattern of the debate, but perhaps a dramatic opening may be provided by the European opinions of C. J. Latrobe. Latrobe was a Frenchman who together with Count de Pourtales visited the United States in 1832 as the guest of Washington Irving. It was during this visit that Irving, together with James Paulding as well as his two French guests, first visited the Catskill Mountain House, a chronic "must" of any grand tour of nineteenth century America.[17] Latrobe's opinions, for all their validity, were representative of a type of foreign comment that could infuriate the hypersensitive Americans of the last century, if only because they *did* come from a foreigner.

"The United States taken as a whole," he flatly stated right from the start, "is far from possessing a fair proportion of what we should term picturesque scenery." The American States lack "those details which render them essentially picturesque." European countries, on the other hand, are picturesque

not only because the works of man, by which they are thickly diversified, has made them so, but because the natural disposition of the surface—broken ground, bare rock, wood, water, verdure, mountains and valleys, alternating in quick succession—has stamped that peculiar character upon them. But the abrupt outlines of surface, so usual in the Old World, and the interminable interchange of the various elements of the picturesque, are of much rarer occurrence in the New.

Most sections of America do not meet those requirements of the picturesque, including, as Latrobe went on to enumerate, the Mississippi Valley, the great coastal plain of the Atlantic seaboard, the regions of our great forests and mountains, and (surprisingly enough) New England. The far-flung forests of America are especially important to the over-all impression of unpicturesqueness:

In a continent where the forest still covers so large a portion of both mountain and plain, where the undisturbed ribs of rock are hidden within the mountain sides by the swelling and even outlines of the mould, protected and increased by the forests of ages, there must be monotony.

And in one terse sentence Latrobe put his finger on a defect of American scenery that was expressed by almost every other critic of the nineteenth century: "What nature has to a certain degree denied, man has hitherto done but little to remedy." [18] All in all, Latrobe's critique was a good example of that persistent negative criticism that proved singularly offensive to most nineteenth century Americans.

Latrobe, however, had not been completely negative. Perhaps sensing he had gone too far, he noted exceptions to his general indictment of the American landscape, exceptions which must have been especially comforting to the citizens of New York State:

Still do not misunderstand me. Though you cannot, in speaking of these vast regions, say that the general character of their scenery is picturesque,—yet go more into detail, and you will find, though they may be far apart, scenes of the most exquisite beauty, fully justifying the application of the epithet. The course of the Hudson abounds with them from its source till it meets the ocean. [19]

We would be unwise, I think, to assume that Latrobe made that concession out of a respect for his host's feelings and his known opinions about the beauties of the Hudson; for as we have noted earlier, the exceptional beauty of the Hudson Valley was universally assented to during the nineteenth century. And so was the particular beauty of Kaaterskill Clove that Latrobe singled out for special praise: few critics of the nineteenth century had anything but praise for this particular region of the Catskills.[20]

But Latrobe made one other concession that almost outweighed all his previous objections to American scenery. Believing that America was generally deficient in the picturesque with the exception of the Hudson Valley and the Catskill Mountains, he yet held that the American landscape was richly endowed with all the elements of "the sublime." And as an example he chose the very thing that had been most detrimental to the picturesque aspect of the American landscape—"the dark mantle of primeval forest" that could be seen from the summit of the Allegheny Mountains. "Well may America be proud of such scenes," he concluded. "All bear the impress of sublimity. The feelings which they convey to the human mind may be less pleasing and less definite [than the picturesque], but they are more durable." [21] And with this opinion about the forests of America the critical Frenchman at last found himself in complete agreement with most nineteenth century Americans.

Latrobe's point regarding the sublimity of the view from the summit of the Allegheny Mountains was probably an allusion to one of the most famous views of the American landscape and one that he in fact visited with Washington Irving during the 1832 trip up the Hudson, the view from the Catskill Mountain House. While we may question Irving's opinion that this view affords "one of the finest prospects in the world," [22] or smile at Cooper's hyperbolic statement that it affords a panorama of "all creation"; still we cannot question a more recent commentator's opinion that "it is the view that made the Catskills famous" [23]; and anyone visiting the scene in the middle of the twentieth century can still agree with the American Geographical Society in saying that it "can easily claim to be one of the most inspiring views of the national domain east of the Rocky Mountains." [24] As the *pièce de résistance* of the whole scenic wonderland of the Catskills and the goal of literally tens of thousands of people during the summer months of the nineteenth century, the view became the focus of the long romantic debate on the nature of the "sublime" in American scenery.

The literature on the subject is vast enough to fill a separate volume, for half of America must have tried at one time or another to describe the immeasurable view with yards of shimmering adjectives.[25] Rhetoric fell from the ledges of Pine Orchard like water from the mighty Falls of the Kaaterskill. Undaunted by the self-imposed task of attempting to describe what was commonly called "the indescribable," visitor after visitor was seduced into the literary posture by the alluring prospect of capturing the highest prize of nineteenth century aesthetic theory, the ineffable category of the "sublime." We need refer only to one classic example to reveal the major content of that endlessly repetitious, nineteenth century obsession. The following dates from the 1830s and was penned by Willis Gaylord Clark, co-editor with his brother Lewis Clark of the *Knickerbocker Magazine*, an early organ of the American romantic movement.

Good Reader! expect me not to describe the indescribable. I feel now, while memory is busy in my brain, calling up that vision to my mind, much as I did when I leaned upon my staff before that omnipotent picture, and looked abroad upon its God-written magnitude. It was a vast and changeful, a majestic, an *interminable* landscape; a fairy, grand, and delicately-colored scene, with rivers for its lines of reflections; with highlands and the vales of *States* for its shadowings, and far-off mountains for its frame. Those particolored and varying clouds I fancied I had seen as I ascended [the mountain], were but portions of the scene. All colors of the rainbow; all softness of harvest-field, and forest, and distant cities, and the towns that simply dotted the Hudson; and far beyond where that noble river, diminished to a brooklet, rolled its waters, there opened mountain after mountain, vale after vale, State after

State, heaved against the horizon, to the north-east and south, in impressive and sublime confusion; while *still beyond*, in undulating ridges, filled with all hues of light and shade, coquetting with the cloud, rolled the rock-ribbed and ancient frame of this dim diorama! As the sun went down, the houses and cities diminished to dots; the evening guns of the national anniversary [it was the 4th of July] came booming up from the valley of the Hudson; the bonfires blazed along the peaks of distant mountains, and from the suburbs of countless villages along the river; while in the dim twilight,

> "From coast to coast, and from town to town,
>   You could see all the white sails gleaming down."

The steamboats, hastening to and fro, vomited their fires upon the air, and the circuit of unnumbered miles sent up its sights and sounds, from the region below, over which the vast shadows of the mountains were stealing.

Just before the sun dropped behind the west, his slant beams poured over the South Mountains and fell upon a wide sea of feathery clouds, which were sweeping midway along its form, obscuring the vale below. I sought an eminence in the neighborhood, and with the sun at my back, saw a giant form depicted in a misty halo on the clouds below. He was identified, insubstantial but extensive Shape! I stretched forth my hand, and the giant spectre waved his shadowy arm over the whole county of Dutchess, through the misty atmosphere; while just at his supernatural coat-tail, a shower of light played upon the highlands, verging toward West Point, on the river, which are to the eye, from the Mountain House, level slips of shore, that seem scarce so gross as knolls of the smallest size.

In discoursing of the territorial wonderments in question, which have been moulded by the hand of the ALMIGHTY, I cannot suppose that you who read my reveries will look with a compact, imaginative eye upon that which has forced radius upon my own extended vision. I ask you, howbeit, to take my arm, and step forth with me from the piazza of the Mountain House. It is night. A few stars are peering from a dim azure field of western sky; the high-soaring breeze, the breath of heaven, makes a stilly music in the neighboring pines; the meek crest of Dian rolls along the blue depths of ether, tinting with silver lines the half dun, half fleecy clouds.

There is a bench near the verge of the Platform where, when

you sit at evening, the hollow-sounding air comes up from the vast vale below, like the restless murmurs of the ocean.

Listen to those voiceful currents of air, traversing the vast profound! What a mighty circumference do they sweep! Over how many towns, and dwellings, and streams, and incommunicable woods! Murmurs of the dark sources and awakeners of sublime imagination swell from afar. You have thoughts of eternity and power here which shall haunt you evermore.

You can lie on your pillow at the Kaatskill House, and see the god of day look upon you from behind the pinnacles of the White Mountains in New Hampshire, hundreds of miles away. Noble prospect! As the great orb heaves up in ineffable grandeur, he seems rising from beneath you, and you fancy that you have attained an elevation where may be seen *the motion of the world.* No intervening land to limit the view, you seem suspended in mid-air, without one obstacle to check the eye. The scene is indescribable. The chequered and interminable vale, sprinkled with groves, and lakes, and towns, and streams; the mountains afar off, swelling tumultuously heavenward, like waves of the ocean, some incarnadined with radiance, others purpled in shade; all these, to use the language of an auctioneer's advertisement, "are too tedious to mention, but may be seen on the premises." I know of but one picture which will give the reader an idea of this ethereal spot. It was the view which the angel Michael was polite enough, one summer morning, to point out to Adam, from the highest hill of Paradise.[26]

All in all, the passage is an excellent example of Tuckerman's dictum that the American landscape "is on so large a scale as to yield sublime rather than distinct impressions," and that "the very immensity of the prospect renders it too vague for the limner; it inspires the imagination more frequently than it satisfies the eye." No artist ever painted the view per se from the Mountain House; but as the above example displays, writers consumed whole reams of paper trying to capture its "sublimity" in prose. The view lacked, in other words, graphic "picturesqueness." There can be no doubt that Willis Gaylord Clark was mainly interested in conveying what he called the "sublime confusion" of the scene. That is why he deals in such heavily loaded words and concepts as omnipotence, vastness, God-written magnitude, majesty, profound depths, vagueness, insubstantial shapes, mysterious sounds of night, "murmurs of dark sources," "thoughts of eternity and power," and "the motion of the world"—all are standard elements of the prodigious concept of the "sublime."

There were, of course, occasional dissenting voices regarding the nature of the view from the Mountain House; not all commentators were equally convinced of its innate sublimity. To Theodore L. Cuyler, for instance, the view was apparently more "beautiful" than "sublime." In his own words:

There was a dim resemblance in the scene to a sunrise on the Rigi. But alas! no glaciers, no sky-piercing pinnacle of ice, was in sight. No sublimity either, was in our spectacle; but there was *beauty* infinite, beauty beyond aught that we have seen from mountain-top before, beauty beyond the reach of words. The sublime is only to be found at Catskill when a thunder-storm is mustering its battalions and discharging its terrific artillery among the "rattling peaks." At other times, the one sensation that is inspired by every varying view from sunrise to sunset, is that of beauty unending and illimitable. And never is the spectacle so surpassingly beautiful as at the day-dawn of a summer's morn.[27]

No one in the nineteenth century disagreed about the sublime effect of a thunderstorm, for it was the perfect embodiment of all that monolithic confusion and awe-inspiring terror that romantics glorified as unmistakable symptoms of sublimity. Another romantic visitor to the Mountain House, Thomas W. Strong, held, for instance, that "there is a terrific grandeur and sublimity about the mountain storm, when it howls and sweeps around the lofty peaks . . . as if in furious madness."[28] As Elizabeth Ellet said, "the clearing up of a storm seen under these circumstances must be sublime beyond imagination, and well worth a journey to the Mountain House expressly to see."[29] So Thomas Cole also agreed, who deliberately painted the Mountain House under the violent aspect of such a thunderstorm and thereby gave us the most romantic painting that we have of that subject [Figure 19]. But Theodore L. Cuyler was also correct about the nature of sublimity when he cited the necessary presence of "glaciers" and a "sky-piercing pinnacle of ice"—all such exaggerated forms of nature were always deemed essential to the "sublimity" of nature. Agreeing with Cuyler about these deficiencies in the view from the Mountain House, George William Curtis noted in 1852 that

the whole thing is graceful and generous, but not sublime. Your genuine mountaineer (which I am not) shrugs his shoulders at the shoulders of mountains which soar thousands of feet above him and are still shaggy with forest. He draws a long breath over the spacious plain, but he feels the want of that true mountain sublimity, the presence of lonely snow-peaks.[30]

The absence of these features in the view from the Mountain House (and in American landscape as a whole) was therefore a genuine weakness in the "sublimity" of that scene. It is noteworthy that both Cole in his painting and Clark in his writing felt compelled to exaggerate many aspects of the scene in order to achieve a genuine effect of sublimity.

Yet it was Thomas Cole and Willis Gaylord Clark, rather than the critical Theodore L. Cuyler and George William Curtis, who were more typical of the nineteenth century response to what Tyrone Power called "one of the most glorious prospects ever given by the Creator to man's admiration." [31] Most romantics, in other words, chose to consider the scene a true manifestation of the sublime, even when it lacked the romantic props of a thunderstorm or snow-capped mountain. Although William L. Stone and Elizabeth Ellet believed that the scene was certainly sublime when seen during a thunderstorm, they also held that it was equally sublime when seen on the calmest of days. Stone resorted to some rather novel arguments to support this claim. Turning to one of the most respected authorities of the day, Edmund Burke, he found the convenient point of view that (as Stone expressed it) "height has less grandeur than depth, and we are more struck at looking down from a precipice than in looking up to an object of equal height." Stone immediately drew the conclusion that "the correctness of this opinion will not be questioned by those who from below have looked up to the hotel almost without emotion, and who have looked down from these shelving cliffs with giddy head and trembling, breathless interest." [32] The view was therefore intrinsically sublime, and had no need of the adventitious element of the thunderstorm. It was an opinion that was given a summary statement by Park Benjamin when he visited the Mountain House in the summer of 1843:

Station yourself upon that projecting rock that hangs in such terrific altitude over the immense space beneath, but attempt not to give utterance to your feelings—language could not express them. Have you ever stood upon a vessel's deck, lashed to her for security, amid the howling tempest's rage, the winds driving her into the sea's deep chasms, and suspending her on the lofty pinnacle of the waves, the lightning's flashes brightening the surrounding horrors, and showing by its vivid glares the peril of your situation? Have you ever known the mightiness of the tempest's angry mood at such a moment, and felt how utterly inadequate is speech? If so, then stand upon this high-poised rock and learn that it is not the *awfully* sublime alone that seals the lips, but that nature in her *calmest* mood can subdue the mind to silence. [33]

To Park Benjamin, Elizabeth Ellet and William L. Stone as well as to most of the enthralled visitors to the Mountain House, the view from Pine Orchard was incontestably "sublime," and this opinion conformed to the general opinion we have already noted in regard to American scenery as a whole. The standard opinion of Tuckerman and Latrobe that American scenery is lacking in the qualities that produce the "picturesque," but has more than its share of those which constitute the "sublime" was the settled conviction of most patriotic Americans. Bryant believed, for instance, that the very absence of the "picturesque" produced a type of sublimity in America that was unlike anything in Europe. Declaring as early as 1830 that "our scenery has its peculiarities not less strongly marked than those of the old continent," he gave credit for this individuality to the "absence of those tamings and softenings of cultivation, continued for ages, which, while they change the face of landscape, at the same time break up its unity of effect." It is this unity of effect, produced by our "far-flung wilderness," that therefore makes our landscape uniquely American. [34] N. P. Willis made a similar point eight years later in a preface to a magazine that had been brought out to permit people "to compare the sublime of the Western Continent with the sublime of Switzerland." Willis declared:

Either Nature has wrought with a bolder hand in America, or the effect of long continued cultivation on scenery, as exemplified in Europe, is greater than usually supposed. Certain it is that the rivers, the forests, the unshorn mountain-sides and unbridged chasms of that vast country, are of a character peculiar to America alone—a lavish large-featured sublimity, (if we may so express it), quite dissimilar to the picturesque of all other countries.[35]

Yet as we have seen, difficulties remained in this thesis and there were always a few recalcitrant individuals who made the most of them, thus sharpening the terms of the ultimate apotheosis of the American landscape. A notable example was James Fenimore Cooper. We have noted how the Leather-Stocking tales reveal a romantic predilection for the mass effects of the American forest. However, in an essay written specifically on the subject of "American and European Scenery Compared," Cooper's crusty realism came to the fore and he displayed very little interest in those grandiose aspects of mountain scenery that so delighted Irving, Bryant, and Cole and the more othodox romantics of the period. Dismissing this aspect of the subject with the statement that "in the way of the wild, the terrific, and the grand, nature is sufficient of herself," he immediately added, "but Niagara is scarcely more imposing than she is now rendered lovely by the works of man." [36] The addendum was typical of Cooper, for it was one of his central beliefs that "a union of art and nature alone render scenery perfect." [37] In the Leather-Stocking tales we may find a different opinion—Natty Bumppo's primitivistic belief that the most perfect scenery is that which has been least touched by the hand of man. In the essay on American scenery, however, Cooper put his faith in a fusion of nature and art. This emphasis separated Cooper from the majority opinion of his age. However, he was back with more popular opinion in yet another aspect of his thought. Agreeing with Tuckerman and Latrobe about the superiority of the American landscape in its mass effects, he declared:

The greater natural freedom that exists in an ordinary American landscape, and the abundance of detached fragments of wood, often rends the view of this country strikingly beautiful when they are of sufficient extent to conceal the want of finish in the details, which require time and long-continued labor to accomplish. In this particular [i.e. in the presence of mass effect where the absence of polish and detail is not important] we conceive that the older portions of the United States offer to the eye a general outline of view that may well claim to be even of a higher cast, than most of the scenery of the Old World.[38]

Or more tersely stated:

Of a cloudy day, a distant view in America often bears the likeness to the park in a very marked degree, for then the graces of the scene are visible to the eye, while the defects of the details are too remote to be detected.[39]

But even here Cooper was not in complete agreement with the usual opinion of his age. Both Willis and Bryant believed, for instance, that this superiority of the American landscape in mass effect was the source of its unique "sublimity" and hence its superiority—at least in this category—to European scenery. Not so with Cooper:

As a whole, it must be admitted that Europe offers to the senses sublimer views and certainly grander, than are to be found within our own borders, unless we resort to the Rocky Mountains, and the ranges in California and New Mexico.[40]

Believing that American scenery was deficient in sublimity and grandeur, Cooper went along with the more common opinion that it was also deficient in the "picturesque." "Time, numbers, and labor are yet wanting to supply the defects of nature," he held, "and we must be content, for a while, with the less teeming pictures drawn in our youth and comparative simplicity."[41] But when the continued advance of American civilization *will* produce an improvement, the resulting beauty can only be a "peculiar blending" of "the agricultural and savage"; and while this may be "striking and effective," it still will not be either "picturesque" or "sublime." [42]

Cooper was therefore *sui generis* in his opinions about the American landscape. We have previously intimated that another alternative existed for Cooper (a belief in the primitivistic superiority of the American landscape), a point we shall refer to again; but in respect to the classic formulation of the "sublime" and the "picturesque" Cooper stood in a class by himself. Neither alternative was true for Cooper: the aesthetic value of the American landscape lay somewhere in between the two extremes.

Yet problems remain, for there can be no doubt that Cooper did have a point—the romantic pictures are overdrawn, for instance, and the Catskills have far less grandeur or "sublimity" than European mountains. And it seems equally true that some of the plausibility of Irving's and Cole's descriptions can only be the result of an unconscious readjustment of their European-oriented vocabulary to the less grandiose scenery of the American continent (at least in the East where they drew most of their references). "Rugged clefts and defiles" and "deep umbrageous valleys" only characterized the peaks and cloves of the Catskills when, as James warned, the adjectives remained geared to the surrounding scale of America's own landscape. Such terms only seem plausible when we ignore their European context.

It is noteworthy that even such an enthusiast as Thomas Cole could become somewhat nervous and defensive when going to Europe and directly confronting its majestic landscape. Writing from Europe in 1841 (a few weeks after he had extolled the American landscape before the Catskill Lyceum), he declared:

You may fear, perhaps, that the wonderful scenery of Switzerland will destroy my relish for my own. This will not be the case. I know that when I return I shall yet find beauty. Our scenery has its own peculiar charms, and it is so connected with my affections that it will never lose its power.[43]

After returning home Cole still found it necessary to allay the possible fears of his friends and protested his continued faith in the great beauty of the American landscape:

Must I tell you that neither the Alps, nor the Apennines, no, nor Etna itself, have dimmed in my eyes the beauty of our own Catskills. It seems to me that I look on American scenery, if it were possible, with increased pleasure. It has its own peculiar charm—a something not found elsewhere.[44]

The assertion, however, was delivered *ex cathedra* and without any elaboration, and practically coincides with Cooper's ambiguous position. Turning to Cole's paintings rather than his words, we may find even more tangible evidence of his inner disquietude about the possible inadequacy of the American landscape. It is significant, for instance, that when he started to paint the large allegorical subjects for which the nineteenth century most admired him, he felt it necessary to exaggerate the scenic effects of the Catskills in order to fulfill the deepest promptings of his spirit. In such a painting as "Youth," the second of the "Voyage of Life" series, Cole utilized a specific Catskill setting in the vicinity of the "high Bluff of Jefferson"; but the scene has become all but unrecognizable under the Byronic needs of his highly wrought imagination.[45] The landscape in this painting might well be European; it certainly is no longer American.

Chapter 9

The Romantic Apotheosis

Students of the romantic movement have long been aware that it had a singular way of breaking down the usual boundaries between the arts, and uniting writers, artists, and philosophers in something of a common enterprise. This higher unity was the inevitable result of the ultimate subservience of literary or artistic ideas to a common fund of metaphysical belief. It was this terminal philosophy and its special relevancy to the American environment that permitted the writers and artists of nineteenth century America to join forces in a single romantic glorification of the American landscape.

When Henry T. Tuckerman said that the very vastness and lack of what we may call the "composability" of the American landscape "inspires the imagination more frequently than it satisfies the eye," we may construe his statement to mean that our landscape has more metaphysical than artistic or aesthetic values. The same meaning can be read into Latrobe's statement that our "sublime" forests convey feelings to the mind which are "less pleasing and less definite" than the feelings which come from a "picturesque" landscape, but are on that very account "more durable." Our feelings are "more durable" because they are less sensuous and aesthetic and more metaphysical.

Old Platonic (as well as Christian) distinctions lay at the heart of such romantic notions. They are seen again in Willis Gaylord

Clark's statement that the view from the Mountain House is "indescribable." The scene is "indescribable" because of its "God-written magnitude." The emphasis here is on "God-written." Magnitude alone might frustrate all description simply as a problem in selection, but the nineteenth century romanticist had a qualitative rather than quantitative obstacle in mind. As Park Benjamin suggested, the magnitude of the view from the Mountain House was a revelation of the divine order that had been formed by "the great Creator of the universe" to teach man to submerge himself in "the power and majesty of the Omnipotent." He therefore advised future visitors to the Mountain House not to attempt "to give utterance to your feelings—language could not express them." [1] Not, at least, if the view had evoked what all romantics called the "sublime imagination" and transported the beholder to the speechless realm of the Absolute.

No belief was more essential to the nineteenth century philosophy of nature than this high tenet of formal Idealism. Harriet Martineau expressed it most succinctly when she said that any visitor to the heights of Pine Orchard

gains the conviction, to be never shaken again, that all that is real is ideal. . . . He becomes of one mind with the spiritual Berkeley, that the face of nature itself, the very picture of woods, and streams, and meadows, is a hieroglyphic writing in the spirit itself. . . .[2]

The implications of this cardinal tenet of nineteenth century romanticism are difficult to exaggerate. Frederick A. Sweet has noted, for instance, that the world of nature

which medievalists had regarded as sinful, perhaps because the pagan gods of nature were incompatible with Christianity, now became fully "respectable," as it were, and could be admired for its own sake. Romanticists believed that nature could do no wrong, while the classicist thought nature in the raw was chaotic and must be put in order before it could be considered beautiful.[3]

But the ultimate source of this great historic change in man's attitude toward nature lay in the popular belief in nature's metaphysical reality, or what E. P. Richardson called the abiding belief "that the fundamental reality was spirit." [4] If romanticists believed that nature could do no wrong even when it was "raw" and "chaotic," the reason was that they also believed that nature was the spontaneous manifestation of a divine spiritual order as superior to anything man could create as the "sublime" is to the lower order of the "beautiful."

The implications of this belief for the particular conditions of the American environment are obvious. As William Cullen Bryant said early in the history of the romantic movement:

Foreigners who have visited our country, particularly the mountainous parts, have spoken of a far-spread wildness, a look as if the new world was fresher from the hand of him who made it, the rocks and the very hillocks wearing the shape in which he fashioned them, the waters flowing where he marked their channels, the forests, enriched with a new creation of trees, standing where he planted them; in short, of something which, more than any scenery to which they had been accustomed, suggested the idea of unity and immensity, and abstracting the mind from the associations of human agency, carried it up to the idea of a mightier power, and to the great mystery of the origin of things. [5]

If, in other words, nature is a revelation of divine order, where in all the world is that order more visible than in the American landscape? Where can we find fewer human impediments to the immediate vision of God's first creation? Of what significance is it that the American landscape is poor in human artifice and "romantic association"? Do not such omissions liberate the mind for the much higher associations of a divine rather than human agency? What if the American landscape abounds in the wildest forests on the face of the globe? Can divinity be found, as Emerson asked, in the cultivated field? Can it be seen in the face of the city's blank walls? Is it not true, as Cooper said of the virginal Catskills, that "the hand of God is seen in the wilderness"?

It was this intrinsic harmony between metaphysical aspiration and the more primitivistic aspects of the American wilderness that permitted the final apotheosis of the American landscape. Nor is it conceivable how such an apotheosis could have been achieved on any other basis. American landscape as a whole did not favor such a romantic purpose. And over and above the aesthetic difficulties of the American landscape lay more formidable obstacles that no American artist of the nineteenth century could escape, obstacles that were inherent to American society itself and profoundly inimical to the American artist. The traditional American emphasis on utilitarian values and occupations; the paucity of aesthetic traditions, art museums, teachers, and schools; the bondage of painting to portraiture or topical and historical painting; the hostility of old Puritan notions to a new and more benevolent concept of nature—all were formidable obstacles to any incipient apotheosis of the American landscape. There were, to be sure, mitigating influences: the upsurge of nationalism during the Jacksonian period certainly redounded to the benefit of the American painter and gave him fresh markets and monetary rewards. Yet it is doubtful if this new-found patriotism could have been sufficient in itself to produce an apotheosis of the American landscape without the catalytic discovery of the romantic world of nature and the exclusive metaphysical value of the "uncorrupted" American wilderness. It was this intoxicating discovery that converted every aesthetic deficiency of the American landscape into an *ipso facto* virtue of a higher moral order and even surmounted the philosophical prejudices of a profoundly utilitarian society.

The explanation for this may perhaps best be found in the following remarks of Henry T. Tuckerman. Speaking about the new commitment of the nineteenth century artist to the metaphysical order of nature, he declared:

Numerous modern artists are distinguished by a feeling for nature which has made landscape, instead of mere imitation, a vehicle of great moral impressions. As modern poets have struck latent chords in the heart from a deeper sympathy with humanity, recent limners have depicted scenes of natural beauty, not so much in the spirit of copyists as in that of lovers and worshipers; and accordingly, however unsurpassed the older painters are in historical, they are now confessedly outvied in landscape. And where should this kind of painting advance if not in this country? Our scenery is the great object which attracts foreign tourists to our shores. No blind adherence to authority here checks the hand or chills the heart of the artist. It is only requisite to possess the technical skill, to be versed in the alphabet of painting, and then under the inspiration of a genuine love of nature "to hold communion with her visible forms," in order to achieve signal triumphs in landscape, from the varied material so lavishly displayed in our mountains, rivers, lakes, and forests—each possessing characteristic traits of beauty, and all cast in a grander mould and wearing a fresher aspect than in any other civilized land.[6]

The whole argument hinges upon the metaphysical assumption of a "moral" reality behind the "visible forms" of nature. If we grant this, then all Tuckerman's other points follow with the inexorability of a syllogism. If nature has this reality, for instance, can we not then admit (in the words of Frederick A. Sweet) that it may "be admired for its own sake"? Cannot the artist transfer his allegiance from topical or historical painting to "pure landscape"? And granted the possibility of a direct relationship between the artist and the moral reality behind the "visible forms of nature," what need is there for such intermediary agencies as schools, museums, traditions? Indeed, the very absence of such intermediaries exposes the purity of the original relationship and therefore facilitates its speedy exploitation. And does not the very primitivism of the American landscape provide similar advantages? Such a landscape is "fresher from the hand of him who made it," as Bryant said, and therefore stands forth all the more clearly as what Harriet Martineau called "a hieroglyphic writing in the spirit itself."

It is a point of view that could not have been more consistent with the deepest prejudices of the American mind. Echoing the belief of the American founders that they could build a new utopian society simply by removing the many corrupting influences—social and historical—that stood between themselves and the divine order of nature, the artists and writers of the nineteenth century assumed that they could achieve an apotheosis of the American landscape through the same direct and unmediated confrontation with the surrounding world of nature. It is this conviction that informs every last rhapsodic phrase of the following description by Thomas Cole of his first visit to the Catskill Mountains:

Before us spread the virgin waters which the prow of the sketcher had never yet curled, enfolded by the green woods, whose venerable masses had never yet figured in annuals, and overlooked by the stern mountain peaks never beheld by Claude or Salvator, nor subjected to the canvas by the innumerable dabblers in paint of all past time. All nature is here new to art. No Tivolis, Ternis, Mount Blancs, Plimmons, hackneyed and worn by the pencils of hundreds, but primeval forests, virgin lakes and waterfalls, feasting his eye with new delights, and filling his portfolio with their features of beauty and magnificence, hallowed to his soul by their freshness from the creation, for his own favored pencil.[7]

It is this conviction that lay at the heart of the romantic deification of the American landscape. If, as we have seen, "the scenic mountains of New York," and especially the Catskills, figured more predominantly than any other mountains in America in that high achievement, it is because they were the most convenient and dramatic symbolization of that vast primeval wilderness that had once darkened the great continental shelf of the Atlantic seaboard, and finally, after two hundred years of history, been wrought and molded into an idealized image of a national heritage.

Part III

The Gilded Age

Introduction

Eras of great change are more often seen in hindsight than in their moment of passage, for the present is first of all continuous with the past and the new order is a product of accumulated change. The Civil War marked the end of one period in our story of the Catskills and the beginning of another, but there was little recognition of that momentous change in the years immediately following the war. Charles Rockwell's *The Catskill Mountains and the Region Around*, the most comprehensive history and guidebook of the Catskills ever written, was published in 1867 and reissued in 1873, yet it shows little awareness of the vast changes that were altering the whole face of the Catskills even as it was being written, and it is chiefly used today as a compendium of information on the antebellum years of the resort area. Equally misleading is the authority of the *American Cyclopaedia* as it described the Catskills in 1879. Declaring that "these mountains range parallel with the river only for about 12 m.," it asserted that Stony Clove is "in a portion of the group called the Shandaken mountains" and that "the highest summits are Round Top, High Peak, and Overlook. . . ." We have already had occasion to note the fallacy of those opinions. It is, however, the following paragraph that becomes especially interesting in the light of its 1879 formulation:

Their chief interest [i.e. the mountains] lies in the variety and beauty of their scenery. In a field of very limited area, easy of access and soon explored, they present a multitude of picturesque objects, which have long made them a favorite resort of artists and of those who find pleasure in the wild haunts of the mountains. From the village of Catskill a stage route of 12 m. leads to the "Mountain House," a conspicuous hotel, perched upon one of the terraces of Pine Orchard mountain, at an elevation of 2,500 ft. above the river. Here the traveller finds a cool and quiet retreat, and a convenient starting point for his explorations.[1]

The paragraph could have been lifted from a hundred guidebooks of the antebellum period, but it had very little application to the Catskills of the 1880s.

Within three years of its writing, the vast interior of the mountains had been laced with railroads, altering the whole geography of the resort area. By 1880 the accessible area of the Catskills had expanded four or five times beyond the "very limited area" noted

Figure 45. The Mountain House in the early 1880s after the South Wing reached its maximum size. From a picture folder published by Wittemann Bros., New York, 1884.

above, and it required many days of exploration before its richness and beauty could be exhausted. Though artists still painted in the Catskills, the statement that the mountains are "a favorite resort of artists" is an echo of the antebellum period when the Hudson River School flourished in the immediate area of Kaaterskill Clove and the Catskill Mountain House. Nor, in the light of the railroad history, was the old Beach stage line from Catskill Landing to Pine Orchard the only or even the chief means of transportation to the mountains. The Ulster and Delaware Railroad out of Kingston had already reached Phoenicia in the Esopus Valley by 1879, and within another three or four years masses of people were arriving at the "top of the mountain" *back* of Pine Orchard by way of Stony Clove and Ulster County. Indeed, by 1882 the golden age of arcadian simplicity when the Mountain House ruled the destiny of the mountains in splendid isolation had become a thing of the past: hotels abounded along the new railroad lines; a new class of people, a new culture, had come into being; the "Mountain House and the Region Around" had embarked upon the volatile years of the Gilded Age.

At the start of our story we had found the key to the preëminent fame and status of the Mountain House in the strategic relationship of the Catskill mountains to the full circumference of American life and culture at the start of the antebellum period. We learned that the Catskills were ideally situated in respect to the center of population in 1825 and that the peculiar beauty of the Pine Orchard area made it a natural "proving ground" for the rising nationalism of the American romantic movement. The key to the second phase of our story may be found in the rearrangement of those relationships. Neither the Catskills in respect to the nation as a whole nor the Pine Orchard area in respect to the Catskills as a whole remained the same after the Civil War, and as E. P. Richardson has noted, the romantic movement faded away as "the first and most hopeful moment of our national life" with its "simple world of farmers, merchants and handicraftsmen disappeared under the impact of the gigantic forces of consolidation —the railroad, telegraph, steam power, machine manufacturing, finance capitalism, the mass life of cities—which produced the modern world." [2]

One index of this dramatic change is the remarkable growth and distribution of American population during the interval of 1826–1876. Between these two dates, which are the fiftieth and hundredth anniversaries of American independence, the land area of the United States more than doubled and the total population more than tripled. [3] In 1830 it took two weeks to go from New York City to the frontier on the Mississippi; in 1870 it required only four or five days and the frontier had advanced to the western borders of Minnesota, Nebraska, Kansas, and Texas; and the Pacific Coast states of Oregon and California had already been admitted into the union. [4] Only three states could claim populations of more than a million in 1830; by 1870 fifteen states could make that claim. [5] The density of population during the same period increased from 7.3 people per square mile to 13 people per square mile. [6] Cities continued to attract an increasing percentage of the total rising population, one out of every fifteen living in cities of 8,000 or more in 1830, nearly one out of six in 1860 (by 1890 three out of ten lived in cities of 8,000 or more, and nearly half of that total lived in cities of more than 25,000 people). [7] In 1830 the three largest cities were New York with 202,589, Philadelphia with 161,410, and Baltimore with 80,625. [8] By 1860 New York maintained its lead with more than a million, Philadelphia was second with more than half a million, and Baltimore had 212,000. [9]

At first glance such statistics seem to suggest that the Catskill Mountains had lost their strategic relationship to the rest of the nation; a second glance, however, soon corrects that impression. The great expansion of American territory westward, for instance, was not as important as it seemed to be, for it was accompanied by a startling development in new and more rapid means of transportation. Thanks to the ingenious railroad, it took no more time to reach the Pacific coast in 1870 than it had to reach the Mississippi in 1830. But of even greater significance was the way the distribution of population continued to favor the northeastern part of America. In 1830 Pine Orchard was about 345 miles as the crow flies from the statistical center of American population; in 1870, in spite of the opening of vast new territories and the tripling of the total population, Pine Orchard was still only about 536 miles from the center of population.[10] American population, in other words, continued to be geographically favorable to the development of the Catskills as the most accessible and therefore the most popular resort area in all the United States. The second half of the nineteenth century, to be sure, saw the advent of other centers of recreation and fashionable resort areas: parts of the Adirondacks, Berkshires, and White Mountains began to be developed at this time; people began to frequent such seaside resorts as Long Branch, New Jersey, and Newport, Rhode Island; and an ominous note for the future fate of the Catskills was struck in 1889 when the first Flagler Hotel was built in St. Augustine, Florida. In spite of all these developments, however, the supremacy of the Catskills as the nation's oldest and most popular "vacationland" was never effectively challenged until after the advent of the twentieth century.

While there was little change in the advantageous geographical position of the Catskills in respect to the nation as a whole during the post-Civil War period, there was a drastic cultural transformation that reflected a larger revolution in the whole texture of American life. American historians have long been aware of what Arthur M. Schlesinger, Sr., as early as 1922 called "a new economic and social order" that invaded American life in the 1860s and 1870s.[11] Previously America had been a nation of small farmers, merchants, and "household" manufacturers, innately chauvinistic and isolationist, and finding an appropriate ideological voice in the nativist concepts and sentiments of the romantic movement. The Civil War, however, brought the "gigantic forces of consolidation" and the unleashed might of the Industrial Revolution, accompanied by the rise of great urban wealth, the proliferation of material comforts, the popular demand for greater leisure and travel, and a new international and eclectic culture. The famous Philadelphia Exposition of 1876 in commemoration of the hundredth anniversary of American independence became a symbol of this new culture. Many art historians, for instance, date the end of the Hudson River School and the loss of native patronage for American landscape painting from this Exposition.[12] A new taste, a new class of people, were in the saddle, as Emerson said, and driving mankind. The same phenomenon was noted in respect to the history of the Catskills: previously artists and writers had been the chief agents of discovery and popularization, and they had been drawn into the mountains by the cult of the wilderness and the romantic adulation of American scenery; they were replaced after the Civil War by entrepreneurs and business tycoons who were bent upon the development of the interior of the mountains for the sake of monetary gain. And they were followed by a new and larger class of people that was as different from the previous aristocracy of talent and wealth as Grant was from Jefferson.

In the earlier period such writers as Bryant and Irving went to the Catskills to find literary inspiration, and their names are today inseparably linked with the mountains; they were followed in the second period by Mark Twain and, a little later, Hamlin Garland, both of whom went for social rather than literary reasons and neither of whom is remembered today for any particular association with the Catskills. Thomas Cole left New York City to live in a white clapboard house in the village of Catskill, and he made the mountains a common possession of every lover of American scenery; he was followed in the Gilded Age by his own pupil, Frederick E. Church, who only returned to the Catskills after having made a fortune satisfying the coarse taste of the age for gigantic canvases of the melodramatic sights of the world; and he lived out his last few years in a huge "Persian" palace built on a high bluff of the Hudson. The famous Irish actor, Tyrone Power, visited Pine Orchard out of a respect for its legendary fame and beauty during the era of the "grand tour" of the American landscape; he was followed at the end of the century by Maude Adams and Julia Marlowe, both of whom went to the Catskills to escape the heat of the metropolis, the former settling beyond Pine Orchard in the fashionable summer resort of Onteora Park, the latter joining a new summer colony at Highmount in the northern tip of Ulster County.[13] Jenny Lind, the Swedish Nightingale, was drawn to the Catskills during the 1850s by the fame of the Mountain House; she was followed in the early twentieth century by Amelita Galli-Curci, who joined the rising throng of summer visitors around Margaretville on the East Branch of the Delaware River.[14] Asher B. Durand and the nativist artists of the Hudson River School who settled at Palenville in the 1840s were followed in the early 1900s by the English visionary, Ralph Radcliffe Whitehead, and the eclectic bohemians and sophisticates of the Woodstock Art Colony.[15]

Between the two periods the Catskill Mountains had passed from the pioneer days of the romantic era to what one commentator calls "the gayest and grandest epoch of summer resort history in the Catskills." [16] Where hundreds had previously taken the slow paddle-wheelers up the Hudson to Catskill Landing and transferred to the lumbering coaches of Charles L. Beach for the three- to four-hour drive to Pine Orchard, thousands now boarded parlor cars in Philadelphia and New York and found themselves in less than half the time in the booming resorts of Greene, Ulster, and Delaware counties. As the cities of the East continued to proliferate in size and numbers, and the idea of the summer vacation took hold of more and more segments of the American population, passing from what was called "a mere social fad of fashion for the gratification of the rich" [17] to what was recognized as a "habit" that had become "chronic and confirmed among all classes" by 1904,[18] the Catskills reached their highest pitch of development and fame. In 1870 it was estimated that "not over two thousand persons" went into the mountains; [19] during the 1880s this figure had risen to sixty or seventy thousand visitors annually; [20] by 1907 it had attained the "marvelous proportions" of about 300,000 annually.[21] From a scenic wilderness, rough and remote, limited geographically to the eastern escarpment of the mountains in the vicinity of Pine Orchard, dominated by the solitary splendor of the Catskill Mountain

House, the Catskills had become by the end of the century a teeming thousand-square-mile vacationland of hotels, boarding-houses, and rich summer homes, the refuge of the affluent masses of the Gilded Age, the Playground of the Nation.

Although the "old hotel on the mountain," as it was often called, no longer exercised complete control over the destiny of the mountains, its commanding geographical position and far-flung economic interests still made it the master of the old, historic approach to the mountains from the major entrepôt of Catskill. Even as the resorts of the Catskills expanded westward into the interior of the mountains by way of the Esopus Valley, the lofty Mountain House still remained the largest and most elegant edifice on all the mountains, constantly improving its facilities, surpassing all other establishments in technological innovations, arbitrating taste and fashion, and attracting the most select clientele of the age. Finally challenged by the erection of two super-hotels during the building boom of the 1880s (the Grand Hotel at Highmount and the Kaaterskill Hotel on nearby South Mountain), the Catskill Mountain House lost some of its lustre as the most luxurious hotel in the mountains. This diminution of stature, however, did not extend to its untarnished reputation as the Catskills' oldest, most romantic and historic establishment, and indeed as one of the most famous hotels in all America. Several thousand hotels and boardinghouses attracted the vacationing masses of the late Gilded Age to the Catskills; but only the Mountain House drew untold numbers of these vacationers from "a radius of a hundred miles" to view what had finally become an American classic.[22] Eclipsed as a hotel, the Mountain House had become by the end of the century a historic sight and shrine.

Chapter 10

The Coming of the Railroads

As late as 1866 there was not a single mile of railroads in the Catskills. The abandoned roadbed and tracks of the narrow gauge Catskill-Canajoharie Railroad, built about 1838, were still visible near the village of Catskill. Originally planned to link the Mohawk and Hudson Valleys by way of the northern flank of the Catskills, the railroad soon became embroiled in administrative scandals and had to be abandoned after the laying of only twenty-six miles of track between Catskill and Cooksburg.[1] Thomas Cole's painting called "River in the Mountains" shows this part of the railroad while it was still in use about 1840. Soon after this date, even this part of the railroad was abandoned, and we do not hear of this original railroad again until Charles L. Beach incorporated a section of the old roadbed (from Catskill to Cairo) in his new Catskill Mountain Railroad of the 1880s. The only other railroad that existed in the vicinity of the Catskills in 1866 was the New York-to-Albany line of the Hudson River Railroad built up the eastern bank of the river in the late 1840s. From the time this railroad was first opened it became a favorite means of travel to the Catskills and the Mountain House, taking a good deal of the burden off the overladen steamboats of the Hudson.

The history of the railroads in the Catskill Mountains actually began in 1866 when construction was started on the Ulster and Delaware Railroad from Kingston to Stamford by way of the

Esopus Valley and the East Branch of the Delaware, a distance of seventy-four miles that presented many difficult problems to the engineers of the day. The height of railroad building occurred in the early 1880s: in 1882 the proprietor of the Mountain House opened his Catskill Mountain Railroad from Catskill to Palenville, and in 1883 the New York West Shore and Buffalo Railroad was opened between New York and Kingston, and the Stony Clove line between Phoenicia and Hunter was extended all the way to South Lake, on the very doorstep of the Mountain House. The grand climax of railroad history occurred in 1892 when the Otis Elevating Railroad overcame the barrier of the "Wall of Manitou" directly in front of the Mountain House and linked Beach's Catskill Mountain Railroad with the Stony Clove and the Ulster and Delaware railroads. This formed one continuous route from Catskill to Kingston, Phoenicia, Stony Clove, the Otis Elevating, and thence back to Catskill, a circular trip around the Catskills that could be enjoyed in a single day's outing. The completion of this system gave the Catskills two major ports of entry, two major arteries into the mountains, and placed the Mountain House at their exact point of junction and made it almost as accessible from Kingston (by way of Phoenicia and Stony Clove) as from Catskill (by way of the Catskill Mountain Railroad and the Otis Elevating). The two main arteries into the mountains also linked the Catskills with the two major railroad lines going up either side of the Hudson River as well as the old steamship lines, and made the mountains accessible from every point of the compass, from the budding cities of the Old Northwest to the metropolitan centers of the Atlantic seaboard.

When the Ulster and Delaware Railroad first opened in the spring of 1870 its eastern terminus was Mount Pleasant, near Phoenicia, a distance of twenty-four miles from Kingston. By 1879 it reached Stamford, and a few years later it reached its western terminus in Oneonta (Otsego County), 108 miles from its eastern point of origin on the Hudson River.

The effect upon this undeveloped region of the Catskills was

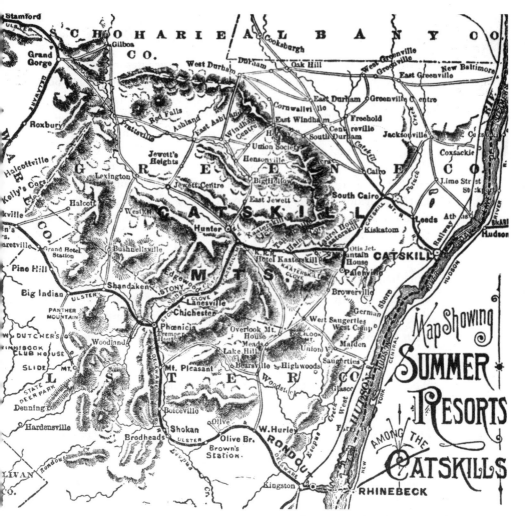

Map 9. Map of the Catskill resorts, from Hudson River Day Line literature of 1894 (Hudson River Day Line Collection, The New-York Historical Society).

incalculable. As the railroad itself never tired of repeating in its annual guidebooks, "for some fifty years" after the "summer charms" of the Catskills were first discovered, the mountains as a whole "remained practically inaccessible." The only way into the mountains was by way of the old stage line, and the resort area was restricted to one corner of Greene County:

This was the condition of affairs in the Catskills, with slight improvements, down to 1870, when the iron-horse began to sniff the

air of the hills. Here was a charming summer resort wholly undeveloped; even the old Greene county section, which was about
the only part known at all. The wildest and most charming region,
lying in the counties of Ulster and Delaware, was largely unexplored
and completely inaccessible except to the sturdy hunters and bark-
men. The great chain of mountains had never been entered on
this side where the great popular and easy approach for the entire
range was destined to be. The giant Slide Mountain crag, which
had overshadowed every other peak for countless ages, was practically unknown, and its superior height quite unsuspected. Thus
the varied magnificence of this entrancing region which has now
so greatly enhanced the fame of the Catskills, was yet to be revealed.

But then came the building of the Ulster and Delaware Railroad,
even though the mountainous terrain posed many difficulties and
the whole project "was generally considered wild and ill-advised,
with certain failure at the end." Total success crowned these
efforts:

The completion of the road of course proved the great factor
in the development of the Catskills as a popular summer resort.
A new impetus was imparted to the mountain boarding business,
and hotels, large and small, began to rise here and there in the
valleys and on the mountain slopes. It opened a new section of
the range, which rivalled and even surpassed in beauty any other
portion, while the entire region at once became easily accessible.[2]

There can be little doubt that in spite of the inevitable exag-
gerations of all such promotional literature (the "wildest and
most charming region" does *not* lie in Ulster or Delaware counties) the description is a fairly accurate appraisal of the mighty
influence of the railroad upon the subsequent history of the Catskills. As earlier guidebooks often asserted, the railroad "was not
built in advance of its needs, for it was the very thing the people
had been waiting for." [3] The "people" in this context are not
the privileged few who were amply served by the stagecoaches
of the antebellum period; they are the affluent classes of a new
urban society that went to the Catskills en masse and required
the swift comfortable facilities of the modern railroad.

It is also true that the building of the Ulster and Delaware initiated a great era of hotel building in the Catskills. We begin to hear from 1878 onward that whereas the Mountain House was once "the only place for entertainment of the tourist among the mountains," it is now but one of many hotels that "share with the *Father* of these summer resorts in entertaining the increasing flow of visitors to this delightful region." [4] The reference is no doubt an allusion, in part at least, to the building of new hotels in the Mountain House's own sphere of influence in Palenville, Tannersville, and Hunter (first noted in the guidebooks of 1876); [5] but it also must refer to the far more significant construction that was occurring along the line of the Ulster and Delaware Railroad. In 1878 the Overlook Hotel at Woodstock was completed, nine miles from the railroad at West Hurley and a good 500 feet higher than the Mountain House on the same eastern escarpment of the mountains. The following year the Mount Tremper House with accommodations for 200 was opened within sight of the railroad station at Phoenicia. In 1880 came the first hotel that exceeded the Mountain House in size and elegance, the Grand Hotel at Pine Hill, 42 miles from Kingston, with its own railroad station and a capacity of 450 guests. Indeed, so many hotels were being built in this area at this time that Walton Van Loan had to add a special section to his yearly *Catskill Mountain Guide* to take cognizance of them (though he still devoted most pages to the Mountain House and its immediate vicinity). In 1879 he already noted that "good hotels" may be found as far west as Stamford, the "present terminus" of the Ulster and Delaware Railroad. [6] The railroad itself noted in an advertisement in the same guidebook that it "is annually attracting an increasing number of tourists" and that it has provided a way of getting into the mountains that "is nearer, cheaper and more picturesque than any other, and requires much less conveyance by stages to visit the many romantic lakes, trout brooks and other points of interest in the mountains." [7] There is much more truth than fiction in that resounding claim, and it contained an implicit threat to the continued hegemony of the Catskill Mountain House and its surrounding satellites in the old resort centers of Greene County.

That threat materialized in no uncertain manner in the year 1880. The opening of the Grand Hotel alone must have sounded like the tocsin of fate to Charles L. Beach, for it broke the fifty-six-year record of the Mountain House as the largest and most luxurious hotel in all the Catskills and it symbolized the advent of all of Ulster and Delaware counties into the viable resort area of the mountains. But the year 1880 saw even greater threats to the continued supremacy of Pine Orchard and the old resorts of Greene County. The Stony Clove Railroad was constructed between Phoenicia and Hunter, linking the Ulster and Delaware Railroad with the new resorts of the Schoharie Valley. The new railroad bypassed the whole line of transportation from the village of Catskill to Pine Orchard and threatened to isolate the Mountain House altogether from the expanding resorts of both Ulster and Greene counties.

But the gravest threat of all occurred in the concluding weeks of 1880 when an army of men encamped on the heights of South Mountain and started construction of a colossal 1,200-room hotel deliberately built, as the story goes, to ruin Charles L. Beach and the Catskill Mountain House. It stood a very good chance of achieving its purpose. Built within two miles of the Mountain House with accommodations for 1,000 guests, the new "Hotel Kaaterskill" was presided over by George W. Harding, who in turn was one of the chief exponents of the Ulster and Delaware and Stony Clove railroads. Harding was determined to do everything possible to reduce the importance of the village of Catskill as a major port of entry and to deflect all traffic to the new railroads through Ulster County and Stony Clove, even going so far as to encourage those who came from Albany or Saratoga to pass on by Catskill to Rhinecliff and Kingston before entering the mountains. To Charles L. Beach the year 1880 must have been something of a nightmare.

In 1880 the master of the Mountain House was seventy-two years old, an advanced age for encountering the malevolent forces of George W. Harding and the formidable challenges of the railroads. We mistake our man, however, if we assume the power

Figure 46. Hotel Kaaterskill (1881–1924). From the Ulster & Delaware's pamphlet, *The Catskill Mountains* (Roundout, N.Y., 1909), p. 100.

that had once revolutionized the transportation of the Hudson Valley was in any way diminished or that the aggressive septuagenarian still could not enter the lists of fierce economic combat. Though he could perhaps only intuit the fact from some deep level of undiminished vitality, Charles L. Beach in 1880 still had twenty-two years of dynamic life ahead of him. This was more than enough time to master the intricacies of a new age of transportation and to reassert his authority over the destiny of Greene County. Nurtured, rather than ravaged, by change and conflict, the unconquerable lord of Pine Orchard was still "remarkably well and vigorous" long after he had completed his work some seventeen years later.[8] It is no wonder that in 1880 he still had the power to move mountains—as least figuratively— by changing their temporal relationships with the geography of all the past. Seizing the gauntlet of Harding's harsh challenge, he forged in two years' time (1880–1882) his own line of railroads from Catskill Landing to Cairo and Palenville (requiring

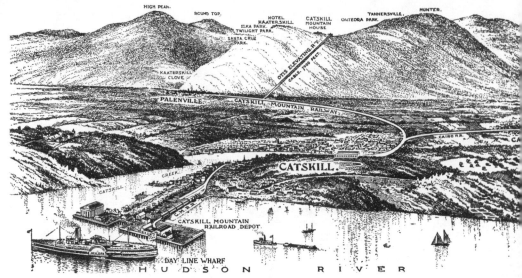

Figure 47. The transportation system during the heyday of the Catskills. From *Van Loan's Catskill Mountain Guide* (New York, 1909), p. 6.

the building of a great wharf and depot at the river's edge as well as railroad stations at Cairo, Palenville, and the base of Sleepy Hollow); and within the next decade he pulled off the railroad coup of the era by building the Otis Elevating Railroad straight up the "Wall of Manitou" (1892) and connecting that line with the "Kaaterskill Railroad" (an 1883 extension of the Stony Clove line that terminated at South Lake), thus linking his own system of railroads with the Ulster and Delaware system and uniting the port of Catskill with the expanding destiny of the interior resorts of the mountains. He negated Harding's attempt to deflect all traffic to Kingston and the Ulster and Delaware Railroad, and restored the preëminence of the Mountain House as the most accessible and spectacularly situated hotel in all the Catskills. The triumph was not without its mitigating circumstances, for it fell under the shadow of the imminent catastrophes of the twentieth century and was short-lived; but during Beach's lifetime it was complete, and it placed him at the pinnacle of his career.[9]

Charles L. Beach organized the Catskill Mountain Railroad Company in September, 1880, personally investing $100,000 in the enterprise (or "more than one fourth of the entire cost of the road"),[10] and thereby becoming its first president. Work on the new railroad began in earnest in the following spring, and in another year's time it was almost completed. The first announcement of the opening of the Catskill Mountain Railroad appeared in Walton Van Loan's *Catskill Mountain Guide* of 1882:

The Catskill Mountain Railroad, which will be ready for travel about the middle of June, will reduce the time from Catskill Landing to the Hotel about *two hours*. The heat, dust and mud incident to the stage ride of former years will be avoided. The Locomotives and Cars will be new and equipped with the most approved brakes and other appliances for the safety and comfort of passengers. During the season of Summer travel there will be at least four trains each way daily, making close connections at Catskill Landing with the steamers "Albany" and "Vibbard" of the Hudson River Day Line, the Catskill Night Boats, and the principal trains of the New York Central and Hudson River Railroad. Passengers for the Catskill Mountain House will leave the railroad at Mountain House Station and take C. A. Beach's Carriages to the Hotel.[11]

A similar advertisement that appeared the same year in Wallace Bruce's *The Hudson River by Daylight* declared that the railroad would be "ready for Summer travel about the last of June, 1882," and then noted that "this will be the Shortest, Quickest, Cheapest, and most desirable route for Summer Travel to the Catskill Mountain House . . . and other points of the Catskill Mountain region lying in Greene County."[12] It was a pronouncement that was framed in deliberate competition with the Ulster and Delaware Railroad, for the Stony Clove extension of this railroad had been completed as far as Hunter in 1881, and it had already become the leading approach to the resorts of Greene County.

Although the Catskill Mountain Railroad was only a three-foot-wide narrow-gauge railroad and therefore required a relatively narrow roadbed, it still posed many unexpected engineering (as well as administrative) problems, and as the month of June came and went it was apparent that it could not open with the advent of the tourist season. The new Hotel Kaaterskill (which had opened the previous season) lost no time in chiding the master of the Mountain House for the delay of the new railroad. "Those who have in charge the construction of the road from Catskill," the hotel's official magazine declared on July 1, 1882, "will have to stir themselves if they would have it completed this year. The season is steadily advancing and there is no time to be wasted." [13] Work was continuing furiously and by August 19 *The Kaaters-kill* had to recognize the fact that "the Catskill Mountain Railroad is completed" and—more significantly—"the Catskills are more easy of access." [14] So eager had the new railroad been to cash in on the season's unprecedented hordes of tourists and vacationers that it opened operations even before it had time to complete its station at the foot of Sleepy Hollow. This is how Lucy L. Lillie reported the event:

A curious scene presents itself at the railway terminus. Although nothing is finished yet, the traveller demands swift locomotion, and so things have been put in working order in advance of their completion. With High Peak rising grandly at his back, with the rush of a mountain torrent in his ears, with a stretch of richly rolling country to right and left, silent with the silence of majestic supremacy, the ticket agent of the railroad sits out-of-doors, with a little pine table before him whence he distributes tickets. And round about are the travellers: young ladies in the latest style of summer costume, young men with alpenstock and Knickerbockers, elderly people in search of health or quiet, or amusements for their younger ones—all either waiting for the mountain stages or the train down to Catskill Landing. . . .[15]

Starting at Catskill Landing, where people disembarked from the steamboats or the ferries from the Oak Hill Station of the Hudson River Railroad, the Catskill Mountain Railroad traversed the whole course of the town of Catskill and followed the old roadbed of the Catskill-Canajoharie line to the village of Leeds and the resort center of South Cairo, a distance of seven miles. Turning southwest at that point, the railroad proceeded another two miles when it encountered a junction with a four-mile spur that terminated at Cairo, a depot for such resorts as Acra, Durham, and Freehold. The main line of the Catskill Mountain Railroad continued southwest along the base of the mountains to the Mountain House Station, 520 feet above sea level, and then proceeded another few miles to the terminal station of Palenville at the base of Kaaterskill Clove, a total of sixteen miles from the Hudson River. From Palenville, vacationers could take stages up Kaaterskill Clove to Haines Falls, the Laurel House or the rail head of the Stony Clove line; and guests of the Hotel Kaaterskill could transfer to the hotel's own stages and drive up a new private road to the top of South Mountain.

The railroad thus brought to an end the old stage line that had been under the control of the Beaches since 1823, and it practically eliminated all traffic over the historic road that went from Catskill to Pine Orchard with the exception of the last few miles up Sleepy Hollow. Local traffic continued to use this old dirt road during the winter months, however, for the Catskill Mountain Railroad was a strictly seasonal operation that went into hibernation with the close of each summer.

In 1885 the railroad was reorganized and Alfred Van Santvoord, a close friend of Charles L. Beach and an official of the Hudson River Day Line (who also had interests in Beach's "Catskill-Tannersville Railroad," built in 1899), became president. Beach himself became vice-president.[16] The change reflects the difficulties that harassed the history of the railroad throughout its brief career. Unlike the Stony Clove Railroad, the Catskill Mountain Railroad could never make the transition from a narrow-gauge to a standard-gauge railroad (the Ulster and Delaware had always been that): it lacked both demand and financial wherewithal. The fact supports the contention of contemporary citizens of Catskill that the railroad was never financially solvent and that Charles L. Beach actually lost a great deal of money through it.[17] Such losses, on the other hand, were not untypical of all railroad promotion in nineteenth century America, and in Beach's case they were entailed by the fact that the railroad had come too late in the history of the Catskills to undergo the usual evolution toward amalgamation with other lines and a broader base of financing. Practically, however, it achieved its purpose, as even Beach's archenemy, George W. Harding, had to admit: "Since the railroad was opened about a week ago," he noted in the official columns of *The Kaaterskill,* "all the hotels have been benefited, and many have been full to overflowing." [18] It was a statement that could be repeated each summer for the next two decades.

The opening of the Catskill Mountain Railroad had gone a long way toward reëstablishing Catskill as the main port of entry for the Mountain House and the old resorts of Greene County: the Ulster and Delaware no longer threatened to deflect all traffic to Kingston and the inland route through Phoenicia and Stony Clove. Charles L. Beach was not the man to be satisfied with a partial triumph, and he still found ample reasons for disquietude. The Hotel Kaaterskill, for instance, took literally thousands of people from Sleepy Hollow to its own new road from Palenville to the top of South Mountain (however much their traffic increased the revenues of the Catskill Mountain Railroad). The Mountain House itself stood in a kind of no man's land between the railroads of the valley below and the railroads of the upper plateau that terminated at South Lake, thus requiring the continued use of the primitive stagecoach to its doors (an important fact when hotels began to be built within walking distance of the new railroads and people refused to patronize such a hotel as the Overlook House because it required a nine-mile stage ride). But perhaps the greatest source of Beach's disquietude, containing and symbolizing all others in its own incontrovertible image, was the great "Wall of Manitou." It still interposed a 3,000-foot barrier between Catskill and the new resorts of western Greene County and prohibited the final integration of the whole of Greene County into one unified system of transportation that could be dominated, as in ages past, by his own "hotel of hotels" on the strategic heights of Pine Orchard.[19] All these problems were solved in the construction of the Otis Elevating Railroad and a one-mile spur to South Lake.

Beach's job required the forging of a single line of railroads from the end of the Stony Clove-Kaaterskill line at South Lake to the Mountain House, and then down the "Wall of Manitou" to the Catskill Mountain Railroad. It required exactly two years to do so: 1892–1893.

When George Harding completed the Kaaterskill extension of the Stony Clove line from Hunter to South Lake in 1883, Beach's first reaction was to bridge the remaining one-mile gap to the Mountain House by means of a wagon road. This meant that Beach had to enter into negotiations with his arch-enemy, the owner of the Hotel Kaaterskill, but Beach had no choice if he were to make the Mountain House accessible to the masses of visitors who preferred to enter the Catskills by means of the Ulster and Delaware system. Nor did George Harding have any choice if he wished to encourage the clientele of the older resort to use his railroad. After a tortuous exchange of letters Harding finally permitted Beach to construct a one-mile wagon road, cleared, grubbed and graded, for the sum of $250. The advantage

Figure 48. The Laurel House Station of the Kaaterskill Railroad (later the Ulster & Delaware Railroad). Early spring, 1961. Author's photo.

Figure 49. The Otis Elevating Railroad (1892–1918). Probably a photograph by J. Loeffler. The Mountain House is barely visible against the sky.

ultimately proved to be on Beach's side of the bargain, for after the construction of the Otis Railroad Beach converted the wagon road into a railroad (1893) and thus linked his own railroad system with that of the Ulster and Delaware.[20]

The completion of Beach's railroad system thus waited upon the building of the Otis Railroad, and the ten-year delay between 1882 and 1892 is perhaps significant. Although the Otis Elevating Railroad was a triumph of mechanical engineering and soon became known as "the sensation of the Catskills"[21] when it was finally opened in 1892, there is some indication that the eighty-four-year-old Beach saw it to completion with something less than total enthusiasm. An old romantic respect for the primitivistic beauties of the mountains that he had absorbed before the years of the Civil War probably stood in the way of total acceptance. We are told by someone who knew him personally that as long as he lived "he kept the mountain forests inviolate and would not permit the cutting of a single tree on any property under his control except when absolutely necessary, regarding the despoliation of the primitive woodland as an act of vandalism." It is not surprising to learn that "to him the innovations of the incline railway up his mountain, and other changes demanded by the increasing population of the region, seemed a desecration of nature to which he never became fully reconciled." [22] In the 1880s and 1890s, however, Beach had no choice if he were to maintain the supremacy of the Mountain House, and in 1891 while visitors were still using the tortuous three-mile stage route up the precipitous curves of Sleepy Hollow, he cut a 7,000-foot gash straight up the face of North Mountain and cleared the ground for the trestles and tracks of the Otis Elevating Railroad.

The Otis Elevating was not the first such railroad in the world; Switzerland and Italy (Mount Vesuvius) each had an "incline" railway; [23] but the Beach railroad was apparently the first of its kind in America.[24] It was built by the Otis Cable Company which also built the well-known El Dorado Trucking Elevator at Weehawken as well as the later incline railways on Mount Beacon (on the lower Hudson) and on Prospect Mountain (Lake George).[25] *The* Otis Elevating, however, was this pioneer line in the Catskills, and in length, elevation, and carrying capacity it was said to exceed "any other incline railway in the world." [26] A station called "Otis Junction" connected the elevated line with the Catskill Mountain Railroad at the base of the mountains; after 1893, when Beach built the narrow gauge line from South Lake to within 300 feet of the Mountain House, another station called "Otis Summit" connected the incline railroad with the Ulster and Delaware system. A boardwalk connected the summit station with the Mountain House. The station at the base of the mountains is still standing (1963), though it is now a private home. The original gash down the mountain side is visible either from the top or bottom of the mountain and provides a vent for a modern power line. Present-day visitors may also see the foundations of the brick powerhouse and other remains of "Otis Summit."

This "remarkable piece of engineering" operated on the relatively simple principle of counterbalancing cars and cables. Two pairs of cars (with a passenger and baggage car each) started simultaneously from the top and bottom; they were attached to each end of double cables and passed each other at the halfway point on the mountain. The cars and cables were hoisted and lowered by two 100-horsepower engines that were housed on the summit of the mountain. An operator stood in a picturesque tower on the top of the engine house and was "in electric communication" with each car, controlling their various movements with the aid of three huge levers. The cars had a carrying capacity of 75 to 100 passengers and were opened on all sides "so that no part of the magnificent panorama, extending for miles and miles on every side, is lost to view." [27] They could be run every fifteen minutes if the traffic demanded it, and they rose 1,600 feet from the base of the mountains to the 2,250 foot level of the Mountain House in less than ten minutes at the cost of 75 cents per person. To nineteenth century Americans it was a miraculous way of ascending the eastern escarpment of the Catskills, and it had an extraordinary effect upon the surrounding communities of the Hudson Valley. With the completion "of this quick and easy means of access," as the *Rand, McNally Guide* noted in 1893, "large bodies of excursionists now rush up the mountain two or three times a week, dine at the hotel [at a hastily inaugurated excursionist rate of $1.00 per dinner], scramble around the park, and rush back again at night, tired and noisy, but happy." [28]

The post-Civil War revolution in the history of transportation in the Catskills was now complete. In 1822 Erastus Beach had taken a full "day of toil" to lead the first pleasure party from Catskill to Pine Orchard. [29] In 1892 Charles L. Beach could make the same journey—if it could be called that any longer—in forty to fifty minutes. [30] During the 1830s and 1840s the trip to the Mountain House by way of the improved road up Sleepy Hollow required three to four hours' stage time—or the same time that it took a person to go all the way from New York City to Pine Orchard after 1892.

The latter point is especially remarkable. From 1823 to 1850 (when the east shore railroad was first opened) people traveling from New York City to Pine Orchard could use only steamboats and stagecoaches. Day steamers from New York to Catskill Landing commonly required seven hours throughout their history (night steamers required about twice that time); the stage ride to the summit required another three to four hours. The total time between New York and Pine Orchard in the period 1823–1850 was therefore ten to eleven hours. Passengers commonly left the metropolis in the early morning and arrived at the Mountain House at dinnertime or just after dark. Between 1850 and 1882 when people could take the Hudson River Railroad to the Oak Hill (or east shore) Station of Catskill, the time from New York City was reduced by three to four hours, thus permitting people to go to Pine Orchard in about the same time as it had previously taken them to go by steamer from the metropolis to Catskill Landing.[31] From 1883 to 1892 when both the Catskill Mountain Railroad and the West Shore Railroad (up the Hudson) were in operation, people could go from the city to the summit in five and a half hours (or eight and a half by the steamers of the Day Line).[32] From 1892 until 1915 or 1916 when the Otis Elevating was in operation, people could finally go from New York City to the Mountain House in exactly the same time that it required the people of the antebellum period to go from the nearby village of Catskill. Twelve miles of stagecoach travel in 1823 had become the equivalent in time of 125 miles of railroad travel in 1892. As the Mountain House proudly announced throughout the remaining years of the century, the hotel was now "three and one-half hours from New York City."[33]

The consequences were immeasurable. The reduced time of travel restored the primacy of the original route from Catskill into the resorts of Greene County; it made daily excursions and weekend visits common occurrences; it established a record for swift and comfortable travel into the mountains that was never excelled until the middle of the twentieth century;[33] it democratized the institution of the summer vacation; and it guaranteed the continued supremacy of "the pioneer hotel of the mountains" throughout the greatest years of their history.

Chapter 11

The Flush Years of the Catskills

"In a faded letter lying before me," Lucy C. Lillie wrote in *Harper's Magazine* in 1883,

and which is dated from Greenwich Street, in New York, fifty years ago, the writer says:

"I could wish the Hudson were in better condition for my trip to Catskill. I shall be four or five days in going, but I will start well prepared for the journey."

I wonder what the anxious gentleman of that day would say were he to sit in his own library on this morning, and listen to and observe the changes in his beloved Catskill since that period of green fields and wide-spreading orchards, fine old country estates and farms that stretched down to the very water's edge? . . . A great arena of summer traffic has developed. Boats and trains are coming and going, the bustle of arrival and departure stirs all the "Point," animating the village in the way peculiar to American towns near a "resort," and the whole community to a new-comer seems to be on the alert for signs of travel. . . . One longs to leave the concentration of village life, the bustle of the wharves and station behind one, and be up and away to the hills, whose everlasting beauty is the background for this picture of activity, thrift, and speculative longing.

Twenty years earlier (c. 1860), when she had made her first trip to the Catskills, it had been altogether different. She had arrived at Catskill by way of the all-night steamer from New York and then transferred to "a large lumbering old coach":

Our driver was a man of amiable though meagre physiognomy, and he idled over his employment in a way that gave the child beside him ample opportunity to fill her eyes and heart—indeed, perhaps, to touch some glimmerings of her soul—with the majesty, the gigantic wonders, of the scene before her. High upon every side rose the mountains, their pathways cleft with gorge and ravine, their indomitable silence broken only by the rushing of their many waters, or the quiet summer wind moving through the pines. God's grace and bounty spoke through it all, in the green splendor of their height and depth, their width and vastness.

Now, however, all has changed. "Those old days have passed away. Progress has come sweeping over the country, setting much at defiance. . . ."

What would the writer of the letter before me say were he to arrive at the "Point" in Catskill on a summer's morning of 1882? Everything bespeaks not only bustle and enterprise, but the ex-

Figure 50. The Mountain House about the time of the Civil War, before the extension of the South Wing. Photograph by J. Loeffler, Tompkinsville, Staten Island, N.Y.

hilaration of something new, since the railroad has been established from the Landing up to Laurenceville, just at the mountain's foot. . . . The train rushes down into the placid loveliness of the shore where the boat lands, with little shrieks and starts and various signs of its being new to this experience, and I think it is disappointing to most people to be met with so much bustle and crudity when their destination is such an old and grand region.[1]

But the "bustle and crudity," as Lucy C. Lillie well knew, was there to stay, for the "old and grand region" had changed once and for all. As early as 1843, N. P. Willis observed that the village of Catskill had lost its rural character and become a "resort," the steamboat having given it "too easy an access to the metropolis." No place, he complained, "can be rural, in all the *virtues* of the phrase, where a steamer will take the villager to the city between noon and night, and bring him back between midnight and morning."[2] What would he have said if he had joined Lucy Lillie on the Catskill Mountain Railroad in 1882, or a decade later sped from New York to the summit of the mountains in three and a half hours and found all the Catskills a burgeoning resort of 300,000 vacationers! For the age of the railroad—from 1882 to 1915 or 1918—were the flush years of the Catskills.

This does not mean that the railroads supplied the *only* means of transportation during these fabulous years. The heyday of the resort history of the Catskills required every and all means of transportation that man had ever devised until the advent of the automobile and airplane. Saddle horses, carriages and stages of every type and description abounded at all the railroad stations and were still used for both pleasure and business in all the more inaccessible regions of the mountains. Steamboats still performed a herculean task, supplementing the work of the railroads. By the 1890s these boats had attained a maximum length of 341 feet and could accommodate more than 2,500 passengers on a single trip up the Hudson.[3] During the summer season two boats per day arrived at the congested wharves of Kingston and Catskill, one in the early morning and one in the middle of the afternoon; and both made connections with the Ulster and Delaware and Catskill Mountain Railroads.

It was these railroads, however, and the major trunk lines of the Hudson Valley that made the flush years of the Catskills a logistical possibility. As early as the 1880s six trains a day left New York City for the mountains, three on the older East Shore line and three on the West Shore. Several more arrived from Albany (and points west) and from Boston (terminating at the town of Hudson). Fifty years before only two steamboats and a small fleet of stagecoaches were needed to transport the modest number of "travellers" to and from the Mountain House and the few resorts of Greene County. By the end of the century swift trains maintained a shuttle service up both banks of the Hudson carrying thousands of excursionists and vacationers to every part of the Catskills from every part of the compass, making possible a new pattern of summer travel (where wives and children remained in the mountains for weeks and months at a time, while husbands and fathers commuted on weekends), and providing a complex range of facilities and attractions from drawing rooms and parlor cars to express trains, holiday and "husband specials," and weekly excursion rates.

There can be no doubt that the flush years of the Catskills were to a great extent a triumph of the railroads. As the Hudson River Railroad never tired of asserting during the 1890s, the few people who had once ventured to explore the recesses of the mountains on foot and horseback were now "succeeded by countless thousands of health and pleasure-seekers from far and near," and "that which was once a long journey of fatigue and discomfort is now a short ride of interest and pleasure." [4] But the railroads and the advance of technology are only a part of the story. There is no *ipso facto* connection between a new efficient mode of transportation and "thousands of health and pleasure-seekers." The last phrase refers to ends rather than means, to motives, values, and social mores that enjoy their own existence and may even be opposed to the technical or material facilities of any given epoch. The motives that took "the few" to the Catskills on foot or horseback during the early antebellum years were not the same as those that impelled the masses of the railroad epoch. The summer vacation, now taken for granted as an established custom, was an innovation of the Gilded Age that reflected the aspirations as well as technological achievements of a new secular society. The railroads made that innovation a practical possibility and even encouraged it, but they did not guarantee it: the ultimate warrant of such a new custom resided in the values and beliefs of a new urban-industrial society.

Before the advent of modern America, people never thought of going to the mountains or countryside for vacations: most people were already there! An agricultural people had no need of going "to the country" in quest of recreation and pleasure: fishing, hunting, boating, hiking, were already familiar and even necessary aspects of everyday life and did not have to be ritualized into seasonal migrations. Nor could pleasure and leisure be sought as their own ends even if everyday life permitted such a quest: a pioneer society governed morally and ethically by the Puritan restrictions of Jonathan Edwards and the utilitarian aridities of Benjamin Franklin equates pleasure and recreation with sin and wastefulness. Leisure and the graces of life can only be the fruits of an advanced stage of civilization and a highly sophisticated moral and social philosophy. America lacked those prerequisites until the advent of the nineteenth century. By the 1820s the developing wealth and sophistication of the urban centers of the Atlantic seaboard made it possible for at least the upper classes to travel for rest and recreation, and it was therefore at this time that the Catskill Mountain House first arose as a center of fashion.

This new culture was aided and abetted by the philosophical rise of romanticism and its subversion of older American beliefs and values. The aesthetic interests and values of romanticism undermined the grim utilitarianism of "Poor Richard's" Gospel of Work, and romanticism's new religion of nature undermined the Puritan conception of nature's innate depravity. Both together had the effect of encouraging one to go to nature at one's leisure and enjoy a higher mode of existence, both physically and spiritually, irrespective of the older moral and utilitarian taboos. Primitivism, the cult of the wilderness, and the glorification of natural scenery (the latter conceived as a patriotic duty) also encouraged this happy endeavor. Writers and artists led the way, luring the rich and well-born with a seductive metaphysic of art and culture. Throughout the antebellum period the promotional literature of the Mountain House confined itself to extracts from the writings of its famous visitors "for the information and amusement of the lovers of natural scenery." [5] The closest thing to an advertisement that the Mountain House permitted itself was something like Park Benjamin's concluding adjuration: "Come, then, ye multitudes of uneducated mortals, and from this great book [of nature] store your minds with deep reflections, leading to wisdom and happiness." [6] This is not the type of appeal that could attract the "multitudes" of the later Gilded Age, but it did work magic on the first generation of visitors to the Catskill Mountain House, and it was these people who prepared the way for the less philosophical masses of the later era. The idea of the summer vacation, in other words, brought the "multitudes" of the Gilded Age, but that idea was the outgrowth and legacy of the earlier romantic movement.

This in turn was not an instantaneous development; the romantic movement did not suddenly end: many of its attitudes and beliefs—an aesthetic concern for the "sublime" and "picturesque" aspects of nature, a primitivistic bias against the city and urban life—persisted into the Gilded Age and even into the twentieth century. But the romantic movement's core of metaphysical conviction vanished with the new beliefs and values of our modern urban-industrial society. Philosophically, romanticism with its glorification of the pantheistic heresy and its secular emphasis on the world of nature represented a liberalization of religious dogma. The step from theism to pantheism is significant enough; but the next step from pantheism to outright secularism which characterized the post-Civil War period brought that logical de-

velopment full cycle and completed the evolution from religion
to our modern temper of secular naturalism. The new orientation
was an indispensable feature of the Gilded Age and the "gayest
and grandest epoch of summer resort history in the Catskills."
The metaphysical and aesthetic orientation of the previous period was necessarily restrictive and selective, geared to talent and
fashion and exactly attuned to the scenic primitivism of the undeveloped Catskills. But the arrival of the postwar masses was
dependent upon the extended development of modern technological facilities throughout the mountains and the emergence of
a common philosophy of unsophisticated hedonism. The former
plea of the romantics—to go to the mountains to find "deep reflections, leading to wisdom and happiness"—now yielded to an
appeal that defied no one's comprehension and applied equally
to all segments of the population—go in quest of "health and
pleasure."

The new secular dispensation did not arise without a struggle.
The long arm of Puritan asceticism and deep-rooted habits of
utilitarian necessity still contended for the American conscience.
The summer vacation came more and more into being, but it
was preceded and accompanied by an elaborate literature of apol-
ogy that still had to neutralize Puritan prejudice by appealing
to the new shibboleth of science. "There is a science of summer
rest," the Ulster and Delaware Railroad informed its patrons in
its annual publications, "and the sooner this fact is realized and
reckoned with the better it will be for those who live in the
temperate zones." [7] Then followed several pages of psychological,
biological, clinical, and medical reasons why an annual vacation—
especially in the higher altitudes of the Catskill Mountains—is
a scientific necessity. The elaborate argument, we need not add,
encountered a most receptive audience and exerted a profound
influence. By the turn of the century the summer vacation had
achieved the following status:

The Summer vacation is no longer a fad, but a necessity; no
longer a mere luxury for the rich, but an inestimable reality for
the poor. No man or woman will care to contradict these state-

ments in these opening years of the new century. From every point of view they will be freely conceded. To ignore the fact is madness that can be indulged in only at the peril of the transgressor. If such a vacation a hundred, or even fifty years ago, was less important or imperative to the people of that period, it was because of the different conditions in social and business life that prevailed in those days of moderation and comparative composure. No such tension of human existence, no such hustling competition, nor any of the hot conflicts that now dominate the efforts of men and women in every walk of life were even dreamed of in the days of our ancestors. Nor is the average man or woman of to-day more liberally endowed with strength and resistance than at that time. Neither in brain nor physique do we find any material change in normal conditions. We must, therefore, meet the exigency of the situation by the conservation of forces. There must be a time for rest and relaxation, complete and unreserved; a period in which to regain and build up lost energy and vital force. This is the sanitary aspect of the vacation on its practical and serious side. Natural laws cannot be set aside with impunity.

But there is also another phase, and it pertains more directly to the aesthetic side of our nature. We need change, and cannot live on monotony or systematic routine. Every one of the five senses needs a new diet and a change of regime. This cannot be had in the atmosphere or horizon of the town home, even with an entire cessation of work and business. All must be changed— the air, the scenery, the environment, the room, the food, the people we meet, the sounds we hear; all these must be different, to make the rest complete and secure the benefits desired. These things we have learned during recent years in the ethics of a Summer vacation which are being studied by careful observers and scientists.[8]

It is noticeable that even when introducing the "aesthetic" reasons for a vacation, the argument is still utilitarian and clinical. During the romantic era aesthetic motives were either considered their own end or the corollaries of moral and metaphysical principles.

The muted reference to the "tension" of urban life in the above passage usually gained a fuller expression in the literature of the period and provided one of the strongest arguments for the necessity of a vacation. "A breath of Nature, uncontaminated by the

dregs of city civilization is the unfailing panacea" for lost strength
and vitality, according to the Ulster and Delaware Railroad:

> We must run away from bricks and mortar, the noise and dirt
> of the town and all its pleasure as well for a time, and go out
> among the hills and rocks, the green trees and fields, the waving
> meadows and orchards, the wild flowers and the filmy ferns, and
> bathe in the fresh air and pure sunshine of the country. . . . In
> the quiet of the grand cathedral of its Maker, even the soul forgets
> the battles, the downfalls, the cuts and scars of life's great contest
> and becomes something purer, stronger and more worthy of its
> origin.[9]

With this theme we are back in old familiar territory, for the
argument against the city is a legacy of the primitivistic bias of
the earliest romantics. When about 1833 Asher B. Durand wrote
to his friend Thomas Cole in the Catskills complaining about
periodic depression and loss of vitality, Cole replied: "You must
come to live in the country. Nature is a sovereign remedy. Your
expression is the result of debility; you require the pure air of
heaven." Art, health, spirits—everything would be served, Cole
concluded, if Durand "could consistently leave the city." [10]
Charles Rockwell's poem, "The Catskill Mountain House," is also
full of this primitivistic bias ("There it stands, to bless the pil-
grim / From the city's heated homes, / Worn and weary with
life's contest, / To this mountain height he comes.").[11] To Rockwell, Cole, and most romantics the city was not only unhealthy,
it was immoral and unnatural—i.e. contrary to God's "natural"
order of life.

The high metaphysical viewpoint of the romantics thus persisted into the age of secularism. It lingered, however, at the cost
of vitality and conviction. There is something fatuous about a
railroad tycoon singing the praises of "waving meadows and orchards," and the phrase itself betrays its own lack of conviction.
The real belief of the age is best seen in a simple statement of
secular purpose. Such is the following: "To the dweller in a great
city, weary of work and worn with the tumult of life, there are
few places in the whole range of American scenery so attractive

and refreshing as the Catskill Mountains." [12] The phrase, "in the whole range of American scenery," covers a great deal of territory; but we must remember that even in the second half of the nineteenth century most of the mountainous areas of the country were still *terra incognita* to the average American, and only the Catskills were immediately accessible to the centers of population. It is this fact that even lends credence to the following extravaganza: "It seems as if the gods, in their inscrutable wisdom, had ordained that this great city [of New York] should grow up in the vicinity of the Catskills, that it might have within easy reach, a place of recreation unsurpassed in the splendor of its scenery." [13] It is this accessibility of the Catskills to the masses of the urban seaports that made these mountains the playground of the nation during the Gilded Age.

Although much of the literature on the health-restoring properties of the Catskills was manifestly propagandistic, designed above all to circumvent the antihedonistic prejudices of an older American morality, a good deal of it was based on fact. The debilitating effect of the city, especially during the summer months,

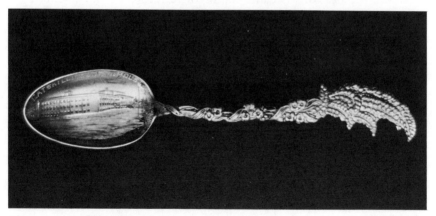

Figure 51. A Mountain House souvenir spoon of the 1890s (approximately actual size). Another such spoon made by J. T. Henderson, Catskill, N.Y., and considered to be one of the "handsomest" and "heaviest" spoons of the period, is reproduced in *Souvenir Spoons of America* (New York, The Jeweler's Circular Publishing Company, 1891), p. 45.

was a harsh reality to the urban population of the Gilded Age. As early as 1838, N. P. Willis discovered that there is "no place so agreeable as Catskill, after one has been parboiled in the city." Willis was talking about New York City when he made that statement, but he might just as well have been talking about Philadelphia, Baltimore, Boston, or any other city of the Eastern coast. The American summer is generically oppressive in any part of the country, but in the great ports and harbors of the Atlantic seaboard where water condensation provides a high degree of humidity, it is apt to be intolerable. Year after year the Mountain House claimed without exaggeration that "the temperature is always 15 to 20 Degrees Lower than at Catskill village, New York City or Philadelphia." The change is indeed remarkable and may be accounted for in terms of the very physiography of the mountains. Composed of high compact mountain peaks and a rich profusion of deep cloves and shady valleys, the mountains are a natural hygroscopic laboratory converting the hot moisture of the day into the cool air of the night. Liberally endowed with refreshing streams and rivulets, devoid of humidity, and requiring extra sleeping blankets during the hottest summer season, the Catskills became the favorite refuge of the sweltering masses of the East.

Relief from the enervating heat of the city, however, was only one aspect of this mass movement to the mountains; the American summer during any year of the late nineteenth century had other terrors. Year after year from 1824 until well into the twentieth century the annual brochures of the Mountain House never failed to inform the public that "the atmosphere is delightful, invigorating and pure, the great elevation and surrounding forests rendering it *absolutely free from Malaria*," and that any visit to the Catskills "affords relief to sufferers from Chills and Fever, Asthma, Hay Fever, Loss of Appetite and General Debility." [14] Such exalted claims remind us of the picturesque labels on old patent medicine bottles, and we strongly suspect they warrant the same lack of serious consideration. But they were anything but frivolous to the long-suffering nineteenth century, and they allude

—especially in the italicized words—to a grim reality that had a profound influence on the post-Civil War history of the Catskill Mountains.

From the seventeenth century until the early years of the present century, malaria and its related pestilence, yellow fever, were the twin horrors of the American summer. Originating in the West Indies and Africa, they were imported into North America with the Negro slave and became such an endemic part of American life that they soon came to be called "the American plague." [15] Typically tropical diseases, they created the greatest havoc in the alluvial and coastal plain seaports of the eastern seaboard from New York to New Orleans. One such epidemic struck Philadelphia in 1793 and was so severe that some historians say it "doomed the supremacy of Philadelphia among American cities." [16] But no area was immune: yellow fever was known to penetrate into western New York State, central Pennsylvania and southeastern Ohio,[17] and malaria extended its depredations as far north as Wisconsin.[18]

These classic horrors of the American summer were augmented during specific periods of the nineteenth century by a new deadly disease with world-wide ramifications, the dreaded cholera. Originating for the most part in India and the Far East and thriving on the filth and squalor of nineteenth century seaports, cholera followed the waterways of the world and struck six disastrous blows in five successive decades. The first epidemic originated in India, passed on to Russia, ravaged Great Britain, and arrived in America by way of Canada in the spring of 1832, creating at Bellevue Hospital in New York City, for instance, what has been called "one of the main horrors of American medicine." [19] This was the year, and very season, that Washington Irving first visited the Catskill Mountain House. The epidemic was in full swing, "extending about the country, and spreading great alarm," according to his brother Pierre, "so that the whole course of business, as well as pleasure, was interrupted." Many of the towns through which Irving passed were "in the first stage of panic and outbreak." This was fortunately still not the case in Catskill (and never was at the Mountain House), and Irving determined to complete his tour of Pine Orchard.[20]

The second major outbreak of cholera started in India and China in 1841, spread to Europe in 1847, and reached America by way of several vessels from France in 1848. New York was able to quarantine the disease, but it escaped out of New Orleans, went up the Mississippi Valley and thence spread throughout the country. It arrived at the village of Catskill in the summer of 1849.

A third outbreak in 1850 again originated in the Orient, entered Europe in 1853, and reached America the following year by way of immigrant ships that found "the door open in a less vigilant New York."[21] The epidemic was unusually severe, both throughout North and South America. In the village of Catskill during the summer of 1854 it created an unforgettable nightmare. The disease coincided with a torrid season of drought and forest fires and struck down 300 people. "Men were walking the street and a few hours later were dead." Panic gripped the town and a great many people, including, it was said, ministers and doctors, fled into the mountains and were safe.[22] Fortunately, this worst of cholera epidemics was also the last: although three more epidemics reached America in 1866, 1867, and 1873, they were relatively mild, and there is no indication that the village of Catskill suffered any further from this great scourge of the nineteenth century.

Yellow fever and malaria remained an implicit threat throughout the century, the latter, for instance, being especially prevalent along the whole coast of Long Island during the 1890s.[23] Speculation about the causes of these diseases can only be described as medieval. As late as 1887 a presumed authority on malariology ridiculed the notion that the lowly bite of the mosquito could have anything to do with such malevolent diseases, and held instead that they were caused by the phases of the moon or perhaps electricity.[24] It was not until 1898–1899 that Ross and Grassi discovered that malaria is transmitted by the *Anopheles* mosquito, and it was not until the early 1900s that W. C. Gorgas proved in Panama that the disease could be totally eradicated.

What *was* known, however, was where the disease did *not* occur, and also what general geographic and climatic conditions favored its absence. It was known to be a tropical disease that favored hot, swampy, low-lying areas and that its incidence diminished with altitude and a cooler, more temperate climate. Cholera was also known to favor "low-lying places on alluvial soil near rivers" and to diminish with altitude and on land "standing high or on a rocky foundation." [25] Much was made in the second half of the nineteenth century of "the hygienic importance" of altitude and the therapeutic necessity of spending as much time as possible during the summer in the mountains.[26] While much of this opinion was intuitive rather than scientific and mistook secondary for primary causes, it *was* consistent with the fact that the Catskills were *"absolutely free from Malaria."* The advice given to James Silk Buckingham when this distinguished English parliamentarian contracted malaria in New York City in 1838 was well taken—"embark at once upon the Hudson river, and go straight to the village of Catskill, without halting at any intermediary point, but on landing there . . . ascend the mountains and pass a night or two at the Mountain House the elevation of which secures a cool and bracing atmosphere, while all the lower parts of the country are steeped in sultry heat." [27]

In time science would discover the validity of that popular prescription. We have learned in the twentieth century, for instance, that the Anopheles mosquito cannot thrive where there are few people or cattle (for it feeds on blood), that it rarely appears at an elevation more than two to three thousand feet above sea level, that it requires an absence of bright sunshine (injurious to the mosquito's breeding) and wind (which breaks its horizontal flight), and that extensive areas of low-lying swamps (its natural breeding ground) are almost a necessity. All these conditions account for the relative security of the Catskill Mountains during the pestilential years of the nineteenth century. If people misapprehended the causes of that security, they were fully aware to the point of idolatry of its effect. With a wisdom that exceeded knowledge they believed that "the best summer resort for the average dweller of the cities and plains in every hygienic aspect of the case, is the higher altitudes, the mountainous regions of the country." [28]

The quest for health and the need to escape the pestilential conditions of nineteenth century cities thus exerted a profound influence on the rise of the Catskills as "the nation's playground." The movement began as early as the mid-1820s when, as Basil Hall noted, "during the hot season of the year—when the greater part of the United States becomes unhealthy, or otherwise disagreeable as a residence, even to the most acclimated natives, as the local expression is—the inhabitants repair to the North. . . ." [29] But it was during the Gilded Age when more than one out of every ten Americans were living in cities of 25,000 or more inhabitants that the quest for safety and comfort during the pestilential weeks of the summer season became a mass movement helping to actualize the institution of the summer vacation and the greatest era in the history of the Catskills. By the 1890s it could truly be said:

To-day the Catskills are among the most popular of all the health-giving and pleasure-resorts in this broad land. Not alone do the dwellers in cities within easy access of them make them the Mecca of their summer pilgrimage, but even from the far-off West and distant North people go there to rest and drink in new vitality with every breath.[30]

These, then, were the flush years of the Catskills. In the last two decades of the nineteenth century "when the Catskills were about the only mountain country available for the fortnight vacation," [31] the invasion of vacationers from the metropolitan centers of the East as well as "the far-off West and the distant North" kept the mountains in a constant turmoil of construction and expansion. Demand chronically exceeded supply. Lionel De Lisser noted in 1894 that "the popularity of the Catskill mountains as a summer resort has increased so rapidly of late years, that the accommodations of the boardinghouses have been severely taxed and the securing of comfortable quarters for the summer, in this region, has become a serious question." [32] The building of the large private parks in the vicinity of Kaaterskill Clove was one reply to this chronic shortage. The super-hotels of the 1880s were another obvious answer to the same burgeoning demand for accommodations. Equally important, however, was the conversion of farms into boardinghouses. The discrepancy between the easy profits of the hotel business and the marginal returns of agriculture was not lost upon the natives of the Catskills. Farmhouses that were located some distance from established resort centers, towns, and villages, according to a first-hand report of 1909, "were apt to look neglected and often were vacant." Those that were closer to the popular cloves and railroads and "had been transformed into summer hotels and boardinghouses" looked exceedingly prosperous. [33] For many vacationers who could not afford the luxury of the larger hotels and were sentimental about the American past, the reconverted farmhouses allowed them to enjoy an illusion of rural existence without facing its stark hardships. Farmhouses that could accommodate ten to twenty-five paying guests were a ubiquitous feature of the Catskill landscape at the turn of the century. Agriculture and farming decayed, thousands of acres that had been cleared for grazing and crop cultivation began to revert to second-growth hardwood, creating in the end a landscape that is far more wooded and wild today than it was at the beginning of the process seventy-five years ago; but the Catskills prospered as they had never before or since. In 1905 there were at least 900 hotels, farmhouses, and boardinghouses within reach of the Ulster and Delaware Railroad alone, affording accommodations for something like 25,000 guests at one time. [34] If we add to these figures the many more thousands who patronized the older resorts of Greene County, we may accept without question an estimated total of 300,000 annual visitors to the Catskills during these great years of the late nineteenth century. It was a time of high fulfillment in the history of the mountains, a time when the Catskill Mountain House, as we shall now see, became "one of the greatest hotels of the country." [35]

Chapter 12

"One of the Greatest Hotels of the Country"

Each year more rooms were added to satisfy the demands of the growing clientele from all over the world.

—CHARLES L. BEACH

I

"A massive and elegant structure of wood."

As late as 1878 when the Mountain House opened for its fiftieth season it could say, as it had always said from the time it first appeared on the edge of the mountains, that it was the "largest and leading hotel of the Catskill region, and the only first-class house on the mountains."[1] The post-Civil War boom in the history of the Catskills was in full swing, for it had begun right after the conclusion of the war, and it gained increased momentum as the summer vacation became a common practice of the new urban-industrial classes of the victorious North.[2] New hotels and boardinghouses kept pace with the boom, and by the late 1870s it was already apparent that the long monopoly of the Mountain House had come to an end and that many new hotels competed with what was constantly described as "the *Father* of these summer resorts in entertaining the increasing flow of visitors to this delightful region."[3] Most of these establishments were very modest in scale, the vast majority accommodating only twenty to one hundred guests. By 1879 the statement that the

258

Figure 52. *On the Road from Kaaterskill Hotel*, E. Heinemann, 1884. From the engraving in A. E. P. Searing, *The Land of Rip Van Winkle* (New York, 1884), p. 35.

Figure 53. Colonnade of the Mountain House. From a photograph in *Catskill Mountain House*, an undated brochure published by the hotel during the management of John K. Van Wagonen in the 1920s, p. 2.

Figure 54. The piazza of the Mountain House. From a photograph in *Catskill Mountain House* (undated brochure), p. 8.

Mountain House was the "only first-class house in the mountains" was becoming somewhat apocryphal, for both the Mt. Tremper House at Phoenicia and the Overlook House at Woodstock were already in existence and both were "first-class" hotels by any standard of the age. Both of them together, however, could not match the size of the Mountain House, and in every other respect—fame, history, grandeur of setting, diversity of facilities, range of economic interests—the Mountain House was still the "largest and leading hotel of the Catskill region."

It was the following decade that first effectively challenged that claim. By 1883, as a publication of the West Shore and Buffalo Railroad asserted, there were "four great hotels" in the Catskills: the Prospect Park (400 guests), the Grand Hotel at Pine Hill (450), the Kaaterskill (800) and the Mountain House (400).[4] Since the Prospect Park was located in the town of Catskill on the banks of the Hudson it offered very little challenge to the large mountain resorts. But both the Grand Hotel and the Kaaterskill were erected with greater technological knowledge and financial resources than the original Mountain House, and in respect to size and elegance of appointment the pioneer hotel had finally been "somewhat eclipsed," as the Rand McNally *Guide* declared. Yet as the *Guide* also admitted, the "flourishing" Mountain House was still "the best known," and not even the elaborate but short-lived Kaaterskill (1881–1924) could rob the Mountain House of its preëminent position as the most historic hotel in all the Catskills.[5] Although the Kaaterskill was designed to outstrip the pioneer hotel, it actually had the opposite effect of promoting the resort business of the whole area, including the Mountain House's; and the two hotels enjoyed an equal share of the most glamorous and select clientele of resort society.

To help maintain its position through so many years of resort history, the Mountain House was periodically enlarged and renovated "as business increased." The hotel also had to be periodically modernized to keep abreast of technological developments. Because of its humble beginnings and piecemeal evolution (10 rooms in 1824 to more than 300 in the 1880s), the hotel acquired its own indigenous charm and character. Advantages, however, are always counterbalanced by disadvantages, and by the time the hotel achieved its final form (probably by 1880, in the light of our scanty evidence), it possessed one or two generic features that placed it at a distinct disadvantage vis-à-vis the towering Kaaterskill or the cavernous Grand Hotel. The Mountain House had become a victim of what was ordinarily one of its chief assets, its great age. Each successive renovation retained the imprint of the hotel's first humble beginnings, and as room was added to room, wing to wing, there was less and less structural possibility of emulating the high vaulting halls and lounges, the baronial dining rooms and soaring ballrooms that came to characterize the new extravagant colossi of the Gilded Age. The Mountain House became an impressive maze of multitudinous rooms and corridors, of unexpected nooks and corners, of sudden en-

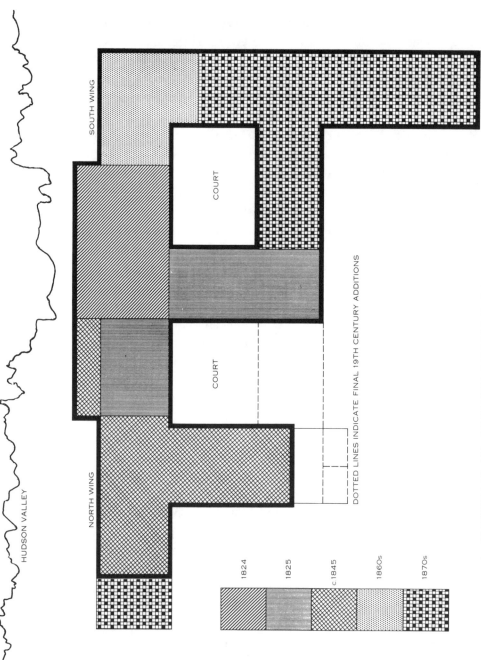

HUDSON VALLEY

NORTH WING

SOUTH WING

COURT

COURT

DOTTED LINES INDICATE FINAL 19TH CENTURY ADDITIONS

1824

1825

c. 1845

1860s

1870s

A. SKETCH PLAN, GROWTH OF THE CATSKILL MOUNTAIN HOUSE

PREPARED BY THE AUTHOR FROM ROUGH PLANS DRAWN BY CLAUDE MOSEMAN IN THE 1940s

trances upon outside courts and annexes; but it lacked for this very reason a modern note of internal capaciousness.

This was especially noticeable in the main entrance and lobby of the hotel, neither of which seemed to have been commensurate with the over-all grandeur of the building. The entrance was narrow and admitted upon an enclosed porch with a low ceiling. The lobby also had a low ceiling, perhaps ten feet high, certainly not more than twelve feet; and it could only have been about thirty feet wide—a small area for handling the four to five hundred guests (not to mention staff) that the hotel eventually accommodated. George William Curtis noted as early as 1852 that the main lobby or "parlor" of the hotel "seemed to have been dislocated by some tempestuous mountain ague . . .

There are eight windows, and none of them opposite to any of the others: folding-doors which have gone down the side of the room in some wild architectural dance, and have never returned, and a row of small columns stretching in an independent line across the room, quite irrespective of the middle. It is a dangerous parlor for a nervous man.[6]

A card room (perhaps 23′ x 15′) and a telephone room (c. 12′ x 12′) were placed off the right side of the lobby, and the combined width of these rooms plus the lobby was forty feet—or, in other words, the total width of the original centralmost part of the hotel that had been built in 1825. Since a ballroom was constructed on the floor above this (40′ x 65′ with a twelve-foot ceiling), and the next or third floor was used for bedrooms, the ceiling of the lobby could never be raised without demolishing and rebuilding the whole wing. The narrow width of the lobby was also assured by the presence of two open courts that flanked each side of the wing. As the hotel grew in size, these courts evolved from outer to inner courts and were surrounded by the great north and south wings of the hotel, so providing a necessary source of light for all the "inside" rooms of the building and prohibiting any expansion of the lobby into these available spaces. In this manner first steps bind second steps, and the advantages of

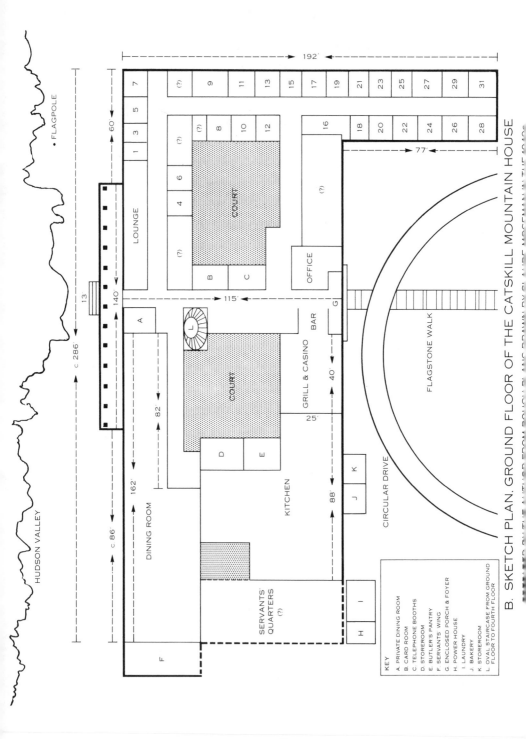

B. SKETCH PLAN. GROUND FLOOR OF THE CATSKILL MOUNTAIN HOUSE

KEY
A PRIVATE DINING ROOM
B CARD ROOM
C TELEPHONE BOOTHS
D STOREROOM
E BUTLER'S PANTRY
F SERVANTS' WING
G ENCLOSED PORCH & FOYER
H POWER HOUSE
I LAUNDRY
J BAKERY
K STOREROOM
L OVAL STAIRCASE FROM GROUND
  FLOOR TO FOURTH FLOOR

one period become the insurmountable obstacles of a second period.

The same problem reappeared in the size and location of the main staircase. The original staircase of the Mountain House arose near the rear north corner of the small ten-room structure of 1824. The substantial addition of 1825 retained this staircase and enveloped it on its northern and southern sides, making it impossible to change the staircase during all the subsequent additions to the hotel. In the end the Mountain House contained two elevators; [7] but the original small spiraling staircase of 1824 remained unaltered even after the Mountain House had become one of the largest and most impressive buildings of the Hudson Valley.

The hallways and bedrooms of the Mountain House also remained proportionately small during all later additions. The main 168' hallway of the second floor, for instance, was 5'6" wide; its 52' extension into the north wing was only 4' wide. Corridors throughout the hotel varied between these two dimensions. Bedrooms ranged in size from the smallest ones on the fourth floor (two 9 x 10 and two 7 x 10) to the choice corner rooms on each floor of the southeastern corner of the hotel (15 x 15). [8] The Mountain House also appears to have had few suites or luxury apartments. The dormitory style of the earliest house of 1824 left a structural imprint upon later additions, creating an aspect of cellular uniformity throughout the sleeping quarters of the finished hotel. Before the Civil War the bedrooms of the Mountain House were said to be "of a better size, and more comfortably furnished, than the sleeping-rooms usually appropriated to travelers at the fashionable watering-places;" [9] but after the Civil War when the new huge hotels were under construction, the same bedrooms must have appeared inadequate.

Expansion of the hotel began in 1825 when two wings (containing fifty rooms) were added to the northern and southern sides of the original building. The ground floor of the northern wing probably absorbed a previous shedlike attachment that housed the kitchen and dining room, establishing a pattern that

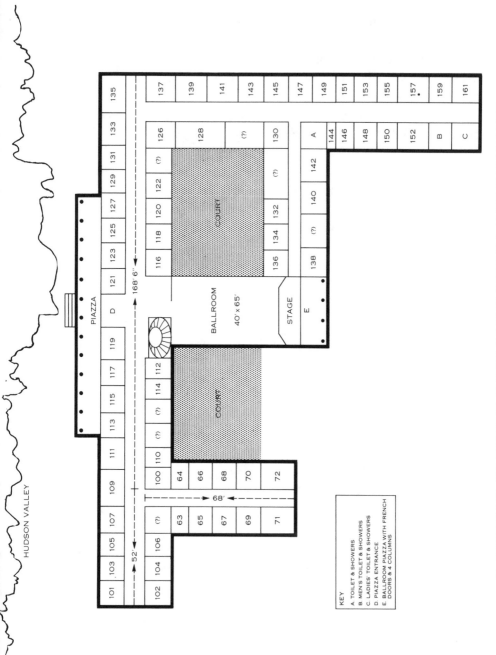

HUDSON VALLEY

PIAZZA

168' 6"

52'

68'

BALLROOM
40' × 65'

COURT

COURT

STAGE

KEY

A. TOILET & SHOWERS
B. MEN'S TOILET & SHOWERS
C. LADIES' TOILET & SHOWERS
D. PIAZZA ENTRANCE
E. BALLROOM PIAZZA WITH FRENCH
   DOORS & 4 COLUMNS

C. SKETCH PLAN, SECOND FLOOR OF THE CATSKILL MOUNTAIN HOUSE

PREPARED BY THE AUTHOR FROM ROUGH PLANS DRAWN BY CLAUDE MOSEMAN IN THE 1940s

was to be maintained in all subsequent enlargements of this part of the building. The second major expansion occurred some time between 1839 and 1845 when Charles L. Beach first leased and then bought the hotel. By 1844 the new north wing of 1825 was enlarged on its Hudson River side so that it formed one continuous front (and a 140-foot piazza) with the older building, and a new north wing was added in the shape of a "T," at least 50 x 130 feet. In another year or so, Beach also ripped off the Federalist appurtenances of the original house (the peak of which was no longer over the center of the new 140-foot piazza), built a new fourth floor, added a classical portico and the famous thirteen Corinthian columns. With the addition of the new north wing the former outside wall of the old wing was broken through and the dining room extended through the length of the new wing, forming what was called a room "large enough for a feudal banqueting hall" and containing "a range of pillars for the whole length down the center." [10] In time this great room reached a length of 162 feet and could seat four to five hundred people at a single sitting. It introduced a note of spaciousness which together with the beautifully shaped ballroom was rather exceptional to the Mountain House. The expansion of the dining room was accompanied by a proportionate expansion of the main kitchen of the Mountain House. When this truly "baronial" kitchen finally stopped growing, it contained almost as much cubic space as the dining room and occupied eighty-eight lineal feet of the rear wall of the Mountain House. So the north wing became the "business end" of the hotel, and it finally terminated in a maze of ancillary sheds and outbuildings that provided facilities for a cooler and ice house, a laundry, a powerhouse, and a bakery.

While the northern side of the Mountain House continued to expand during the antebellum period, providing facilities for new servants' quarters as well as the increasing culinary needs and utilities of the all but self-sufficient establishment, the southern side apparently remained unchanged until about the time of the Civil War when a small wing was first added to the southeastern corner of the hotel. The best picture of the new addition is a

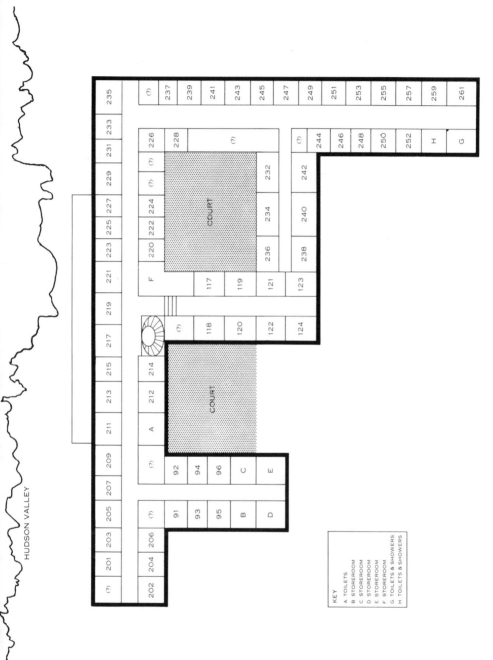

HUDSON VALLEY

KEY

A TOILETS
B STOREROOM
C STOREROOM
D STOREROOM
E STOREROOM
F STOREROOM
G TOILETS & SHOWERS
H TOILETS & SHOWERS

D. SKETCH PLAN. THIRD FLOOR OF THE CATSKILL MOUNTAIN HOUSE:

PREPARED BY THE AUTHOR FROM ROUGH PLANS DRAWN BY CLAUDE MOSEMAN IN THE 1940s

photograph by J. Loeffler and Co., the firm that always made the stereoscopic views of the Mountain House [Figure 50]. As this picture shows, the three-story wing was skillfully integrated with the older part of the house and extended sixty feet from the piazza to the new southeastern corner of the building, and then about another sixty feet toward the rear (or southwestern corner). Several doors permitted access from the ground floor to the nearby cliffs and paths of South Mountain. The corner rooms of this new wing were some of the largest in the hotel and doubtless some of the most expensive.

By 1879 this wing was extended another 132 feet, making a grand total of 192 feet from the piazza to the rear of the hotel.[11] The remarkable addition was undoubtedly a reflection of the burgeoning demand of the great flush years of the Catskills. The new wing was used exclusively for patrons and guests of the hotel, and was kept isolated from the "business end" of the hotel on the other side of the circular drive. Architecturally, it conferred something of a deception upon the Mountain House. When viewed from the vicinity of the flagpole or the great boulder that still stands on the edge of the cliff on the southeastern corner of the lawn, the wing emphasized the classical cubical lines of the Mountain House and concealed the horseshoe-shaped indentation formed in the rear by the two obtruding wings. Viewed from this angle alone, therefore, the Mountain House looked like a "massive and elegant structure of wood"[12] boldly confronting a sixty-mile sweep of the Hudson Valley with the classic composure of a Greek temple.

With the completion of the south wing the Mountain House achieved its final shape and form with the exception of two extensions that united both the north and south wings to the rear of the old building at its main entrance. The extension uniting the south wing with the old building was probably completed concurrently with the south wing or shortly thereafter. The new addition sealed off the exposed side of the southern court and converted it into a four-sided inner courtyard. The same conversion was repeated on the north side of the house when a forty-

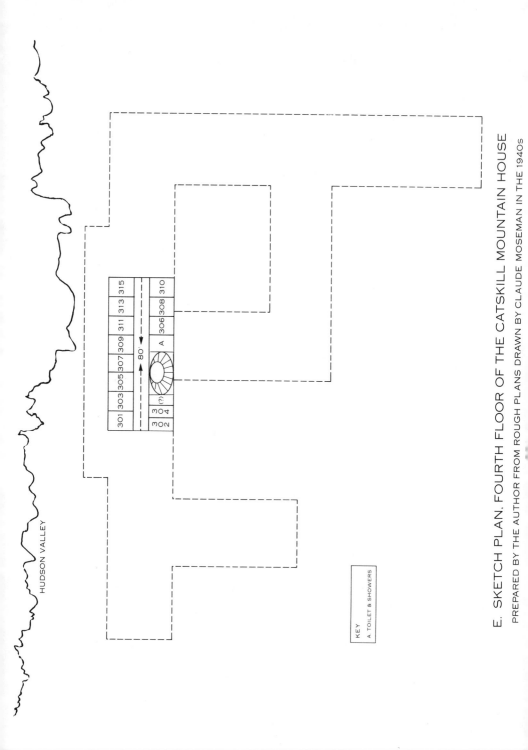

HUDSON VALLEY

301 | 303 | 305 | 307 | 309 | 311 | 313 | 315

← 80 →

302 | 304 | 306 | 308 | 310 | 312 | 314 | 316

A

300(?)

A

306 308 310

302
304

KEY

A TOILET & SHOWERS

E. SKETCH PLAN. FOURTH FLOOR OF THE CATSKILL MOUNTAIN HOUSE

PREPARED BY THE AUTHOR FROM ROUGH PLANS DRAWN BY CLAUDE MOSEMAN IN THE 1940s

foot extension united the kitchen wing and the main entrance of the hotel. Both courts were now completely "enclosed" and therefore totally invisible from any exterior point of view.

Although the Mountain House still had more than half a century of active life ahead of it and minor changes continued to be made around the edges of the dynamic north wing (as well as inside the hotel where constant "improvements" had to be made), the long history of this "large and irregular building . . . built in different parts at different times" [13] apparently came to an end with the major additions of the late 1870s. The greatest number of people the hotel could ever accommodate was about five hundred, a figure that was quoted by a publication of the New York Central Railroad in the year 1908.[14] A statement made by Lucy C. Lillie in 1883, that the hotel could accommodate "very comfortably eleven hundred souls," is clearly misleading unless it is meant to include servants as well as guests.[15] The Mountain House itself boasted that it had one employee for every guest; if so, its total accommodations might reach Mrs. Lillie's figure of 1,100 people. In the light of the three hundred-odd rooms of the hotel, however, this seems doubtful. What appears most likely is that the figure which was most constantly quoted in the late nineteenth century—400 paying guests—is the reliable one. But this figure first began to appear in the timetables, brochures, etc., of the period from the year 1879, or, in other words, from the time the great south wing was completed.[16] This evidence is therefore consistent with all the pictorial evidence we have that the Mountain House attained its full and final form not later than the year 1880.

II
"All the Comforts and Luxuries"

The evidence of the period also shows that the Mountain House reached a pinnacle of material splendor. The hotel always maintained that it had "all the comforts and luxuries of the best hotels in our large Cities," but during the post-Civil War period

Figure 55. *Rear View of the Mountain House*, Walter Launt Palmer, August 9, 1883 (watercolor, 6¾″ x 13¾″). Collection of Norman S. Rice, Albany, N.Y.

this boast could only be fulfilled at the expense of major techno-logical improvements and the complete modernization of the hotel. In 1873, for instance, Charles Rockwell noted that "a recent effort of the well-directed enterprise and wealth of Mr. Beach" was the installation of telegraphic service between the Mountain House and "other lines throughout the land." [17] The techno-logical marvel permitted patrons to make instantaneous reserva-tions from almost every part of the Union and required the erection of twelve miles of telegraph poles all the way from the village of Catskill. [18] The Mountain House continued to main-tain its own Post Office within the hotel—for letter-writing was then as now an indispensable feature of resort life—but much of its ordinary business was now conducted by telegraph (an ad-vantage that was not ignored by the hotel's publicity agents).

The coming of electricity was another notable triumph of the period. Year after year while such established hotels as the Laurel House continued to be "lighted throughout with gas," the Moun-tain House proudly informed its public that "the hotel is lighted throughout by electric lights." [19] Besides providing such services as "call and return call bells" throughout the hotel, electricity turned the Mountain House into one of the gayest and most brilliantly lit buildings in all the Catskills. To the people who had been brought up on gas illumination and could even remember the days when kerosene and candles provided the main source of flickering light, the sudden apparition of the Mountain House, vividly illuminated on the dark crest of the mountain, was a sight never to be forgotten. "Here on the very summit of the highest mountain peak," the astonished Lucy C. Lillie exclaimed in 1882 after arriving at the hotel just after dark,

we come upon a great lawn and terrace illumined by electric light, a hotel all doors and windows and vivid animation. A band is playing; there is a vista of a long room with whirling figures, while everything round and about is suggestive of youth and brilliancy, fashion and luxury. What a surprising change is this! [20]

The Mountain House devised all kinds of ingenious distractions with the new means of illumination. One of these required

Figure 56. Rear view of the Mountain House, as it had evolved by c. 1910. From a photograph in *Catskill Mountain House* (undated brochure), p. 7, captioned "Casino and Tennis Courts."

the inauguration of an evening ritual involving the use of a gigantic carbon searchlight. As the annual advertisements of the Mountain House said, "A Powerful Searchlight, on the east front, will be operated from 9 to 11 P.M., reflecting its light over twelve thousand square miles of the Hudson River Valley." [21] What actually happened was that at the appointed hours the guests assembled on the ledges of the Mountain House and watched the gigantic searchlight probe the dark recesses of the Hudson Valley as it tried to intercept the passing steamships of the Hudson Night Line. Every now and then a cheer from the guests would announce another capture as one of these great vessels—the *Berkshire*, the *Trojan*, the *Rensselaer*, and even the freighters, *Poughkeepsie* and *Benjamin B. Odell*—flicked its lights by way of surrender to the great light of Pine Orchard. [22]

Another exciting technological triumph of the period was the installation of telephone service. The telephone had come to the village of Catskill in 1881, [23] and the enterprising Mr. Beach soon extended its service to the great white edifice on the top of the mountain. It was another "first" for the Catskill Mountain House and it was attended by initial rites and ceremonies that were talked about for years in the resorts of the Catskills. Attending the opening ceremonies, presiding and officiating and all but deifying the glamorous event, was none other than the inventor himself, Alexander Graham Bell. Accompanied by his wife and a group of enthralled visitors, the inventor was led by Charles L. Beach to the main office of the hotel on the south side of the lobby where a direct line had been established between the first bulky telephone of the Mountain House and a similar apparatus in the village of Catskill. After the first magical words had been transmitted to the far banks of the Hudson, a popular concert artist of the day consecrated the occasion by singing "Nearer, My God, to Thee," and then the assembled guests formed a line into the inner office and took turns speaking into the miraculous instrument. [24] Telephone service never became extensive in the Mountain House (we find no advertisements saying "telephone service in every room"), but in time public telephone booths were installed in a specially designed room off the south side of the lobby, and the Mountain House henceforth announced that it had a "Long Distance Telephone."

Services and facilities of every type and description were added to the normal resources of the Mountain House during this period as it strove to maintain its traditional reputation as the "most modern equipped hotel in the Catskills." Besides the telegraph, telephone, and post office (the latter with daily mails), it continued to maintain its own book and stationery shop; [25] it provided new game rooms, a bowling alley (in a separate annex), and billiard room; it supported a resident orchestra and a resident physician; it built an outdoor playground for children (supervised by attendants); it inaugurated a Rathskeller Service ("evenings from 9:30 to 11:30"); and it continued to maintain an "unexcelled" cuisine by employing a French chef and guaranteeing a constant supply of fresh dairy products, meats, and vegetables (fresh vegetables, butter and eggs were "delivered daily from the fertile gardens at the base of the mountains"; fresh milk and cream came from the hotel's own "herd of choice Alderney cows" on the top of the mountain; and fish, poultry, meat, and game were all delivered early each morning from New York City and stored in "perfectly appointed coolers" [26]). At one time or another the Mountain House also contained a solarium, beauty parlor, grille, casino, and bar.

III
"Its own Park of 3,000 acres of magnificent Forests."

The landed resources and outdoor facilities of the Mountain House also reached their highest stage of perfection during the second half of the nineteenth century. When the hotel first opened its doors in 1824 it possessed 300 acres of the choicest land of the Catskills. Subsequent years saw a constant expansion of these original holdings until they finally came to embrace (during the late 1870s and early 1880s) 3,500 acres of both North and South Mountains. About 1885 there was a reduction in this total amount of acreage (3,000 acres in that year);[27] and 1894 saw another reduction;[28] but from the 1870s until 1930, when the hotel sold all but about 300 acres to New York State, the Mountain House never had less than 2,780 acres embracing "about five square miles of forests and farming lands."[29] These vast holdings stretched from the valley below to the peak of North Mountain, and included both North and South Lakes, Palenville Overlook, and "seven miles of graded carriage roads,"[30] and many more miles of trails and footpaths.

Expansion and improvement of the trails and footpaths continued without abatement throughout the Gilded Age. Lucy C. Lillie noted in 1882, for instance, that their "variety seems endless, and new pathways are opening on every side."[31] In 1894 a new path was added to the already existing trails to South Mountain,[32] and in 1909 "a number of new trails" were opened "to points of interest" that had not been heretofore accessible, and all the old trails ("marked by nearly a century of foot-prints, to the famous outlooks") were "worked over and improved."[33]

The network of scenic carriage roads going from the base of Sleepy Hollow to South Lake, the Laurel House, and Haines Falls, was also expanded and improved throughout the flush years of the Catskills. In 1880 a carriage road (a coöperative venture of many hotels) was built from the new Overlook Hotel near Woodstock, along the crest of the mountain to the head of Plattekill Clove, affording "easy access back and forth between the Catskill Mountain House and the Overlook Mountain House."[34] Stage travel to and from the various hotels of the Catskills was a favorite diversion of the period, lending an extra note of gaiety to the life of the mountains. Each stage carried from eight to twelve persons, all of whom were "usually in the best of holiday spirits; well supplied with tin horns, streamers, flags, songs, and witticisms."[35] To provide for this transportation (and also travel to and from the various railroad stations), the proprietor of the Mountain House maintained an elaborate livery service both in Catskill and at the Mountain House. In 1896, for instance, a "New first-class Livery Service, Single Horses, Surreys and Mountain

Figure 57. West view from the Mountain House looking toward barns and stables. From a photograph in *Catskill Mountain House* (undated brochure), p. 11.

Figure 58. West view from the Mountain House, c. 1910. Photograph in the collection of Mabel Parker Smith.

Wagons" was established by Charles L. Beach.[36] Huge barns and stables located near the rear gates of the hotel always sheltered the equipment of this elaborate livery service.[37]

North and South Lake continued to be two of the most valuable assets of the great "Mountain House Park." Besides their intrinsic aesthetic appeal, they provided good fishing and boating, since both lakes were "plentifully stocked with various Kinds of Fish, and well supplied with Boats, Canoes, etc." [38] Boating facilities were commonly controlled by private business firms operating under a franchise of the Mountain House. During the early 1900s "the boat livery privilege" was granted "to Messrs. Byles and Hoff, of Bayonne, New Jersey," who furnished "canoes, out-riggers, and row boats of the most approved pattern." [39] Most boating activities centered on South Lake where the Mountain House also maintained a large pavilion for special entertainments and festivities and where the young and gay, half a century ago, always collected late in the evening for the final moonlit revelries of a long summer's day.

IV

"The favorite summer resort on the river."

The domain of the Mountain House became fused during these years of high fulfillment with the contiguous domain of its great rival, the Hotel Kaaterskill, converting all the top of the mountains into one great park "of forest and lawn . . . traversed in all directions by shady walks and pretty drives." [40] The whole of Pine Orchard was now a single resort area where "aesthetic furnishings, luxurious tables, seductive music, charming companions, well-graded drives, shaded walks, a bracing air and glorious views, offer everything to be desired in the way of eating, drinking, dancing, flirting, making merry, and enjoying life to the utmost." [41]

Yet while "these great mountain houses" conjointly ruled the most important resort area in all the mountains and became the twin luminaries of the Gilded Age, it was the Mountain House,

Figure 59. The board walk to South Lake used in the early years of the 20th century. From a photograph in Catskill Mountain House (undated brochure), p. 4.

the "pioneer summer mountain hotel," [42] that always remained "the favorite summer resort on the river." [43] Still occupying what was "universally acknowledged to be the most desirable location in the Catskills" [44] and retaining its ancient reputation as the "noblest wonder" of the Hudson Valley, it remained for the rest of the century "the favorite with a multitude of visitors. . . ." [45]

These included throughout the Gilded Age the most distinguished visitors in all the mountains. Fame, fashion, wealth, and talent abounded in the Catskills during these great years,[46] and the Hotel Kaaterskill certainly had its share of what it called "the largest wealth, the wisest statesmanship, the most enterprising business interests, the most genuine scholarhip, the greatest culture, elegance, and refinement" in all the nation.[47] But the Mountain House had its great age and history on its side, and though it was outclassed by the Hotel Kaaterskill in size and elegance, the "grand old landmark" [48] never lost its preëminent position as the Catskills' foremost center of fame and fashion. By 1884, as one historian of the Catskills enthusiastically noted, the registers of the hotel had been inscribed with "the names of nearly all of the men and women famous in every circle of life within the last 50 years." [49] But the same statement could have been repeated twenty-five years later when the Mountain House stood at the very apex of its long illustrious history.

A few examples may suffice to suggest the scintillating atmosphere of the Mountain House during these final years of the nineteenth century. The new era began appropriately enough in 1881 when ex-President Ulysses S. Grant arrived at the Mountain House. After leaving the White House in 1877 Grant made a triumphant tour of Europe, returning to America in the fall of 1879. In the summer of 1881 he took up residence in New York City, and it was at this time that he made his memorable visit to the Mountain House. The visit coincided with the last period of Grant's life: harassed by public calumny, pecuniary want, and ill health, he made repeated visits to northern New York State, and in the summer of 1881 he sought "the salubrious air of the Catskills." Local report says he first went to the newly opened Hotel Kaaterskill where he spent two days on South Mountain and then transferred to the Mountain House for a fortnight's stay.[50] The transfer was typical of the relative status of the two leading hotels of the mountains during the Gilded Age. While the ex-President was staying at the Mountain House, the Stony Clove Railroad was completed to Hunter and Grant interrupted his vacation to attend the opening ceremonies. It was an important day in the history of the mountains, and Grant's comings and goings to and from the Mountain House and the ensuing banquets and festivities were long remembered by the assembled guests.

Within two or three years of Grant's memorable visit the incumbent President, Chester A. Arthur, paid a visit to the Mountain House, accompanied, it was said, by his daughter, Nellie, whose bantam-high arrogance made her a source of acute discomfort to the other children of the hotel.[51] But then, nothing seems to have gone well during President Arthur's visit, however much his name added to the distinguished record of the Mountain House. It was a time when the aging heroes of the Civil War were still being lionized on every public occasion, and perhaps because Arthur's record included no distinguished service on the field of battle, he was given no royal treatment upon his arrival at the Mountain House. A handsome and impressive, though never popular, President (he failed to gain his party's nomination after his first term in office), his administration was hounded by civil service scandals (especially in New York State) which may have also accounted for his cool reception. In any event, the only ceremony that greeted his arrival (in one of Charles L. Beach's four-horse coaches) was the hoisting of an extra flag on the cliffside mast of the Mountain House.[52]

Things were altogether different when about the summer of 1890 General William Tecumseh Sherman and his elderly sister arrived at the Mountain House. His arrival had been eagerly anticipated, and by the time he descended from the stage at the west entrance all the guests and employees of the hotel had as-

Figure 60. General William T. Sherman at the Mountain House, c. 1890. Photograph in the collection of Mary Van Wagonen Rising.

sembled to give him a rousing welcome. The occasion was still sharp in the memory of a citizen of Catskill sixty years after he had first witnessed it:

We gave him a big welcome, shouting and cheering and singing, with the whole house gay with flags and bunting of every description. From the time we heard he was coming we rounded up everything we could find for decoration and it was a great sight when we finished . . . the colors were everywhere all over the building.[53]

It was as if the famous march through Georgia had occurred only yesterday. But it hadn't, and a quarter of a century later the aging tired general (Sherman died within months of his visit to the Mountain House) found the vigorous reception a bit too much for him. Especially exhausting were the indefatigable demands of a brigade of female autograph hunters. Seeing the predicament of the general, a young employee of the hotel suggested that he retire to his chambers and there prepare a sheet of signatures which could be cut up and handed out on demand with a minimum of discomfort. The general was delighted with the stratagem and reportedly spent the remainder of his stay at the Mountain House in a state of happy retirement. Throughout the earlier ordeal, Sherman's elderly sister had retreated to the front piazza of the hotel where she sat rocking and knitting, completely ignoring the distress of her famous brother.

On another memorable occasion at the Mountain House public adulation was deliberately sought rather than discouraged, for the personage in question was none other than that consummate master of public relations, the volatile, improper, and improbable Oscar Fingal O'Flahertie Wills Wilde. The saga of this famous aesthete's visit to America and his diversionary tour through the Catskills is one of the most beguiling and incongruous in the history of the mountains. But then, this was just as Wilde wanted it.

The young iconoclast and unquestioned genius arrived in New York for an extended lecture tour of the United States in the first week of January, 1882.[54] Wilde was a youthful twenty-five years old and had still to write his brilliant plays and poetry, but he had already acquired notoriety if not fame through the tremendous popularity of the 1881 production of Gilbert and Sullivan's *Patience*. The operetta satirized the new aesthetic movement of which Wilde was the avowed leader, and he was immediately identified as the prototype of the play's poet, Bunthorne. Wilde exploited this gratuitous publicity for all it was worth and arrived in America with all the outlandish manners and dress of the fabricated poet who "walked down Picadilly with a poppy / or a lily in his med-i-e-val hand." [55] Pictures were widely circulated wherever he went and there was not a major city in the north or west that could not identify Oscar Wilde as a long-haired eccentric who sported green velvet breeches, silk hose, silver-buckled pumps, and who stared languidly at a golden sunflower.

The Catskill phase of Wilde's American tour started on a hot sultry day in early August when he boarded the luxurious steamer,

Mary Powell, for a leisurely trip up the Hudson. At every public landing crowds of homespun Americans elbowed their way aboard to stare at the exotic exponent of art for art's sake, and editors throughout the Hudson Valley hailed his passing in varying tones of fascination and abhorrence. In Woodstock (according to a local historian), "reporters made it plain that no red-blooded American male had any business approving of Wilde—an attitude which Wilde, inspired showman that he was, did his best to encourage." [56] The journey was almost as eventful as the famous 1860 voyage of the *Daniel Drew* when the Prince of Wales (later King Edward VII) was fêted up and down the river.

Wilde arrived with his traveling companion, D'Oyley Carte, at the Hotel Kaaterskill on the afternoon of August 15, and that evening entertained the guests by giving his lecture on "The Decorative Arts." It was Wilde's inimitable manner to interrupt his lecture with caustic comments about the people and culture around him, a deliberate stratagem to arouse "the lily and sunflower furore" that gave him such notorious publicity throughout his American tour. His conduct at the Kaaterskill had apparently been true to form, for rumor has it that one "anti-Wildean beaned the Englishman with an immense sunflower" and that when Wilde took it upon himself to criticize the design of the hotel china the owner gave him "the invitation to leave if he didn't like the place." [57] Such stories, however, may well be apocryphal, for *The Kaaterskill* finally expressed nothing but praise for the young aesthete,[58] and Wilde himself "assured reporters that he was charmed by the Catskills and would return for a longer stay." [59]

Return he did, and that was the time he probably made his memorable visit to the Catskill Mountain House. A former resident of Catskill (and childhood ward of Charles L. Beach) who was present on that occasion, remembers it as "the sparkling episode" of the summer of 1883.[60] The date is probably correct, for after returning to England after his first tour of America (early in 1883) Wilde made a second trip to America in August of the same year to attend the opening of a new play. The play, however, failed after only a week's run and Wilde returned to England the end of September.[61] During the interval he undoubtedly returned to the Catskills and at that time visited the Mt. Tremper House in Phoenicia as well as the Mountain House. It was the height of the resort season and Wilde was not one to stay in the city when the world of fashion had moved to the Catskills.

Events at the Mountain House were idyllic compared to "the lily and sunflower furor" that attended Wilde's earlier visit to the Kaaterskill. In 1883 he came as a guest rather than a professional lecturer, and Wilde apparently readjusted his conduct accordingly. Sunflowers reappeared on the scene, but this time without malice aforethought, for the improbable Wilde joined in the presentation of an amateur theatrical in which each youthful actor appeared "black mantled, peak-capped, [and] armed with the most bucolic of blooms, a gaudy sunflower apiece." [62] The play was the idea of a fellow guest called Annie Phelps, a dramatic reader who was the nineteenth century equivalent of our present-day Cornelia Otis Skinner. She was joined by a young man who was to become one of the luminaries of American law and government, George Wharton Pepper.[63] The lyrics of the play or playlet were probably written by the sixteen-year-old Pepper, for he later confessed a life-long interest in writing "occasional" and light verse. In any event, it took no "Lord of Language" as Wilde called himself, to write such uninspired lyrics as "We are the Peak Sisters, / We come from Pike's Peak, Long's Peak and Peekskill, / But more recently from High Peak . . ." *The Peak Sisters*, as the playlet was called, was the gentlest of satires on the life of the summer resort ("And on the broad piazza / You could every evening spy / Groups of gay young people / Safe from Mother's eye. . . ."), and Wilde's contribution was limited to acting as honorary coach and mentor. As late as the 1940s, however, the principals still remembered that long-ago evening in the white and gold ballroom of the Mountain House when the young Oscar Wilde circulated among guests and players and

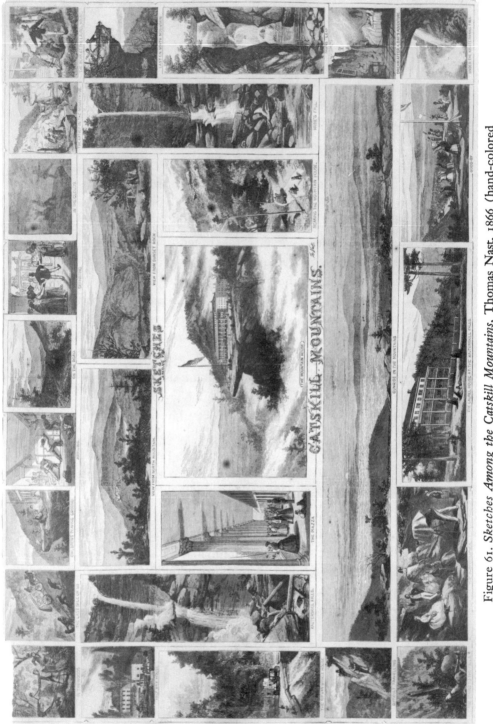

Figure 61. *Sketches Among the Catskill Mountains*, Thomas Nast, 1866 (hand-colored double-page engraving, 14" x 21"). Author's collection. Published in *Harper's Weekly*,

Figure 62. "The Piazza," Mountain House;
Thomas Nast, 1866 (detail of Figure 61).

Figure 63. "Arriving," Mountain House;
Thomas Nast, 1866 (detail of Figure 61).

Figure 64. "Departing," Mountain House;
Thomas Nast, 1866 (detail of Figure 61).

turned an amateur theatrical into one of the most sparkling episodes of their lives.

War heroes, presidents, literary idols, inventors, great merchants, lawyers, journalists, composers—they all went to the Mountain House in the flush years of the Catskills. Thomas Nast, the German immigrant who became "one of the greatest influences in American journalism," [64] went to record his impressions of the hotel for *Harper's Weekly*. Charles K. Harris, one of the most popular ballad composers in American history, went as a guest about the time he became famous with that perennial favorite, "After the Ball is Over" (1892). But the names of the great and near-great who visited the Mountain House during this period need no further illustration to substantiate the hotel's supreme record as a mecca of distinguished visitors. "Were we to repeat the names of all the celebrities in art and literature, and of the distinguished foreigners, who have stopped at this hotel," a commentator noted as early as 1881, "we should be obliged to enlarge this book much beyond the scope we intend it should embrace. To relate all the anecdotes of this place would fill volumes." [65]

V
"This shrine of summer pilgrimage."

It was a time of apotheosis for the Catskill Mountain House. In another decade or so new forces in American life would begin to bypass this hotel. In 1900–1910, however, all the past history and fame of the hotel suddenly began to have an accumulative force that had never been known before and that finally gave the Mountain House a status that is all but unique in the history of American resorts.

Beginning about 1892 when the Otis Elevating was opened and the Mountain House stood entrenched at the very apex of the great flush years of the Catskills, the hotel began to possess a new magnetic attraction that could not be duplicated in any other part of the mountains. The Otis itself had something to do with this phenomenon, for it acted as a lodestar to all the towns and villages of the Hudson Valley and brought thousands of day excursionists to the heights of Pine Orchard. But the Mountain House also began to attract at this time thousands of visitors from all the other resorts of the Catskills. Some of this traffic was a normal part of everyday life throughout the mountains as a whole, for people traveled from hotel to hotel merely in quest of diversion and recreation. But the volume of such traffic that terminated at the doors of the Mountain House was out of all proportion to the usual pattern of the mountains. The 3,000-acre domain of the Mountain House had become, in fact, a resort within a resort.

On any clear summer's day two or three hundred people milled about the front ledges of the Mountain House; hundreds more clambered about the trails of North and South Mountains; as many more sauntered along the lakes and streams and wandered through the secluded nooks and dales of Glen Mary. Weekends saw such an invasion of tourists and sightseers that the Mountain House had to provide special dining facilities. For every guest who registered at the hotel, three or four more came to enjoy its scenery and facilities and to bask in the glow of its fame and history. All the rock ledges round and about the Mountain House, from the famous "protruding platform" in front of the hotel to the high abutments of Artist's Rock, Newman's Ledge and North Point, became a prodigious repository of finely chiseled names and dates that went back to the earliest decades of the nineteenth century. Great age and all the rich associations of past history had become a part of the visible inheritance of the Catskill Mountain House, drawing not only the rich and fashionable, but the enchanted multitudes. At the very peak of its power and influence, on the threshold of a new and unpredictable century, "one of the greatest hotels of the country" had also become all but deified as a "shrine of summer pilgrimage." [66]

Figure 65. Full-page advertisement, 1905. From the Ulster & Delaware's pamphlet, *Catskill Mountain Resorts* (Roundout, N.Y., 1905), p. 176.

Part IV

The Twentieth Century

Introduction

Houses live and die: there is a time for building
And a time for living and generation
And a time for the wind to break the loosened pane
And to shake the wainscot where the field-mouse trots
And to shake the tattered arras woven with a silent motto.

—T. S. ELIOT

A century and a half ago, near the start of our story, the Catskills were a 3,000-square-mile preserve of unclaimed wilderness
close by the volatile centers of American population along the
tidal bays and inlets of the Atlantic seaboard. Dark and heavy
with primeval stands of virgin hemlock, feared by the supersti-
tious Dutch farmers of the Hudson Valley, laden with legend
and Indian lore, they were bypassed by the restless pioneers of
the old trans-Allegheny West and remained the undisturbed haunt
of the lynx and bear, the fleet white-tailed deer, and the far-ranging eagle. Settlement by the white man began, as we have seen,
in the latter part of the eighteenth century, but the wilderness
did not show substantial change until the second quarter of the
next century when American enterprise first appeared in the form
of the tanning industry, and the scenic heights of Pine Orchard
began to attract foreign visitors and the artists and writers of the
romantic movement. The tanneries reduced the wild life of the
mountains and also cleared whole valleys and mountainsides for
the more refined cultivation of the farmer and dairyman. Then

Figure 66. The Mountain House in ruins. Summer, 1961. Author's photo.

came the great age of the large hotels and resorts when manicured golf courses replaced rude pastures, when ancient Indian trails became smooth carriage roads, and whole mountaintops were shaped into private parks and finely groomed estates. The Catskills always remained a characteristic fusion of the wild and domesticated, of smooth lawns and formal drives in the midst of unkempt forests and rushing mountain streams, but by the end of the century they were never less a wilderness, never more a humanly contrived landscape.

A new phase began some time after the turn of the century and by 1918 it had become unmistakable: "the Catskills are passed by," a sensitive observer wrote in that year. "They are actually getting wilder. There are more deer in them than ever before, as many bear." [1] Twenty years later the regressive pattern was writ large on the face of the land: "Fields have gone back to woodlot; the shorn hills have grown new timber." [2] Today everywhere through the Catskills old stone walls wander inexplicably through the deepest forests, their purpose a mystery to all but the oldest inhabitants of the mountains. Faded photographs taken only forty years ago in the Esopus Valley reveal whole communities that are today all but invisible from their surrounding heights, so swiftly has the enveloping forest reclaimed the neighboring fields and pastures. Miles of railroad tracks lie rusting along river valleys, saplings grow between their rotted ties; stations lie abandoned in the woods, pitted and gutted by voracious porcupines of the Catskills, foul haunts of a thousand field mice. Old iron gates hang sagging on their hinges, leading nowhere, mute symbols of past opulence, now hidden by the forest.

But the Catskills are not all haunt and ruin: modern roads lead to small communities that still serve the hunter and tourist; summer camps abound; and each winter sees more skiers on newly opened tows and slopes. Yet over all the region, side by side with the life of the present and infusing that life with its own deep poignancy, lies the heady atmosphere of decay. The Catskills are more suggestive of the past than the future, and the past intrudes itself in a manner peculiarly American, as something that has been hewn all too hastily from the depths of the primeval forest and as carelessly thrown away again. Like the swift furtive flight of the native goldfinch within these darkening forests, a brilliant moment of the past has quickly come and as quickly gone. High open slopes revert to hardwood, villages disappear from view, and the returning wilderness envelops clove and mountain. And what is past can never return, for in the middle of the twentieth century as farms and estates decay and more and more land reverts to wilderness, thousands of acres are being withdrawn from private ownership and placed under the permanent jurisdiction of the paternalistic agencies of the State of New York. Under the protective guise of the Catskill State Forest Preserve an era of human culture is now coming to an end and the mountains are returning full cycle to the first condition of their primeval past.[3] All terminates as the poet sang: "In my beginning is my end."

The advance of the wilderness and the simultaneous decline of the Catskills as a social and cultural center of American wealth and fashion has been an inevitable result of the full continental sweep of twentieth century American civilization.

Throughout the nineteenth century, as we have seen, the Catskills enjoyed a strategic relationship to the abiding centers of American population. The westward movement never altered that relationship, for even as the frontier crossed the Mississippi and penetrated the plains and mountains of the Great American West the overwhelming majority of Americans still remained behind in the great rising cities of the East. The northeastern part of America dominated the cultural life of the nation throughout the nineteenth century, and it was all but inevitable that such cultural phenomena as the fashionable tourism of the Gilded Age and the first school of American landscape painting should have become concentrated in the nearby Catskill Mountains.

It is the twentieth century that has finally revoked those relationships. Territorial expansion *per se* has had, once again, very little to do with this change: the Catskills easily survived the great era of territorial expansion from 1830 to 1870, and since that time there has been very little change in the territorial size of the United States. The significant change has been in the growth and distribution of American population. Between 1870 and 1910 the total population of the nation more than doubled [4] and it took on a geographical configuration that soon spelled the end of the historic position and role of the Catskills. During this period all the remaining states of the continental United States were admitted into the Union (New Mexico and Arizona being the last in 1912), and there was a vast increase of population in the Midwest and in the Pacific Coast states. In 1910 New York still retained the lead with a population of nine to ten million, but Illinois had risen spectacularly to more than five million, Ohio was not far behind with more than four million, Texas had more than three, and Minnesota, Michigan, Wisconsin, and California each had over two million.[5] Throughout this period the statistical center of population moved steadily westward so that by 1910 Pine Orchard was just twice as far from the center (690 miles) as it had been in 1830 (345 miles).[6] This meant that by 1910 the forests of northern Minnesota and the beaches of northern Florida were just as close to the center of population as the Catskills, and it was not long before the new railroads of the country had translated this statistic into a living reality. About 53,000 miles of railroad had already been laid during the period 1840–1870, mostly in the East; between 1870 and 1910 about 200,000 more miles were laid, and they extended to every part of the nation.[7] Each region of the country now became equally accessible to every other region, and travel and vacation habits changed as resorts sprang up throughout the country.

This was especially noteworthy after 1915 when the automobile and the airplane began to exert their tremendous influences on American life. Between 1898 and 1915 the automobile evolved from a "plaything of the rich" into "a widely used pleasure and business vehicle." In 1895 there were only four automobiles registered in America; by 1900 there were 8,000; by 1915, 2,500,000.[8] A state and federal highway system accompanied this revolution, affording opportunities for mass travel throughout the nation, and creating as early as the 1920s great real estate booms in the farthest corners of the continent.[9] In another decade the airplane added its climactic influence. A commercial airline from New York to San Francisco was established in 1920; by 1930 airline companies served all the major cities of the country and one could fly from coast to coast in thirty-six hours (in the 1940s, sixteen hours; in the 1950s, seven hours).[10] This completed the twentieth century revolution in the history of transportation; and it also terminated the outstanding position of the Catskills in the history of American travel and resorts.

Fanning out over every part of the nation, masses of tourists and vacationers now discovered great areas of natural beauty that could not be duplicated in any region of the Atlantic seaboard. The scenic beauty of the West came as a revelation to hordes of freely moving Americans. Discovery began in the 1870s when many artists of the Hudson River School made brief excursions into the Rockies and Sierras at the invitation of the newly opened transcontinental railroads. By the end of the century, the whole nation knew that the most formidable mountains of America lay along the high peaks and passes of the Continental Divide. In the three Western states of Colorado, California, and Washington alone one could find a total of sixty-three peaks above 14,000 feet (including the highest in the continental United States, Mt. Whitney);[11] in the Appalachian Mountains, by con-

trast, the highest peak is only 6,684 feet (Mt. Mitchell in North
Carolina), and there are only a handful that rise above 5,000 feet
(Marcy, Washington, Clingman's Dome, and Katahdin). The
Catskills have only one peak slightly over 4,000 feet (Slide) and
the vast majority (thirty-six peaks in all) lie between 3,000 and
4,000 feet above sea level.

The superiority of the Western landscape soon gained official
recognition in the establishment of the National Park Service. In
1872 Yellowstone was set aside by a special act of Congress "as a
public park or pleasure-ground for the benefit and enjoyment
of the people," and became the first National Park in American
history.[12] Between 1890 and 1919 fifteen more Parks were established, and only one of these (Acadia in Maine) was located
east of the Mississippi. There are indeed few areas in the East
that can compare with the scenic wonders of these great Parks
of the West. Yellowstone, for instance, is almost three times as
large as the Catskill State Park and it contains a profusion of
geysers, boiling springs, mud volcanoes, petrified forests, canyons, lakes and streams, huge herds of wild animals and high
waterfalls that are completely foreign to the Eastern landscape.
Sequoia (established in California in 1890) boasts the world's
largest and oldest trees plus Mt. Whitney and the magnificent
scenery of the High Sierras. Glacier National Park (Montana,
1910) displays more than two hundred glacier-fed lakes, sixty
glaciers, rugged mountain scenery and innumerable precipices
thousands of feet deep. Yosemite (California, 1890), comparable
to the best of European scenery, is a fairy-tale region liberally
endowed with giant sequoia groves, deep pastoral canyons and
high lacy waterfalls (the largest is at least six times higher than
the Kaaterskill Falls). As millions of vacationing Americans have
come to realize since the opening decades of the twentieth century, the West is true lord of the American landscape.

None of this was known in the early nineteenth century when
American geography was restricted to the littoral mass of the
Allegheny Mountains, and the low-lying Catskills captured the
imagination of the nation through the romantic sensibility of
Washington Irving. Nor were the wonders of the West appreci-
ated in the 1840s and 1850s when the Mountain House had be-

come "the noblest wonder of the Hudson valley" and the geographical center of "one of the grandest and most picturesque of the mountain ranges of the United States." [13] Nor was popular appreciation yet crystallized in the post-Civil War period when the Western landscape was at least familiar to American landscape painters. Aesthetic appreciation was still restricted to the Eastern seaboard and especially the romantic Catskills. Throughout the flush years of the Gilded Age, masses of Americans still believed with William Cullen Bryant that "there are few places in the whole range of American scenery so attractive and refreshing as the Catskill Mountains." [14]

It is the twentieth century that has seen the final revocation of that classic opinion as well as the complete demise of the Catskills as a cynosure of American travel, art, and recreation. The balance of power in this as in other things has shifted westward with the vast geological tilt of the nation—up into the high plateaus of the Rockies or Sierras and down into the huge valleys of California or the deep canyons and exotic deserts of Arizona and New Mexico, where nature's largesse has finally fulfilled the age-old expectations of a grandeur uniquely American and a formidable landscape that needs no romantic apologia for its self-evident "sublimity."

The fate of the Catskills in the twentieth century involves the dissolution of all those nineteenth century relationships that first projected them into the limelight of American culture, and it returns for its most eloquent expression to the heights of Pine Orchard and the venerable white edifice that always carried the main burden of the area's history. The Catskill Mountain House never closed its doors until well after the advent of World War II, but like all the other resorts of the Catskills it had already lost its aura of fashion and fame by the 1920s, and from the 1940s on it enacted the full decay of the Catskills in one last chapter of embattled ruin, finally succumbing to the entrenched forces of a new American culture during one memorable week in January, 1963, exactly one hundred and forty years after it had first appeared on the brow of the mountain.

Chapter 13

Years of Decline,
1918–1942

Time was when the Catskills were about the only mountain country available for the fortnight vacation. The White Mountains were a little far away, and the Adirondacks an unexplored wilderness. The West was unknown. Now it is but a day from Broadway to Montreal. A trip to be talked about means at least Australia or the Ural Mountains. Therefore the Catskills are passed by.

—T. MORRIS LONGSTRETH (1918)

I
Early Signs: 1894–1918

The years between World War I and World War II were years of declining fortune in the history of the Mountain House and the resorts of the Catskills; but change, as we have noted before, is never sudden, and certain events of the period 1894–1918 already foreshadowed the more precipitous events of the 1920s and 1930s.

As early as 1894—the year the Mountain House announced a reduction in rates for the first time in its history—a writer on the Catskills made the observation that while there had been no diminution in the total number of visitors to the Catskills, several of the largest hotels were not doing so well as formerly, and he concluded that "the days of the great hotels may have gone by. . . ."[1] The Panic of 1893 certainly injured the large hotels and threw patronage to the small boardinghouses; but unlike earlier years when a sudden depression hit the Catskills, there were signs that the large hotels never regained their former equilibrium after the economic blight of 1893–97, and our commentator of 1894 may therefore have been substantially correct in his prediction of the end of an era. The economic collapse of the last decade of the century came at the very apex of the flush years of the Catskills, and it may have been the harbinger of other changes and initiated a long chain reaction of accelerating doom.

In any event, it was not long before there were other portents of declining fortune. In 1899 the Otis Elevating Railroad broke its connection with the Ulster and Delaware [or Kaaterskill] Railroad at the top of the mountains, thus severing the single line of railroads that had been forged in 1893 and breaking the economic links between Catskill and the interior resorts of Greene County. The immediate cause of the severance was the conversion of the narrow gauge Stony Clove-Kaaterskill line into a standard gauge railroad, an act of vengeance as well as technological improvement on the part of George W. Harding; but the fact that Beach could not restore the connection by converting his own railroad into a standard gauge and had to resort instead to the building of a competitive and uneconomical narrow gauge line from Otis Summit to Tannersville was incontrovertible evidence of the declining fortunes of the oldest resort in the Catskills.

Less symptomatic, but certainly highly symbolical of a passing era, was the "strange coincidence" of the almost simultaneous deaths in 1902 of "two of the most noted and historic personages identified with the history and development of the Catskills as a Summer resort," our own master of the Catskill Mountain House, the ninety-four-year-old Charles L. Beach, and his antagonist, the ruthless lord of the Hotel Kaaterskill, George W. Harding.[3] The two encompassed the full range of Catskill resort history from the early pioneer days of the romantic 1820s and 1830s to the great flush years of the competitive 1880s and 1890s. It was the native-born Beach who was always hailed as "that venerable old pioneer of the Catskills" and who remained the paramount figure. While he met and mastered the crass commercial challenges of the Gilded Age almost as brilliantly as Harding, he also exemplified as Harding did not the more benign and historic culture of the antebellum period. A colorful figure of early New York State history who always remained "a mountain enthusiast of the most dogmatic type, with a vast fund of reasoning for the supremacy of the Catskills over every other and any other mountains on the globe," [4] he fortunately did not live to see the cultural extinction of his beloved Catskills and died on the very threshold of the cataclysmic changes of the twentieth century.

Those changes announced themselves with more and more frequency in the years immediately following Beach's death. Minority groups fresh from the shores of Europe began to replace the native American stock of the fashionable Gilded Age. In 1908 Ernest Ingersoll noted in a Rand McNally guidebook that "Tannersville has become the resort of a very mixed and rapidly moving summer population, and is a great resort, in particular, of our Israelitish brethren, who love to gather where they can be together." [5] In the western Catskills the community of Griffin's Corners changed its name to Fleischmanns in honor of a well-known German restaurateur who started a new summer colony in that area. [6] Not long after Italians and Armenians began to arrive at Haines Falls and Tannersville, Shandaken became a favorite of Cubans and South Americans, and the Esopus Valley from Phoenicia to Oliverea became a favorite resort of first generation German immigrants.

The phenomenal rise of the automobile as a mass means of transportation hastened the advent of these as well as other profound changes during the early years of the twentieth century. By 1907 New York City was full of automobiles, [7] and by 1909 the automobile had become such a popular means of travel to and from the Catskills that the Mountain House had to build its first "Automobile Garage." [8] The event symbolized a great historic change from public to private means of transportation and foretold the end of the Catskill Mountain Railroad as well as every other aspect of the Mountain House's system of transportation from Catskill to Pine Orchard. Stagecoach traffic up the old classic route of Sleepy Hollow had long since disappeared, but by 1916 or 1917 when the abandoned Rip Van Winkle House finally went up in smoke, most traffic had also disappeared from both the Catskill Mountain Railroad and the Otis Elevating, and the burning of the old Inn of Sleepy Hollow seemed to bode some final, irrevocable ruin.

II
1918 to 1930

It actually took some years to fulfill that dire prognostication, but there can be no doubt that the year 1918 was the *de facto* beginning of the end. The year saw the death of Charles L. Beach's last son and heir, the total extinction of both the Catskill Mountain Railroad and the Otis Elevating Railroad, and the advent of a new American culture under the impact of World War I.

When Charles L. Beach died in 1902 he was succeeded by two sons, Charles and George H. Beach, who became the joint owners and managers of the Catskill Mountain House. As things turned out, the long fruitful years of fame and accomplishment had already been consumed in the life of the father: Charles Beach died in 1913 after only eleven years as co-manager, and George H. Beach died five years later.[9] Ownership then passed into the hands of the collateral descendants of Erastus Beach, whose memorable visit to the ledges of Pine Orchard in the year 1823 first began our history; and so the end of World War I saw the end of the seventy-nine-year rule of Charles L. Beach and Sons.

Perhaps even more significant was the final demise in 1918 of both the Otis Elevating and Catskill Mountain Railroads. This terminated a ninety-five-year history of transportation that began with Erastus Beach's establishment of the first livery service to the Catskill Mountain House. The Otis Elevating had closed down for lack of patronage as early as 1915 or 1916, and when World War I broke out it gave the owners a chance of redeeming some of their investment by selling all the rails, fly wheels, steel drums, wire cable, and hoisting equipment to the federal government for ultimate conversion into weapons of war.[10] The scrapping of the Otis was also the signal for the termination of the Catskill Mountain Railroad. All traffic over the thirty-six-year-old railroad ceased in 1918, but the death pangs of the railroad extended into the mid-1920s when the line fell into receivership and the last of its rolling stock (two locomotives and four boxcars) was finally liquidated.[11] The demise of these transportation enterprises was a serious blow to the economy of the whole region.

The downward trend of the Catskills, confirmed by these dramatic events of 1918, continued without abatement during the 1920s. It was a time when each loss or failure of some hotel or enterprise became permanent, without any possibility of recovery or regeneration. This was seen again in the sensational fate that overtook the Hotel Kaaterskill in the late summer of 1924. This great 1,200-room rival of the Mountain House which had once claimed to be the largest and most luxuriously appointed mountain hotel in the world, had lapsed into a second-rate hostelry, catering to the new minority groups of the Catskills, as early as 1920 when it came under the ownership of one Harry Tannenbaum. Then one evening in early September, 1924, only a week after the close of the summer season, the $1,500,000 structure burned to the ground in a brief two-hour holocaust that could be seen as far away as the State of Massachusetts.[12] Since it had already become a monolithic relic, a jaded *déclassé* monument to the extravagant years of the Gilded Age, it had outlived its purpose and was never rebuilt. With its passing, moreover, about half of the developed area of Pine Orchard—known during its heyday as a picturesque region where "tally-hoes are whirling down the rocky mountain roads, bugle sounds come echoing up, acres of tennis courts are crowded at once, and on distant mountain sides equestrians are following tortuous and romantic bridle paths or halting by rustic bridges, overlooking gorges and precipitate waterfalls—"[13] this 12,000-acre tract with its lawns, golf courses, observatories, reservoirs, and elaborate network of roads connecting such diverse points as the Laurel House and the Mountain House and their combined scenic delights and resources, fell into neglect and ruin, and reverted to a state of wilderness.

Meanwhile, the Mountain House, which celebrated its hundredth anniversary the year the forty-three-year-old Hotel Kaaterskill burned, fought bravely on throughout the 1920s under the management of John K. Van Wagonen, the husband of Mary L. Beach, a granddaughter of Charles L. Beach.[14] Life at the old resort was ostensibly as rich and full as in previous years, the hotel still supported such facilities as a post office, telegraph service, long-distance telephone, and resident physician; it maintained a full range of activities from boating, bathing, and fishing, to mountain climbing, golf, and tennis;[15] thousands of sightseers still came by automobile (if not by the Otis Elevating or Catskill Mountain Railroad) to admire "the world-famous view"; but the mood and tone were noticeably altered and decline was felt in a thousand subtle ways—in the number of fashionable people who did *not* return the following year, in the reduction of accommodations from 500 to 300 people,[16] in the lack of expansion or improvement of house and grounds. And then in 1929 came the great Crash of Wall Street and another new decade of spiraling misfortune.

III

1930 to 1940

In August of 1930, ten months after the bottom had fallen out of the stock market, the Catskill *Examiner* brought out a special edition of its newspaper to acknowledge its one hundredth anniversary and to commemorate a century of progress in the history of the Catskills. Catching the spirit of the occasion, which was inevitably optimistic and self-congratulatory rather than realistic, in spite of the general state of business, the owner and manager of the Mountain House inserted the following advertisement:

CATSKILL MOUNTAIN HOUSE. "The World Famed View." The oldest and most modern hostelry in America's favorite summer playground. Built in 1823—Each year since improved and made more modern.

Artists, Writers of prose and poetry, have contributed to the fame of this hotel of hotels—Presidents, Cabinet Members, Senators, Congressmen, Princes and others of Royal Blood have visited and remained at the Catskill Mountain House.

Situated on an overhanging cliff, and nestling in the shelter of a bristling crag, this Hotel is a bit of modernity on the face of wildest nature.

Easy of access by modern transportation. Plenty to do—games, sports, mountain climbing, exploring and sight seeing. Plenty of opportunity for rest, recreation—Large playgrounds on property.

Its cuisine is as famous as the view.[17]

So the Mountain House had advertised throughout the flush years of the nineteenth century when such exalted claims were still joined with a respect for truth. The traditional claims of the Mountain House, however, were already impugned by the changes of the 1920s, and in 1930 its classic stance suddenly degenerated into the braggadocio of modern advertising. In June of 1930, a good two months before the Catskill *Examiner* went to press, John K. Van Wagonen, who had recently bought out the interests of Louis J. and Charles T. Beach, was compelled to reduce the vast landholdings of his "hotel of hotels" to one-fifth of their classic dimensions, and thereby eliminated the historic "Mountain House Park" that had always been one of the hotel's chief claims to fame; a few weeks later he relinquished ownership of the hotel altogether and so brought to an end the ninety-one-year tenure of the family and descendants of Charles L. Beach.

What local pride and the Catskill *Examiner* could not admit, or perhaps even honorably perceive at this early stage, was that America had recently embarked upon the most severe depression of its history and that this new blow to the resort industry of the Catskills had finally created a *situs in extremis* that could never again be retrieved by the declining forces of private enterprise.

In any event, as of June 11, 1930, when the deed of purchase was recorded in the Clerk's Office of Greene County, the major part of the great "Mountain House Park" with its valley frontage of over three miles and its "miles of graded carriage roads and trails" became the public property of the State of New York. And within three more weeks the State consolidated its control over the old resort area by becoming owner of a substantial part of the contiguous domain of the former Hotel Kaaterskill.[18] In another thirty years the State purchased all remaining territory on both North and South Mountains, and the whole of Pine Orchard— to and including the Catskill Mountain House and the famous rock ledges of the "protruding platform"—became the permanent corporate possession of "the people" of the State of New York, terminating finally, completely, and "forever" [19] the great era of private enterprise.

The original purchase of 1930 (all but one-fifth of the property of the Mountain House) contained 2,197.93 acres and cost the people of New York State $26,375.16 or $12.00 per acre.[20] This block of land, which the State rightly called "one of the finest recreation spots in the entire Catskill region," [21] extended north of the point where the Sleepy Hollow road entered the grounds of the Mountain House and included most of North Lake and much of the summit of North Mountain (and therefore all such promontories as Artists' Rock, Prospect Rock, Newman's Ledge, and the favorite locations of the artists of the Hudson River School). The State soon marked and improved the old-established trails of the Mountain House, and it subsequently built a public campsite complete with roads, trailer sites, fireplaces, and a caretaker's cottage on the shores of North Lake. The campsite, however, occupied but a fraction of the total area acquired by the State and public usage was made conditional to the preservation of the surrounding wilderness. The acquisition by the State of New York of the heights of Pine Orchard was actually the fulfillment, in whatever unexpected form, of the fondest hopes of that "mountain enthusiast of the most dogmatic type," Charles L. Beach, who always regarded "the despoliation of the primitive woodland as an act of vandalism" and could never make his peace with the gradual disappearance of the wilderness during the flush years of the Catskills.[22]

Meanwhile the Catskill Mountain House continued to function as a hotel, though shorn of its scenic assets and reduced to the original boundaries of 1824 and 1825. Ownership throughout the 1930s was in the hands of two local businessmen, Milo Claude Moseman, a banker of Tannersville, and Clyde Gardiner, a lawyer and friend of Moseman. The banker was apparently the major figure in the new partnership, for he eventually acquired complete ownership of the hotel and was fated to bring the history of the Mountain House to a melodramatic conclusion. The hotel survived the great depression years, for the newcomers, and especially the enthusiastic Claude Moseman, rediscovered some of the faith and conviction, if not craft and opportunity, of

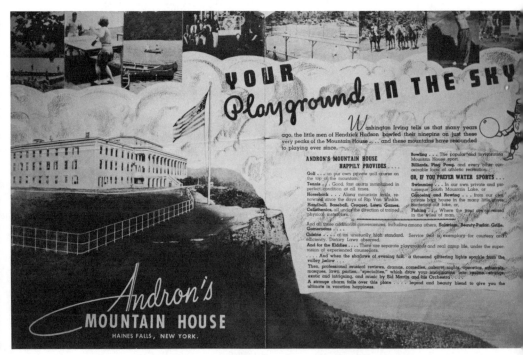

Figure 67. An Andron advertisement of the late 1930s.

the redoubtable Charles L. Beach. The declining fortune of the Catskills, however, had to be recognized in the leasing of the hotel to Jacob, Eli, and David Andron, of New York City, who changed the name of the hotel to "Andron's Mountain House." The change that had come to the Hotel Kaaterskill as early as 1920 reached the Mountain House in the thirties. It adopted a kosher cuisine, thus limiting its clientele.[23]

Though operating within a new cultural context, the Androns made a valiant attempt to maintain the traditional standards of the Mountain House. As in the ages past, an office was reëstablished during the spring and summer months in New York City,[24] and the Androns circulated elaborate brochures that included useful information on the latest automobile routes to the Catskills.[25] At the hotel itself the Androns featured their "own golf course on top of the mountain," tennis, horseback riding, handball, baseball, croquet, lawn games, calisthenics ("all under the direction of trained instructors"), bowling, Ping Pong, swimming ("in our private and picturesque South Mountain Lake"), canoeing, fishing, and rowboating ("from our own private boat house"); a playground for children ("under the supervision of experienced counsellors"); "professional" musical revues, dramas, comedies, cabaret nights, operettas, minstrels, masques, lawn parties, "specialties," and "music by Sid Martin and his Orchestra."[26] The Mountain House had become, in fact, an early forerunner and prototype of the large kosher hotels that were to spring up in the southern foothills of the Catskills after World War II.

The years under the Androns seemed to be highly prosperous to some commentators. The following, for instance, is Carl Carmer's impression of the 1930s:

Now motorcars and buses transport visitors to the Catskill Mountain House. The ledge before the old pillared veranda is crowded every summer with hundreds of guests who look out over a peaceful farming countryside not much changed since the days when nearly all of America's dignitaries and the great majority of the nation's honored guests made pilgrimages to this high shrine. The enormous public rooms have not changed and plaster busts of Daniel Webster and Henry Clay and other gods of American democracy stand in dignity in the early American parlors.[27]

The aura of prosperity, however, was highly deceptive to any-one knowing the long declining years of the past and the im-minent blows of the future. The number of sightseers visiting the hotel was not a particular sign of its traditional vitality, for hundreds of people would still visit the hotel after it had been forced to close its doors; and the fact that the early American parlors were still the same as ever could be a sign of stagnation and decay rather than stability and vigor. Truth is, the old hotel was under eclipse even as Carmer described it: the carrying charges and maintenance of the huge building were severe bur-dens throughout the depression years; the hotel used less internal space with each passing year; renovation or "improvement" was haphazard and improvisatory; shoddiness spread like a dry rot through the antiquated halls and parlors. The brochures of the Androns were illusory: the Mountain House was a monolithic white elephant, the relic of an insupportable past. By the end of the decade it was ripe for a fall, and history soon obliged without mercy in the cataclysmic blows of World War II.

IV
1941 to 1942

The summer of 1941 provided one unforgettable image for a visitor to the Mountain House: on the huge veranda of the hotel a twenty-piece band in blazoned uniforms of scarlet and gold played round after round of polkas and waltzes as eldery visitors sat in the shade of the nearby trees and a happy throng of swirl-ing, chattering youngsters spilled from the veranda to the green swath of lawn along the mountain's edge. It was one of the last images of a long fading elegance, soon to be gone forever.[28]

In December of that year the Japanese attack on Pearl Harbor plunged America into World War II, and the immediate curtail-ment of all normal peacetime pursuits and pleasures soon proved fatal to the Catskill Mountain House. Anticipating that end, the

Androns made no attempt to renew their lease on the hotel during the winter of 1941–42 and retreated forthwith from the scene
of impending catastrophe. The sanguine Claude Moseman, however, could not believe that such a venerable edifice had come to
the end of its time. Unable to lease the hotel again or find anyone
to relieve him of the burden of running it, he himself became the
administrative head of the hotel and re-opened it for the summer
of 1942 under his own management. With an enthusiasm that far
exceeded his practical knowledge, Moseman hastened the very
end he hoped to avoid, and turned the season of 1942 into an unmitigated fiasco.[29] Henceforth, though Moseman never ceased
to believe otherwise until he died some sixteen years later, there
was no hope for the hotel.

The coming of early spring, 1943, saw none of the activities
on the heights of Pine Orchard that usually preceded the opening of the Mountain House.[30] While the slopes of North and
South Mountain softened to the touch of returning spring, the
huge graying structure remained lifeless on the edge of the
mountain, its doors and windows still locked and boarded up to
protect them against the ravages of the previous winter. The old
inhabitants of all the villages below began to take concern. The
annual opening of the "familiar white landmark" on the distant
rim of the mountains had always been a sure sign of returning
spring and another year of life and hope in the towns and villages
of the Catskills. Now for the first time in almost a century and a
quarter this "old landmark and pioneer summer mountain hotel"
showed no signs of life. It was as if the Catskills had lost their
soul.

Chapter 14

Years of Embattled Ruin, 1942–1962

There is a profound appropriateness in the final years of the Mountain House. History had passed it by and it had to go, but in the Catskills this end did not betoken any necessary act of commemoration or atonement: the past recedes in the Catskills as it does in America as a whole, without expiation or the metaphysical overtones of loss and grief. When things are no longer useful they are simply discarded and left to rust and rot and pass into the earth again: death comes mechanically. When the Mountain House expired as a hotel it could have been left to rot on the mountain's edge, as the Overlook Hotel still crumbles on the edge of the mountains above the village of Woodstock. It could also have met the fate of the old Lexington Hotel and been converted into a summer camp, dying piecemeal and in abject violation of its true form and meaning, the prey of an alien host bent upon the extraction of its last ounce of ravaged utility. At any moment of its history it could also have met the fiery end of the Hotel Kaaterskill and the Mt. Tremper House, consumed by a blind stroke of simple, catastrophic misfortune, leaving nothing more for history to say. The Mountain House was spared all these conventional ends and awaited its own unique dispensation. Known for its charmed existence from the time it first arose "as an exhalation" on the very edge of the precipice, it met its final hours in an appropriate incantation of sacrificial love and martyrdom.

Figure 68. The piazza, Mountain House. Early spring, 1961. Author's photo.

That ritualistic end was the result of the fanatical devotion of one extraordinary individual, Milo Claude Moseman. A lifelong bachelor and benign eccentric who was born and bred in the heart of the resort region on the top of the mountains, Moseman spent the summers of his childhood working as a bellboy in the Mountain House when it was at the very pinnacle of its fame and glory; and the experience marked him for life: the great white edifice became the symbol of his most secret hopes and aspirations, and he grew into manhood obsessed with the dream of one day becoming lord and master of "the noblest wonder" of the Hudson Valley. For such a dream, fate often reserves the most unexpected of fulfillments. As a leading banker of the resort region, Moseman had become something of a local Maecenas, dispensing aid far beyond the call of duty and the dictates of sound business practices to the hard-pressed innkeepers and landlords of upper Greene County. When the finances of the Mountain House fell into arrears at the beginning of the great depression, Moseman fell into the seductive trap that awaits all such men who love not wisely, but too well, and mistook the tocsin of fate for the clarion call of opportunity. He assumed ownership of the "famous cloud-capped palace," hoping to preserve it against destruction. It was an alliance of love that could end only in disaster; but disaster, as Moseman himself may well have divined in some deep level of his being, is the inevitable dénouement of any great drama of love and sacrifice.

I

Decade of Undecided Fate,
1942–1952

Moseman's heroic struggle began in 1942 when he first closed the doors of the Mountain House. For the next ten years he had but one aim: to maintain and preserve the Mountain House by every means at his command pending its ultimate sale to some responsible agency or philanthropic institution that could relieve him of his unequal burden and preserve the hotel against any threat of destruction. In the end he had to capitulate and help to destroy what he most loved; but from 1942 until the latter part of 1951 he won a temporary reprieve in the fated end of the old hotel and was able to maintain the large building and its last four or five hundred acres as he originally found them. If the Mountain House ever had a chance of being saved, it was during this last decade when Moseman's valiant efforts still provided the opportunity. But the opportunity was ignored, and then it was too late.

Prima facie the most likely source of salvation was the Conservation Department of the State of New York. Ever since the Conservation Department had acquired ownership of most of North Mountain and a substantial part of South Mountain (1930), it had cast a covetous eye on the remaining property, if not buildings, of the Mountain House. South Lake was still owned by the hotel and it threw a wedge between the northern and southern holdings of the Conservation Department, violating the geographical unity of the area and causing considerable administrative embarrassment. The State of New York had been deeply concerned about the ultimate disposition of this property throughout the 1930s, and when it found the Mountain House in a vulnerable position after 1942, it opened negotiations for a possible settlement. After much hard bargaining—the State offering $30,000, Moseman and his partner demanding $35,000, a compromise of $32,500 being decided upon—Moseman suddenly astonished everyone by breaking off negotiations. At the very last moment an ill-timed remark had reminded Moseman of the sacred trust to which he had committed himself, and he would not permit any further reduction in the remaining property of the Mountain House. Like a much earlier romanticist (and equally difficult person), James Fenimore Cooper, Moseman was also unnerved by the conviction that the admission of the general public would desecrate and defile the hallowed precincts of Pine Orchard. This belief was not shared by Moseman's partner, Clyde Gardiner, who was eager to take advantage of any offer of the Conservation Department. An altercation ensued between the two partners. Moseman remained obdurate and Gardiner finally forced Moseman to buy out his interest in the partnership and become complete owner of the Mountain House.

The next round of negotiations with the State of New York occurred with Moseman alone, and this time the impractical dreamer was even more difficult. The State opened negotiations by offering a resounding $60,000, but this was for everything that Moseman owned, both the hotel and all its remaining property; and the offer threw the hard-pressed Moseman into an abject state of confusion. At one time, for instance, Moseman offered to sell everything but the actual building and the old Mountain House Road. The State gave in about the building, but demanded ownership of the road (it led directly into the center of the property); to allay Moseman's fears about not controlling the avenue of approach to the Mountain House, the State offered him an easement over the road. Moseman found this unsatisfactory and offered in turn to retain ownership of the road while giving the State a permanent easement. This finally exasperated the officials of the State beyond endurance, and they broke off negotiations and never returned until death had removed the apparently irrational source of all their frustrations.[1]

Milo Claude Moseman, however, was not as irrational as he appeared to be. Only one interest dominated Moseman's erratic behavior during all those negotiations: the preservation of the Mountain House. But this was an interest that the State could not acknowledge and which it was powerless to act upon even if it *did* acknowledge it. Since the State was acting under the authority of the Constitution of the State of New York and was restricted by the specific provisions of the Land Acquisitions Act, it was absolutely prohibited from buying any land that contained standing buildings. Throughout the negotiations, in other words, the Conservation Department was never interested in buying the actual buildings of the Mountain House; and when it tried to bribe Moseman into submission by offering the extremely liberal amount of $60,000 for *all* the remaining property of the Mountain House, everyone concerned in the negotiations knew that this meant the preliminary destruction of the Mountain House. There was no question here of praise or blame: the State acted in good faith and, indeed, up to the very limits of its constitutional authority. Some other state or federal agency may have been able to buy the Mountain House without its preliminary destruction (The National Council of Historic Sites is one such agency), but not the Conservation Department of the State of New York; and as long as the Conservation Department was the only negotiator, Moseman was a man who had been caught on the horns of a dilemma: if he sold to the State he would become financially solvent but would lose the Mountain House; if he did not sell he would retain the Mountain House but still face the original problem of its costly maintenance (and probably lose it through eventual bankruptcy). Nor would the latter problem have been solved even if Moseman had been able to sell everything but the actual buildings. Moseman therefore had no recourse but to break off negotiations and await or pray for future developments.

Throughout this whole period of negotiations the general public remained oblivious of or indifferent to the unresolved fate of the Mountain House. Sightseers and tourists still visited the famous sight during the warm summer months, but the melancholy scene provoked surprisingly little comment or discussion in the local press and there was no sign on the horizon of any forthcoming aid or organized protest. The reaction of the general public was perhaps best conveyed by the nonchalant attitude of an Albany newspaperman who visited the Mountain House in the fall of 1950:

If you are wondering [he wrote for his readers in the *Times-Union*] where to take the family in your automobile over the weekend, may we suggest (to the oldsters, at least) that they recharge their nostalgic batteries with a trip down to the old Catskill Mountain House, atop South Mountain in the Catskills. Sure, it still stands there, but gradually falling into decay and oblivion. Instead of the old manner of arriving at the "World Famous View," when one took the Day Boat to Catskill Landing, thence by narrow gauge railroad to the foot of the mountain, once more transferring to the Otis inclined railway to the plateau on which stood the formerly famous hotel, one arrives at one's destination by driving around the mountain and coming in on it from the rear flank.

To behold the marvelous view from in front of the hotel (for a slight sum) one drives to Haines Fall, and a little beyond the village, turns right and continues until one sees one of the two lakes on the expanse of property.

One arrives at the rear of the hotel which is almost as ornate as the front. The last promoters of the famous hotel were the Andron family which renamed it "Andron's Catskill Mountain House," featuring good food and all kinds of physical and mental recreation.

Today the buildings are in charge of H. E. Lockwood, of Tannersville, who drives there every day and collects the small toll charge for enjoying the incomparable view. . . .

Today the hotel is boarded up as is the famous piazza where millionaires rocked to get an appetite for the famous meals which were served there. It is owned by a corporation which, apparently has no plans for the future. However, the hotel may last for several years or it might suddenly go to pieces like the old "one-hoss shay." But the view from the ledge in front of the hotel will remain throughout eternity.[2]

One month after this was written the threat alluded to in the next to the last sentence of a sudden ending to the Mountain House almost became a reality. On November 26, 1950, a violent hurricane raged through the Catskills doing widespread damage to the unattended hotels and boardinghouses of the mountains. The Mountain House as a whole escaped surprisingly well, but it received one perverse, demonic blow: the storm struck full force against the front façade of the hotel and destroyed at least a half of its famous columns. For the first time in more than a century the Mountain House was now deprived of the beautiful colonnade that had always symbolized its architectural elegance. Moseman later salvaged the fragments of the shattered capitals and stored the remains of the columns inside the hotel for safe-keeping; but the columns were never replaced, and as time went by the consecutive disappearance of each remaining column kept progress with the stage by stage destruction of the whole building. Though it was not realized at the time, the loss of the first columns in November, 1950, marked the beginning of the end for the Catskill Mountain House.[3]

Six months later the desperate circumstances of the Mountain House suddenly became common knowledge throughout the Hudson Valley. On June 21, 1951, an article appeared in the Catskill *Examiner-Recorder* under the alarming title, "August 1 Final Date for the Fate of Famed Catskill Mountain House." Moseman had apparently informed the newspaper of his previous negotiations with the State of New York and his inability to fulfill those negotiations because, as the newspaper said, "he would not approve destruction of the world-famous hotel." But Moseman's main intent in contacting the newspaper at this time became more apparent in the following paragraph:

Moseman stated that if he does not receive constructive help in solving the Mountain House problem by August 1, he intends to commence furthering his plans in the sale of lots bordering the lake. . . . The general over-all scheme is a summer resident colony with stores, summer theatre, and restaurant.

As the newspaper pointed out, "the pertinent question of what is to be done with the House itself, was not answered by Moseman." The newspaper's final comment was that "the main house itself is structurally sound" and "for the past few seasons the house has been utilized as a tourist attraction with admittance fees charged, which seems a regrettable end for one of the country's potentially prize attractions." [4]

In a surprisingly short time this fear suddenly proved—or so it seemed—baseless. On July 5, 1951, the *Examiner-Recorder* informed a startled public that Moseman had decided to completely restore the Mountain House to its original condition. While this was certainly the best possible way of answering "the pertinent question of what is to be done with the House itself," it ominously failed to say *how* this was to be done; for despite Moseman's earlier appeal, he was never able to "receive constructive help in solving the Mountain House problem." The public could only assume that he had been able to solve the problem through his own private means of financing.

Figure 69. "Catskill Mountain House, Otis Summit, Catskill Mountains, New York." From a postcard (Charles W. Hughes, Mechanicville, N.Y., c. 1922).

Whether he had or not hardly mattered to the editors of the *Examiner-Recorder*. The important thing as far as they were concerned was that Moseman had said the Mountain House would be restored: the fact had unlimited commercial implications:

The announcement by Claude Moseman of Tannersville that the restoration of the Mountain House is likely, is good news for Greene County. For the once proud resort, once world famed for its splendor, can build a new age in the resort business for Greene County.

The beauty of the Catskills that brought people from all over the world to spend their vacations here is everlasting. But beauty alone is not enough to attract the modern vacationist and tourist.

The rehabilitation of the Mountain House could serve as a striking example of faith in Greene County as a great resort area. We have what it takes, if we are willing to do something about it.

Success to the Mountain House. May it always stand as a proud marker atop North Mountain, overlooking our Hudson Valley, and one of the finest scenic sights in the world.[5]

How blind, alas, is the vision of commerce! The possibility of a commercial renaissance in the Catskills had long since disappeared with the last receding echoes of the nineteenth century. It was a time for poetical, not commercial, truth. Even Moseman knew this, whose main interest in the restoration of the Mountain House was not the revitalization of business, but simply the preservation of a shrine. If this poetical truth had been kept in mind, perhaps the commercial interests of the Catskills would

Figure 70. The beginning of the end: the Mountain House after a hurricane of November 26, 1950, destroyed most of the columns. From a newspaper photograph in *The Knickerbocker News*, Albany, N.Y., March 28, 1952.

not have missed the true facts of the case, as any visit to the Mountain House could have plainly revealed. Such, in any event, is the testimony of a poet and naturalist who visited Pine Orchard within weeks of the *Examiner-Recorder's* announcement of "a new age in the resort business for Greene County:"

> I had never realized until today [Vernon Haskins said in the fall of 1951 after a visit to the Mountain House], just how great and how magnificent this place must have been in the days gone by. As I wandered through the corridors and the ballroom and the dining room of this dying giant of a place, I was far from being happy. My heart was heavy as I saw the dying of one of America's great historical points of interest. The place was thronging with many people. I got to studying the folks there. I heard no loud laughter, no fun-making. So it was with a heavy heart that I turned away from what might have well been a national shrine.[6]

It took poets, writers, and artists, rather than businessmen, to appreciate the true condition of the Mountain House and put out a call for help. On November 20, 1951, the following appeal appeared in the *New York Times*, written by Hans Huth, Assistant Curator of the Chicago Art Institute:

> The Catskill Mountain House is falling to pieces. The fine Greek Revival pediment once rested on thirteen Corinthian columns; now only five remain, together with a few emergency props. Once again it is obvious that private ownership is unable to support one of New York State's, indeed one of the country's, outstanding landmarks. Help by public agencies or interested societies must be sought.
>
> In 1823 a group of far-sighted citizens subscribed to the erection of a temporary building to house tourists coming up from Catskill to enjoy the view from the ridge, 2,400 feet above the Hudson valley. After Washington Irving's "Rip Van Winkle" described it so eloquently the view became famous all over the world.[7] Soon the primitive abode was no longer adequate and the main part of the present building was erected, three stories in height and 140 feet in length. The interior was most elegantly appointed, and the Mountain House became one of the great attractions for those who were imbued with the romantic spirit of the period.
>
> Soon it became the fashion to visit the hotel, which was becoming more luxurious with each season. Visitors to the hotel were aroused

early in the morning to observe the sunrise. Innumerable are the accolades found in travel books of the nineteenth century, both native and foreign, of those who came to admire the "eagle's nest."

Only with the advent of the automobile did the number of visitors willing to put up with the limited comforts of the old frame building begin to dwindle. Gradually it became apparent that the old mansion, once so hospitable, could no longer serve as a hotel and compete with newer and better buildings. Therefore about a decade ago it became necessary to close the Mountain House.

But in spite of disuse and neglect the house still stands, dominating the ridge, and in its majestic surroundings it is one of the most impressive sights of the Greek Revival period. Interest in the paintings of the Hudson River School has grown year by year, and if this interest is genuine it should not prove difficult to find means to support one of the sites which played such an important role in the movement. It would be criminal not to maintain this landmark, which has lost not one iota of its inspirational value. Why lament the ruins of Europe when we have our own to be saved? Probably for no exorbitant cost the most important parts of the present building could be converted into an historical museum which would tell of the past, and at the same time serve as a recreational spot for visitors. The National Council for Historic Sites in Washington might be willing to accept suggestions from those willing to help and might perhaps channel these into some cooperative effort. But it is necessary to hurry, else the building will fall into complete ruin this winter, and the Hudson valley be deprived of one of its most impressive features.[8]

It was an eloquent and compelling appeal, but the need of haste was even more imperative than the writer realized. The shadow of doom had already foreshortened the last golden hours of opportunity. The Mountain House did not fall into complete ruin during the winter of 1951, but it might just as well have: some time during December, six months after the distraught Moseman had made his final appeal to the public, nine years and four months after he had first been forced to close the doors of the hotel, he decided to sell the two great wings of the Mountain House to William Woodward of Hudson, New York, for the desperately needed sum of about $70,000. Woodward in turn contracted with the Bell Wrecking Company of the same city to destroy the great wings for salvage, the wrecking operations to commence in the spring of 1952. By this reckless measure Moseman hoped to liquidate his debts and still have ample resources for completely restoring the oldest and most central part of the original Mountain House. Perhaps this is what he had had on his mind when he led the Catskill *Examiner-Recorder* to assume some five months earlier that "the restoration of the Mountain House is likely." No doubt the impractical dreamer had hoped until the last moment that it would not be necessary to sacrifice at least two thirds of the great building to preserve the remaining third. By the end of the year, this had in fact become mandatory, and the momentous decision was made public. Moseman could at least console himself with the fact that it was a much better solution than the one that had been previously offered by the State. If he had yielded to the State in the 1940s he would have been $60,000 richer, but he would have destroyed the Mountain House in toto. Now he had about $70,000 and could preserve the most historical part of the House. Or so he avidly believed. He had no way of knowing in late 1951 that the sacrifice had been made in vain and that he had terminated a full decade of undecided fate by plunging the Mountain House toward a final *Götterdämmerung*.

II
Decade of Wreckage and Ruin,
1952–1962

The snows had not melted in the early spring of 1952 when the Bell Wrecking Company first began to arrive on the heights of Pine Orchard. For nine previous springs the great hotel had remained lifeless during the traditional season of its annual awakening, and the people of the Hudson Valley had grown accustomed to its long unnatural hibernation. Could not they clearly perceive, after all, that the great graying mass of a building still clung to the mountain's edge as it had from time immemorial?

Was it not still a fixed part of the landscape, as secure and permanent as the familiar contour of the surrounding peaks and cloves? But the spring of 1952 created a difference; people looked with new eyes; and many went to Pine Orchard itself, provoked by new realities. Toward the end of March an Albany newspaper sent a woman reporter to the scene, and the news went out to all the State: "The ring of hammers echoes from South Mountain—rooms that played host to the world's great and near-great crumble to dust under wreckers' crowbars—and a hotel whose fame has become a legend is undergoing a change." [9]

"Undergoing a change" hardly seems the phrase to describe the event, but the people at Pine Orchard did not know what we know today and they felt no need of stronger expressions. All still assumed that the destruction of the wings was preliminary to the restoration of the central part of the Mountain House. Moseman's plans, first announced the previous summer, had become common knowledge: he was going to restore the classic veranda with its thirteen Corinthian columns, the ballroom, and a total of about forty rooms in the oldest part of the house. The hotel would still be a resort center, however diminished in size, grounds, and facilities; and it would thereby continue to maintain itself as "one of the country's outstanding landmarks." A few local citizens such as Vernon Haskins and Mabel Parker Smith who were more sensitive to the general deterioration of the old resort area (or an occasional stranger such as the Curator of the Chicago Art Institute who had the unclouded vision of an outsider) were filled with deep misgivings. Most, however, assumed the feasibility of Moseman's intent and simply agreed with the Albany newspaperwoman that the Mountain House was "undergoing a change." It took another year of destruction to arouse a general sense of apprehension, and it wasn't until the people in the villages below could actually look up and *see* the gutted ruins that apprehension turned into a measure of outrage.

The huge sprawling north wing was destroyed first, and its

Figure 71. Where the North Wing joined the central part of the Mountain House. The cupola atop the central part admitted light to the central stairwell. The four tall windows at the right are off the ballroom. Early spring, 1961. Author's photo.

destruction took all the summer and all the fall of 1952. The demolishment included about one third of the northern end of the veranda, the original wing that had been added in 1825, and the whole of Beach's addition of about twenty years later. Left standing was a servants' wing that had been attached at a much

later date to the northern end of the building (and which remained conspicuously isolated from the rest of the Mountain
House throughout the next decade). The northern wing was
probably demolished first because it contained all the utilities and
kitchen facilities of the hotel and therefore yielded the greatest
salvage value. The removal of this wing opened up an area (giving access to the front ledges from the rear of the hotel) that
had not been seen since the early 1840s; but despite Moseman's

Figure 72. Sixteen hundred feet below the Mountain House. The isolated building on
the right was a servants' wing that formerly joined the great North Wing. The Otis
Summit Station was located in the slight depression at far right. Late fall, 1961. Author's
photo.

original intentions, the area remained ever after an unsightly slag-heap of discarded rubble and ruin, an offensive monument to human wantonness. Stanton W. Bell, in charge of wrecking, declared that the operation had never intended to be "a clean up job" and that his contract with Woodward permitted him "to take out what he wants and leave the rest." [10] The contract, needless to say, was fulfilled to the letter, leaving a sight in 1953 that could only be described in the following terms:

From Catskill, looking westward on bright mornings, there is a vacant spot against the sky where, for a hundred years, the broad North wing of the Catskill Mountain House has shouldered the heavens.

With the disappearance of the North wing from the skyline the eastern gable of the long servants' quarters, a building of comparatively late date showing end-on to the cliff, stands out now in greater prominence than ever before. It is well preserved and will be retained. Missing from the scene since early in the wrecking process, however, is the brick engine house of the long-abandoned Otis Elevating Railway. Only the foundation of that remains close to the great slash up the mountain-wall which is the fast-fading evidence of that world-famous ascent.

From Palenville, looking almost straight up to the overhanging ledge of South Mountain, the brooding structure once celebrated as the world's most beautiful hotel is now a spectacle to grip the heart and tighten the throat. Shorn of its North wing, the remaining bulk of the house, once gleaming white, now weathered to dull gray, is sad enough, but in Palenville, whence a few gaunt uprights of the demolished section have been seen slicing the sky since wrecking operations were suspended last November, the sight has cut deep into the feelings of those who live beneath it. [11]

Soon after this was written the Bell Wrecking Company returned to Pine Orchard and began the destruction of the south wing. By the time the company ceased operations in October of 1953 the Mountain House had become a melancholy ruin that was to offend the skyline—and conscience—of the Catskills for another decade. For some reason or other the southeastern corner of the building was left standing (perhaps because the contract had expired or the corner simply was not worth salvaging).

Figure 73. Looking west over the remains of the North Wing. The columns off the ballroom have just been removed by the New York State Conservation Department. Late summer, 1962. Author's photo.

Viewed from the southeast, therefore, the building now looked as it had about the time of the Civil War. With this exception the Mountain House now roughly corresponded to the fifty-room structure of 1825, and it was this remaining part that Moseman planned to preserve as a deluxe summer resort.

The destruction aroused deep feelings of regret in the nearby villages of Greene County and an occasional expression of outrage, but it never produced anything like an organized vote of protest or any co-operative attempt to come to the rescue of the Mountain House or the distraught Moseman. Scores of people displayed the narrow limits of their interest by requesting pieces of the building as mementoes and souvenirs; others visited Pine Orchard to purchase desirable furnishings (cornices, paneling, etc.) for their own private residences. On one memorable day Mr. Vincent Astor appeared on the ledges of Pine Orchard, drawn by curiosity as well as a sense of personal loss. "It can't go," Mr. Astor was reported as saying. "It's been a part of my life as long as I can remember traveling up and down the Hudson River." [12] So it had been to every aristocrat of the Hudson Valley; but Mr. Astor was one of the last of his species to visit the famous landmark: the Mountain House was doomed, and its fate could never be rescinded by the pale efficacy of human regrets.

There is often a strange period in the declining years of men of talent and vigor when life reasserts itself with feverish intensity, as if the long dark curtains of the night may still be parted by a final act of defiance. Such were the last few years of Claude Moseman between the end of 1953 and the fall of 1958. Once the wreckers had departed and the Mountain House stood in naked ruins upon the mountain's brow, the extraordinary Moseman threw himself into what poets call "the last battle of the Norse gods," a final consuming "struggle without hope." [13] Mustering his last remaining strength and resources, he gathered together a group of friends and workers and made a heroic attempt to push through his plans for the ultimate restoration of the Mountain House. He hired an architect and went into daily consultations with interior decorators. Building permits were taken out; elaborate blueprints were drawn for all phases of the renovation. One plan after another was conjured up, discarded, reintroduced, and finally shelved. At one time he called for a summer theater; then a museum, or perhaps an art gallery. Weeks later he was completely absorbed in plans for relandscaping all the grounds of the hotel; later again he became enthusiastic about possible plans for a swimming beach and a cabin colony on the shores of South Lake. [14]

The phantasy prevailed for several years, for Moseman had the capacity of arousing intense enthusiasm and devotion in all his friends, and he had on his side the irresistible force and appeal of the majestic ruins of the Mountain House. But as plan proliferated into plan and one scheme after another was fervently adopted and as quickly discarded, no work itself was ever started on the actual renovation of the Mountain House, and each passing year brought fresh evidence of the intrinsic madness of the whole adventure. Toward the end of the period Moseman surprised his friends by suddenly selling all of South Lake and most of the remaining property of the Mountain House to a New York City real estate firm by the name of "Carpathian Vacation Camp, Inc." It was one of the last desperate and contradictory acts of an impractical dreamer who had finally all but destroyed that which he had dedicated himself to preserve. Perhaps to escape that conclusive tragedy he relapsed into despondency and died in the late fall of 1958, leaving the wreckage of his dreams on the shattered heights of Pine Orchard.

From 1958 to 1960 the hulking ruins of the Mountain House still pierced the skies above the mountain's edge, distinctly visible on any clear day from the distant towns and villages on the eastern banks of the Hudson. People from remote states of the union who revisited it to commemorate some resplendent memory of youth or childhood arrived with fond anticipation and departed in stunned silence. Young campers and hikers on their first vacations in the mountains stumbled upon it with curiosity and awe, and were eager to know its history. Even in ignominious death the gaunt remains were redolent of past glory. The rear façade of the building still retained its huge Corinthian columns and presented an imposing spectacle of massive, decaying elegance. Seen from any distant vantage point, surrounded by forest and mountain, the classical remnants of the building evoked the image of some wild ruin of ancient Arcadia. Close by, it became more American: a huge mortal frame of wood, violently sacked and gutted, ringed with debris, an abandoned derelict defiling the surrounding landscape. To enter the building was to be presented with a ubiquitous obscenity: barroom scrawls were carved wantonly on paneled doors; dark corners were filled with the stench of marauding animals; piles of refuse and garbage blocked doorways and corridors; furniture and equipment lay broken and looted by thieves and vandals. In the

Figure 74. The corner of the South Wing facing the Hudson Valley. Late summer, 1962. Author's photo.

darkened ruins of the main office one came upon an old iron safe that had been scarred and wrenched by prying crowbars, the name of "C. L. Beach" still etched upon its broken surface. Upstairs in the once beautiful ballroom one found an old upright piano lying forlornly on its side, the object of perverse destruction. The tall and elegant windows of the ballroom lay hanging on their heavy broken hinges, warped and shattered by a thousand winds and rains.

To be alone in the ruins of the Mountain House was to know how a giant building died. Silence filled the dry depths of the labyrinthine ruins like some fearful, unseen presence: it riffled the dust as you groped haltingly down the long dark corridors; it caught the loosened board by the unseen step; it ascended the untrod stairwell and waited expectantly in each empty room and chamber. And then, borne by the unseen wind, the silence suddenly materialized into a palpable threat of violence: in some distant recess of the lower building a door slammed with more than human force. And that was all. One waited and listened. In another moment, close by, there was a low wrenching squeak, like the lifting of a ponderous lid. Then as the wind rose the whole building shook and trembled, and things gave way: a metal sheet clanged against the upper eaves of the building and broke free; something fell muffled, heavy, in the deep rubble of the north wing. One turned to leave. But the wind subsided as capriciously as it had begun; and silence returned, ominous, expectant, pregnant with all the agony of an imminent catastrophe. The Mountain House awaited its final hours.

Figure 75. The rear of the Mountain House from the circular drive. Both the North Wing (left) and the South Wing (right) have been removed. Early spring, 1961. Author's photo.

Figure 76. The ledges in front of the Mountain House. Early spring, 1961. Author's photo.

During the winter of 1960-61 the ruins of the Mountain House were sold by the heirs of Claude Moseman to the same New York City real estate firm that had previously purchased South Lake and is surrounding acreage. This gave "Carpathian Vacation Camp, Inc." all the remaining buildings and land (about 260 acres) of the Catskill Mountain House property, and it caused considerable consternation among the personnel of the Conservation Department of the State of New York. The Conservation Department, having tried unsuccessfully to get control of this property from Claude Moseman in order to consolidate its holdings on North and South Mountain, now had lost out to a private corporation which planned to develop "a sort of summer 'cabin colony'" in the very heart of the State's great forest preserve and in direct competition with one of its most valuable public campsites.[15] Fortunately for the State of New York, as well as the general public whose welfare was most directly concerned, Carpathian was never able to fulfill any of its plans regarding the Catskill Mountain House property; and within another year (spring, 1962) the company gladly turned for relief to New York State, and the Conservation Department acquired full and final ownership.

The announcement of the sale was made in the *New York Times* on Monday, April 9, 1962, the twentieth anniversary of the last season of the Mountain House. Taking its cue from a terse news bulletin issued by the Conservation Department, the *Times* gave little indication of the momentous nature of the purchase and merely offered the ambiguous information that the Mountain House, "now in ruins," was a "historic resort hotel" and the "one-time summer White House of President Ulysses S. Grant." [16] The purchase was made under New York's "Park and Recreation Land Acquisitions Bond Act" and cost the people of the State $61,000. It gave the State a total of 2,458 acres—or

Figure 77. The gutted remains of the South Wing. Early spring, 1961. Author's photo.

Figure 78. The piazza, showing a column that fell during the winter of 1960–61. Early spring, 1961. Author's photo.

almost the whole—of the "Catskill Mountain House Park" that had been established by Charles L. Beach during the heyday of the Catskills.[17] Since the State had already acquired most of the property of the former Hotel Kaaterskill, this final purchase of the property of the Mountain House also gave the State complete control over the whole historic resort area of Pine Orchard. It was thus an event of major historical significance that may well symbolize the passing of an era. The whole of the "pioneer resort area" of the Catskill Mountains had now passed from private to public ownership and become the common possession of the new socialized American citizenry of the twentieth century. Though the event marked the ending of a great cultural epoch, it was an inevitable development that also contained the seeds of all future regeneration. As a man of wisdom has said, "If we want things to stay as they are, things will have to change." [18]

That change occurred at Pine Orchard in 1962; and though it promised a new lease on life for this oldest region of the Catskills, it also entailed one particular sacrifice, the ultimate and irrevocable necessity of which we may forever question—the total destruction of the Catskill Mountain House.

For some weeks after the State acquired ownership of the Mountain House the impressive ruins still clung to the ledges of Pine Orchard, yielding reluctantly to each passing storm, dying slowly and majestically. The long years of neglect and full exposure to wind and rain had dangerously weakened the internal frame of the building, and the State began to fear for the safety of the innumerable sightseers who still insisted on exploring its labyrinthine depths. When "No Trespassing" signs failed to discourage the public, the State erected a fence around the building and forbade admission even to the grounds of the hotel. But still the public came; and since the old veranda of the hotel provided the easiest means of access and also happened to be the weakest and most dangerous part of the whole structure, the State sent wreckers to the scene during the summer of 1962 and removed every last vestige of the famous columns and piazza of the Mountain House. Now all ornament and grace had disappeared from the once beautiful structure with the exception of four remaining Corinthian columns that still supported the pediment over the rear porch. Identical with the famous thirteen columns of the front piazza, the four rear columns had never been exposed to the slashing storms of the eastern escarpment and were almost as sound as the day they were first installed more than a century past. In a final gesture of piety the State carefully removed three of the best columns and gave two to the Greene County Historical Society near the town of Catskill and one to a rural museum in the mountain community of Durham. There they repose to this day, the last and only remnants of the once "noblest wonder" of the Hudson valley.

Figure 79. The Mountain House ballroom, sometime between 1902 and 1913. The three men in the group at left are Charles L. Beach's sons, George H. and Charles Beach (who ran the hotel between 1902 and 1918), and Louis P. Schutt (who became assistant manager when John K. Van Wagonen took over the hotel after 1918). The women in the same group include the wives of these three men as well as Miss Mary L. Beach (who later married John K. Van Wagonen) and Miss Sarah Beach, daughters of Charles L. Beach. Photograph in the collection of Mary Van Wagonen Rising.

Figure 80. The western corner of the Mountain House ballroom, showing the stage added in later years. Early spring, 1961. Author's photo.

Postscript
Friday, January 25,1963

The winter of 1962–63 struck New York State with uncommon severity. It came full-throated from the frozen chambers of the north and raged with a violence and destructiveness that had not been known for over a century. On the other side of the continent the State of California took a more than usual interest in the sufferings of the Empire State. Geographically immune to the annual afflictions of the northeastern winter, California now had another reason for exulting in the superiority of its position

Figure 81. The Mountain House immediately after the New York State Conservation Department removed the remaining columns and the piazza. Summer, 1962. Author's photo.

Figure 82. The main entrance of the Mountain House off the circular drive. The French doors off the piazza lead to the ballroom. The distant opening at ground level is 115 feet from the near entrance and faces the Hudson Valley. Early spring, 1961. Author's photo.

Figure 83. Looking west from a window over the ballroom, directly above the entrance off the circular drive, toward the former site of the barns. The column on the right was salvaged and is now in a museum in upstate New York. Early spring, 1961. Author's photo.

vis-á-vis its great Eastern rival: sometime in January, 1963, it had fulfilled the implicit promise of the long memorable westward movement of American population and become the largest state in the Union. For the first time in almost a century and a half New York State was no longer the unchallenged leader of the nation. It was an event laden with the implications of history, and it turned the winter of 1962–63 into a time of symbolic finalities.

By the middle of January the peaks and cloves of the Catskills lay deeply locked and silent under three feet of crusted snow. Dark nights followed somber days and then about the twenty-third the overladen skies fell quietly to earth again, enveloping all the countryside in a fresh mantle of white driven snow and bending low the heavy boughs of spruce and pine in the dense forests of North Mountain. The time had come for the enactment of one last drama on the high encrusted ridges of Pine Orchard. Acting in necessary secrecy, known only to a few officials in the surrounding villages, five or six members of the New York State Conservation Department rose in the dead of night on January 24, drove to the vicinity of Haines Falls, put up road blocks, then parked their cars at South Lake and trudged through the deep snow to the moonlit ruins of the Mountain House. Everything had been perfectly timed and co-ordinated; the signs and omens of success could not have been more auspicious: the moon shone brightly—there was hardly need of flashlights; everything round about from the forests above to the villages below lay securely protected under a fresh mantle of snow— there was no need to fear any disastrous conclusion to their mission; dawn had not yet broken—there was ample time for a full day's work; in all the towns and villages, above and below, the people slept. The hour had come, that deathlike hour of deep suspension when the heavy wheel of night first turns to feel the nascent touch of day.

People learned later that it had taken only one well-placed match to ignite the desiccated ruins of the Mountain House. An hour later as the eastern sky grew luminous with departing star and planet, a monstrous red flame shot above the darkened ridge of the mountain, visible to all the awakening towns and villages of the Hudson Valley, dread beacon of another alarming catastrophe in the old resort region of the Catskills. People left their homes in the dawn's growing light and searched the familiar skyline for some identifying landmark. Then peak and clove came full-face into the morning sun, and they knew: it was the greatest landmark of all, the Catskill Mountain House, their own expiring glory.

Figure 84. The burning of the Mountain House by the New York State Conservation Department, Friday, January 25, 1963, 6:00 A.M. Photo courtesy of Edward G. West, Shandaken, New York.

Figure 85. Four days after the New York State Conservation Department burned down the remnants of the Mountain House, January 29, 1963. Author's photo.

DINNER

❧

Stuffed Egg

Chicken Mulligatawney   Consomme Celestine

Radishes   Pickled Onions   Sweet Mixed Pickles
    Spiced Watermelon   Sour Gherkins   Dill Pickles

Boiled Salmon, Venitienne

Sliced Cucumbers   Potatoes Persilade

Boiled Smoked Beef Tongue, Sauce Piquante

Chicken Saute, Hongroise
                    Sweetbread Cutlet, Sauce Perigueux

Macaroni au Gratin   Banana Fritters, Lemon Sauce

Grape Juice Punch

Prime Ribs of Beef au Jus   Loin of Veal, Demiglace

Boiled New Potatoes   Mashed Potatoes
Carrots and Peas   Creamed Spinach   Succotash

Crab Meat Salad   Lettuce   Mayonnaise Dressing

Bread Pudding, Fruit Sauce

Peach Pie   Raspberry Meringue Pie
    Assorted Cakes   Charlotte Russe   Banana Ice Cream

Fresh Peaches   Watermelon   Plums   Peanuts
    Almonds   Ripe Cherries   Cluster Raisins   English Walnuts

Cheese:-   Cream   American   Swiss
    Bents Water Crackers   Uneeda Biscuits

    Coffee   Tea   Postum   Kaffee Hag   Cocoa
        Iced Tea   Iced Coffee

❧

THURSDAY JULY 17, 1924

John K. Van Wagonen, Manager
L. P. Schutt, Associate Manager

Appendix

Rate Policy of the
Mountain House

Rates at the Mountain House were always consistent with its reputation as one of the foremost hotels of the country. When in 1843 N. P. Willis wondered "how the proprietor can have dragged up, and keeps dragging up, so many superfluities from the river level to the eagle's nest," the answer was, by charging high prices. Most patrons recognized the necessity of these prices and agreed with Harriet Martineau that it was worth paying something extra to have one's "bodily wants" well provided for on such an inaccessible mountaintop. The policy of charging high prices also guaranteed the select clientele of the Mountain House; less affluent or fashionable people were forced to patronize the farms and boardinghouses of the surrounding valleys and plains where accommodations were always cheaper than in the mountain hotels. But rates at the Mountain House were even high by comparison with the usual mountain standards. Before the Civil War they were on a level with "most of the fashionable summer resorts in the United States [e.g. Saratoga Springs], $2.50 per day." Yet the Laurel House, which was also a mountain hotel, charged only about half that amount (Richards, *Appleton's Illustrated Hand-Book of American Travel*, 1857, 148). Auxiliary fees at the Mountain House always added substantially to the basic charge: coach fare to and from Catskill and a trip to the falls, for instance, added another four or five dollars. Such prices may seem ridiculously low to us today, but in 1846 "two maiden ladies from Philadelphia" would not stay in a farmhouse near the Kaaterskill Falls until the proprietor had reduced his price from $5.00 *per week each* to $2.00! (*Van Loan's Catskill Mountain Guide*, 1892.)

By 1879 we learn that "the price of board in the Catskills varies from five dollars a week to three dollars and a half." (Rusk, *An Illustrated Guide to the Catskill Mountains*, 12.) The Laurel House charged a maximum price of $3.50 per day at this time; the Mountain House, by comparison, charged a minimum of $4.50 per day. C. Richards, *Appleton's Illustrated Hand-Book of Summer Resorts*, 1876, 15–16.) Concurrent prices at the Overlook Hotel (considered one of the better hotels of the Catskills) were $3.00 per day or $15 to $20 per week. (*Van Loan's*, 1879, 70.) In 1881, perhaps to undercut the high prices of the new Hotel Kaaterskill, the Mountain House announced a "great reduction in rates" and dropped its $4.50 rate to $2.50 or $3.00 per day. (Richard's *Appleton's Hand-Book of American Summer Resorts*, 1881, 16.) At the same time it announced special low rates for the pre-season month of June ($2.50 per day or $14 to $17.50 per week). (*Van Loan's*, 1881, 6.) This meant that even during midsummer the rates of the Mountain House for 1881 were slightly lower than those of the Overlook ($3.00 to $3.50 per day or $15 to $20 per week) and substantially lower than those of the Kaaterskill ($4.00 per day or $21 to $25 per week), the highest in the Catskills. (*Ibid.*, 88.) At the same time, such second-class hotels as the Laurel House charged $12 to $20 per week, or about $1.70 to $2.85 per day. (*Appleton's*, 1881, 16.)

In another year or so, perhaps because it discovered that its policy of undercutting the Kaaterskill did not work, the Mountain House restored its high rates of $17 to $25 per week, and it maintained these rates (with minor variations) throughout the remaining years of the century. Concurrent rates at the Kaaterskill remained slightly higher; but the two hotels plus the Grand Hotel at Pine Hill were all considered in a class by themselves—a triumvirate of superhotels (the Overlook had been forced to close its doors in 1891).

From 1880 onward the Mountain House also began to give fuller recognition to seasonal variations. In 1883, for instance, rates were $3.50 per day or $17.50 to $21 per week from June 15 to July 15; they were $4 per day or $21 to $24 per week from July 15 to September 1; and during the months of September they were lowered again to $3.50 per day or $21 per week. (*Van Loan's*, 1883, 7.) The seasonal variation became a common policy of all the hotels of the Catskills. By the early 1890s visitors could be "comfortably accommodated from June 1st to 20th at $2 per day" in all but the large luxury hotels. (*Van Loan's*, 1892, 12.)

In 1893 rates at the Mountain House were raised to $4 or $5 per day (concurrent prices at the first-class Prospect Park Hotel in Catskill were a comparative $3 to $4 per day). (Ernest Ingersoll, *Rand, McNally and Company's Illustrated Guide to the Hudson River and Catskill Mountains*, 1893, 188.) The following year, however, we learn that "it is now no secret that several of the largest and finest hotels in the region have not done so well as formerly, since people have found what excellent treatment they can get in the country, at reasonable prices"; and the Mountain House announced a reduction in rates. (N.Y. Central and Hudson River Railroad, *Health and Pleasure on America's Greatest Railroad*, 1894, xli.) The Panic of 1893 undoubtedly helped to cause this reduction in rates. By 1900, however, prosperity had returned, and the rates of the Mountain House were back to the high 1893 level of $4 to $5 per day (Ingersoll, 1900, 192) and they remained there until the season of 1904 when there was a slight reduction to $3 to $4 per day or $21 to $25 per week. The season of 1904 also saw the now common reduction for the three week period prior to July 4. (The Ulster and Delaware Railroad, *The Catskill Mountains*, 1904, 179.)

From 1905 until about World War I the daily rate stayed firmly at $4 per day and the Mountain House maintained the usual seasonal variations. The hotel also provided at this time special rates for children and servants. Children under ten in rooms with parents or maids paid $12 per week or $2 per day. Maids occupying servents' rooms or taking meals at children's tables paid the same rate as children. By 1908 these rates had risen to: children under ten in rooms with parents or maid, $14 per week or $2.50 per day; maids with children at dinner, $14 to $17.50 per week, $3 per day. If children took their meals "at regular table," they paid the same as adults. (*Van Loan's*, 1908, 12.)

Throughout most of the antebellum period the season at the Mountain House regularly went from June 1 to October 1. Beginning in 1883, the season was gradually shortened through each successive year until most of June and September had been eliminated. By the early 1920s the season usually began at the end of June (the 27th or 30th) and ended on Labor Day or the first week of September. (Ulster and Delaware Railroad, *The Catskill Mountains*, Kingston, N.Y., 1891 ff., annual advertisements of the Mountain House.) In other words, the annual season of the Mountain House showed that the summer vacation had become a general practice restricted to the two summer months of July and August.

Catskill Mountain House

C. M. LEVETT, MUSICAL DIRECTOR

PROGRAM

1   Fox Trot—"You Left Me Out In The Rain"....Witmark

2   Fox Trot—"Home In Pasadena".......Clark and Leslie

3   Waltz—"The Land of Broken Dreams".........Remick

4   Fox Trot—"Lonely Little Melody".............Harms

5   Vocal Solo—"Aria from Samson & Dalila"..Mrs. H. Hahn

6   Fox Trot—"California Here I Come".........Witmark

7   Waltz—"A Kiss In The Dark"............... . Harms

8   Fox Trot—"Why Did I Kiss That Girl" Shapiro, Bernstein

9   Fox Trot—"Home, James. Home".......Clark and Leslie

10   Waltz—"Memory Lane".......................Harms

11   Fox Trot—"Driftwood".................Irving Berlin

12   Fox Trot—"Twelve O'clock at Night" .....Ager, Yellen

Saturday Evening, July 19, 1924   8:30 O'clock

Notes

(See bibliography, which follows, for complete citations.)

PART I—THE ANTEBELLUM PERIOD

CHAPTER 1—*The Setting*

1. Lord and Lord, p. 49.
2. Channing, vol. 5, p. 82.
3. Lord and Lord, pp. 220–21.
4. Clifton Johnson, p. 34.
5. Denison, "The Great River of the Mountains," p. 7.
6. Taylor, "Travels at Home," p. 17; also Rockwell, p. 252.
7. Willis, "The Catskill Mountains"; also Rockwell, pp. 219–20.
8. Martineau in Rockwell, p. 224.
9. Trollope, p. 291.
10. Bryant in Durand and Wade, p. 9.
11. Washington Irving, *Spanish Papers*, vol. 2, pp. 482–83; also Rockwell, p. 164.
12. Bryant in Durand and Wade, p. 9.
13. Richards, *American Summer Resorts* (1876), p. 33. According to the WPA guide, *New York, A Guide to the Empire State*, p. 14, one of the first hotels in the Adirondacks was built in 1859 on St. Regis Lake by Paul Smith.
14. Richards, *American Travel* (1857), p. 144.
15. Henry A. Brown, "The Catskills," in Bryant, ed., *Picturesque America*, II, 133.
16. *History of Greene County*, p. 125.
17. Hough, p. 323.
18. Posselt, *The Rip Van Winkle Trail*, p. 6.

19. *Ibid.*
20. Haring, p. 261.
21. De Lisser, *Picturesque Catskills,* p. 61.
22. Haring, p. 263.
23. Vedder, *Official History of Greene County* of 1927, p. 57, says
    that the pioneers of Hunter built a road down the mountain
    "after the Revolution." Since this clearly does not refer to the
    old Indian route down the Kaaterskill Clove, the only other pos-
    sible route in the vicinity, it must refer to the maps of 1802 and
    1819.
24. Spafford, p. 330.
25. To those who are familiar with the geography of the Catskills a
    question might arise at this point regarding the status of Kaaters-
    kill Clove as an obvious route into the mountains. Any topo-
    graphical map of the Catskills immediately shows that the Kaaters-
    kill Clove is a much more formidable vent in the mountains than
    either Sleepy Hollow ravine or Plattekill Clove. Since the Kaaters-
    kill Clove is in the same neighborhood as Sleepy Hollow and is
    in fact today the main automobile route into the mountains north
    of Kingston and has, in other words, supplanted the old Sleepy
    Hollow route as the main artery into the Catskills, we may well
    question why it never acquired that status in the nineteenth cen-
    tury. We know, indeed, that some kind of road was built down
    the clove as early as 1823 (*History of Greene County,* p. 45)
    and that this road was a favorite walk as well as ride for legions
    of sightseers during the nineteenth century. Yet the fact remains
    that it never became a major artery until the advent of the auto-
    mobile. The combined resources of the tanners and the proprietors
    of the Mountain House in maintaining an excellent road up Sleepy
    Hollow ravine might suggest an explanation for the prime im-
    portance of this famous toll road. But that cannot account for
    even the earliest settlers' of Hunter and Tannersville choosing to
    build their first roads down Sleepy Hollow rather than Kaaters-
    kill Clove.

    A more plausible explanation—and perhaps the only one—is
    that Kaaterskill Clove posed insurmountable engineering prob-
    lems. Even today the road cannot be maintained without chronic
    repairs and the constant vigilance of highway engineers. One
    can easily imagine how impossible it was before modern tech-
    nology. All the evidence of the nineteenth century points to the
    fact that this famous gap in the "Wall of Manitou" was as un-
    tamable as it was picturesque. Landslides and washouts through-

out the nineteenth century were as predictable as each returning spring. In 1887, for instance, "an enormous mass of rock fell, blocking both roadway and creek," and "blasting had to be resorted to before the creek could resume its former course or the road be travelled." (De Lisser, *Picturesque Catskills*, p. 19.) De Lisser noted in the 1890s that bridgebuilding "seems to be a constant and necessary occupation along the creek, as the Kaaterskill (when swollen by rain and freshets) carries before it, in its wild rush down the clove, everything not built in the most substantial manner." (*Ibid.*, p. 35.) In 1910 Ernest Ingersoll noted that "each winter" at one particular place near the head of the clove, "the road is torn from the hillside and hurled into the abyss 600 feet below." (Ingersoll, *Illustrated Guide*, p. 190.) In 1918 T. Morris Longstreth noted during a walking tour of the clove that "a part of the road had slipped away to a less dizzy level. I found that nearly every winter some part said farewell, and that every spring it was rather the custom than otherwise to remake some portion of the highway to take the place of the departed." (P. 101.) Much earlier, in the 1860s, Rockwell noted that the road was the scene of many "accidental deaths." (P. 329.) The Sleepy Hollow Road, on the other hand, was always easy to maintain compared to the route up the Kaaterskill Clove; and it was never known to have been the scene of a single serious accident.

26. "The Old Mountain Road . . . shortened the haul from tannery to the Hudson by thirty-two miles. It gave the tanners the much-needed eastern outlet. The older way through Mink Hollow was at once abandoned. The toll road prospered . . . and best of all, the tanneries were able to reduce the cost of haulage." (Haring, p. 264.)

27. Richards, "The Catskills," p. 145.

28. Rockwell, pp. 324–25.

29. Ripley and Dana, vol. 4, p. 126. Durand and Wade had helped to publicize the erroneous notion that Round Top was the highest peak in the Catskills (p. 3); and in 1854 T. Addison Richards propagated the same deception by declaring that "all the loftiest peaks" were found in the vicinity of the Mountain House ("The Catskills," p. 145.)

30. In 1879 Walton Van Loan said that "a year or so ago" the owner of Hunter Mountain accidentally discovered (with the use of a carpenter's water level) that a mountain peak in the southern Catskills was higher than either his own mountain or Round

Top. "Not until then did it get noised about, and afterwards proved to be a fact, that the Slide Mountain is the highest of the Catskill range," p. 64).

31. Evers, "The Shandaken Mountains," p. 1.

32. Cooper, *The Pioneers*, pp. 299–302.

33. Searing, p. 461; also Haring, p. 807. There are people in Woodstock, N.Y., who still believe that Cooper's description refers to the Overlook Mountain.

34. A. T. Goodrich, p. 38.

35. One of these, the legend of Norsereddin and Chief Shandaken, is especially interesting. Shandaken (whose name is still perpetuated in a twentieth century township of that name) was an Indian chief of the seventeenth century who used the platform and the surrounding plateau as the summer headquarters of his tribe. The legend asserts that Chief Shandaken had a beautiful daughter who was murdered by a swarthy "Egyptian" called "Norsereddin" when the latter was refused the hand of the princess in marriage. Norsereddin was subsequently pursued by Shandaken, captured, and burned at the stake at the exact place where the Mountain House was later erected. As De Lisser noted, in describing this legend, "Who can foreshadow the changes of time? The red men have departed and the tourist and woodsman have taken their places; on the camp ground of Shandaken gleam the white pillars of a famous summer house, and the idle lounger, seated upon the table rock, dreams not of its story of love, hatred and anguish." (De Lisser, *Picturesque Catskills*, p. 38.)

36. A good deal of this lore has to do with the loyalist Indians of the American Revolution who used the Catskills as a base of operations during their predatory raids upon the villages of the Hudson valley. The aim of the hostile Indians was not simply one of destruction, but to capture men, women, and children and transport them to Canada where the Indians received a liberal bounty for each live captive. The first night of the long flight to Canada was often spent in some hidden recess of the mountains, and on one memorable occasion it was spent on the famous "rock platform" of Pine Orchard. The story is still well-known in the Catskills and much too involved to relate here. Suffice it to say that the hero of the story, one David Adell (whose original stone house is still standing in the valley below the Mountain House), was abducted on one horrendous evening in 1781 and dragged to the heights of Pine Orchard where he spent his first anguished night of captivity. He subsequently survived the har-

rowing trip to Canada and lived to tell the story to his own friends and relatives in the town of Catskill. (One version of this story appears in Searing, pp. 70–71; another in Rockwell, pp. 68–73.)

37. Such is the opinion of Captain Basil Hall who was presumably told by citizens of Catskill that Pine Orchard "had long been the resort of picnic parties from New York and Albany" even before the founding of the Mountain House. (Hall, vol. 1, p. 95.)

38. *American Landscape*, p. 10.

39. Hall, vol. 1, p. 95.

CHAPTER 2—*The First Two Decades of the Mountain House*

1. Spafford, p. 245.
2. *Ibid.*, p. 414.
3. Levasseur, vol. 1, p. 111.
4. Beach.
5. *History of Greene County*, p. 78.
6. How this manuscript came to light is told by Mabel Parker Smith, "Beach, Symbol of America," p. 6-A.
7. Beach.
8. *Ibid.*
9. Van Loan (1908), p. 45.
10. Mabel Parker Smith, "Mountain House Was Side-Line," p. 1. Mrs. Smith's conclusion is also supported by the treasurer in the account book of the Catskill Mountain Association. The only references to Erastus Beach pertain to his livery service and stage-coach business.
11. As late as 1950, for instance, E. S. Van Olinda declared that the Mountain House was acquired by the Beach family "in 1825."
12. Mabel Parker Smith, "Mountain House Was Side-Line," p. 1.
13. *Catskill Mountain Scenery*, p. 29.
14. *History of Greene County*, p. 78.
15. Rockwell, p. 335.
16. *History of Greene County*, p. 7.
17. Vedder, *Official History of Greene County*, p. 98.
18. Beach.
19. *History of Greene County*, p. 79.
20. Beach. DeWitt Clinton visited Pine Orchard with his family on August 28, 1823 ("Diary," the New-York Historical Society).
21. Barrett, *The Eagle Guide*, p. 15; also *Catskill Mountain Scenery*, p. 29.

22. Samuel Chichester is given sole credit for the building of the first Mountain House by both Nathaniel Bartlett Sylvester (p. 313) and the anonymous author of the 1896 *Commemorative Biographical Record of Ulster County* (p. 1316). However, the account book of the first treasurer of the Catskill Mountain Association makes no reference to Chichester. All references pertain to Wells Finch. One can understand how Chichester could come to receive sole credit for the construction of the hotel, for his later career was much more distinguished than Finch's, and his name is immortalized today in the town of Chichester, near Phoenicia, where his sons ran a large chair factory. But the evidence of the account book is conclusive, and it is the obscure Wells Finch, rather than the well-known apprentice, who must receive major credit for the construction of the first Mountain House.

23. Spafford, p. 414. The costs of the hotel and its furnishings must have almost exhausted the capital assets of the Catskill Mountain Association. Between June 1823 and June 1824 the builder received a total of $3,097.72. The lathing and plastering of the house, contracted separately, cost another $725. The furniture and accessories of the hotel—including such items as floor matting ($80), window blinds ($24), two mirrors ($42), card tables ($10), wallpaper ($45), chairs ($90), and sofas ($70)—added another five or six hundred dollars. If we add to these costs such miscellaneous items as the laying of a stone foundation ($171), the purchase of old buildings at Pine Orchard ($65), the surveying of the land ($17), the purchase of paint ($168.60), and the rebuilding of the road up the mountain (about $1,000 between September and December of 1823), we can understand the necessity of the association's request for an increase in capital stock, granted by the state in 1824. (Account Book of the Treasurer of the Catskill Mountain Association.)

24. Rockwell, p. 174.

25. Catskill Mountain Scenery, p. 29; and Gordon, p. 470. The contract for this enlargement was won by one Henry Pins who worked from the fall of 1824 to the early spring of 1825. (Account Book of the Treasurer of the Catskill Mountain Association.)

26. This is the firm opinion of Mrs. Mabel Parker Smith who discovered that there is "almost complete lack of information about the various stages of its growth on the part of those who have

lived all their lives literally or figuratively in its shadow." ("Lines of First Mountain House Emerge.")

27. Clark, "Impressions of the Scenery of the Catskills," pp. 1–6; also Rockwell, p. 214; and Martineau in Rockwell, p. 226.

28. Mabel Parker Smith, "Mountain House Was Side-Line," p. 5-A. (The original quotation appeared in *The Bower of Taste*, a Boston magazine of 1829.)

29. Willis in Rockwell, p. 220.

30. Martineau in Rockwell, p. 229.

31. *Ibid.*, p. 224.

32. T. Dwight, p. 26.

33. Cooper, *Home as Found*, p. 56.

34. Bartlett Cowdrey, "William Henry Bartlett and the American Scene," p. 390.

35. Bryant in Durand and Wade, p. 10.

36. A. T. Goodrich, p. 37.

37. The various booklets, about forty pages in length, usually appeared without dates or names of editors or publishers. The first (*The Scenery of the Catskill Mountains*) appeared during the 1840s; the second, under the same title, appeared about 1845; the third, under the same title, appeared in 1864; and the fourth (under the title of *Catskill Mountain Scenery*) appeared some time after 1896. All had substantially the same content.

38. *Hudson River Guide* (1835), p. 232. The Mountain House is still the center of attention in Disturnell's *Gazetteer*, p. 324.

39. Willis, *American Scenery*, vol. 1, pp. 105–06.

40. *Ibid.*, p. 77.

CHAPTER 3—*The Early Years under Charles L. Beach*

1. Beach.

2. *Ibid.*

3. One of the first published accounts of this episode was Vail's; other accounts appeared by Mabel Parker Smith, "Beach Exploits Historic Developed Region," and by Wilstach, pp. 153–54.

4. Mabel Parker Smith, "Beach Exploits Historic Region," p. 1.

5. Quotation from Beach's "Autobiography." Other information on the mail and stage lines from Wilstach, pp. 152–53.

6. *Scenery of the Catskill Mountains* (c. 1845).

7. The author is indebted for most of this information to an unpublished speech by Mrs. Mabel Parker Smith called "The Mountain House Columns."

8. Richardson, Plate No. 96.

9. The phrase is the Rev. David Murdoch's (Rockwell, p. 244). George Harvey (1800?–1878), who resided in this country from 1820 to 1849 or 1850 and lived for a period on the lower Hudson near Washington Irving, apparently spent much time in the vicinity of the Mountain House. Other than the aforementioned "The Catskill House, N.Y.: A Day View," he painted two other views of the subject entitled "The Mountain House by Moonlight," and "Sunrise, Above the Clouds, from the Catskill Mountains," both of which were exhibited by the artist during the course of a lecture tour he made in Europe in 1849 (*Illustrations of Our Country*, pp. 31–32). In a list of paintings accompanying an announcement of a picture book that Harvey once planned to publish, we find two more works pertaining to the Catskills, "Kaatskill Landing, from the East Bank of the Hudson" (now in the New-York Historical Society) and "Morning Sky—Mountains from Near Kaatskill Village" (Shelley, "George Harvey and His Atmospheric Landscapes of North America," p. 112.

10. Richards, "The Catskills," p. 146. The metropolitan elegance and luxury of the Mountain House did not impose undue formality on the dress and manners of its pleasure-seeking visitors. "The Mountain House," George William Curtis observed in the 1850s, "is really unceremonious. You are not required to appear at dinner in ball costume, and if you choose, you may scramble to the Falls in cowhide boots and not in varnished pumps," p. 38.

11. Richards, *American Travel* (1857), p. 145.

12. Elizabeth F. Lummis Ellet in *Scenery of the Catskill Mountains*, pp. 24–25; also Rockwell, p. 232. Not everyone agreed with Mrs. Ellet about the excellent cuisine. In 1838 a very critical Englishman, James S. Buckingham, found that "the table" of the Mountain House was "like all the American tables of hotels, steam boats, and boardinghouses that we had seen, more remarkable for superabundance of food than skill or delicacy in preparing it." And he concluded that "though the native Americans are generally insensible to the defects of their culinary preparations, all persons who have travelled in Europe return deeply convinced of their national inferiority in this particular," pp. 253–54.

13. Murdoch in Rockwell, p. 248.

14. Taylor, "Travels at Home," p. 18; also Rockwell, p. 255. The subject provoked a mountain of descriptive analysis. One example may suffice to convey the tone and mood of this literature.

James Silk Buckingham, a member of the British Parliament, during a visit of early spring, 1838, wrote:

On the morning of Monday the 18th of June, we were all stirring at daylight, in order to enjoy the prospect of the rising sun. On looking out of the windows, the scene that presented itself was most remarkable, and totally different from any thing I had ever before witnessed. The sky above us was a bright clear blue, slightly mottled with white fleecy clouds, as in the finest summer mornings of England. But of the earth beneath us, nothing was to be seen except the rocky platform on which our habitation was built, and a small portion of the brow of the hill on which this stood. All the rest of the great expanse before us, extending to a distance of from 40 to 50 miles, was covered with a thick sea of perfectly white billows, as if there had been a general deluge, and we were occupying the summit of the Ararat which alone rose above the wide waste of waters around us. This was a compact and continuous stratum of fleecy clouds, which were below our feet instead of above our heads, and which literally covered the earth as with a canopy, and shrouded it entirely from our view. The waves of this cloudy sea assumed, too, so much the appearance of huge billows rolling, the one after the other in succession, from west to east, that excepting in the colour of the element, which here was of snowy whiteness instead of blue, it was like looking down from a ship's mast-head on the turbulence of the southern ocean in a tempest off the Cape of Good Hope, or like a view of the great sea, seen in its most violent agitation from the summit of the Table Mountain that overhangs the promontory named. It was altogether the most striking and impressive scene I had ever beheld, and could never be forgotten if life were prolonged to a thousand years.

While we were gazing with unspeakable admiration on this singular and beautiful cloudy sea, the increasing light of the eastern horizon, betokened the near approach of the sun. All eyes were accordingly turned to that direction, and in a few moments the bright and splendid orb rose up from his eastern bed, with a fulness of glory, that seemed like the dawn of a new creation. There were accumulated, in the immediate quarter of the heavens where the sun arose, a series of strata in the clouds, of different shapes, densities, and distances, which produced a variety of lights and tints, from the palest amber to the deepest purples; and caused the straight edges of some, and the wavy or undulated edges of others, to be tipped with the brightest lustre, sometimes of silver—sometimes of paler, and sometimes of deeper gold, so as to form altogether one of the most gorgeous and splendid skies that could be imagined; while overhead in the zenith, and in every other quarter but the east, a serene azure, over which sailed clouds of fleecy whiteness, completed the beauty of the picture. At the same time, the billowy surface of the cloudy sea beneath our feet, still completely hiding every spot of the earth from our view was made so radiant with the slanting beams of the rising sun thrown horizontally along its waves, that they looked like a sea of the brightest snow, heaving and rolling in some places in rounded surges, and in others flinging up their spiral points to the sky, like the conflict of opposing streams, or the spray of a vast cataract. Altogether the scene was as indescribable as it was splendid and sublime, and we dwelt upon it with an intensity of admiration which almost made the head ache with the pleasure of the sight.

About an hour after sunrise, we began to discover a partial breaking away of the cloudy awning, or rather the opening of patches and spaces in it, which bespoke its approaching dis-solution. . . . At ten o'clock the mist had so cleared away over the Hudson, that its stream became visible, but no portion of the green banks of the river could be seen on either side, so that it was like a mighty stream winding its way through a bed of clouds. . . . By noon, the whole of the clouds below us were dissipated, and the full glory of a meridian sun beamed down upon one of the most extensive and beautiful landscapes that could well be conceived. (Pp. 255–59.)

15. Taylor, "Travels at Home," p. 19; also Rockwell, p. 258.
16. G.E.L. (Ellis Gray Loring?) in *Scenery of the Catskill Moun-tains* (c. 1845), pp. 29–30. The weather always had a profound effect upon the mood of the Mountain House. Such was a cold foggy day in June, 1838:

We passed the whole of Sunday at the Mountain House, as completely shut out from the world below, as if we had been elevated to another planet; for the mist or fog continued so intense during the greater part of the day, that we could rarely see the foundations of the house we occupied; and at some moments the mist so completely enveloped the house, that not a particle of the ground around or near it could be distinguished, so that our dwelling was like an aerial mansion suspended among the clouds. I never remember to have been placed in a situation in which I felt so strongly the impression of complete isolation from the world. (Buckingham, p. 252.)

17. Rev. Theodore L. Cuyler in Rockwell, pp. 259–62.
18. Rockwell, p. 265.
19. *Examiner-Recorder*, Centennial Edition, p. 17.
20. Beach.

CHAPTER 4—*The Old Mountain Road*

1. Brown in Bryant, ed., *Picturesque America*, vol. 2, pp. 118–22.
2. The name by which Henry A. Brown called this ravine, Rip Van Winkle's Glen, was unusual. It was more commonly called Sleepy Hollow, and it was not Irving, but his public, who bestowed that name upon the ravine below the Mountain House. The Sleepy Hollow that Irving referred to is the scene of his famous *Legend of Sleepy Hollow* in the neighborhood of Tarrytown, New York. Though the Tarrytown Sleepy Hollow is more generally known today and is actually the authentic hollow—at least according to Irving's intentions—the Catskillian Sleepy Hollow was actually far better known throughout most of the nineteenth century. As a writer for Harper's declared as late as 1883, "Those who have seen the Catskill ravine outnumber those who have seen the valley of the Pocantico (in Tarrytown) a thousandfold; and few of these thousands will ever doubt but that the only true and original Sleepy Hollow is that in which Rip Van Winkle slept his wondrous sleep so long ago." ("The Genesis of the Rip Van Winkle Legend," *Harper's New Monthly Magazine*, vol. 67, p. 167.) Today, however, it is the Tarrytown Sleepy Hollow that attracts the "thousands" and the name has been restored to its proper location. But the cost, alas, has been the decline and fall of the Catskills as "a shrine of summer pilgrimage."
3. Van Loan (1897), p. 10.
4. A. T. Goodrich, p. 38.
5. *Traveller's Steamboat and Railroad Guide*, p. 46.
6. Mabel Parker Smith, "Recalls Trip," p. 3.
7. Hall, pp. 93–94.
8. Van Loan (1881), p. 7.
9. Mabel Parker Smith, "Recalls Trip," p. 3.

10. Clark in Rockwell, pp. 215–16.
11. Ellet in *Scenery of the Catskill Mountains* (c. 1845), p. 24; Rockwell, p. 231.
12. Buckingham, p. 250.
13. Mabel Parker Smith, "Recalls Trip," p. 3.
14. Van Loan (1879), p. 7.
15. Taintor, p. 57.
16. Clark in Rockwell, p. 210.
17. Tyrone Power, in Rockwell, p. 217.
18. *Traveller's Steamboat and Railroad Guide*, p. 46.
19. Gordon, p. 470.
20. Buckingham, p. 249. Buckingham's harsh criticism of the road stood in marked contrast to his opinion of his American driver. Here he has nothing but praise:

> The driver managed his team not only with great skill, but with great tenderness also; for he permitted them to halt for breath in the steep ascent every five minutes at least; and when they had sufficiently rested, said to them, "Come, my joys, set out again," as if he had been addressing men instead of cattle; and the horses understood these good English phrases quite as well as the unmeaning sounds of "gee-whoap, gee-whoap, and weather-ho!" with which English carters and ploughmen accost their beasts; and once or twice he said, "Now mind, if you don't get us well up the hill, I must get others that will." They set out invariably at the word of command, and the whip was not once used, nor its sound ever heard, from the commencement to the end of the journey; and I confess, I thought the substitution of the vocal organs for the last a great improvement, and one worthy of universal imitation. [P. 251.]

21. Taylor, "Travels at Home," p. 18; also Rockwell, p. 253.
22. Sims (1892), p. 30.
23. *Scenery of the Catskill Mountains* (c. 1845), back page of booklet.
24. Lillie, "The Catskills," pp. 522–23.
25. James, *American Scene*, pp. 154–57.
26. Brown in Bryant, ed., *Picturesque America*, vol. 2, p. 122.
27. Haring, p. 65.
28. Lillie, "The Catskills," p. 534.
29. Munroe, p. 25.
30. Ingersoll, *Illustrated Guide* (1893), p. 192.
31. Pierre M. Irving, vol. 3, p. 27.

32. *Ibid.*

33. *Ibid.*, p. 28.

34. *Ibid.*, p. 53.

35. *Ibid.*, p. 54.

36. *Ibid.*, p. 27.

37. "Rip's Rock" became a standard tourist attraction of Sleepy Hollow. A poem on the subject appeared in De Lisser's *Picturesque Catskills*, p. 58 ("High upon old Kaaterskill's crest/ Is a rock, where one may rest/ Safely hid from hue and cry;/ Hen-pecked husbands, hither hie." And so forth). With the aid of a photograph that appeared in the same book, the author visited the rock in 1961 and discovered several ornate initials carved into its upper surface. The rock is located a short scramble above and to the left of the old foundations of the Rip Van Winkle House.

38. Haring, p. 64.

39. *Scenery of the Catskill Mountains* (c. 1845), p. 38.

40. Mabel Parker Smith, "Recalls Trip," p. 3.

41. Rockwell, p. 180.

42. *Ibid.*, p. 281.

43. Ellet in *Scenery of the Catskill Mountains* (c. 1845), p. 28; Rockwell, p. 241.

44. Lillie, "The Catskills," p. 530.

45. Rockwell, p. 180.

46. Lossing, *Hudson River*, p. 155.

47. Richards, *American Travel* (1870), p. 46.

48. *History of Greene County*, p. 330.

49. Haring, pp. 66–67.

50. Ingersoll, *Illustrated Guide* (1900), p. 191.

51. Clifton Johnson, p. 173.

52. Haring, p. 67.

53. Clifton Johnson, p. 173.

54. Gallt, p. 46.

55. Longstreth, p. 105. How Longstreth found out that the Rip Van Winkle House burned down about 1917 affords an amusing anecdote. He was traveling on foot around the Catskills collecting material for his book when he decided to try to find out if the citizens of Palenville knew anything about Irving's story of Rip Van Winkle. Choosing the first house he came to, he knocked on the door and asked the lady of the house if she happened "to have a Rip Van Winkle handy." The answer: "Sure!" she exclaimed. "I know what you mean. But it burned down last year."

The ruins is up the next hollow about a mile." When Longstreth explained that all he needed "was a copy of the book for a few minutes," the puzzled woman exclaimed, "Book—book? I don't know as there's any book about it. But the Rip Van Winkle burnt down last year. The ruins—."

56. Vedder, *Official History of Greene County*, p. 99.

57. Haring, p. 67; and Mabel Parker Smith, "Recalls Trip," p. 3.

58. Posselt, *Rip Van Winkle Trail*, p. 78.

59. Mabel Parker Smith, "Recalls Trip," p. 3.

CHAPTER 5—*The Scenic Domain of the Mountain House*

1. Ellet in *Scenery of the Catskill Mountains* (c. 1845), p. 28; also Rockwell, p. 242.

2. Rusk, p. 81.

3. *Ibid.*, p. 79; also Van Loan (1881), p. 12.

4. Van Loan (1881), p. 16.

5. Van Loan (1897), p. 14.

6. Mulholland, pp. 28–31.

7. Van Loan (1879), p. 17.

8. Bartlett, an Englishman, was not strictly a member of the Hudson River School, but his painting is faithful to that style.

9. Ellet in *Scenery of the Catskill Mountains* (c. 1845), p. 27; also Rockwell, p. 238.

10. Van Loan (1879), p. 18.

11. Richards, *American Travel* (1857), pp. 294–95.

12. Van Loan (1897), p. 12.

13. The pipeline went from the headwaters of the creek to a reservoir near Glen Mary, then between the two lakes and up the hill to the north wing of the Mountain House.

14. Ellet in *Scenery of the Catskill Mountains* (c. 1845), p. 25; also Rockwell, p. 234.

15. Rockwell, pp. 281–83.

16. The work that Thomas Cole did on this first visit to the Catskills, including the preliminary sketches for these three historic paintings, is itemized in a typed copy of a "Note Book" that is in the manuscript collection of the New-York Historical Society. Page 29 contains references to six sketches of views around West Point, including three sketches of Fort Putnam. Page 31 contains references to sketch No. 17, "View of Catskill Falls" (which Cole deemed "a magnificent scene"); sketch No. 18, "View from under the projecting rock of Catskill Falls"; sketch No. 19, "The

View of Catskill falls from above looking below," and "another view from under the projecting rock"; sketch No. 20, "Mountain Lake Catskill—very singular effect"; sketch No. 21, "View of the Mountain House Pine Orchard from the road below"; and sketch No. 22, "View of the Catskill Mountains from the village of Catskill."

17. Ellet in *Scenery of the Catskill Mountains* (c. 1845), p. 28; Rockwell, pp. 241–42.

18. Since Van Loan says in 1881 (p. 427) that the trip required five hours during the era of improved carriage roads, it probably took about three hours by the Otis Elevated.

19. Rockwell, p. 285.

20. *Ibid.*, p. 286.

21. Van Loan (1881), p. 20.

22. *Ibid.*

23. Rockwell, p. 30.

24. Richards, *American Travel* (1857), p. 147.

25. Lossing, *Hudson River*, p. 165.

26. Rockwell, p. 30.

27. Posselt, *Rip Van Winkle Trail*, p. 114.

28. Van Loan (1881), p. 21.

29. *Ibid.*, p. 22.

30. *Ibid.*

31. One legend regarding the origin of the falls is still featured in anthologies of Catskillian literature (e.g., Bellows, *The Legend of Utsayantha and Other Folk-Lore of the Catskills*). Another legend was used by Bryant in his poem, "Kauterskill Falls."

32. The author discovered dates going back to 1810. Some of the earliest visitors to the falls were the pioneer geologists of New York State. Dr. Samuel Latham Mitchell (1764–1831) of Columbia University visited the falls before 1800 and wrote a description that is referred to by Mease, pp. 455–58. Amos Eaton (1776–1842), Professor of Sciences at the Rensselaer Polytechnic Institute in Troy, probably visited the falls shortly after the turn of the century. Henry Edwin Dwight paid a visit in 1819 and wrote a description that appeared in an article entitled "Account of the Kaatskill Mountains," pp. 17–21. These and other possible early visitors are mentioned briefly by Chadwick, pp. 19–21.

33. Posselt, *Rip Van Winkle Trail*, p. 124.

34. "Descriptive Journal of a Jaunt up the Grand Canal; Being a Letter from a Gentleman in New-York, to a Lady in Washington, in August, 1825," p. 382.

35. Hale, "Early Art of Thomas Cole," p. 37.
36. Bryant, ed., *United States Review and Literary Gazette*, vol. 2 (1827), p. 255.
37. Brown in Bryant, ed., *Picturesque America*, vol. 2, p. 125.
38. The author has not been able to track down Church's painting, but it was mentioned by George H. Daniels, general passenger agent of the New York Central, p. 15.
39. Cropsey's painting, "Kauterskill Falls," is No. 223, in Maria Cropsey's "Catalogue."
40. McEntee's painting, "Kaaterskill Falls," is No. 39 in his catalogue.
41. Weir lists: No. 276, "Kauterskill Falls," 1862; No. 309, "A Sketch of Kauterskill Falls"; No. 384, "A Recollection of Kauterskill Falls," 1864; No. 575, "Kauterskill Falls," 1871; and No. 577, "Kauterskill Falls," 1871. A painting now hanging in the Metropolitan Museum of Art entitled "Kauterskill Falls" is actually a view of Haines Falls.
42. Van Loan (1892), p. 13. If the phrase "the next season" refers to the year 1847, Charles L. Beach is probably in error about the exact year of this incident. In Mrs. Elizabeth Ellet's account of 1849 or 1850 there is no indication of any hotel at the head of the falls. When Bayard Taylor visited the falls in 1860 he said that the hotel had been built since his "last visit," or 1851 ("Travels at Home," p. 18). According to a story told by Charles Rockwell, on the other hand, the Laurel House was already in existence by 1850, and this date supports the contention of *History of Greene County* that "in 1850 the Laurel House was built, with a capacity of accommodating 25 guests. . . ." (P. 338.) All evidence therefore points to 1850 rather than 1847 as the probable date of the first Laurel House. Charles Rockwell's story, noted above, refers to a dramatic incident in the early history of the falls, and warrants full quotation:

> In the forenoon of July 20, 1850, Mr. C. B. F., a young man from Utica, aged nineteen, and weighing nearing two hundred pounds, was standing on the inclined surface of a rock, at the head of the Lower Falls, at the Laurel House, with two young friends near him, when he slipped and went over the falls, eighty feet, into the rocky basin below. There was at the time a high freshet, to which fact Mr. F. was probably indebted for the saving of his life, as the force of his fall was thus greatly lessened. One leg was broken above the knee, as was also the shoulder-blade. By deep wading through the lake, and much

effort, Mr. Peter Schutt obtained help from the Mountain House, Mr. Beech (sic), the proprietor, coming from a sick bed, and the old attache of the house, Mr. Thorp, known as "The bear-hunter," aided in the difficult task of carrying the injured man up the steep banks, and recently described to me what then occurred. It was ten o'clock P.M., when with much effort and exposure, two physicians arrived. By skillful medical attendance, aided by a vigorous, youthful constitution, and the kind and devoted care and nursing of Mrs. Schutt, wife of the proprietor of the Laurel House, Mr. F. was in six weeks able to leave for home. One year later he is on the register of the house, as "alive and kicking," he being then a visitor there; and he is, I understand, still living. [P. 331.]

43. Richards, *American Travel* (1857), p. 148.
44. Rockwell, p. 327.
45. Van Loan (1879), p. 26. There is also a notice of this new addition in an advertisement of the Laurel House at the end of Rockwell (1873).
46. "The Kaaterskill," vol. 1 (1882), p. 2. The author estimates that not more than a hundred now visit the falls during any summer.
47. Richards, "The Catskills," pp. 149–50.
48. The poem is quoted in full in Rockwell, pp. 332–35.
49. *Ibid.*, pp. 289–93.

PART II—INTRODUCTION

1. Born, p. 42.
2. Tuckerman, *Artist-Life*, p. 116.
3. Van Loan (1879), p. 11.
4. W. Gilpin, p. 343.

CHAPTER 6—*The Discovery of the Romantic Motif*

1. Brown in Bryant, ed., *Picturesque America*, vol. 2, p. 117.
2. Hale, "American Scenery in Cooper's Novels," p. 321.
3. Blair, pp. 53–54, 58–59; Burke, pp. 82–83; W. Gilpin, pp. 334–35.
4. Wallace Bruce, *Along the Hudson with Washington Irving*, p. 11.
5. Washington Irving, *Rip Van Winkle*, pp. 19–20.
6. Pierre M. Irving, vol. 3, p. 28.
7. Washington Irving in *Home Authors and Home Artists*, p. 71.

8. *Ibid.*, p. 72.
9. James, *American Scene*, p. 831.
10. Clark in Rockwell, p. 210.
11. Wendell, p. 186.
12. Hale, "American Scenery," pp. 329–30.
13. Cooper, *Deerslayer*, p. 3.
14. Haring, p. 69.
15. Allen Johnson, vol. 4, p. 403.
16. Born, p. 46.
17. Lloyd Goodrich, p. 9.
18. Lillie, "Two Phases of American Art," pp. 206–10.
19. Hale, "Early Art of Thomas Cole," pp. 39–40.
20. Lillie, "Two Phases of American Art," p. 206.
21. Bryant, *Orations and Addresses*, p. 13.
22. Greene, p. 93. Cole's instantaneous success was also well attested by his friend and biographer, Louis L. Nobel: "The whole affair of the three pictures was very gratifying, and well suited to raise hopes. They were not raised in vain. Through the kindness of his new friends, the attention of the public was enlisted, and the way opened to success. He soon received abundant commissions, some from distant cities. 'His fame spread like fire,' said Durand, in conversation on that subject, many years afterwards. . . ." (Noble, p. 58.)
23. Hale, "Early Art of Thomas Cole," p. 22.
24. James Grant Wilson, pp. 43–44.
25. *Ibid.*, p. 51.
26. Godwin, *William Cullen Bryant*, vol. 1, p. 381.
27. Bryant, *Orations and Addresses*, p. 41.
28. Godwin, *William Cullen Bryant*, vol. 1, p. 381.
29. *Ibid.*, p. 367.
30. Bryant, *Orations and Addresses*, p. 41.
31. Godwin, *William Cullen Bryant*, vol. 1, p. 384.
32. *Ibid.*, vol. 2, p. 37, footnote.
33. Brooks, *Washington Irving*, p. 362.
34. Rockwell, p. 183.
35. The painting was given to the New York Public Library, New York City, by Bryant's daughter, Julia, in 1904. (Seaver, p. 36.)

CHAPTER 7—*The Hudson River School of Painting*

1. Richardson, p. 7. (The James Thomas Flexner quotation under the title is from his *That Wilder Image*, p. 267. Flexner's book

was read much too late to form any influence on the present work, but the author could not resist inserting this very appropriate epigram just before releasing his manuscript to the publisher.)

2. McCormick, p. 11.

3. Richardson, p. 7.

4. Sweet's *Hudson River School* contains an excellent survey of the diverse members of the Hudson River School and their far-ranging geographical interests.

5. *Ibid.*, p. 11.

6. There is remarkable unanimity of opinion among American art historians regarding Cole's role in the founding of the Hudson River School: Sweet, *Hudson River School*, p. 12; Lloyd Goodrich, p. 10; Seaver, p. 1; and Francis, p. 113; all say that to Thomas Cole belongs the honor of establishing the first school of American landscape painting.

7. "The Kaaterskill," vol. 1 (1882), p. 2.

8. Lillie, "Two Phases of American Art," p. 211.

9. Sweet, *Hudson River School*, p. 96.

10. Lillie, "Two Phases of American Art," p. 211.

11. Such, for example, is the opinion of F. J. Mather, Jr., who said that Church's "less pretentious transcripts" of the Catskill Mountains "are perhaps, if not the most amazing," then the "finest pictures" he ever made, pp. 304–05.

12. There is some difference of opinion among the experts as to the priority of importance among these four artists. Sweet lists Doughty, Cole, and Durand as "the leaders" of the school ("Asher B. Durand," p. 142, whereas Bartlett Cowdrey excludes Doughty for Kensett in "The Return of John F. Kensett," p. 134. There is never any disagreement, however, about Cole and Durand being two of the main leaders of the school.

13. Cole made an all-out effort about 1833 when he and Durand had an exchange of letters about the matter (John Durand, p. 141).

14. Sweet, "Asher B. Durand," p. 144.

15. Durand's friend and colleague, D. Huntington, is the authoritative source of this opinion: "As far as I can learn, he was the first artist in the country that painted direct from nature" (John Durand, p. 81).

16. *Ibid.*, p. 184.

17. *Ibid.*

18. This was probably the first picture book, planned by a native American artist and devoted exclusively to the American land-

scape, that appeared in the United States. It was almost exclusively the work of Asher B. Durand. It failed, however, after the first and only issue. Besides Durand's "Catskill Mountains," this original issue contained works by Thomas Cole, R. W. Weir, and William J. Bennett; and a preface by Durand's friend, William Cullen Bryant. (Mather, pp. 297–98.)

19. Evers, "Shandaken Mountains," p. 1.
20. Rusk, p. 27.
21. Evers, "Shandaken Mountains," p. 1.
22. John Durand, p. 184.
23. Evers, "Shandaken Mountains," p. 1.
24. Brooks, *Times of Melville and Whitman*, p. 13. The high prices at the Mountain House kept the artists from staying there during protracted periods of work in the mountains, but the registers of the hotel show a fair representation of the Hudson River School for at least occasional visits of one or two nights' duration. In 1853, for instance, Sanford R. Gifford and Jervis McEntee each spent a night at the hotel (June 21 and July 3 respectively), and Jaspar F. Cropsey stayed for the unusual length of seven days (Aug. 3–10). In the following year Frederick E. Church made two separate visits (July 12 and 19), Benjamin B. G. Stone appeared for one night (July 16), and John W. Casilear accompanied by Jonathan Sturges, the art patron, spent two nights at the hotel (July 22–23). In 1855 Church reappeared for another visit (July 21), and McEntee registered for the first two days of August. During the summer of 1861 Gifford and T. Worthington Whittredge had dinner together at the hotel (July 26), and Church and Casilear again put up at the hotel (July 27 and Aug. 17–18 respectively). The season of 1862 saw another visit by Whittredge (Aug. 22) and what was probably the first visit of Régis F. Gignoux (Sept. 7). If the registers of the Mountain House were available for the earlier decades of the century, we would undoubtedly find a similar pattern of at least occasional visits by members of the Hudson River School.
25. The Dutch language and culture were extremely tenacious throughout the Hudson Valley. As late as 1857 we hear that the village of Catskill "is essentially a very *Dutch* appearing village; and here, as well as at many other Dutch towns upon the Hudson, the old inhabitants still retain their mother tongue, and the perpetual jabber, so easy to recognize, is frequently heard." (*Traveller's Steamboat*, p. 46.)
26. Richards, "Catskills," p. 151. The opinion is supported by a state-

ment made to Longstreth by a citizen of Palenville that there were "no summer people here then [i.e. before the Civil War] except artists." (Longstreth, p. 110.)

27. John Durand, pp. 185–86.
28. Richards, *American Travel* (1857), p. 147.
29. Van Loan (1897), p. 40.
30. De Lisser, *Picturesque Catskills*, p. 33. Page 35 contains a picture of Hall's house.
31. Born, p. 139.
32. Lillie, "Two Phases of American Art," p. 211.
33. Sweet, *Hudson River School*, p. 94.
34. Weir.
35. Groce and Wallace, p. 606.
36. De Lisser, *Picturesque Catskills*, p. 30.
37. Mabel Parker Smith, "Sherman Won Atlanta," p. 8.
38. The author encountered these illustrations, or engraved copies of paintings, wherever he went in the Catskills, from a Beach family household in Catskill to the old Bogart house deep in the forest at Palenville.
39. Sweet, *Hudson River School*, p. 113.
40. This is the somewhat ambiguous opinion of Lloyd Goodrich (pp. 8–9).
41. Sweet, *Hudson River School*, p. 35.
42. *Ibid.*
43. Born, p. 38.
44. Called "In the Catskills," it is reproduced in Sweet, *Hudson River School*, p. 38.
45. McCormick, p. 12.
46. Allen Johnson, vol. 10, p. 342.
47. Metropolitan Museum, *John F. Kensett.*
48. Sears, p. 127.
49. *Catalogue of Paintings by the Late Jervis McEntee, N.A.*
50. A painting called "In the Wilds of the Catskills" (reproduced in Sweet, *Hudson River School*, p. 112) is an example of an early work painted in the tradition of the Hudson River School before Wyant came under the influence of Inness.
51. Allen Johnson, vol. 10, p. 342.
52. Born, p. 59.
53. Downes, p. 69.
54. Bartreaux, "W. H. Bartlett," p. 436.
55. "It was once a matter of common knowledge that artists were copying Bartlett. . . ." Bartlett Cowdrey, "William Henry Bart-

lett," p. 392. The unsigned, undated painting of the Catskill
Mountain House owned by the author is probably a copy of
Bartlett's painting of the same subject.

56. Larkin, p. 204.

CHAPTER 8—*The Romantic Debate*

1. Seaver, p. 13.
2. Hale, "American Scenery," p. 323.
3. Cooper, "American and European Scenery Compared," p. 69.
4. W. Gilpin, pp. 15–16.
5. *Ibid.*, p. 11.
6. Seaver, p. 14.
7. Taylor in Rockwell, pp. 252–53; also "Travels at Home."
8. Godwin, *William Cullen Bryant*, vol. 1, p. 367.
9. Washington Irving in *Home Authors and Home Artists*, p. 73.
10. Longstreth, p. 99.
11. James, *American Scene*, pp. 150–54; or "New York and the
    Hudson," pp. 827–31.
12. James, *American Scene*, pp. 146–47; or "New York and the Hud-
    son," p. 824.
13. Seaver, p. 14.
14. W. Gilpin, pp. 28 ff.
15. For a fuller discussion of these distinctions, see Van Zandt, "The
    Scotch School," pp. 156–59.
16. Henry T. Tuckerman, "Over the Mountains, or the Western
    Pioneer," *Home Authors and Home Artists*, pp. 115–16.
17. This was especially true during the antebellum period, but even
    as late as 1882 Wallace Bruce still noted that "no European
    traveler ever thinks of leaving it unvisited." Wallace Bruce, *Hud-
    son River by Daylight*, p. 74.
18. Latrobe, pp. 37–38.
19. *Ibid.*, p. 39.
20. Rockwell's opinion that the Kaaterskill Clove afforded "one of
    the wildest and most romantic rambles in the world" was voiced
    again and again by nineteenth century travelers, p. 183.
21. Latrobe, p. 41.
22. Pierre M. Irving, vol. 3, p. 27.
23. Longstreth, p. 68.
24. Angelo Heilprin, "Catskill Mountains," p. 194.
25. As Benson John Lossing said in 1866, "That view has been
    described a thousand times. I shall not attempt it. Much rhetoric,

and rhyme, and sentimental platitudes have been employed in the service of description. . . ." *Hudson River*, p. 327. Think what the record became after another fifty years!

26. Clark in Rockwell, pp. 212–15.
27. Cuyler in Rockwell, p. 260.
28. Strong, p. 20.
29. Ellet in *Scenery of the Catskill Mountains* (c. 1845), p. 27; Rockwell, p. 239.
30. Curtis, p. 36.
31. Tyrone Power in Rockwell, p. 217.
32. Stone in Rockwell, p. 174.
33. Park Benjamin in *Scenery of the Catskill Mountains* (c. 1845), pp. 18–19; Rockwell, p. 221.
34. Bryant in Durand and Wade, pp. 5–6.
35. Willis, *American Scenery*, vol. 1, p. iii.
36. Cooper, "American and European Scenery Compared," p. 56.
37. *Ibid.*
38. *Ibid.*, p. 54.
39. *Ibid.*, p. 61.
40. *Ibid.*, p. 52. Cole, of course, did not believe this. In one of his poems about the Catskills he declared: "Though not the loftiest that begert the land,/ They yet sublimely rise. . . ." (De Lisser, *Picturesque Catskills*, p. 25.)
41. Cooper, "American and European Scenery Compared," p. 55.
42. *Ibid.*, p. 61.
43. Cole in Rockwell, p. 287.
44. *Ibid.*
45. Hine, p. 49.

CHAPTER 9—*The Romantic Apotheosis*

1. Benjamin in *Scenery of the Catskill Mountains* (c. 1845), p. 18; Rockwell, pp. 221–22.
2. Martineau in *Scenery of the Catskill Mountains* (c. 1845), p. 21; Rockwell, p. 227. George Harvey, the English artist who painted "The Mountain House by Moonlight" and "Sunrise, above the Clouds, from the Catskill Mountains," expressed the same metaphysical belief when he said the view from the Mountain House is an "analogy of the moral world within us." *Illustrations of Our Country*, p. 33.
3. Sweet, *Hudson River School*, p. 8.
4. Richardson, p. 21. The implications of this belief from the point

of view of the artist were eloquently expressed by Asher B. Durand: "It is only through the religious integrity of motive, by which all real artists have ever been actuated, that it [art] still preserves its original purity, impressing the mind through the visible forms of material beauty with a deep sense of the invisible and immaterial, for which end all this world's beauty and significance, beyond the few requirements of our animal nature, seems to be expressly given. . . ." (John Durand, p. 214.)

5. Bryant in Durand and Wade, pp. 5–6.
6. Tuckerman, *Artist-Life*, p. 80.
7. Cole in Rockwell, p. 282.

PART III—INTRODUCTION

1. Ripley and Dana, vol. 4, p. 126.
2. Richardson, p. 20.
3. *Information Please* (1954), p. 211 (for land area); and Lord and Lord, pp. 220–21 (for population).
4. Lord and Lord, p. 79; Martin, II, 10 (map of the U.S., 1870).
5. *Information Please* (1954), p. 222.
6. Hansen (1961), p. 465.
7. Schlesinger, *Political and Social Growth*, p. 66.
8. Channing, vol. 5, p. 82
9. Martin, vol. 1, p. 508.
10. In 1830, the center of population was 18 miles west-southwest of Moorefield, West Virginia. In 1890, it was 48 miles east by north of Cincinnati, Ohio. (Hansen, p. 465.)
11. Schlesinger, *New Viewpoints*, p. 248.
12. Richardson: "After the centennial, romantic art became un-fashionable and rapidly disappeared," p. 21. Also Bartlett Cowdrey: "European Influence was suddenly felt by the American art-loving public in 1876 when a quantity of foreign paintings were shown at the Philadelphia Centennial Exposition. It caused a lessening of interest in the works of Cole, Durand, and Kensett and others of the older Hudson River School group." "John Frederick Kensett," p. 13.
13. Hamm, pp. 165–83.
14. *Catskill Mountain News*, Centennial Edition, Aug. 15, 1963, p. 13. Galli-Curci died in November, 1963.
15. Anita M. Smith, pp. 40–50.
16. Mabel Parker Smith, "In the 80s They All Came."
17. Sims (1891), p. 5.

18. Sims (1904), p. 7.
19. Hudson River Day Line, *Summer Tours* (1907), pp. 137–38. The figure, however, may be excessively low.
20. *Twilight Park in the Catskills*, p. 6; and Munroe, p. 7.
21. Hudson River Day Line, *Summer Tours* (1907), pp. 137–38.
22. Van Loan (1908), p. 13.

CHAPTER 10—*The Coming of the Railroads*

1. Hough, p. 323. According to the official newspaper of the Hotel Kaaterskill, the ground for the railroad "was broken with ceremonies at Catskill in 1831, the company was organized in 1835, the contracts were given out in 1836, the projectors were denounced as swindlers in 1838, and the road was opened to Cooksburg, twenty-six miles, in 1839." "The Kaaterskill," vol. 3. A more sober account may be found in Arthur C. Mack, "Reminder of the Past," pp. 88–95.
2. Sims (1905), pp. 35, 39.
3. Sims (1892), p. 32.
4. Van Loan (1878), p. 10.
5. For example, Richards, *American Summer Resorts* (1876), p. 17, and *History of Greene County*, pp. 338–39.
6. Van Loan (1879), p. 69.
7. *Ibid.*
8. Van Loan (1897), p. 51.
9. The cost of this achievement was the total commitment of Beach's wealth to the resort industry of the Catskill Mountains. Up until this time Beach's main economic wealth had been devoted to the transportation enterprises of the Hudson Valley and therefore the life of all New York State. Now it was devoted to but a part of that life, and to a very local and seasonal part at that. The change in strategy was to prove disastrous to later heirs of Charles L. Beach, for as the resort industry of the Catskills declined under the shattering impact of a new American culture, so the total legacy of Charles L. Beach had perforce to suffer a similar eclipse. In 1860, however, none of this was in the offing; the Catskills were embarking upon the most prosperous years of their history and no one could possibly foresee the cataclysmic changes of World War I or the ultimate demise of the fabulous resorts of the Catskills.
10. Beach.
11. Van Loan (1882), p. 7.

12. Wallace Bruce, *Hudson River by Daylight*, p. 81.
13. "The Kaaterskill," July 1, 1882.
14. "The Kaaterskill," Aug. 19, 1882.
15. Lillie, "The Catskills," p. 527.
16. Beach.
17. Such was the opinion of Mr. Charles G. Coffin, a Catskill lawyer and member of the Greene County Historical Society, as told to the author.
18. "The Kaaterskill," Aug. 19, 1882.
19. *Examiner* Centennial Edition, Aug. 14, 1930, p. 21.
20. In six years' time (1899) Harding retaliated by changing the Kaaterskill Railroad to standard gauge, thus severing the link with Beach's railroad. Beach in turn retaliated the same year by building the narrow gauge "Catskill-Tannersville Railroad" from Otis Summit to Tannersville. The history of these various railroad manipulations is one of the most tortuous in the regional history of American railroads. For help in avoiding gross errors the author is indebted to Gerald M. Best and John B. Hungerford of California, and to Eugene C. Dauner of Port Ewen, N.Y.
21. New York Central and Hudson River Railroad Co., p. 203.
22. Hendricks, p. 46.
23. New York Central and Hudson River Railroad Co., p. 204.
24. Haring, p. 66.
25. *Examiner-Recorder*, April 16, 1953, p. 1.
26. Van Loan (1897), p. 4.
27. New York Central and Hudson River Railroad Co., p. 204.
28. Ingersoll, *Illustrated Guide* (1893), p. 188.
29. *Catskill Mountain Scenery* (after 1896), p. 29.
30. Van Loan (1897), p. 5.
31. Van Loan (1879), p. 9, for instance, says that the village of Catskill is "three to four hours" from New York City by way of the Hudson River Railroad—half the time of the old steamers.
32. Van Loan (1883), p. 7. The combined railroad and steamship facilities of the 1880s provided a remarkable variety of ways and means of getting from the metropolitan centers to the Catskills. In 1883 after the West Shore Line had opened and the Ulster and Delaware had been extended from Hunter to South Lake, people could leave New York at 9:00, 11:00 A.M., or 3:30 P.M. on the east shore line; or 8:30, 11:00 A.M., and 3:30 P.M. on the west shore; and making connections with the same train out of Kingston, they arrived at South Lake at either 2:53, 5:30 or 10:00 P.M. People could also go on to Catskill and make connections with the Catskill Mountain Railroad for the Greene County approach

to the mountains. Or they could take an Albany Day Line steamer, leave New York at 8:30 and arrive at South Lake at 5:30 by way of the Ulster and Delaware Railroad from Kingston. Or they could take an evening boat and arrive the next morning. During the 1880s people could also leave Philadelphia at 8:20 A.M., take a through parlor car to Phoenicia, and change to the narrow gauge Stony Clove Line which arrived at South Lake at 4:00 P.M. (after 1899 when the Stony Clove Line became standard gauge, through cars could be had all the way without any change whatsoever). A limited express also left Philadelphia at 1:30 P.M. and joined at Kingston with another train that had left Philadelphia at 1:00 P.M. and arrived at South Lake at 10:00 that night. People could also leave Boston at 8:30 A.M., arrive at the town of Hudson at 3:10 P.M., cross the river by one of Beach's ferries, make connections with the Catskill Mountain Railroad, and arrive at Pine Orchard by 6:00 P.M. After the opening of the Otis Elevating in 1892 all scheduled routes to and from Pine Orchard by way of the entrepôt of Catskill had an hour and a half taken off. [Information on the transportation facilities of the 1880s is scattered throughout all the guide books of the era; a good deal of the above, however, came from the very elaborate information provided on the last page of "The Kaaterskill," Aug. 15, 1883.]

33. New York Central and Hudson River Railroad Co., p. xl.
34. Until about 1953 automobiles took at least four hours to go from New York to the summit of the Catskills. The opening of the New York State Thruway reduced that time to two and a half to three hours.

CHAPTER 11—*The Flush Years of the Catskills*

1. Lillie, "The Catskills," pp. 521–23.
2. Willis in *Scenery of the Catskill Mountains*, pp. 17–18; Rockwell, p. 219.
3. The *New York*, for instance, had a length of 341 feet and could carry 2,500 to 4,500 people! (Hudson River Day Line, *The Most Charming Inland Water-Trip*.)
4. Daniels, p. 7.
5. Statement on the cover of *The Scenery of the Catskill Mountains* (1840s).
6. *Ibid.*, p. 19.
7. Sims (1894), p. 7.

8. Hendricks, p. 5.
9. Sims (1905), pp. 9–10.
10. John Durand, p. 141.
11. The full poem (twelve stanzas) appears in Rockwell, pp. 322–23.
12. Brown in Bryant, ed., *Picturesque America*, vol. 2, p. 133.
13. Schile, preface.
14. Van Loan (1897), p. 12.
15. This was especially true of yellow fever. Adams, vol. 5, p. 504.
16. *Ibid.*
17. Krout and Fox, *Completion of Independence*, p. 305.
18. Heiser, p. 446.
19. Adams, vol. 1, p. 369. Much data was also obtained from *The Encyclopaedia Britannica*, vol. 6, p. 264.
20. Pierre M. Irving, pp. 31–32.
21. Adams, vol. 1, p. 369.
22. Gallt, p. 208.
23. Heiser, p. 446.
24. Adams, vol. 3, p. 329.
25. *Encyclopaedia Britannica*, vol. 6, p. 264.
26. Sims (1909), p. 13.
27. Buckingham, pp. 236–37.
28. Sims (1909), p. 15.
29. Hall, vol. 2, p. 9.
30. Daniels, p. 5.
31. Longstreth, p. 31.
32. De Lisser, *Picturesque Catskills*, p. 70.
33. Clifton Johnson, p. 171.
34. Sims (1905), p. 115. The 25,000 figure is a rough estimate based upon the tables listed on pp. 116–39.
35. *New York Hotel Review*, Jan. 1909, p. 22.

CHAPTER 12—*"One of the Greatest Hotels of the Country"*

1. Van Loan (1878), p. 6.
2. "The number of visitors to the Catskill mountains has increased ten fold during the past fifteen years" [1864–1879]. "While, until about 1865 they might have been counted in hundreds, since that time each season has added to the numbers, so that now thousands annually visit this region." Rusk, pp. 5, 11.
3. Van Loan (1879), p. 10.
4. New York West Shore and Buffalo Railroad Co. (1883), p. 21.
5. Ingersoll, *Illustrated Guide* (1893), p. 188.

6. Curtis, p. 39.
7. Lillie, "The Catskills," p. 533. There were 37 rooms that were 12 x 15, mostly located on the third floor; there were 22 rooms which were 9 x 12, seven on the second floor and fifteen on the third. Sixteen more rooms were 9 x 15, scattered on the first three floors. Eight rooms on the second floor were 8 x 14. Eight more on the second and third floors were 10 x 15. Nine rooms were 10 x 12, seven 10 x 10, six 10 x 14. The remainder (about thirty) varied in size from 9 x 14 (four) to 12 x 17 (one). The choicest rooms were on the second and third floors facing the Hudson Valley. About forty rooms faced the two open courts (which were landscaped with lawns, walks, and shrubs). At one time about 100 rooms were furnished with private baths, but the majority of the guests were forced to use separate men's and ladies' rooms scattered throughout the hotel.
8. *In the Catskills*, p. 38
9. Ellet in *Scenery of the Catskill Mountains* (c. 1845), p. 24; Rockwell, p. 232.
10. *Ibid.*
11. The extension is visible in an illustration of the Mountain House that appears on page 6 of Van Loan (1879).
12. Richards, *American Travel* (1857), p. 145.
13. Ellet in *Scenery of the Catskill Mountains* (c. 1845), p. 24; Rockwell, p. 232.
14. Timetable of the New York Central Lines, "In the Catskill Mountains, reached by the West Shore Railroad and Connections" (1908), p. 28.
15. Lillie, "The Catskills," p. 533.
16. The earliest reference to 400 guests that the author has found appears in Rusk, p. 7.
17. Rockwell, p. 327.
18. New Yorkers could also use the booking office that the Mountain House maintained in the city during the spring of each year after the turn of the century.
19. Consult, for instance, the correlative advertisements of the Laurel House and Mountain House in Sims (1905), pp. 170, 176.
20. Lillie, "The Catskills," p. 532.
21. Sims (1904), p. 179.
22. Barr.
23. *History of Greene County*, p. 125.
24. Mabel Parker Smith, "In the 80s They All Came," p. 7-A.
25. For one six-year period it was run by Walton Van Loan, later

the author of the celebrated Catskill Mountain Guide. Van Loan
(1908), p. 65.

26. *Catskill Mountain Scenery* (after 1896), p. 36.
27. Link.
28. New York Central and Hudson River Railroad, p. xl.
29. Ingersoll, *Illustrated Guide* (1908), p. 188.
30. Mabel Parker Smith, "Feud Between the Mountain House," p. 3.
31. Lillie, "The Catskills," p. 533.
32. Van Loan (1897), p. 13.
33. Van Loan (1909), p. 13.
34. Van Loan (1881), p. 87. Traffic over the new road rose and fell
    with the fate of the Overlook House, and when the hotel closed
    its doors in 1891 it was not long before the road was permanently
    abandoned. By 1918 Longstreth noted that "washouts, new trees,
    deserted flagstone quarries, decaying cabins mark the re-occu-
    pancy by the wilderness," p. 33.
35. *History of Greene County*, p. 330.
36. Van Loan (1896), p. 12.
37. These barns were never painted by the artists of the Hudson
    River School (though they were rudimentarily suggested in
    some of the paintings of the Mountain House done from North
    Mountain), and the author has seen only two photographs that
    barely suggest their former size and location.
38. Van Loan (1897), p. 12.
39. Sims (1905), p. 176; and Van Loan (1909), p. 13.
40. New York Central and Hudson River Railroad, pp. 199–200.
41. West Shore Railroad, p. 41.
42. Sims (1916), p. 83.
43. Wallace Bruce, *Hudson River by Daylight* (1876), p. 441.
44. Link, p. 483.
45. Ferris, p. 169.
46. Onteora Park, for instance, claimed at various times such dis-
    tinguished visitors and residents as Maude Adams, Mark Twain,
    Hamlin Garland, Brander Matthews, William T. Tilden, Jr.,
    Henry L. Stimson, R. H. Macy, and a host of socialites, theatrical
    producers, and prominent people from all walks of life. During
    its first three years of operation (1881–1883) the Hotel Kaaterskill
    housed such dignitaries as John Greenleaf Whittier, Lily Langtry,
    John Wanamaker, Herbert Spencer, General George B. McClel-
    lan, Thomas A. Edison, Joseph Pulitzer, Oscar Wilde, and Gen-
    eral Ulysses S. Grant.
47. *The Kaaterskill*, Sept. 15, 1882.

48. Sims (1892), p. 66.
49. *History of Greene County*, p. 338.
50. Mabel Parker Smith, "In the 80s They All Came," p. 7-A.
51. *Ibid.*
52. *Ibid.*
53. Mabel Parker Smith, "Sherman Won Atlanta," p. 8.
54. Wilde, *Decorative Art*, p. 176.
55. I am indebted for this part of the story to an article by Alf Evers, "Oscar Wilde Agreed to Lecture in Woodstock," p. 5.
56. *Ibid.*
57. *Ibid.*
58. *The Kaaterskill*, Aug. 19, 1882.
59. Evers, "Oscar Wilde," p. 5.
60. I am indebted for this part of the story to Mabel Parker Smith, "In the 80s They All Came," p. 7-A.
61. Wilde, *Impressions*, pp. 15–16.
62. Mabel Parker Smith, "In the 80s They All Came," p. 7-A.
63. Besides heading a famous law firm in Philadelphia, Pepper served two terms in the United States Senate, taught law at the University of Pennsylvania, Yale, and Berkeley College; became a Fellow of the American Academy of Arts and Sciences, a member of the American Philosophical Society, and President of the American Law Institute; and was the author of many books, including *Philadelphia Lawyer* (1944). (*Who's Who in America*, vol. 24, 1946–47, p. 1844.)
64. Allen Johnson, vol. 13, p. 392.
65. Schile, p. 66.
66. Brown in Bryant, ed., *Picturesque America*, vol. 2, pp. 116–17.

PART IV: Introduction

1. Longstreth, p. 31.
2. WPA guide, p. 407.
3. By September 30, 1963, the State Forest Preserve had grown to 238,389.69 acres or 37 percent of the total land area of the Catskill State Park (Fosburgh, "New York State's Forest Preserve," p. 18.
4. *Information Please* (1954), p. 211.
5. Lord and Lord, pp. 220–21.
6. Hansen, p. 465.
7. Lord and Lord, p. 238.
8. Faulkner, p. 133.

9. Wish, vol. 2, p. 455.

10. Lord and Lord, p. 163.

11. *Information Please* (1954), p. 213.

12. *World Book Encyclopaedia*, vol. 12, p. 5424.

13. Richards, *American Travel* (1857), p. 144.

14. Brown in Bryant, ed., *Picturesque America*, vol. 2, p. 133.

CHAPTER 13—*The Years of Decline*

1. De Lisser, *Picturesque Catskills*, p. 10.

2. Ulster and Delaware Railroad, "Announces the Improved Train Service."

3. Hendricks, p. 45.

4. *Ibid.*, p. 40.

5. Ingersoll, *Illustrated Guide* (1908), p. 165.

6. *Ibid.*, p. 172.

7. Faulkner, p. 134.

8. Van Loan (1909), p. 12.

9. *Examiner*, Centennial Edition, p. 19.

10. Haring, p. 67.

11. Vedder, *Official History of Greene County*, pp. 143–44.

12. Mabel Parker Smith, "Owner States Portion," p. 3.

13. *The Kaaterskill*, Aug. 15, 1883.

14. Van Wagonen's marriage to Mary L. Beach occurred at the Mountain House on June 29, 1911, and was attended by some of the most impressive ceremonies the hotel had ever seen. The wedding party and its distinguished guests left the town of Catskill by special train in the early evening and ascended the mountain by means of the Otis Railroad. During the slow ascent the party was caught under the playful illumination of the hotel's giant searchlight. Arriving at the Mountain House, the party found it fully bedecked for the occasion, the great ballroom being especially beautiful under a rich canopy of mountain laurel and roses. An orchestra from New York City was imported for the occasion, and the festivities came to an end in a gala ball. ("Summer Night's Wedding," Greene County *Recorder*, June 30, 1911.) Van Wagonen was the assistant manager of the Mountain House under George Beach, the last son of Charles L. Beach. When this son died in 1918 and ownership passed into the hands of Louis J. and Charles T. Beach, Van Wagonen became full manager.

15. Catskill Chamber of Commerce, p. 24.

16. *In the Catskills*, p. 38.

17. *Examiner*, Centennial Edition, p. 21.

18. By a deed dated June 6, 1930, and recorded June 30, 1930, in the Book of Deeds (No. 255, p. 571) of the Clerk of Greene County, the State bought exactly 619.6 acres from Harry Tannenbaum for $6,176.

19. The Act of the New York State Constitution that governs the acquisition of such land stipulates that it "shall be kept forever as wild forest lands" (Article XIV, Section 1 of the Constitution).

20. Book of Deeds, No. 255, p. 485, Greene County Clerk's Office, Catskill, N.Y.

21. Haring, pp. 165–66.

22. Hendricks, pp. 45–46.

23. Carmer, p. 325.

24. During the 1930s it was kept at 11 West 42nd Street.

25. After 1931 New Yorkers could leave the city by way of the George Washington Bridge and ascend the Hudson via route 9W, or go up the Westchester County parkways and cross the Hudson at Bear Mountain or Poughkeepsie.

26. Brochure in possession of the author.

27. Carmer, p. 325.

28. It is an anecdote of Mrs. Elsie S. Feistmann of Jackson Heights, N.Y.

29. Such is the opinion of Moseman's closest friends.

30. A writer for the Albany *Knickerbocker News*, Katherine A. Van Epps, declared in the March 29, 1952, issue of her newspaper that "The Mountain House was last open in 1945, when Mr. Moseman and his partners ran it as a 'boarding house.'" This opinion, however, clearly seems to be erroneous. All Moseman's friends interviewed by this author declared that the hotel closed at some earlier date; and one of Moseman's closest friends, Mrs. Elsie S. Feistmann, whom Moseman asked to manage the hotel during its last season, told the author that the year 1942 is the more likely date. This date is also confirmed by the *Ulster County Townsman*, Jan. 31, 1963, which said that the hotel "shut its doors in 1942." In the light of these authoritative opinions, the author has adjudged that the year 1942 was in fact the final year of the Mountain House.

CHAPTER 14—*Years of Embattled Ruin*

1. The author is indebted to Mr. Edward G. West, friend of Claude Moseman and member of the New York Conservation Department, for the details of these negotiations.

2. Van Olinda.

3. Mabel Parker Smith, "Lines of First Mountain House."

4. *Examiner-Recorder*, June 21, 1951.

5. "Hope for the Mountain House."

6. Haskins.

7. Irving's tale described Sleepy Hollow, not the view from Pine Orchard. Mr. Huth alludes to James Fenimore Cooper's description in *The Pioneers*.

8. Huth.

9. Van Epps, p. 4–B.

10. *Examiner-Recorder*, April 1, 1954.

11. Mabel Parker Smith, "Lines of First Mountain House."

12. *Ibid.*

13. Hone, p. 405.

14. The author is indebted to Mrs. Elsie S. Feistmann and Mrs. Ridi Kolb, friends and co-workers of Claude Moseman, for details regarding the final activities of the owner of the Mountain House.

15. Barr.

16. *New York Times*, April 9, 1962.

17. New York State Conservation Department, "News Bulletin," April 9, 1962, pp. 1–2. The Conservation Department also tried to purchase the Laurel House and its property at this time, but was not successful until the fall of 1965 when it finally paid $75,000 for 89.32 acres plus the buildings of the hotel and the once-famous Kaaterskill Falls.

18. Lampedusa, p. 35.

Bibliography

Abbot, Arthur P. *The Hudson River Today and Yesterday*. New York: De La Mare, 1915.

Adams, James Truslow, ed. *Dictionary of American History*. 5 vols. New York: Scribner, 1946, 2nd rev. ed.

Albany Institute of History and Art. *Catalogue of Valuable Oil Paintings. Works of the famous artist, Sanford R. Gifford . . . to be sold without reserve, by order of executors on April 11th and 12th, 28th and 29th. . . .* New York, 1881.

———. *The Works of Thomas Cole, 1801–1848* (exhibition catalogue). Albany, N.Y., 1941.

American Art Union. *Exhibition of the Paintings of the Late Thomas Cole at the Gallery of the American Art Union.* New York, 1848.

The American Landscape (engravings by Asher B. Durand; preface and descriptive text by William Cullen Bryant). New York: E. Bliss, 1830.

Art News, Aug. 18, 1906 (obituary of Benjamin Bellows Grant Stone).

Bacon, Edgar M. *The Hudson River from Ocean to Source*. New York: Putnam, 1907.

Barr, Daniel. "Once Regal 'Mountain House' Finished, At Last," Albany *Times-Union*, Oct. 2, 1960.

Barrett, Richard S. *The Eagle-Guide to the Catskill Mountains*. Brooklyn, N.Y.: Eagle Press, 1905.

———. *Greene County, Catskills, New York*. Catskill Chamber of Commerce, c. 1919.

———. *The Land of Rip Van Winkle, Greene County, Catskills.* C. 1920.

Barteaux, Eleanor. "W. H. Bartlett, of 'Bartlett Prints,'" *Dalhousie Review*, Vol. XXIV, No. 4, Jan., 1945.

Beach, Charles L. "Autobiography of Charles L. Beach" (unpublished manuscript in possession of Mrs. Charles A. W. Beach, Catskill, N.Y.).

Beattie, William. *Memoir of the Life of W. H. Bartlett.* London: [G. Virtue?], 1855.

Beers, F. W. *Atlas of Greene County, New York.* New York: Beers, Ellis and Soule, 1867.

———. *County Atlas of Ulster, N.Y.* New York: Walker and Jewett, 1875.

Bellows, Arnold Hill. *The Legend of Utsayantha and Other Folklore of the Catskills.* Margaretville, N.Y.: The Catskill Mountain News, 1945.

Benjamin, Park. "Catskill Mountain House," *New World* (magazine), July, 1843.

Benjamin, S. G. W. *Art in America.* New York: Harper, 1880.

Blair, Hugh. *Lectures on Rhetoric and Belles Lettres.* London: Cadell and Davies, 1819.

Boas, George, ed. *Romanticism in America.* Baltimore: Johns Hopkins, 1940.

Born, Wolfgang. *American Landscape Painting.* New Haven: Yale, 1948.

Brodhead, John Romeyn. *History of the State of New York.* 2 vols. New York: Harper, 1871.

Brooks, Van Wyck. *The Times of Melville and Whitman.* New York: Dutton, 1947.

———. *The World of Washington Irving.* New York: Dutton, 1944.

Brown, Henry Collins. *The Lordly Hudson.* New York: Scribner, 1937.

Bruce, Henry. "Old Catskill," *Harper's Magazine*, Vol. LX.

Bruce, Wallace. *Along the Hudson with Washington Irving.* Poughkeepsie, N.Y.: Haight, 1913.

———. *The Hudson. Sketches and Poems about the Catskills, Adirondacks, Highlands, and Tappan Zee.* Boston: Houghton Mifflin, 1881.

———. *The Hudson. Three Centuries of History, Romance and Invention.* New York: Bryant Union, 1913.

———. *The Hudson River by Daylight.* New York: American News, 1872, 1875, 1876, 1882.

———. *The Hudson River Guide and Map. Showing Prominent Residences and Historic Landmarks of the River.* New York: Bryant Union, 1903.

Bryant, William Cullen. *A Funeral Oration Occasioned by the Death of Thomas Cole.* New York: Appleton, 1848.

————. *Orations and Addresses.* New York: Putnam, 1873.

————, ed. *Picturesque America: or, The Land We Live In. A delineation by pen and pencil of the mountains, rivers, lakes, forests, waterfalls, shores, canyons, valleys, cities and other picturesque features of our country.* 2 vols. New York: Appleton, 1872–74 (introduction by Bryant).

————, ed. *The United States Review and Literary Gazette,* Oct. 1, 1827.

Buckingham, James Silk. *America, Historical, Statistic, and Descriptive.* 3 vols. London: Fisher, 1841.

Buckman, D. L. *Old Steamboat Days on the Hudson River.* New York: Grafton, 1907.

Burke, Edmund. *Philosophical Inquiry into the Origin of Our Idea of the Sublime and Beautiful.* Baltimore: Neal, 1833.

Burroughs, John. *In the Catskills.* Boston: Houghton Mifflin, 1910.

Carmer, Carl. *The Hudson.* New York: Farrar, 1939.

Catalogue of Paintings by the Late Jervis McEntee, N. A. (executor's sale). New York, 1892.

Catskill Chamber of Commerce. *The Greene County Catskills.* 1924.

Catskill Mountain Association. *Treasurer's Accounts.* (One volume with entries by Ezra Hawley for the years 1823–43 and entries by Charles L. Beach for the years 1845–46, 1876, 1879, and 1886.) Manuscript Room of the State Library, Albany, N.Y.

Catskill Mountain House, Beachview, New York. (12-page picturebook.) Buffalo, Cleveland, and New York: Matthews-Northrop, c. 1922.

"Catskill Mountain House," *Bower of Taste,* Vol. 2, Boston, 1829.

"Catskill Mountain House, First Built in 1823, Has Inspired Famous Writers," *Greene County Examiner-Recorder,* Catskill, N.Y., Centennial Edition, Aug. 14, 1930.

Catskill Mountain House. *Registers.* (Volumes covering the years 1853–69, 1902–13, and 1915–16.) Vedder Memorial Library, Greene County Historical Society, Coxsackie, N.Y.

Catskill Mountain News, Margaretville, New York. Centennial Edition, Aug. 15, 1963.

Catskill Mountain Scenery. (Pamphlet by the Mountain House, after 1896.)

Catskill Mountain Summer Resorts. Containing selected lists of hotels, boarding houses, and farm houses where summer guests are entertained. New York: American Resort Assn., 1902.

"Catskill Prospects," *New York Herald Tribune*, July 5, 1954.

The Catskills. (Illustrated.) New York: Wittemann, 1889.

Chadwick, George H. *Geology of the Catskill and Kaaterskill Quadrangles*. Part II, *New York State Museum Bulletin*, No. 336, June, 1944.

Channing, Edward. *A History of the United States*. 6 vols. New York: Macmillan, 1912–25.

Clark, Willis Gaylord. "Impressions of the Scenery of the Catskills," *The Literary Remains of the Late Willis Gaylord Clark*, ed. by Lewis Gaylord Clark. New York: Burgess, Stringer, 1844.

Clearwater, Alphonso T. *The History of Ulster County, New York*. Kingston, N.Y.: Van Deusen, 1907.

Coffin, Robert Barry. *The Home of Cooper and the Haunts of Leatherstocking*. New York: Russell, 1872.

Cole, Thomas, "The Falls of the Kaaterskill in Winter," *New York Evening Post*, March 29, 1843.

———. "Lecture on American Scenery," *The Northern Light*, Vol. I, May, 1841. (Delivered before the Catskill Lyceum, April 1, 1841.)

Commemorative Biographical Record of Ulster County. New York and Chicago: J. H. Beers, 1896.

Conningham, Frederick A. *Currier and Ives, An Illustrated Check List*. New York: Crown, 1949.

Cooper, James Fenimore. "American and European Scenery Compared," *The Home Book of the Picturesque*. New York: Putnam, 1852.

———. *The Deerslayer* (Mohawk Edition). New York: Putnam.

———. *Home As Found*. Chicago and New York: Bedford, Clark, c. 1838.

———. *The Pioneers* (Mohawk Edition). New York: Putnam.

Cowdrey, Bartlett. "The Hudson River School and Its Place in American Art," *American Collector*, Vol. XIV, No. 4, May, 1945.

———. "John Frederick Kensett, 1816–1872, Painter of Pure Landscape," *American Collector*, Vol. XIV, No. 1, Feb., 1945.

———. "The Return of John F. Kensett," *The Old Print Shop Portfolio*, Vol. IV, No. 6, Feb., 1945.

———. "William Henry Bartlett and the American Scene," *New York History*, Vol. XXII, No. 4, Oct., 1941.

Cowdrey, Mary Bartlett. *American Academy of Fine Arts and American Art-Union, 1816–52*. 2 vols. New York: New-York Historical Society, 1955. (With a history of the Academy by Theodore Sizer, of the Art-Union by Charles E. Baker, and a foreword by James Thomas Flexner.)

Cowdrey, Mary Bartlett. "Jaspar F. Cropsey, 1823–1900, The Colorist of the Hudson River School," *Panorama*, Vol. I, May, 1946.
———. *National Academy of Design Exhibition Record, 1826–1860*. 2 vols. New York: New-York Historical Society, 1943.
Cropsey, Maria. *Catalogue. Of the collection of oil paintings and water colors by the gifted American artist, the late Jaspar F. Cropsey, belonging to the estate of Maria Cropsey*. New York: Silo Art Galleries, 1906.
Curtis, George William. *Lotus-Eating: A Summer Book*. New York: Harper, 1852.
Daniels, George H. "In the Catskill Mountains via the New York Central and Hudson River Railroad" (pamphlet). 1893.
Darby, William. *A Tour from the City of New York to Detroit, in the Michigan Territory, Made Between the 2nd and the 22nd of September, 1818*. Brooklyn, N.Y.: Kirk and Mercein, 1819.
De Lisser, R. Lionel. *Picturesque Catskills, Greene County*. Northampton, Mass.: Picturesque Publishing Co., 1894.
———. *Picturesque Ulster*. Kingston, N.Y.: Styles and Bruyn, 1896.
Denison, Merrill. "The Great River of the Mountains," *Scenic and Historic America*, Vol. V, No. 3, May, 1940.
"Descriptive Journal of a Jaunt Up the Grand Canal; Being a Letter from a Gentleman in New York, to a Lady in Washington, in August, 1825," *The Atheneum Magazine*, Oct., 1825.
De Witt, William C. *People's History of Kingston, Rondout, and Vicinity*. New Haven, Conn.: Tuttle, Morehouse, 1943.
Disturnell, John. *A Gazetteer of the State of New York*. Albany: Van Benthuysen, 1843.
———. *New York State Guide*. Albany: Disturnell, 1843.
———. *The Northern Traveller*. New York: Disturnell, 1844.
Douglas, Edward M. *Gazetteer of the Mountains of the State of New York*. Washington, 1927.
Downes, William Howe. *The Life and Works of Winslow Homer*. Boston: Houghton Mifflin, 1911.
Dunlap, William. *History of the Rise and Progress of the Arts of Design in the United States*. 2 vols. New York: Scott, 1834.
———. *Diary*. (5 volumes for the years 1797–98, 1819–20, 1833–34, in the manuscript collection of the New-York Historical Society.)
Dunn, Esher H. "Thomas Cole—A Man and His Mountain," *The Conservationist*, April–May, 1963.
Durand, Asher B., and E. Wade, eds. *The American Landscape*, No. 1. New York: Bliss, 1830. (With a prospectus by the editors and a preface by William Cullen Bryant.)

Durand, John. *The Life and Times of Asher B. Durand*. New York: Scribner, 1894.

Duyckinck, E. A., and G. L. Duyckinck, eds. *Cyclopaedia of American Literature*. 2 vols. New York: Scribner, 1855.

Dwight, Henry Edwin. "Account of the Kaatskill Mountains," *American Journal of Science*, 1820.

Dwight, Theodore. *The Northern Traveller*. New York: Carvill, 1828.

Dykeman, George A., ed. *Choice Bits of Scenery in the Catskills. From the photographs taken by local artists*.

Evers, Alf. "Oscar Wilde Agreed to Lecture in Woodstock in 1882," *Record Press*, Woodstock, N.Y., Nov. 15, 1962.

———. "The Shandaken Mountains and Asher Durand," *Ulster County Townsman*, Vol. 7, No. 1, Woodstock, N.Y., Jan. 5, 1961.

———. "Thomas Cole Climbs Overlook," *Record Press*, Woodstock, N.Y., June 20, 1963.

Encyclopaedia Britannica. 11th Edition. 29 vols. Cambridge, England: Cambridge, 1911.

Faulkner, Harold Underwood. *The Quest for Social Justice*. New York: Macmillan, 1931.

Ferris, R. *The Catskills: An Illustrated Handbook*. Kingston, N.Y.: Ferris, 1897.

Fielding, Mantle. *Dictionary of American Painters, Sculptors, and Engravers*. New York: Struck, 1945.

Flexner, James Thomas. *That Wilder Image*. Boston: Little, Brown, 1962.

———. *The Light of Distant Skies, 1760–1835*. New York: Harcourt, Brace, 1954.

Flick, Alexander C., ed. *History of the State of New York*. 10 vols. New York: Columbia, 1933–37.

Fosburgh, P. W. "New York State's Forest Preserve," *The Conservationist*, Vol. XVIII, No. 3, Dec. 1963–Jan. 1964.

Francis, Henry S. "Thomas Cole: Painter of the Catskill Mountains," *Bulletin of the Cleveland Museum of Art*, Vol. XXIV, July, 1937.

French, J. H. *Gazetteer of the State of New York*. Syracuse, N.Y.: R. Pearsall Smith, 1860.

Gallt, Frank A. *Dear Old Greene County*. Catskill, N.Y., 1915.

"George H. Beach Visits Pasadena," *New York Hotel Review*, New York, Jan., 1909.

Gilpin, Henry Dilworth. *Northern Tour: Being A Guide to Saratoga, Lake George, etc*. Philadelphia: Carey and Lea, 1825.

Gilpin, William. *Forest Scenery*. Edinburgh, 1834.

Godwin, Parke, ed. *Prose Writings* (of William Cullen Bryant). 2 vols. New York: Appleton, 1884.
———. *William Cullen Bryant.* 2 vols. New York: Appleton, 1883.
Goodrich, A. T., ed. *The Northern Traveller.* 2nd ed. New York: Goodrich, 1826.
Goodrich, Lloyd. *A Century of American Landscape Painting, 1800–1900* (exhibition catalogue). New York: Whitney Museum, 1938.
Gordon, T. F. *Gazetteer of the State of New York.* Philadelphia: Collins, 1836.
Gould, Jean. *Winslow Homer, A Portrait.* New York: Dodd, Mead, 1962.
Greene, George Washington. *Biographical Studies.* New York: Putnam, 1860.
Groce, George C. and David H. Wallace. *The New-York Historical Society's Dictionary of Artists in America, 1564–1860.* New Haven: Yale, 1957.
Guyot, A. *Map of the Catskill Mountains.* New York: Scribner, 1880.
Hale, Edward Everett. "American Scenery in Cooper's Novels," *Sewanee Review,* Vol. XVIII, July, 1910.
———. "The Early Art of Thomas Cole," *Art in America,* Vol. IV, 1916.
Hall, Capt. Basil. *Travels in America in the Years 1827 and 1828.* 3rd ed. 3 vols. Edinburgh: Robert Cadwell, 1830.
Halsey, R. T. Haines. *Pictures of Old New York on Dark Blue Staffordshire Pottery.* New York: Dodd, Mead, 1899.
Hamm, Margherita A. *Eminent Actors in Their Homes.* New York: James Pott, 1902.
Hansen, Harry, ed. *The World Almanac.* New York: *New York World-Telegram,* 1956–63.
Hardt, Anton. *Souvenir Spoons of the 90's.* Privately printed, 1962. (Reprint of the original edition of 1891.)
Haring, H. A. *Our Catskill Mountains.* New York: Putnam, 1931.
Harris, Harold. *Treasure Tales of the Shawangunks and the Catskills.* 1955.
Hart, James D. *The Oxford Companion to American Literature.* New York: Oxford, 1941.
Hartmann, Sadakichi. *A History of American Art.* 2 vols. Boston: Page, 1902.
Harvey, George. *Harvey's Illustrations of Our Country. With an Outline of Its Social Progress, Political Development, and Material Resources, Being an Epitome of a Part of Eight Lectures which the Artist had the Honor of delivering before the Members of the Royal*

Institution of Great Britain, in 1849, and subsequently before many other Literary Societies of England and Scotland, entitled The Discovery, Resources, and Progress of North America, North of Virginia, illustrated by more than Sixty Pictorial Views. Boston: Dutton and Wentworth, 1851.

Haskins, Vernon. Quoted in *Greene County Examiner-Recorder*, Catskill, N.Y., Jan. 17, 1952.

Hatch, John Davis. *The Works of Thomas Cole, 1801–48* (exhibition catalogue). Albany: Albany Institute of History and Art, 1941.

Haunts of Rip Van Winkle, Or Rambles Among the Catskill Mountains. New York: Brown, 1886.

Heilprin, Angelo. "The Catskill Mountains," *American Geographical Society Bulletin*, Vol. XXXIX, 1907.

Hendricks, H. *Guide to the Catskill Mountains.* New York: New York American System of Information Bureaus, 1903.

Heiser, Victor. *An American Doctor's Odyssey.* New York: Grosset, 1936.

Hickey, Andrew S. *The Story of Kingston.* New York: Stratford House, 1952.

Hine, Charles Gilbert. *Hine's Annual.* New York: [privately printed], 1907.

———. *The West Bank of the Hudson River, Albany to Tappan; Notes on Its History and Legends, Its Ghost Stories and Romances.* (Newark? N.J., 1907.) Also published in *Hine's Annual*, 1906.

History of Greene County. New York: Beers, 1884.

Home Authors and Home Artists; or, American Scenery, Art, and Literature, Comprising a Series of Essays by Washington Irving, W. C. Bryant, Fenimore Cooper, N. P. Willis, Bayard Taylor, H. T. Tuckerman, F. L. Magoon, Dr. Bethune, A. B. Street, Miss Field, etc. New York: Leavitt and Allen, 1852.

Hone, Joseph. *W. B. Yeats.* London: Macmillan, 1942.

"Hope for the Mountain House" (editorial), *Greene County Examiner-Recorder*, Catskill, N.Y., July 5, 1951.

Hough, Franklin B. *Gazetteer of the State of New York.* Albany: Boyd, 1873.

The Hudson Illustrated with Pen and Pencil. New York: Appleton, 1875.

The Hudson. Illustrated with pen and pencil; comprising sketches, local and legendary, of its several places of interest; together with the route to Niagara Falls; forming a companion for the pleasure tourist. New York: Strong, 1852.

Hudson River Day Line. *Hudson River by Daylight.* New York: 1912.

———. *The Most Charming Inland Water-Trip on the American Continent.* New York: Stillson, 1903.

———. *Summer Excursion Routes and the Catskill Mountain Resorts.* 1907, 1911.

———. *Summer Tours.* 1907.

The Hudson River Guide. New York: Cotton and Disturnell, 1835, 1839.

Huth, Hans. "Preserving a Landmark," letter to *The New York Times*, Nov. 20, 1951.

In the Catskills. Devoted to Boarding-Houses and Hotels of the Catskills, Shawangunks and Mountains of Sullivan County. June 10, 1922.

Information Please Almanac. New York: Macmillan, 1954.

Ingersoll, Ernest. "At the Gateway of the Catskills," *Harper's Magazine*, Vol. LIV.

———. *Illustrated Guide to the Hudson River and Catskill Mountains.* Chicago and New York: Rand McNally, 1893, 1897, 1898, 1900, 1901, 1903, 1907, 1910.

Irving, Pierre M. *The Life and Letters of Washington Irving.* 4 vols. New York: Putnam, 1862–64.

Irving, Washington. *Rip Van Winkle and the Legend of Sleepy Hollow.* New York: McKay.

———. *Rip Van Winkle and Sleepy Hollow.* New York: Kaaterskill, 1884.

———. *Spanish Papers and Other Miscellanies.* Pierre M. Irving, ed. 2 vols. New York: Putnam, 1866.

Isham, Samuel. *The History of American Painting.* Rev. ed. New York: Macmillan, 1942.

James, Henry. *The American Scene.* New York: Scribner, 1946.

———. "New York and the Hudson: A Spring Impression," *North American Review*, Vol. CLXXXI, 1905.

Johnson, Allen, and Dumas Malone, eds. *Dictionary of American Biography.* Centenary Edition. 22 vols. New York: Scribner, 1946.

Johnson, Clifton. *The Picturesque Hudson.* New York: Macmillan, 1909.

The Kaaterskill. (Journal of the Hotel Kaaterskill), Vol. I, No. 1, July 1, 1882; No. 6, Aug. 5, 1882; No. 7, Aug. 12, 1882; No. 8, Aug. 19, 1882; No. 12, Sept. 15, 1882; Vol. II, No. 25, Aug. 15, 1883; Vol. III, No. 30, July 2, 1884. [Privately printed by the Hotel Kaaterskill.]

Killner, Sydney. "The Beginnings of Landscape Painting in America," *Arts in America*, Vol. XXVI, No. 4, Oct., 1938.

Knapp, Samuel L. *The Picturesque Beauties of the Hudson River and Its Vicinity. Illustrated in a Series of Views, from Original Drawings, taken expressly for this Work, and engraved on Steel, by distinguished Artists*. 2 vols. New York: Disturnell, 1835.

Krout, John Allen, and Dixon Ryan Fox. *The Completion of Independence, 1790–1830*. New York: Macmillan, 1944.

Lampedusa, Giuseppe di. *The Leopard*. New York: New American Library, 1961.

Larkin, Oliver W. *Art and Life in America*. New York: Rinehart, 1949.

Larsen, Ellouise Baker. *American Historical Views on Staffordshire China*. New York: Doubleday, 1939.

Latrobe, Charles Joseph. *The Rambler in North America*. 2 vols. New York: Harper, 1835.

Lesley, E. Parker. "Thomas Cole and the Romantic Sensibility," *The Art Quarterly*, Vol. V, 1942.

Levasseur, A. *Lafayette in America in 1824 and 1825; or a Journal of a Voyage to the United States*. Trans. J. D. Godman. 2 vols. Philadelphia: Carey and Lea, 1829.

Lillie, Lucy C. "The Catskills," *Harper's New Monthly Magazine*, Vol. LXVII, No. 400, Sept., 1883.

———. "Two Phases of American Art," *Harper's New Monthly Magazine*, Jan., 1890.

Link, William F. *The Hudson by Daylight*. New York: Link, 1885. (Advertisement of Mountain House.)

Longstreth, T. Morris. *The Catskills*. New York: Century, 1918.

Lord, Clifford L., and Elizabeth H. Lord. *Historical Atlas of the United States*. New York: Holt, 1944.

Lossing, Benson John, ed. *Harper's Encyclopaedia of United States History*. 10 vols. New York: Harper, 1907.

———. *The Hudson, from the Wilderness to the Sea*. New York: Virtue and Yorston, 1866.

Mack, Arthur Carlyle. *Enjoying the Catskills. A practical guide to the Catskill Mountain Region for the Motorist, Camper, Hiker, Hunter, Fisherman, Skier, and Vacationer*. New York: Funk and Wagnalls, 1950.

———. "Reminder of the Past," *Railroad Magazine*, Vol. 48, No. 1, Feb., 1949. (Article on the Catskill Mountain Railroad.)

McCormick, William B. "The Hudson River Men, the First Real

American School of Painting," *Arts and Decoration,* Vol. VI, No. 1, Nov., 1915.

McDannald, Alexander Hopkins. *The Storied Hudson.* New York: Hudson River Night Line, 1927.

Martin, Asa Earl. *History of the United States.* 2 vols. Boston: Ginn, 1928.

Martineau, Harriet. *Retrospect of Western Travel.* London: Saunders and Otley, 1838.

Mather, F. J., Jr. "The Hudson River School," *American Magazine of Art,* Vol. XXVII, June, 1934.

Mease, James. *A Geological Account of the United States.* Philadelphia, 1807.

Metropolitan Museum of Art. *Catalogue of a Loan Exhibition of Paintings by Winslow Homer.* New York, 1911.

————. *Descriptive Catalogue of the Thirty-Eight Paintings . . . of J. F. Kensett. . . .* New York, 1874.

Meyer, Fritz. *Catskill Mountain Album.* New York, 1869.

Michigan State Library. *Biographical Sketches of American Artists.* Lansing, Mich., 1924.

Morrison, John H. *History of American Steam Navigation.* New York: Stephen Daye, 1958.

Mulholland, W. D. *Catskill Trails.* (Recreation Circular 9) Albany, N.Y.: State of New York Conservation Department, 1928, 1948.

Munroe, Kirk. *Summer in the Catskill Mountains.* New York: New York West Shore and Buffalo Railroad, 1883.

Munsell, Joel. *Munsell's Guide to the Hudson River by Railroad and Steamboat.* Albany, N.Y.: Munsell, 1859, 1863.

Murdock, Rev. David. *The Dutch Dominie of the Catskills.* New York: Derby and Jackson, 1861.

New York American Resort Association. *Catskill Mountain Summer Resorts. Containing selected list of hotels, boarding houses and farm houses where summer guests are entertained.* New York: American Resort Assn., 1902.

New York Central and Hudson River Railroad Co. *Health and Pleasure on "America's Greatest Railroad."* New York, 1894.

New York, West Shore and Buffalo Railroad Co. *Summer in the Catskill Mountains.* New York, 1883.

Newgold, Wilbert. "Changes Evoke Nostalgia in Hudson Valley," *The New York Times,* Oct. 16, 1960.

Noble, Louis L., ed. *The Course of Empire, Voyage of Life, and Other Pictures of Thomas Cole.* New York: Cornish, Lamport, 1858.

"Oscar Wilde Agreed to Lecture in Woodstock in 1882," *Record Press*, Woodstock, N.Y., Nov. 15, 1962.

Outing in the Catskills. New York: Sylvanus Lyon, c. 1893.

Owen, George W. *The Leach Club; or the Mysteries of the Catskills*. Boston and New York: Lee and Shephard, 1874.

Peckham, Harry Houston. *Gotham Yankee, A Biography of W. C. Bryant*. New York: Vantage, 1950.

Peirce, James. "A Memoir on the Catskill Mountains," *American Journal of Science*, 1820.

Pinckney, James D. *Reminiscences of Catskill*. Catskill, N.Y.: Hall, 1868.

Posselt, Eric. *The Rip Van Winkle Trail, A Guide to the Catskills*. Haines Falls, N.Y.: Arrowhead, 1952.

———, and Arthur E. Layman. *Guide to the Catskills*. New York: Arrowhead, 1949.

Power, Tyrone. *Impressions of America*. Philadelphia: Carey, Lea, 1836.

"Railroading in [Greene] County was at Zenith during the [*Catskill Daily*] *Mail's* Early Days," *Catskill Daily Mail*, 75th Anniversary Edition, July 10, 1956.

Ratsch, Carl. *Return to the Catskills*. Oak Hill, N.Y.: Big Acorn Press, c. 1946.

Rhodes, James Ford. *History of the United States*. 4 vols. New York: Harper, 1899.

Richards, T. Addison. *Appleton's Illustrated Hand-Book of American Travel*. New York: Appleton, 1857, 1870.

———. *Appleton's Illustrated Hand-Book of American Summer Resorts*. New York: Appleton, 1876, 1881.

———. "The Catskills," *Harper's New Monthly Magazine*, Vol. IX, No. L, July, 1854.

Richardson, Edgar P. *American Romantic Painting*. Robert Freund, ed. New York: Weyhe, 1944.

Ripley, George, and Charles A. Dana, eds. *The American Cyclopaedia*. 2nd rev. ed. 16 vols. New York: Appleton, 1873–81.

Rockwell, Rev. Charles. *The Catskill Mountains and the Region Around*. New York: Taintor, 1867. Rev. ed. 1873.

Ruedemann, Rudolf, John H. Cook, and David H. Newland. *Geology of the Catskill and Kaaterskill Quadrangles, Part I*. New York State Museum Bulletin, No. 331, Dec., 1942.

Rusk, Samuel E. *An Illustrated Guide to the Catskill Mountains*. Catskill, N.Y.: Rusk, 1879.

The Scenery of the Catskill Mountains. As described by Irving, Cooper, Bryant, Willis Gaylord Clark, N. P. Willis, Miss Martineau, Tyrone Power, Park Benjamin, Thomas Cole, and other eminent writers. New York: Fanshaw, c. 1845.

The Scenery of the Catskill Mountains. As described by Irving, Cooper, Bryant, W. G. Clark, N. P. Willis, Miss Martineau, Tyrone Power, Park Benjamin, Thomas Cole, Bayard Taylor and others. Catskill, N.Y.: Joesbury, 1864.

The Scenery of the Catskill Mountains. (1840s.)

Schile, H. *The Illustration of the Catskill Mountains.* New York: Schile [1881?].

Schlesinger, Arthur M. *New Viewpoints in American History.* New York: Macmillan, 1922.

———, and Dixon Ryan Fox, eds. *A History of American Life.* 12 vols. New York: Macmillan, 1927–44.

———, and Homer Carey Hockett. *Political and Social Growth of the American People.* 3rd ed. 2 vols. New York: Macmillan, 1940–41.

Searing, A. E. P. *The Land of Rip Van Winkle: A Tour through the Romantic Parts of the Catskills, Its Legends and Traditions.* New York: Putnam, 1884.

Sears, Clara Endicott. *Highlights Among the Hudson River Artists.* Boston: Houghton Mifflin, 1947.

Seaver, Esther Isabel. *Thomas Cole, 1801–1848, One Hundred Years Later* (exhibition catalogue of the Wadsworth Atheneum, Hartford, and the Whitney Museum of American Art, New York). Hartford, Conn.: Case, Lockwood, 1949.

Seton, Anya. *Dragonwyck.* Boston: Houghton Mifflin, 1943.

Shames, Sylvia. "Sold on the Auction Block," *Chichester Summer League Bulletin,* No. 4, 1952 (unpublished newsletter).

Sheldon, G. W. *American Painters.* New York: Appleton, 1879.

Shelley, Donald A. "George Harvey and His Atmospheric Landscapes of North America," *The New-York Historical Society Quarterly,* Vol. XXXII, Apr., 1948, No. 2.

Shepherd, William R. *Shepherd's Historical Atlas.* 8th ed. London: George Philip, 1956.

Simmons, Benjamin F. *Souvenir Spoons of America.* New York: Jewelers' Circular Publishing Co., 1891.

Sims, N. A. *The Catskill Mountains. The Most Picturesque Mountain Region on the Globe Reached by the Ulster and Delaware Railroad.* Kingston, N.Y.: Freeman, 1891, 1892, 1894, 1904, 1905, 1907, 1908, 1909, 1910, 1913, 1914.

Smiley, Daniel. "Mountains of the Catskills—A Guide and Record," *The Conservationist*, Vol. XVI, No. 1, Aug.–Sept., 1961.

Smith, Anita M. *Woodstock History and Hearsay*. Saugerties, N.Y.: Catskill Mountain Publishing, 1959.

Smith, Mabel Parker. (All articles appear in the *Greene County Examiner-Recorder* unless otherwise cited.) "Artists, Writers Spread Early Fame of Mountain House," Sept. 26, 1957.

———. "August 1 Final Date of Famed Catskill Mountain House," June 21, 1951.

———. "Beach Exploits Historic Developed Region, Loses to Progress He Advanced," May 14, 1953.

———. "Beach, Symbol of America, From Log House to Palace," Apr. 30, 1953.

———. "Beaches, Father and Son, Active in Many Ventures," Aug. 9, 1956.

———. "1824 Visit of Lafayette Gala Event for Catskill," Aug. 9, 1956.

———. "Feud Between the Mountain House and the Kaaterskill," Jan. 24, 1952.

———. "In the 80's They All Came to the Mountain House," Apr. 16, 1953.

———. "Lines of First Mountain House Emerge; Wreckers Resume," Apr. 9, 1953.

———. "The Mountain House Columns." Address delivered before the Monday Club of Catskill, N.Y., Apr. 18, 1955. (Manuscript copy in the Catskill Public Library.)

———. "Mountain House Was Side-Line to Great Beach Dominion of Early Transportation," May 7, 1953.

———. "Mountain House Wrecking Lags, No Clean Up in Sight," Aug. 27–Sept. 10, 1953.

———. "Owner [of Mountain House] States Portion of Hotel to be Dismantled," Jan. 24, 1952.

———. "Recalls Trip Over Stage Road to Mountain House," Jan. 17, 1952.

———. "Sherman Won Atlanta, Near Surrender to Female Pen Brigade at Mountain House," Apr. 23, 1953.

———. "Thomas Cole Wrote of Mountain House," Jan. 17, 1952.

Snow, Julia D. Sophronia. "Delineators of the Adams-Jackson American Views, Part I, Thomas Cole, N. A.," *Antiques*, Nov., 1936.

Soby, James Y., and Dorothy Miller. *Romantic Painting in America*. New York: Museum of Modern Art, 1943.

Souvenir of the Catskill Mountains (13-page folder). New York, [189–?].

Spafford, Horatio Gates. *Gazetteer of the State of New York.* Albany, N.Y.: Southwick, 1813.

———. *Gazetteer of the State of New York.* Albany: Packard, 1824.

State of New York Conservation Department. "News Bulletin," Apr. 9, 1962.

"State to Buy Hotel in Catskills Used by Ulysses Grant," *The New York Times,* Apr. 9, 1962.

"Summer Night's Wedding," *Greene County Recorder,* Catskill, N.Y., June 30, 1911 (marriage at the Mountain House of Mary Lindsay Beach and John K. Van Wagonen).

Swan, Mabel M. *The Atheneum Gallery, 1827–1873.* Boston, 1940.

Sweet, Frederick A. "Asher B. Durand, Pioneer American Landscape Painter," *Art Quarterly,* Vol. VIII, No. 2, Spring, 1945.

———. *The Hudson River School and the Early American Landscape Tradition.* Chicago: Art Institute, 1945.

Sylvester, Nathaniel Bartlett. *History of Ulster County, New York.* Philadelphia: Everts and Peck, 1880.

Taintor, Charles Newhall. *The Hudson River Route. With descriptive sketches of cities, villages, stations, scenery, and objects of interest.* New York: Taintor, 1883.

Tarr, Ralph S. *The Physical Geography of New York State.* New York: Macmillan, 1902.

Taylor, Bayard. "The Hudson and the Catskills," *Home and Abroad.* 2nd ser. New York: Putnam, 1862.

———. "Travels at Home," *New York Tribune,* July 12, 1860.

Thompson, John Bodine. "The Genesis of the Rip Van Winkle Legend," *Harper's New Monthly Magazine,* Vol. LXVII, No. 400, 1883.

The Traveller's Steamboat and Railroad Guide to the Hudson River. New York: Philips and Watson, 1857.

Trollope, Mrs. Frances. *Domestic Manners of the Americans.* London: Whittaker, Treacher, 1832.

Tuckerman, Henry T. *Artist-Life: or Sketches of American Painters.* New York: Appleton, 1847.

———. *Book of the Artists.* New York: Putnam, 1867.

Twilight Park in the Catskills (pamphlet). New York: King, c. 1884.

Ulster and Delaware Railroad. *The Ulster County and Delaware Railroad Announces the Improved Train Service over the New Standard Gauge Line to All Points on the Stony Clove and Kaaterskill Railroads* (pamphlet). New York: American Book Note, 1899.

Vail, R. P. H. "Along the Hudson in Stagecoach," *The Outlook*, June 24, 1905.

Vanderwater, Robert J. *The Tourist, or Pocket Manual for Travellers on the Hudson River, the Western Canal, and Stage Road.* New York: Harper, 1830.

Van Epps, Katherine A. "Catskill Mountain House Being Restored," *The Knickerbocker News*, Albany, N.Y., March 29, 1952.

Van Loan, Walton. *Van Loan's Catskill Mountain Guide.* New York: Aldine, 1879, 1881; New York: Rogers and Sherwood, 1890, 1892, 1897; New York: Dudley Press, 1908, 1909; [publisher unknown]: 1876, 1882, 1883, 1884.

Van Olinda, E. S. "World Famous Beach House," *Times-Union*, Albany, N.Y., Oct. 19, 1950.

Van Zandt, Roland. "The Scotch School of Aesthetic Theory and the Natural Description of the Oregon Trail," *The Southwestern Journal*, Vol. IV, 1949.

Vedder, Jessie Van Vechten. *Historic Catskill.* Catskill, N.Y. [privately printed].

———. *Official History of Greene County.* Catskill, N.Y., 1927.

Verplanck, William E., and Moses W. Collyer. *The Sloops of the Hudson.* New York: Putnam, 1908.

Von Siegl, Rudolf R. *Catskill Region Touring and Resort Map.* Rhinebeck, N.Y., 1952.

Weir, John F. *A Memorial Catalogue of the Paintings of Sanford Robinson Gifford, N. A.* New York: Metropolitan Museum, 1881.

Wendell, Barrett. *A Literary History of America.* New York: Scribner, 1931.

West, Edward G. "The Catskills," *The Conservationist*, Oct.–Nov., 1962.

West Shore Railroad. *Summer Homes and Excursions. Embracing Lake, River, Mountain and Seaside Resorts Accessible by the Picturesque Double Track West Shore Railroad.* [n.p.], 1888.

Who's Who in America, Vol. 24, 1946–47. Chicago: Marquis, 1946.

Wilde, Oscar. *Decorative Art in America.* New York: Brentano, 1906.

———. *Impressions of America.* Sunderland, England: Keystone Press, 1906.

Willis, Nathaniel Parker. *American Scenery.* (Drawings by W. H. Bartlett.) 2 vols. London: Virtue, 1840.

———. "The Catskill Mountains," *The New Mirror*, Sept. 9, 1843.

Wilson, H. *Wilson's Illustrated Guide to the Hudson River.* 8th ed. New York, 1850.

Wilson, James Grant. *Bryant and His Friends*. New York: Fords, Howard, 1886.

Wilstach, Paul. *Hudson River Landings*. Indianapolis: Bobbs-Merrill, 1933.

Wish, Harvey. *Society and Thought in America*. 2 vols. New York: Longmans, Green, 1952.

W.P.A. *New York, A Guide to the Empire State*. New York: Oxford, 1940.

The World Book Encyclopaedia. 18 vols. Chicago: Field Enterprises, 1958.

Index

Acadia National Park, 296
Acra, New York, 234
Adams, John, 31
Adams, Maude, 222–23
Adirondack Mountains, 12, 151, 161, 174, 183; Homer in, 185; resorts of, 221; Wyant in, 184
Aesthetics: art-for-art's sake, 283, 284; Romantic, 152–55, 189–209, 210–15, 247–48, 249, 297; utilitarianism, 249–50. *See also* Art
Africa, 253
"After the Ball is Over" (Harris), 288
Agriculture, 8, 15, 246, 257, 291, 292, 293
Airplanes, 295
Aix-en-Provence, France, 172
Albany, New York, 9, 10, 24, 44, 230, 323; Gifford and, 179; Hudson River Railroad and, 225, 245; mail service, 52, 53, 54; sleighs to, 50–52; State Office, 114
Albany (vessel), 233
Albany County, New York, 20
Albany *Times-Union* (newspaper), 316–17
Alison, Sir Archibald, 156
Allegheny Mountains, 5, 8, 199, 291, 296

Alps Mountains, 196, 209
American Cyclopedia, The, 21, 217–18
"American and European Scenery Compared" (Cooper), 206
American Geographical Society, 200
American Landscape (Bryant), 41
American Landscape (periodical), 175
American Revolution, 8, 20, 26, 29, 192–93
American Scenery (Bryant publication), 188
American Scenery (English publication), 138, 186
American Scenery (Willis), 43, 44
American Scenes (Bartlett), 41, 112
André, John, 192
Andron, David, 307
Andron, Eli, 307
Andron, Jacob, 307
Andron's Mountain House, 307–08, 309, 316. *See also* Catskill Mountain House
Anopheles mosquito, 254–55
Apennine Mountains, 196, 209
Appalachian Mountains, 8, 12, 121, 151, 158, 295
Appleton & Company, D., 188

Appleton's Illustrated Hand-Book of American Travel, 12, 61, 96; on North and South Lakes, 115, 117; on Palenville, 178; on tanneries, 125

Architecture, 37–38, 54–57, 60–61, 316; Church estate, 173, 222; James on, 194; Laurel House, 142, 143, 150; Mountain House renovations, 261, 263, 265, 267, 269, 271, 320

Arizona, 294, 297

Arkville, New York, 185

Art, 27, 36, 46, 70, 79, 109–10, 121; colonies, 175–78, 182, 183, 218, 219, 223; commercial, 186, 188, 189; Hudson River School, 170–88 (*See also* Hudson River School of Landscape Painting); portrait, 171, 173, 174; Romanticism and (*See* Romanticism); waterfall studies, 129, 130–39. *See also* Aesthetics; *and see individual artists*

Arthur, Chester Alan, 281

Arthur, Nellie, 281

Artist's Grotto, 123

Artist's Rock, 109, 289, 305

Ashley's Creek, 115

Ashley's Falls, 115

Association, aesthetic doctrine of, 153–54, 191–95

Astor, Vincent, quoted, 327–28

Athenaeum (periodical), 131–32

Athens, New York, 16

Atlantic Coast, 5, 7, 10, 26, 101, 103, 109, 152; coastal plain, 198; diseases of, 253; forests of, 160; "three most important sights," 41. *See also specific place names*

Automobiles, 71, 72, 86, 99, 303; cultural influence of, 295, 300, 321; Kaaterskill Clove route, 123–27, 129; Kaaterskill Falls route, 149–50

Bakeries, 62, 267

Baltimore, Maryland, 7, 220, 252

Bartlett, William Henry, 36, 37, 41, 55, 186; Bear's Den vista and, 112; Kaaterskill Falls and, 138; South Lake and, 117–18, 120

Bartow, Maria, 172

Bastion Bridge, 126

Bastion Falls, 126

Bayonne, New Jersey, 278

Beach family, 29, 32

Beach, A. F., 54, 70

Beach, Charles (son of Charles L.), 301

Beach, Charles A., 72

Beach, Charles L., 29–30, 31, 32, 223, 284, 330, 334; quoted, 33, 34, 142, 258, 305–06; Catskill Mountain Railroad and, 32, 72, 73, 86, 97, 225, 226, 231–32, 235, 240; death of, 299–300; guidebooks and, 42, 54; Mountain House management, 44, 45–70, 230, 258–89, 304, 307; Mountain House modifications, 36, 37, 54–57, 61, 267; Mountain House livery service, 277, 278, 281; technological improvements, 272–75

Beach, Charles T., 304

Beach, Erastus, 29, 30, 31, 240; heirs, 301; New York livery business, 49; stagecoach line, 32, 44, 46, 47, 48, 71–72, 86

Beach, G. L., 54, 70

Beach, George H., 301

Beach, Louis J., 304

Beach, Mary L., 303

Beach and Company, C. L., 70

"Beach Mountain House, the Artist Sketching" (Cole painting), 57

Bear's Den, 110, 112, 114

Bearsville, New York, 19

Bell, Alexander Graham, 274

Bell, Stanton W., quoted, 326

Bellevue Hospital, New York City, 253

Bell Wrecking Company, 322, 326

Benjamin, Park, 42; quoted, 205, 211, 247

Benjamin B. Odell (vessel), 274

Bennett, William J., 36, 186

Benton, Caleb, 31

Berkeley, George, 211

Berkshire (vessel), 274

Berkshire Hills, 221

Black Head Mountain, 73

Black Snake Bridge, 79, 99

Blue Hills (Shandaken Mountains), 22, 217

Boating, 117, 278, 303, 307

Bogart's Farm, 122

Bogart Road, 123

Born, Wolfgang, quoted, 162, 179, 183, 185

Boston, Massachusetts, 7, 15, 46, 182, 245, 252

Bridges, 85, 86

Brockett's Boardinghouse, 125

Brook Farm, 176

Brooklyn, New York, 67, 68

"Brook in Mink Hollow, The" (McEntee painting), 184

Browere, Albertis De Orient, 179, 180

Brown, Henry A., 73, 88, 188

Bruce, Wallace, 233

Bryant, William Cullen, 36, 73, 88, 188; quoted, 10, 12, 27, 41–42, 145–46, 164, 168, 185, 192–93, 205, 212, 214, 297; romanticism and, 22, 157, 160, 161–62, 166, 168–69, 206, 207, 222

Buckingham, James Silk, quoted, 82, 84, 255

Burger's Hotel, 123

Burke, Edmund, 156, 204

Burr, Aaron, 31, 34

Buttermilk Falls and Ravine, 125

Byles and Hoff Company, 278

Byron, George Gordon, Lord, 156

Cairo, New York, 34, 130; railroads, 225, 231, 232, 234

California, 207, 220, 294, 295, 297, 337

Cambridge, Massachusetts, 185

Canada, 50, 253

Canajoharie, New York, 225

Candles, 68, 273

Cape Horn (on the Old Mountain Road), 79

Carmer, Carl, quoted, 307–08

"Caroline Affair," 50

Carpathian Vacation Camp, Inc., 329, 332–33

Carte, Richard D'Oyly, 284

Casilear, John William, 129, 176, 183

Catskill, New York, 13, 21, 22, 23, 28, 42, 43, 80, 92; Catskill Landing, 73, 76, 80, 81, 219, 223, 231, 233, 234, 241, 315; Catskill Mountain Railroad and, 225, 226, 232–35, 236, 244–45; cholera epidemic, 254; Cole house in, 110, 162–63, 172, 178–79, 180, 222; Irving House, 49; livery service, 29, 30, 32, 46, 69; Moore in, 181, Prospect Park Hotel in, 260–61; Sherman in, 282; stage lines, 32, 44, 46, 47–48, 52, 70, 72–73, 76, 80, 91, 97, 218, 219, 223, 242–43; telephone service, 274; trade and, 15, 16, 44, 46–47, 224; Wilde in, 284–85

Catskill-Canajoharie Railroad, 225, 234

Catskill Creek, 15, 175

Catskill *Examiner-Recorder* (newspaper), 303–304, 320; on Mountain House "restoration," 317–18, 322

"Catskill Falls" (Fenn engraving), 138–39

Catskill Lyceum, 208

Catskill Mountain Album (Meyer), 186

Catskill Mountain Association, 19–20, 29, 31–33, 44

Catskill Mountain Guide (Van Loan), 139, 229, 233

Catskill Mountain House: acreage, 275–76, 304–06, 313–15, 329, 332, 333–35; altitude, 80, 218; American aesthetics and, 152, 154–55, 175, 177, 180, 184, 199–200, 201, 202, 204–05, 297; Andron management, 307–08, 309; automobile garage, 300; building of, 5, 19, 20, 23, 26–27, 28–29, 30, 31, 32, 33–34, 36–41, 265; burning of, 3–5, 339–41; capacity, 260, 261, 271, 303; capital stock, 29, 32, 36; climate, 252; closing of, 297, 308–09, 310, 312, 321; demolition, 323–26; Gilded Age guest list, 222, 280–88 (*See also individual names*); livery service, 276, 278; Moseman management, 306, 309, 312–19, 321–22, 327, 328–29, 332; opening, 45, 71; railroad encirclement, 226, 230, 232, 236, 299; renovations, 261, 263, 265, 267, 269, 271, 320, 328–29

"Catskill Mountain House" (Cole painting), 166

"Catskill Mountain House" (Cropsey painting), 180, 185

"Catskill Mountain House" (Harvey watercolor), 57

"Catskill Mountain House, The" (Rockwell), 250

Catskill Mountain Railroad, 235–41, 244, 245, 315; building of, 32, 72, 73, 86, 97, 225, 226, 232–35; closing of, 300, 301–02, 303

Catskill Mountains, 5, 10–12, 19, 29, 43, 103; extent, 12–13, 218–19; fires, 68–69; freedom from malaria, 255–56; Grant in, 280–81; post-Civil War development of, 143, 155, 186, 217–24, 242–57, 258, 297; railroads and, 85, 86–87, 218–19, 225–41; *Rip Van Winkle* and, 88–93, 193; the Romantic Movement and, 151–55, 156–69, 171–88, 190, 193, 194–95, 215, 222, 250, 297; Sherman in, 281–83; sublimity (aesthetic concept) and, 196, 199–209; twentieth century, 291–98, 320, 340; Wilde in, 283–85. *See also specific place names*

"Catskill Mountains" (Bennett drawing), 186

"Catskill Mountains" (Durand painting), 175

"Catskill Mountains, N.Y." (Gifford painting), 184

Catskill Mountains and the Region Around, The (Rockwell), 21, 94, 217

Catskill Night Boats, 233

"Catskills from Kingston, The" (McEntee painting), 184 [94

Catskill State Forest Preserve, 293–

Catskill State Park, 12, 124, 296

Catskill Steam Transportation Company, 70

Catskill-Tannersville Railroad, 235, 299

"Catterskill Falls" (Currier and Ives), 138–39

Cauterskill, New York, 56

Caves, 110, 131–32, 136, 147

Cézanne, Paul, 172

Chalmers, Thomas, 67

Charleston, South Carolina, 7

Chicago Art Institute, 320, 323

Chichester, Samuel, 34

Childe Harold's Pilgrimage (Byron), 156

China, 254
Cholera, 253
Christianity, 210, 211, 212, 247
Christ Presbyterian Church, Catskill, 56
Church, Frederick Edwin, 139, 171, 172, 180, 184; estate, 173, 222
Church services (Mountain House), 67–68
Church's Ledge, 124
Cincinnati, Ohio, 7
Civil War, 69, 78, 96, 185; Adirondack settlement after, 12, 151; Catskill development after, 13, 20, 22, 143, 155, 186, 217–24, 242–57, 258; heroes of, 280–83; Stone in, 180
Clark, Lewis, 200
Clark, Willis Gaylord, 42, 204; quoted, 81–82, 84, 158–59, 200–03, 210–11
Claude (Lorrain), 119, 194, 215
Clay, Henry, 308
Clermont, New York, 29
Clermont (vessel), 9
Clingman's Dome, 296
Clinton, DeWitt, 34
Cole, Thomas, 11, 22, 36, 42, 60, 109–10, 129, 194; quoted, 95, 118–19, 123, 146–48, 164, 190, 191, 192, 208–09, 215, 250; Bear's Den vista, 112; death of, 57, 164, 176, 179, 181; Bryant and, 161–62, 166–69; influence of, 157, 160, 161–69, 171–76, 179, 183, 185, 222; Kaaterskill Falls and, 132, 136, 139, 185–86; railroads and, 225; sublimity concept and, 203, 204, 206, 208; Trumbull and, 120, 164, 173
Colorado, 132, 179, 295
Columns (Mountain House), 56, 263, 267, 316–17, 321, 329, 335
Comfort, Hiram, 33
Connecticut, 110, 183

Cook, Apollas, 31
Cooksburg, New York, 225
Cooper, James Fenimore, 28, 36, 41, 42, 130, 209, 313; quoted, 23–25, 26, 165, 191, 199, 206, 207–08; Cavern of Kaaterskill Falls and, 131–32, 136; cult of the wilderness and, 159–61, 165–66, 169, 196, 206, 208, 212
Cooperstown, New York, 160, 161
Cranch, Christopher Pearse, 176
Crawford Notch, New Hampshire, 121
Cropsey, Jaspar F., 112, 139, 180, 185
Croswell, Edwin, 31
Cuisine, 39, 62, 144, 275; Andron's, 307, 316; kitchen facilities, 267, 271, 289, 325; Palenville, 178
Cult of the wilderness, *see* Wilderness, cult of the
Culture, 27, 41, 45, 70; European sources of, 189–209; Gilded Age and, 219–24, 246–51, 294; schism in American, 46, 87–88, 145, 189, 213; twentieth century, 291–98; the wilderness and, 152–54, 157–58, 164, 171, 190, 194–95, 196, 210–15, 222, 247. *See also specific aspects, e.g.,* Aesthetics
Cumberland Gap, 121
Currier and Ives, 112, 138–39
Curtis, George William, 176–77; quoted, 204, 263
Cuyler, Theodore L., quoted, 203–204

Dams, 145
Daniel Drew (vessel), 284
Dead Ox Hill, 79
"Decorative Arts, The" (Wilde), 284
Delaware County, New York, 12, 15, 185, 223, 228, 230

Delaware River, 13, 15, 22, 25; East Branch, 223, 226

Delaware Water Gap, 121

Delhi, New York, 48

De Lisser, Lionel, quoted, 256–57

Depression, 33, 298–99, 303, 304, 308, 312

Detroit, Michigan, 161

Devil's Dans Kammer, 11

Dimock (coach driver), 51

Disease, 252–55

Domestic Manners of the Americans (Trollope), 10

Donnelly and Company, J. M., 70

Doughty, Thomas, 163, 165, 173, 182–83

Dripping Rock, 126, 127

Druid Rocks, 106

Dunlap, William, 164, 173

Durand, Asher B., 41, 183, 250; quoted, 177–78; Romantic Movement and, 163, 164, 165, 168–69, 173–78, 223

Durham, New York, 15, 21, 234, 335

Dutch, 130, 177, 193, 291; sailing vessels, 9

Eagle Rock, 106

East Windham, New York, 19

Edward VII, King of England, 284

Edwards, Jonathan, 246

Edwards, William, quoted, 19

Eighteenth century, 130, 291

El Dorado Trucking Elevator, 239

Electricity, 68, 254, 272–74

Elfin Pass, 106

Eliot, Thomas Stearns, quoted, 291

Elka Park, New York, 19

Ellet, Elizabeth F. Lummis, 42; quoted, 61–62, 82, 95–96, 122, 178, 180, 205; on storms, 203, 204

Emerson, Ralph Waldo, 157, 176; quoted, 168, 212

England, 84, 156, 162, 186, 284; cholera in, 253

Entertainment, 39, 61, 62–63, 65–68; facilities for, 275, 278, 302–03, 307; Kaaterskill Falls visits, 144–45; sunrise ritual, 38, 63, 202, 203, 320–21; theatricals, 285, 288

Epidemics, 253

Erie Canal, 8, 46

Erie Railroad, 51, 53

Esopus, New York, 13, 23, 24

Esopus Valley, 22, 176, 219, 224, 226, 243, 300

Europe, 11, 84, 296; American painters in, 172, 179, 182, 183, 184, 185; American Romanticism and, 153, 166, 189–209; cholera in, 253, 254; Cooper in, 160, 161; Grant tour of, 280; immigration from, 300. *See also specific countries*

Evers, Alf, quoted, 22

Fairy Spring, 106

"Falls of Cattskill, New York, The" (Cole painting), 132, 185–86

Fat Man's Delight, 106

Fawn's Leap, 124

Feather Bed Hill, 79

Featherbed Lane, 127

Fenn, Harry, 76, 77, 186; Kaaterskill Falls and, 138–39; *Picturesque America* and, 36, 188

Ferry boats, 70, 73, 76, 234

Finch, Wells, 34

Finger Lakes, 52

Fires, 68–69, 302

First Dutch Church of Brooklyn, 67

Five Cascades, 128, 129

Flagler Hotel, St. Augustine, 221

Fleischmanns, New York, 300

Flexner, James Thomas, quoted, 170

Florida, 221, 294

Flour trade, 9, 15

Fogg Museum, 181

Forest Hymn, A (Bryant), 166

Forests, 16, 34, 291; agricultural decline and, 257, 292; Beach on, 238–39, 305–06; Catskill Park area, 124; cult of the wilderness and, 152, 153, 154, 158, 161, 194–95, 212; fire, 69; Minnesota, 295; Mountain House park, 275–78, 304–05; picturesqueness and, 198; Sequoia, 296; South Lake, 118–19; sublimity concept and, 159–60, 168, 199, 210; twentieth century return of, 100, 292–94

Fort Putnam, 192

France, 197, 254

Franklin, Benjamin, 246

Freehold, New York, 234

"From the Top of Kaaterskill Falls" (Cole painting), 136

Fulton, Robert, 9

Galli-Curci, Amelita, 223

Games, 61, 62, 275, 303, 307

Gardens, 62, 275–78

Gardiner, Clyde, 307, 313–14

Garland, Hamlin, 222

Gazetteer of the State of New York (Spafford), 28–29

Geography, 5, 7, 8, 13; Mountain House and, 26, 27, 103, 218, 220–21, 224, 252, 255, 296

Geology, 13

Georgia, 282

Gifford, Sanford Robinson, 112, 129, 139, 178, 179–80, 184

Gilbert and Sullivan, 283

Gilded Age, 217–24, 294, 297, 300, 302. *See also* Nineteenth century

Gilpin, William, 156; quoted, 153, 191

Glacier National Park, 296

Glen Mary, 114, 115, 289

Goodrich, L., quoted, 162

Gorgas, W. C., 255

Goshen, Connecticut, 30, 51

Grand Gorge, New York, 19, 21

Grand Hotel, Highmount, 224, 230

Grand Hotel at Pine Hill, 229, 260, 261

Grant, Ulysses Simpson, *gen.*, 222, 280–81, 333

Grassi, 254

Great Britain, *see* England; Scotland

Great Smoky Mountains, 12

Greene, George Washington, quoted, 164–65

Greene County, New York, 12, 15, 20–21, 22, 185, 312, 318–19, 327; Clerk's Office, 305; railroads and, 86, 98, 223, 227–28, 229, 230, 231, 233, 236, 241, 245, 257, 299

Greene County Historical Society, 335

Green Mountains, 12, 121, 174

Greenville, New York, 15

Griffins Corners (Fleischmanns), New York, 300

Gulf (ravine), 123, 124

Haight, Jacob, 31

Haines Falls, 71, 105, 122, 127–29, 301, 316; stagecoaches to, 235, 276; winter freezing, 148

Haines' Ravine, 128–29

Hale, Edward Everett, Jr., quoted, 156, 159, 165

Half Moon (vessel), 88

Hall, Basil, 41; quoted, 80–81, 256

Hall, George H., 178

Hall, Rev. Newman, 112

Harding, George W., 230, 231, 232; quoted, 236, 237; death of, 299–300

Haring, H. A., 16; quoted, 93

Harper's Weekly (periodical), 20, 61, 176, 185, 242, 288

Harris, Charles K., 288

Hartford, Connecticut, 132, 136

Harvard University, 181, 182

Harvey, George, 57, 60

Haskins, Vernon, 323; quoted, 320

Hastings, Father, 67

Health, 248–49, 250, 251–56; Mountain House physician, 275, 303

Heinmann, E., 139

Hemlock, 16, 34, 291

Highlands, The, 9, 11, 23–24, 91, 114, 151; historical associations of, 192, 193. *See also specific place names*

Highmount, New York, 223, 224

High Peak, 21, 73, 76, 110, 217, 234; Cooper on, 23, 25, 26; streams of, 124; Sunset Rock and, 105; in winter, 146

High Rock (Palenville Overlook), 105, 106, 123, 176

Hillyer's Ravine, 124

Hinton, J. H., 36

History of American Painting (Isham), 170

History of Greene County, 30, 33

History and Topography of the United States (Hinton), 36

Hoboken, New Jersey, 174

Homer, Winslow, 185–86; Kaaterskill Falls cavern and, 132, 136

Hotels: early nineteenth century, 7, 8, 22, 27, 28, 29, 31, 42–43, 85, 139, 292; Gilded Age, 219, 224, 228, 229, 256–57, 258, 260–61, 292; Panic of 1893 and, 298–99. *See also specific hotels*

Housatonic Railroad, 52

Hubbard, Richard William, 176

Hudson, New York, 46, 47, 179, 245, 321

Hudson River: Cooper on, 25, 26, 160; Latrobe on, 198–99; Irving on, 11, 90–91, 157, 193; nineteenth century importance of, 8–9, 10; the Romantic Movement and, 141, 170, 193; sleigh travel

on, 50–51, 52, 53; steamer traffic, 43–44, 244–45; Wilde trip, 283–84

Hudson River by Daylight (Bruce), 233

Hudson River Day Line, 233, 235, 241, 316

Hudson River Guide, 43

Hudson River Night Line, 274

Hudson River Railroad, 53–54, 70, 225, 234, 241, 245

Hudson River School of Landscape Painting, 61, 87, 88, 112, 119, 127, 151, 295, 305; Cole influence and, 163, 169, 171–76, 182, 183; history of, 170–88, 189, 190, 219, 222, 294, 321; James on, 194. *See also specific artists*

Hudson River sloop, 9, 15

Hudson Valley, 50, 199, 225; building of the Mountain House, 5, 26, 41, 43; historical associations of, 3, 4, 192, 193, 194, 321, 328, 329; Lafayette tour, 29; Lookout Rock view of, 112; nineteenth century importance of, 5, 7, 9, 10, 12, 43, 44, 91, 171, 294; Wilde tour, 283–84. *See also specific placenames*

Hunter, New York, 15, 16, 19, 20, 21, 28, 131; railroads, 226, 229, 230, 233, 281

Hunter Valley, 105

Hurley, New York, 185

Huth, Hans, 320–21

Idlewild, 192

Illinois, 294

Illustrated Guide to the Catskill Mountains (Rusk), 176

Impressions of America (Power), 41

India, 253, 254

Indian Head (Point of Rocks), 105, 123

Indians, 11, 13, 26, 50, 166, 193, 291

Industrial Revolution, 221
Industry, 8, 15–16, 19, 219–20, 221–22; vacationing and, 246. *See also specific industries, e.g.*, Railroads
Ingersoll, Ernest, quoted, 90, 300
Inspiration Point, 105, 125
Irving, Peter, quoted, 92
Irving, Pierre M., 90; quoted, 91, 253
Irving, Washington, 22, 42, 130, 159, 160, 169, 194, 206, 222, 296; quoted, 11, 90–91, 92, 157–58, 166, 199, 208; cholera epidemic and, 253; Latrobe and, 90, 197, 199; the Sleepy Hollow legend and, 77, 87–97, 100, 193, 320
Irving House, Catskill, 49
Isham, Samuel, 170
Italy, 239
Ithaca, New York, 47, 52

Jackson, Andrew, 213
Jacob's Ladder, 110, 114
James, Henry, quoted, 87, 193–94, 208; romanticism and, 158, 193
James Kent (vessel), 29
Japan, 309
Jefferson, Thomas, 222
Jewett, New York, 15
Johnson, David, 176
Jones, Alfred, 176

Kaaterskill, The (periodical), 234, 236
Kaaterskill Clove, 15, 16, 19, 21, 26, 117, 176, 219; Brown description, 73; Hall home in, 178; landscape of, 121–29, 163, 169, 177, 180, 199; private parks of, 257; railroads and, 13, 235; Rip Van Winkle and, 88; Route 23A and, 71; South Mountain and, 103, 105
"Kaaterskill Clove" (McEntee painting), 184

Kaaterskill Creek, 28, 73, 76, 122, 123; Lake Creek and, 127; More's Bridge on, 124
Kaaterskill Falls, 26, 67, 105, 106, 115, 296; Haines Falls and, 128–29; landscape of, 130–39, 144–50, 163, 180, 184, 185–86; Laurel House and, 126, 127, 143–44, 148, 150; South Lake and, 117, 122; winter freezing, 146–50
"Kaaterskill Falls" (Cole painting), 136
"Kaaterskill Falls" (Homer painting), 185
"Kaaterskill Falls" (McEntee painting), 184
Kaaterskill Hotel, 105, 117, 224, 230, 233–34, 238, 305; burning of, 69, 302, 303, 310; capacity, 260; facilities, 261, 278; guest list, 280, 281, 284, 285; New York State purchase, 334; roads, 106, 123–24, 235, 236
Kaaterskill Railroad, 232, 237–38, 299
Kames, Lord, 156
Kansas, 220
Keene Valley, New York, 184
Kemble, Gouverneur, 90
Kensett, John Frederick, 129, 173, 176, 183–84
"Kindred Spirits" (Durand painting), 168, 169
Kingston, New York, 13, 23, 56, 92, 184, 185; railroads, 97, 219, 225, 229, 230, 232, 244–45
Kiskatom Valley, 21, 22, 42, 78
Knickerbocker Magazine, 200
Kosciusko Monument, 192

La Bella Falls, 123
Lafayette, Marie Joseph Paul, Marquis de, 29
Lake Creek, 117, 126, 127, 129

Lake Creek Ravine, 126
"Lake with Dead Trees" (Cole painting), 120, 132
Lake George, 41, 183, 239
Lake Otsego, 26, 161
Lake Superior, 179
Lakes, 13, 22, 43, 103, 296. *See also specific lakes, e.g.,* South Lake
Landscape, 9–10, 20–21, 22–23, 30, 57, 101–50; aesthetics and, 189, 190, 193–94; Brown description of Mountain House approach, 73, 76–77; romanticism and, 7, 11, 27, 61, 63, 70, 136, 145, 151–55, 156–69, 171, 210–15, 219, 222, 247–48; western, 12, 103, 152, 179, 184, 207, 295–97. *See also specific elements, e.g.,* Forests; *and see specific place names*
"Landscape View, Cauterskill Falls from under the Cavern" (Wall painting), 136
Landslide, 123, 128
Lanesville, New York, 184
Last of the Mohicans, The (Cooper), 166
Latrobe, C. J., 90, 206; quoted, 197–98, 199, 205, 210
Laurel House, 117, 129, 139, 142, 235; carriage road, 276, 304; Kaaterskill Falls and, 126, 127, 143–44, 148, 150
Lawrenceville, New York, 244
Leather-Stocking Tales, The (Cooper), 23, 160, 206
Lemon Squeezer, 106
Lexington Hotel, 311
Lexington, New York, 15
Liberty, New York, 13
Life and Letters of Washington Irving (Pierre M. Irving), 90–91
Lillie, Lucy C., 90, 271; on Church, 173; on Cole, 162–63, 164, 172; on electric lights, 273; on Gif-
ford, 179; on paths, 276; on railroads, 87, 234, 242–43, 244
Lind, Jenny, 223
Literature, *see* Travel books; *and see individual authors*
Little Pine Orchard, 79
Lockwood, H. E., 317
Loeffler and Company, J., 269
London, England, 186
Long Branch, New Jersey, 221
Long Island, New York, 254
Long Level (Old Mountain Road), 79, 112, 123
Longstreth, T. Morris, quoted, 193, 298
Lookout Rock, 112
Lossing, B. J., quoted, 96, 125
Lovers' Retreat, 106
Luxury, 7–8, 34, 38–40, 61–62, 224, 271–75, 320–21

M'Cormick, W. B., 183
McEntee, Jervis, 129, 139, 178, 184
McKinstrey, Henry, 31
Mail, 52–54, 81; Mountain House Post Office, 272, 275, 303
Maine, 183, 185, 296
Malaria, 252, 253, 254–55
Manhattan Island, 8
Maps, 20, 78, 79, 101, 103
Margaretville, New York, 21, 223
Marlowe, Julia, 222–23
Martineau, Harriet, 42, 44, 61; quoted, 10, 40, 41, 211, 214
Marvin, George, 47
Mary Powell (vessel), 284
Massachusetts, 15, 69, 110, 302
Meat, 62, 275
Memorial Catalogue (of S. R. Gifford, Metropolitan Museum of Art), 179–80
Mesa Verde, Colorado, 132
Meyer, Fritz, 139, 142, 186
Michigan, 294
Mink Hollow, New York, 19

Minnesota, 220, 294
Mississippi, 7
Mississippi River, 198, 254, 294, 296;
as Western frontier, 5, 12, 152,
196, 220
Mobile, Alabama, 7
Mohawk and Hudson Railroad, 53
Mohawk River, 8, 15, 26
Mohawk Valley, 15, 225
Mohican (Mahican) Indians, 130
Mohican Trail, 175
Montana, 296
Monticello, New York, 13
Moore, Charles Herbert, 181–82
Moran, 171
More's Bridge and Falls, 124
Morgan, Augustus, *maj.*, 49–50
Moseman, Milo Claude, 306, 309,
312–19, 321–22, 327, 328–29, 332
Moses Rock, 31, 122
Mosquitoes, 254–55
Mount Beacon, 239
Mount Etna, 209
Mt. Katahdin, 296
Mt. Marcy, 296
Mt. Mitchell, 296
Mt. Morris, New York, 30, 46
Mount Pleasant, New York, 226
Mount Tremper House, Phoenicia,
229, 260, 285, 310
Mt. Vesuvius, 239
Mount Washington, 196, 296
Mt. Whitney, 295
Mountain House, *see* Catskill
Mountain House
"Mountain House, The" (Fenn en-
graving), 36

Naiad's Bath, 128
Nast, Thomas, 288
National Academy of Design, 136,
182, 183, 184
National Council for Historic
Sites, 315, 321
Nationalism, 213, 215, 219, 221, 247

National Park Service, 296
Nature, 210–15, 246–47. *See also*
Landscape; Wilderness, cult of
the
Nature (Emerson), 157
Nebraska, 220
Newburgh, New York, 47
New England, 157, 161, 176, 180,
198. *See also specific place names*
New Hampshire, 12, 121, 202
New Jersey, 5. *See also specific
place names*
Newman's Ledge, 112, 289, 305
New Mexico, 207, 294, 297
New Mirror (periodical), 36, 186
New Orleans, Louisiana, 7, 253, 254
Newport, Rhode Island, 221
Newspapers, 51–52, 284, 288, 315.
See also specific titles
New York Central and Hudson
River Railroad, 271
New York City, 5, 10, 15, 16, 43,
80, 170, 226; airlines, 295; Albany
sleighs, 50–51; as art center, 171,
173–74, 179, 180, 181; 182, 183,
184, 185, 189; automobiles and,
300; Bryant and Cole arrival in,
161–62, 166, 168, 172; Grant in,
280; health and, 252–53, 254; mail
coaches, 53; Mississippi frontier
and, 220; Mountain House office
in, 307; Mountain House traveling time, 240–41, 242, 244; nineteenth century growth, 7, 8–9, 27,
46, 49, 220, 223, 251; Wilde in,
283
New York *Commercial Advertiser*
(newspaper), 36, 42
New York State, 19, 20, 31, 171,
173; civil service scandals, 281;
forests of, 160, 161, 293–94; mail
routes, 52–54; Mountain House
land purchases, 276, 305, 313–15;
322, 332–34, 335–36; mountains

of, 12, 13; nineteenth century growth, 7, 8, 9, 46; population (twentieth century), 294, 339; public camps, 103, 117, 305, 332; trails, 109, 110, 305; winter (1962–63), 337–41; yellow fever in, 253. *See also specific place names*

New York State Conservation Department, 3, 4, 105, 313–15, 332–33; Laurel House and, 150*n*; North Lake and, 115; trail marking, 109

New York State Constitution, 314–15

New York State Legislature, 31, 32, 51–52

New York Sun (newspaper), 51–52

New York Times (newspaper), 4, 320–21

New York Tribune (newspaper), 170

Niagara Falls, 41, 103, 130, 145, 206

Nineteenth century: Gilded Age of, 217–24, 294; Hudson Valley importance in, 5, 7, 170–88, 189, 294; Romantic Movement of, 27, 70, 87, 88, 136, 151–55, 156–69, 171, 189–209, 210–15, 219, 320

North Carolina, 296

Northeast, population, 7, 294. *See also specific place names*

Northern Traveller, The (Goodrich), 42

North Lake, 80, 110, 114; altitude, 109; campsite, 103, 117, 305; Cole description, 164; ownership, 276, 278; sources, 115, 117

North Mountain, 26, 61, 73, 103, 109, 120, 320; Cropsey on, 185; Gifford and, 180; Mountain House acreage on, 275, 276, 305, 313, 332; Old Mountain Road

and, 76, 77, 79, 239; Spruce Creek on, 117; trails, 112, 114, 289

North Point, 109, 289

Oak Hill, New York, 70, 73, 76, 234, 241

Oberbaugh (woodcarver), 56

Ohio, 253, 294

Old Mountain Road, 71–100

Oliverea, New York, 300

Oneonta, Otsego County, 226

Onteora Park, New York, 223

Oregon, 220

Otis Cable Company, 239

Otis Elevating Railroad, 72, 109, 122, 241, 288–89, 316; Beach and, 232, 236, 238–40; closing of, 301–02, 303, 326; Ulster and Delaware and, 226, 232, 299

Otis Summit, 239, 299

Otsego County, 226

Otsego Lake, 26, 161

Overbaugh, Theodore, 142

Overlook Hotel, Woodstock, 229

Overlook House, 26, 236, 260, 310

Overlook Mountain, 21, 217

Pacific Coast, 220, 294. *See also specific place names*

Palens family, 125

Palenville, New York, 16, 88, 89, 105, 326; art colony, 175–78, 182, 183, 223; Kaaterskill Clove and, 122, 123, 126; Kaaterskill Hotel and, 106, 124, 229; railroads, 226, 231, 232, 235, 236; tanneries, 125

Palenville Overlook (High Rock), 105, 106, 123, 276

Palmer, Walter Launt, 60

Panama, 255

Panic of 1893, 298–99

Paris, France, 161

Park and Recreation Land Acquisitions Bond Act, 314, 333

Patience (Gilbert and Sullivan), 283

Paulding, James, 90, 197

Peak Sisters, The (playlet), 285

Pearl Harbor, Hawaii, 308

Pelham's Four Corners, 71, 78, 122

Pennsylvania, 13, 22, 182, 183, 253. See also *specific place names*

Pepper, George Wharton, 285

Phelps, Annie, 285

Philadelphia, Pennsylvania, 5, 7, 46, 142, 189; Doughty in, 182; population, 220, 223, 252; yellow fever and, 253

Philadelphia Exposition (1876), 221–22

Phoenicia, New York, 21, 22; Mt. Tremper House, 229, 260, 285, 310; railroads, 219, 226, 230, 236

Photography, 188, 269

Picturesque, doctrine of the, 152, 154, 155, 156, 160; America and, 190, 195–99, 297

Picturesque America (Bryant), 12, 36, 73, 88, 188

Picturesque Hudson, The, 98

Pierce, James, 31

Piermont, New York, 51, 53

Pine Hill, New York, 229, 260

Pine Orchard, 13, 19, 42, 295, 302; Catskill road, 20, 32, 71–100, 101; land purchase, 33, 305; landscape of, 21, 22–23, 26, 30–31, 40–41, 43, 70, 101–50, 161, 166, 168, 184, 186, 200, 211, 219, 291; Spafford on, 28–29

Pioneers, The (Cooper), 23–25, 28, 159, 161

Platonism, 210

Plattekill Clove, 19, 184

Point of Rocks (Indian Head), 105, 123

Population: Catskill, 15; nineteenth century concentrations, 5, 7, 13, 27, 46, 219, 220–21, 223, 251, 256, 291, 294; twentieth century concentration, 294, 339; westward movement, 152

Posselt, Eric, 106

Poughkeepsie, New York, 50, 53

Poughkeepsie (vessel), 274

Pourtales, Count de, 90, 197

Power, Tyrone, 41, 42, 84, 204, 222

Powers, James, 31, 33

Powers, John, 47

Prattsville, New York, 16, 19

Prices: board and room (1846), 142; building, 36; Kaaterskill Falls visit, 144–45; land, 32; Mountain House rates, 39–40, 298–99, 343–46 (Appendix); stagecoach fare, 44, 80

Primitivism, 27, 250; Romantic, 154, 206, 208, 214, 247, 248. See also Wilderness, cult of the

Profile Rock, 124

Prospect Mountain, 126, 127, 239

Prospect Park Hotel, 260

Prospect Rock, 109, 127, 139, 305

Pudding Stone Hall, 106

Puritanism, 213, 246, 248

Railroads, 9, 11, 15, 21, 22, 72, 81; abandoned, 293; comfort and, 85–86, 87, 88, 228, 233, 236, 245; continental, 294–95, 296; Gilded Age and, 218, 219, 225–41, 244–45, 246; steam, 53–54. See also *specific railways*

Rand, McNally Guide, 90, 240, 261, 301

Red Hill, 110

Reed, Luman, 170

Rensselaer (vessel), 274

Resorts: early, 5, 8, 10, 12, 13, 19, 20, 21, 22, 26–27, 70, 100, 292; post-Civil War, 221, 223, 230, 244, 257, 258, 260–61, 289, 292; twentieth century, 295, 298. See also *specific place names*

Retrospect of Western Travel (Martineau), 44
Rhinecliff, New York, 230
Richards, Thomas Addison, 176; quoted, 177
Richardson, Edgar P., 57; quoted, 170–71, 211–12, 219–20
Rip's Retreat, 109, 117
Rip Van Winkle (Irving), 77, 87–97, 99, 100, 193; romanticism and, 157–58
Rip Van Winkle Bridge, 173
Rip Van Winkle House, 77, 79, 92–97, 98, 99, 100, 301
Rip Van Winkle's Glen, 88, 91, 95
"Rip Van Winkle's House" (Fenn sketch), 77
Rip Van Winkle Trail, 71–72
Rip Van Winkle Trail, The (Posselt), 106
"River in the Catskills" (Cole painting), 175
"River in the Mountains" (Cole painting), 225
Roads, 293; carriage, 276, 292, 303, 305; Catskill, 15, 19, 20, 22, 26, 31, 32, 71–100, 101, 109, 235, 305, 314; Kaaterskill Clove, 123–27, 129, 235; Kaaterskill Falls, 131; Palenville, 106, 123–24; state and federal, 295
Robinson, Sidney, 50
Rockwell, Rev. Charles, 22, 217; quoted, 21, 33, 94, 96, 125, 250, 272
Rocky Mountains, 12, 103, 200, 207, 295
Romanticism, 87, 88, 151–55; European and American sources of, 189–209; landscape and, 7, 11, 26–27, 61, 63, 70, 136, 145, 156–69, 193–94, 219, 222, 247–48, 296; Rip Van Winkle and, 89–95, 193, 194; view of Nature and, 210–15, 246

Rondout, New York, 184
Rosa, Salvator, 119, 156, 158, 215
Ross, 254
Rossiter, 183
Rossville, New York, 185
Round Top Mountain, 21, 23, 26, 73, 76, 217; Bear's Den view of, 110; fort on, 126; South Lake and, 119; in winter, 146
Route 23A, 71, 123, 127
Rowe and Beach stagecoach firm, 48
Rusk, Samuel E., quoted, 176
Russia, 253

St. Augustine, Florida, 221
San Francisco, California, 295
Santa Cruz Park, 126, 127
Saratoga, New York, 30, 179, 230
Saugerties-on-the-Hudson, New York, 19
Saxe's Farm, 78, 79, 99, 112
Sayre, Francis, 48
Scenery, *see* Landscape
Scenery of the Catskill Mountains, The, 54, 55
Schenectady, New York, 53
Schlesinger, Arthur M., Sr., quoted, 221
Schoharie County, New York, 15, 20
Schoharie Valley, New York, 230
Schutt, Peter, 142, 144–45
Scobie, William, 55
Scotland, 152, 156
Scott, Walter, 156
Scott, Winfield, *gen.*, 50–51
Scribner, Silas, 33
Sears, Clara E., quoted, 184
Sequoia National Park, 296
Servants, 37, 44, 66; quarters for, 267, 271
Seventeenth century, 13, 122, 193
Shandaken, New York, 176, 178, 300

Shandaken Mountains (Blue Hills), 22, 217

Shay's Rebellion, 15

Shelving Rock, 128

Sherman, William Tecumseh, *gen.*, 281–83

Ships, 9, 15; British, 34; cholera and, 253, 254; ferry boats, 70, 73, 76, 234. *See also* Steamboats; *and see specific vessels*

Shokan, New York, 178

Shops (Mountain House), 275

Short Level (Old Mountain Road), 79

Sierra Nevada Mountains, 12, 103, 295, 297

Sketch Book, The (Irving), 92, 157, 159

Skinner, Cornelia Otis, 285

Slavery, 253

Sleepy Hollow, 26, 112, 158; *Rip Van Winkle* and, 88–97, 99, 100, 193

Sleepy Hollow route, 20, 71, 79, 83, 86, 240, 276, 305; railroads and, 232, 234, 235 239, 301

Sleighs, 50–51, 52, 53

Slide Mountain, 21, 228, 296

Smith, Mabel Parker, 323; quoted, 32, 51–52

Smith, Sam, 47

Smugglers Notch, Vermont, 121

South, The, 7, 8, 15, 56. *See also specific place names*

South America, 16, 254

South Cairo, New York, 234

South Durham, New York, 19

South Lake, 33, 86, 97, 105, 110; Cole on, 118–20, 164; Kaaterskill Hotel and, 106; ownership, 276, 278, 313, 328, 329; railroads, 226, 232, 237, 238, 239; sources, 115, 117

South Mountain, 67, 73, 178, 269, 289, 315, 323, 326; Beach and, 30;

Bear's Den view of, 110; forests, 34, 77; Gifford and, 180; Kaaterskill Clove and, 103, 125; Kaaterskill Hotel and, 105, 106, 124, 224, 230, 235, 236; Mountain House acreage on, 275, 276, 305, 313, 332

"Souvenir of the Catskills" (Stone painting), 180

Spafford, H. G., quoted, 28–29

Sphinx, The, 106, 127

Spruce Creek, 117

Spuyten Devil Creek, 11

Stagecoaches, 7, 34, 45, 71, 109, 227, 228, 241; Beach lines, 32, 44, 46, 47–48, 50–54, 70, 71–73, 76–79, 80, 86, 97–98, 218, 219, 223, 235, 239; Clark description, 81–82; Hall description, 81–82; hazards and discomforts of, 82–87, 233, 236; Lillie on, 242–43; Sleepy Hollow legend and, 89, 91, 93, 94, 95, 96, 97; traffic in the 1880's, 244–45, 276, 278, 300–01

Stamford, Connecticut, 47, 48, 225, 226, 229

Steamboats, 9, 10, 11, 43–44, 225, 241; Catskill Landing, 72, 73, 80, 223, 234, 242; election (1843) news race by, 51–52; freighting, 54, 70; Irving on, 90–91; traffic in the 1880's, 244–45; Wilde trip, 283–84

Stone, B. B. G., 180

Stone, William L., 42; quoted, 36, 204–05

Stony Clove, New York, 21, 184, 217, 219, 230, 236

Stony Clove Railroad, 97, 226, 230, 232, 233, 235; opening ceremonies, 281; standard-gauge conversion, 299

Stony Point, New York, 192

Storms, 82, 203, 204–05; hurricane of 1950, 316–17

Strong, Thomas W., quoted, 203

Sturges, Jon, quoted, 168

Sublime, The (aesthetic concept
of), 152, 154, 155; America and,
195–209, 210–15, 297; Cole on,
164, 190; forests and, 159–60, 168,
199, 210

Sullivan County, New York, 12, 20,
22

Sunday, 67–68

Sunnyside (Irving home), 192, 193

Sunrise, 38, 63, 202, 203, 321

Sunset Rock (North Mountain),
110

Sunset Rock (South Mountain),
105, 110, 125

Susquehanna River, 13, 15, 24

Sweet, Frederick A., quoted, 171,
172, 179, 182–83, 211, 214

Switzerland, 206, 208, 209, 239

Tannenbaum, Harry, 302

Tannersville, New York, 16, 131,
229, 300, 306, 317, 320

Tanning industry, 15–16, 19, 20,
125, 291

Tappan Zee, 11

Taylor, Bayard, 194; quoted, 9, 63,
65, 84–85, 192, 193

Telegraph, 272, 275, 303

Telephone service, 274–75, 303

Texas, 220, 294–95

Thanatopsis (Bryant), 157, 166

Thomson, John A., 31

Tompkins and Morgan stagecoach
line, 48, 49–50, 52

Trade, 5, 8, 9, 13, 15. *See also specific trades, e.g.*, Hotels

Transcendentalism, romanticism
and, 154, 157, 176

Transportation: early nineteenth
century, 5, 7, 9, 11, 19, 20, 21,
22, 29–30, 32, 41, 45–46, 50–52, 69,
70; post-Civil War, 220–21, 240–
41, 244–45; twentieth century,
295–96. *See also specific modes,*

i.e., Airplanes; Automobiles;
Railroads; Ships; Stagecoaches

Travel books: accounts of nineteenth century travel, 10–12, 23,
25–26, 121, 187, 188, 200, 321;
guidebooks, 20–22, 28, 41–44, 105,
125, 217–18, 227–28, 229. *See also
specific titles*

Travels in North America (Hall),
41

Triton Cave, 128

Trojan (vessel), 274

Trollope, Frances, quoted, 10

Trumbull, John, *col.*, 120, 164, 173

Tuckerman, Henry T., 206;
quoted, 151–52, 170, 195–97, 202,
205, 210, 213–14

Turner, Joseph M. W., 194

Twain, Mark (Samuel Langhorne
Clemens), 222

Twentieth century, 221, 291–98

Twilight Park, 126, 127, 129

"Two Lakes and the Mountain
House on the Catskills" (Bartlett), 120

Ulster County, New York, 12, 20,
219, 223; railroad guidebooks on,
228; resort development, 230;
Wyant in, 184, 185

"Ulster County Scenery" (McEntee painting), 184

Ulster and Delaware Railroad, 15,
185, 219, 233, 236, 245, 257; construction, 225–26, 228–29, 235;
Old Mountain Road and, 86, 97;
Otis Elevating and, 226, 232, 238,
239; Schoharie Valley and, 230;
on vacationing for health, 248–
49, 250

United States of America, 5, 12,
152–53, 220–21, 251, 294; Canadian dispute (1836), 50; landscape
quality of, 189–209, 210–15;
Westward expansion, 294; Wilde

tour of, 283. *See also specific place names*
United States Congress, 296
United States Insurance Company, 47
United States Navy, 160
Urbanization, 7–8, 220, 246; health and, 251–56; vacationing and, 249–51, 258
Utilitarianism, 213, 246; vacationing and, 248–50

Vacationing, 188, 223–24, 241, 246, 247, 258; health and, 248–49, 256; twentieth century, 295–96. *See also specific resorts and hotels*
Van Bergen, J. C., 31
Van Bergen, Wilhelmus, 29, 31, 33–34
Van Buren, Martin, 50
Van Loan, Walton, 103, 139; quoted, 101, 152, 229, 233
Van Santvoord, Alfred, 235
Van Wagonen, John K., 303, 304
Vedder, J. Van Vechten, quoted, 33
Vermont, 12, 121
Vibbard (vessel), 233
Vilmerung (Dutch painter), 176
Virginia, 7
"Voyage of Life" (Cole series of paintings), 209

Wadsworth Atheneum, Hartford, 132, 136
Wages, 46, 47
Wall, W. G., 136
"Wall of Manitou," 13, 226, 232, 236–37
Wall Street Crash of 1929, 303
Washington, George, 192
Washington State, 295
Waterfalls, 22, 24–25, 43, 79, 103, 127–28; romanticism and, 168,

169; western, 296, 297. *See also specific waterfalls*
Waverley Novels (Scott), 156
Wealth, 27, 45, 221, 222; book publishing and, 186, 188; northeastern concentration, 7, 8
Webster, Daniel, 307
Weehawken, New Jersey, 239
Wendell, Barrett, quoted, 159
West, The, 294; landscape of, 12, 103, 152, 179, 184, 207, 296–97. *See also specific place names*
Western Hotel, New York City, 53
West Hurley, New York, 229
West Indies, 253
West Point, New York, 90, 91
West Shore and Buffalo Railroad, 90, 226, 241, 260
Whitehead, Ralph Radcliffe, 223
White Mountains, 12, 121, 174, 183, 202, 221
Whittredge, Worthington, 129
Wildcat Ravine, 124
Wilde, Oscar, 283–85
Wilderness, cult of the, 152–54, 190, 206, 208, 210–15, 247; Catskills and, 156–69, 171, 194–95, 196, 222, 291–93, 305–06
Williams, Elisha, 33
Willis, Nathaniel P., 41, 42, 61, 207; quoted, 9–10, 39, 43–44, 205–06, 244, 252
Windham, New York, 21
Wines, 39, 145
"Winter Scene on the Catterskills" (Bartlett), 117–18, 120
Wisconsin, 253, 294
"Wolf in the Glen" (Cole painting), 136
Woodstock, New York, 19, 21, 184, 229; Overlook House, 26, 236, 260, 311; Wilde in, 284
Woodstock Art Colony, 223
Woodward, William, 321–22, 326

Woodworking mills, 56
World War I, 298, 302
World War II, 297, 298, 307, 308
Wyant, Alexander H., 184–85
Wyoming, 179

Yale University, 160
Yellow fever, 253, 254
Yellowstone National Park, 296
Yosemite National Park, 296
"Youth" (Cole painting), 209